MW00534127

INDIAN WAR VETERANS

Memories of Army Life
and Campaigns in the West, 1864-1898

Compiled and Edited by

Jerome A. Greene

Savas Beatie

New York and California

© 2007, 2012 by Jerome A. Greene

All rights reserved. No part of this publication may be reproduced, stored in a retrieval system, or transmitted, in any form or by any means, electronic, mechanical, photocopying, recording, or otherwise, without the prior written permission of the publisher. Printed in the United States of America. Any similarities between characters and real life occurrences are completely coincidental.

Cataloging-in-Publication Data is available from the Library of Congress.

First published in hardcover in 2007

ISBN 978-1-61121-113-9

10 9 8 7 6 5 4 3 2 1
First Edition, First Printing

SB

Published by
Savas Beatie LLC
521 Fifth Avenue, Suite 1700
New York, NY 10175
Phone: 916-941-6896

Editorial Offices:

Savas Beatie LLC
P.O. Box 4527
El Dorado Hills, CA 95762
Phone: 916-941-6896
(E-mail) sales@savasbeatie.com

Savas Beatie titles are available at special discounts for bulk purchases in the United States by corporations, institutions, and other organizations. For more details, please contact Savas Beatie, Special Sales, P.O. Box 4527, El Dorado Hills, CA 95762. You may also e-mail us at sales@savasbeatie.com, or click over for a friendly visit to our website at www.savasbeatie.com for additional information.

Dedicated to the memory of Don G. Rickey,
who knew these men.

Books by Jerome A. Greene

Evidence and the Custer Enigma: A Reconstruction of Indian-Military History (Kansas City, 1973)

Slim Buttes, 1876: An Episode of the Great Sioux War (Norman, 1982)

Yellowstone Command: Colonel Nelson A. Miles and the Great Sioux War, 1876-1877 (Lincoln, 1991; Norman, 2006)

Battles and Skirmishes of the Great Sioux War, 1876-1877: The Military View (Norman, 1993)

Lakota and Cheyenne: Indian Views of the Great Sioux War, 1876-1877 (Norman, 1994)

Frontier Soldier: An Enlisted Man's Journal of the Sioux and Nez Perce Campaigns, 1877 (Helena, 1998)

Nez Perce Summer, 1877: The U. S. Army and the Nee-Me-Poo Crisis (Helena, 2000)

Morning Star Dawn: The Powder River Expedition and the Northern Cheyennes, 1876 (Norman, 2003)

Washita: The U. S. Army and the Southern Cheyennes, 1867-1869 (Norman, 2004)

(Co-author with Douglas D. Scott) *Finding Sand Creek: History, Archeology, and the 1864 Massacre Site* (Norman, 2004)

The Guns of Independence: The Siege of Yorktown, 1781 (New York and Staplehurst, UK, 2005)

Fort Randall on the Missouri, 1856-1892 (Pierre, 2005)

CONTENTS

Maps and photos have been inserted through the text for the convenience of the reader. A full-color gallery of rare Indian war veteran-related medals, ribbons, and badges is available online at www.savasbeatie.com.

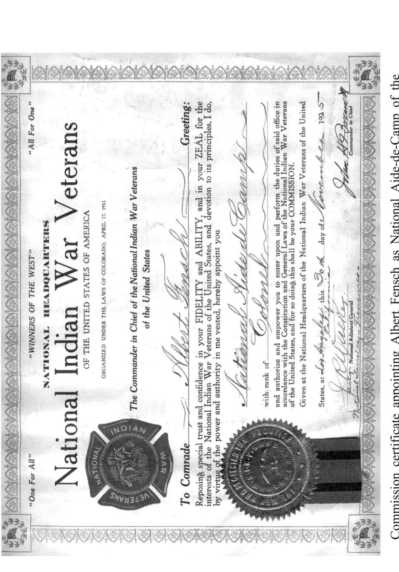

Commission certificate appointing Albert Fensch as National Aide-de-Camp of the National Indian War Veterans and signed by Commander-in-Chief John H. Brandt in Los Angeles, 1925. Editor's Collection.

Preface and Acknowledgments

This book comprises a reader embracing significant personal accounts by army veterans of their life and service on the trans-Mississippi frontier during the last four decades of the nineteenth century, the core period of Indian-white warfare in that region. The essays are drawn from various sources, each as indicated, but with most from the constituency of the National Indian War Veterans Association via the group's periodical tabloid, *Winners of the West*. The first articles, those dealing with veterans' reminiscences of their routine day-to-day experiences on the frontier, are presented in chronological order. Those describing elements of campaign and warfare history are arranged chronologically within geographical areas of the West and constitute the largest part of the book. A few of these essays have appeared elsewhere, although none have previously been widely disseminated.

In all instances, the intent has been to reproduce the content of each essay so that readers might derive the author's original meaning clearly and comprehensively, despite obvious variances in writing technique and ability. Occasionally, minor grammatical, punctuation, and spelling changes have been introduced editorially without brackets to improve readability. Rarely, too, words have been interjected to complete and improve factual representations, such as in giving an individual's full name and/or military rank. (Infrequently, for example, authors of some pieces have referenced brevet or honorary rank in introducing officers, and this has been consistently corrected to reflect proper Regular Army rank usage throughout.) In no way has the substance of an article been altered or otherwise miscast. Footnotes have been scrupulously avoided in the essays for the purpose of insuring an uninterrupted reading experience.

While an ex-soldier might occasionally exaggerate recollected facts or conditions, he might also make factual errors, and in such instances bracketed insertions have been made to correct grievously erroneous data. Also brackets have been used sparingly wherever brief introductory, transitional, and clarifying material was deemed appropriate. In most instances, the titles of individual essays have been changed from the headline format of the original presentations to better convey the content of each. And wherever parts of an article wavered from its purpose or became irrelevant to its subject, those parts were omitted and their omission indicated with ellipses. Finally and importantly, as testimony reflective of the periods during which the veterans performed their service (the 1860s-1890s) and later wrote their pieces (generally the 1920s, 1930s, and 1940s), the references to Indians are often disparaging and occasionally brutally racist. As such, the remarks mirror a temper of thought grounded in ignorance that existed during those times. However objectionable they seem today, they nonetheless provide useful insights into the thinking of this element of early twentieth-century American society, and they have not been sanitized herein.

I wish to acknowledge the following individuals and institutions for their assistance in this project: L. Clifford Soubier, Charles Town, West Virginia; Douglas C. McChristian, Tucson, Arizona; John D. McDermott, Rapid City, South Dakota; James B. Dahlquist, Seattle, Washington; Thomas R. Buecker, Crawford, Nebraska; R. Eli Paul, Kansas City, Missouri; Paul L. Hedren, O'Neill, Nebraska; John Doerner, Hardin, Montana; James Potter, Chadron, Nebraska; David Hays, Boulder, Colorado; Gordon Chappell, San Francisco, California; Dick Harmon, Lincoln, Nebraska; John Monette, Louisville, Colorado; Paul Fees, Cody, Wyoming; Robert G. Pilk, Lakewood, Colorado; Paul A. Hutton, Albuquerque, New Mexico; Neil Mangum, Alpine, Texas; Douglas D. Scott, Lincoln, Nebraska; Thomas Gilcrease Institute of American History and Art, Tulsa, Oklahoma; Little Bighorn Battlefield National Monument, Crow Agency, Montana; and Jack Blades of *Night Ranger*. Special thanks go to Sandra Lowry, Fort Laramie National Historic Site, Wyoming, for her help in providing full and correct names for many of the enlisted men mentioned herein.

My thanks are also extended to everyone at Savas Beatie who helped get this book into print.

Introduction

The Indian War Veterans, 1880s-1960s

They called themselves the "Winners of the West." They were the soldier veterans of the U. S. Army and state and territorial forces in the West, many of them survivors of Indian campaigns between 1864 and 1898, and they regarded themselves as the vanguards of civilization on the frontier. Some had fought Sioux, Cheyenne, Nez Perce, Comanche, Kiowa, and Apache warriors at renowned places like Washita, Apache Pass, Rosebud, Little Bighorn, White Bird Canyon, Bear's Paw Mountains, and Wounded Knee, although the majority who also claimed to be Indian war veterans had performed more routine and unheralded duties during their years beyond the Mississippi River.

While in many ways their service facilitated the economic exploitation of Indian lands wrought by mining and settlement, as well as the internment of the tribes on reservations that followed, like most Americans of the time they embraced concepts of Manifest Destiny, by which they justified their own and their government's actions. Most of them were former enlisted men, drawn together by camaraderie but also for the purpose of bettering living conditions for themselves and their families by championing pension benefits from a seemingly distant and unsympathetically frugal federal government that had extended its largess more charitably to the disabled veterans of the Civil War and the Spanish-American War.

The creation of associations specific to the interests of Indian war veterans followed a course similar to that of other veterans' groups after the period of focus their service represented. Groups composed of veteran officers generally reflected their fraternal interests, as did, for example, the Society of the Cincinnati for those who served in the Revolutionary War; the Society of the War of 1812; the Aztec Club for former Mexican War officers; the Military Order of the Loyal Legion of the United States for former Civil War officers; and several smaller societies observing officer service in Cuba, the Philippines, and China late in the nineteenth century.[1]

Enlisted veteran organizations, generally more concerned with welfare issues, had roots in various municipal and regional relief organizations founded during the Civil War to help needy soldiers and which continued to promote relief programs after the war. In the immediate postwar years, a profusion of groups evolved that eventually (1866-69) merged into a single association, the Grand Army of the Republic (GAR) that included both former Union officers and enlisted men. (A parallel and smaller body, the United Confederate Veterans, later served the interests of those who had fought for the South.)

Much of the GAR's purpose was to provide for the well-being of members and their families, objectives espoused by the Republican Party in the final decades of the nineteenth century, and the organization, which became sizable (400,000 members by 1890) came to register significant political clout. In time, the GAR's rolls gradually fell, and its influence waned during the early decades of the twentieth century; the last annual encampment took place in 1949.

A group formed to promote similar interests for its constituency was the United Spanish War Veterans, which shared ideals of the GAR as applied to officers and enlisted men who had served in the Spanish-American War of 1898, the Philippine Insurrection that followed, and the China Relief Expedition of 1900. Like the GAR, the USWV resulted from the merger of kindred bodies between 1904 and 1908. The goals of the GAR, meantime, inspired the birth of organizations of similar spirit dedicated to the interests of soldiers and sailors whose service postdated the Civil War. In 1888-90, from several such fledgling groups, the Regular Army and Navy Union was founded, mainly by veterans of duty in the postwar West, to provide like needs for soldiers, sailors, and marines without Civil War service, including those yet serving or retired from active duty. In the late 1880s and through the 1890s, garrisons or camps of the Regular Army and Navy Union flourished in cities around the country, as well as at various active army posts.[2]

1   E.g., the Society of the Army of Santiago de Cuba, the Military Order of the Carabao, the Military Order of the Dragon, and the Naval and Military Order of the Spanish-American War.

2   For early veteran groups, see Stuart McConnell, *Glorious Contentment: The Grand Army of the Republic, 1865-1890* (Chapel Hill: University of North Carolina Press, 1992); Mary Dearing, *Veterans in Politics: The Story*

Inspired by these various groups, and desirous of coming together for collateral purposes based upon their shared background and experiences, during the late nineteenth and early twentieth centuries the ex-soldiers of the so-called Indian wars period (ca. 1865-1891) began organizing into several bodies reflective of their common service. With their small and ever-decreasing base, however, they never attained the political strength of the GAR, whose large membership influenced pension legislation as well as the outcome of congressional and presidential elections from the 1870s well into the twentieth century. (Much the same was true of similar bodies of Spanish-American War and World War I veterans.) Beset by limited numbers and resources, the Indian war veterans shared fellowship, longevity, and perseverance, and played much the role of other veterans' groups in sharing reminiscences of their army life, seeking to improve government benefits (albeit with considerably less success), promoting patriotism, and otherwise ensuring that citizens did not lose sight of their contributions to the nation.

The first organization of Indian war veterans was hereditary and fraternal, consisting of retired officers and select enlisted personnel who had shared experiences on the frontier and whose meetings reflected collegiality and an interest in preserving the history of the Indian wars of the trans-Mississippi West for future generations. On April 23, 1896, a group of active and retired army officers convened at the United Service Club in Philadelphia to organize the Society of Veterans of Indian Wars of the United States. Its constitution designated three classes of members consisting of First Class ("Commissioned officers . . . who have actually served or may hereafter serve in the Army during an Indian War . . . [including] any officer of a State National Guard or Militia meeting the above requirements. . . ."); Second Class ("Lineal male descendants of members of the first class," or male descendants of officers who were eligible "but who died without such membership"); and Third Class (Non-commissioned officers and soldiers who have received the Medal of Honor or Certificate of

---

of the G.A.R. (Baton Rouge: Louisiana State University Press, 1952); J. Worth Carnahan, *Manual of the Civil War and Key to the Grand Army of the Republic and Kindred Societies* (Washington, D.C.: U. S. Army and Navy Historical Association, 1889); Robert B. Beath, *History of the Grand Army of the Republic* (New York: Bryan, Taylor and Company, 1889); Harvey S. Eisenberg, "Medals and Badges of the United Spanish War Veterans," *The Medal Collector,* 24 (February, 1973), p. 4; and *The Army & Navy Union, U. S. A.: A History of the Union and Its Auxiliary* (The Army and Navy Union, U. S. A., 1942).

Merit from the United States Government . . . or who have been proffered, or recommended for, a commission, or who have been specially mentioned in orders by the War Department or their immediate commanding officer for services rendered against hostile Indians. . . ." Charter members of the society included William F. ("Buffalo Bill") Cody, who was a colonel in the Nebraska National Guard, and retired Captain Charles King, the army novelist who had campaigned against the Apaches and Lakotas under Brigadier General George Crook.[3]

For reasons not altogether clear, the Society of Veterans of Indian Wars almost immediately evolved into the Order of Indian Wars of the United States, under which title it functioned for nearly fifty years. Chartered in Illinois just months after the Philadelphia meeting, the stated purpose of the group was "to perpetuate the memory of the services rendered by the American Military forces in their conflicts and wars within the territory of the United States, and to collect and secure for publication historical data relating to the instances of brave deeds and personal devotion by which Indian warfare has been illustrated." Membership was restricted to "commissioned officers and honorably discharged commissioned officers of the U. S. Army, Navy and Marine Corps, and of State and Territorial Military Organizations . . . who have been, or who hereafter may be engaged in the service of the United States . . . in conflicts, battles or actual field service against hostile Indians within the jurisdiction of the United States. . . ." The organization also accommodated inclusion of male descendants and provided for honorary and associate memberships.

On January 14, 1897, a meeting of the Order in Chicago elected the first national officers, including as commander retired Ninth Cavalry Lieutenant Colonel Reuben F. Bernard. Later commanders included such formerly prominent retired Indian wars officers as Brigadier General Anson Mills, Brigadier General Leonard Wood, Brigadier General Edward S. Godfrey, Major General Hugh L. Scott, and Lieutenant General Nelson A. Miles. During its half century of existence, the Order of Indian Wars performed valuable commemorative and historical services through its annual dinner meetings, usually held at the Army and Navy Club in Washington, D. C. At a standard gathering, members discussed the Order's business then listened as a companion presented a formal paper on an aspect of Indian wars history based largely on his service. The proceedings were generally published and today constitute important historical data of the organization and the era it

3   *Society of Veterans of Indian Wars of the United States,* Circular of Information (nd, ca. 1896), pp. 1, 3-4, 8.

Pension certificate granted in 1887 to former private Francis G. Barnes, Company I, Fourth Infantry. Barnes's pension was for "Injury to left hand and resulting contraction of muscles of second, third and fourth fingers," for which he was awarded fourteen dollars per month. Barnes died in 1921 in Hamburg, New York.

memorialized. Among the trappings of the society were vellum membership certificates signed by the commander. They bore an elaborate engraving of troops attacking an Indian village, as well as an elitist-sounding sentiment honoring members for "maintaining the supremacy of the United States."

The Order of Indian Wars was most active during the 1910s, 1920s, and early 1930s. Membership peaked at 376 in 1933. By the 1940s, death rapidly took its toll. During World War II Commander Charles D. Rhodes recorded that "we have a difficulty in keeping up interest in the organization. . . . The generation fighting this present war never heard of an Indian war." Staying true to its precepts, however, the Order remained active until 1947, when dwindling membership forced its affiliation with the American Military Institute. During its existence, however, members of the Order of Indian Wars and their descendants accumulated a wealth of historical material that is presently deposited in the research collections of the U. S. Army Military History Institute, Army War College, Carlisle Barracks, Pennsylvania.[4]

Despite its focus on fraternity and history throughout its existence, the Order of Indian Wars frequently supported the causes of several other Indian war veteran groups that existed contemporaneously with it and which were more interested in improving matters respecting the welfare of members and their families. These groups, while likewise bonded by their service fraternity, were driven more by bread-and-butter issues regarding pensions. (Since 2001, a revival group of hereditary companions retaining the title The Order of Indian Wars of the United States has convened annually in

4   *Army and Navy Journal,* September 12, 1896; *By-Laws of the Order of Indian Wars of the United States, Amended to February 20, 1936,* pp. 5-6; *Army and Navy Journal,* January 23, 1897; John M. Carroll (comp., ed.), *The Papers of the Order of Indian Wars* (Fort Collins, Colo.: Old Army Press, 1975), viii (quote); *Proceedings of the Annual Meeting and Dinner of the Order of Indian Wars of the United States Held November Eighteenth Nineteen Hundred and Twenty-six,* p. 18; Rhodes to Brigadier General (ret.) Thomas H. Slavens, June 30, 1944. Don G. Rickey Collection, Evergreen, Colorado; Important Notice to Members of the Order, July 7, 1947. Rickey Collection; "Indian War Veterans," *The Westerners Brand Book* (Chicago), 5 (August, 1948), p. 1. Membership tallies, 1924-45, appear in the annual *Proceedings.* Total membership, 1896-1947, stood at 630. Carroll, *Papers of the Order of Indian Wars,* pp. 273-81. Each member of the Order of Indian Wars received a 14-karat gold membership badge suspended from a ribbon of multi-colored (red, white, blue, and yellow) stripes manufactured by the Philadelphia firm of Baily, Banks, and Biddle. *Military and Naval Insignia and Novelties* (Philadelphia: Baily, Banks and Biddle Company, 1918), p. 5. The colors of the Order of Indian Wars repose in the Manuscripts Division of the U. S. Army Military History Institute.

Washington, D.C. to partake in the tradition of the annual dinner meetings of the original Order; this group presently numbers nearly 200 members.)[5]

Early in the twentieth century, federal invalid pensions for Indian wars service were given to disabled individuals who qualified under a few antiquated laws. That of July, 1892, for example (which was the first designated specifically for Indian wars service), had provided $8 per month to disabled veterans and to widows and children of veterans disabled during Indian wars occurring between 1832 and 1842 ("known as the Black Hawk

5   "Pension" in the late nineteenth century was defined as "a stated allowance to a person in consideration of past services; payment made to one retired from service for age, disability, or other cause; especially a yearly stipend paid by government to retired officers, disabled soldiers, the families of soldiers killed, etc." Thomas Wilhelm, *A Military Dictionary and Gazetteer* (Philadelphia: L.R. Hamersly and Company, 1881), p. 421. For earlier period reference, see also the definition in Henry L. Scott, *Military Dictionary: Comprising Technical Definitions; Information on Raising and Keeping Troops; Actual Service, including Makeshifts and Improved Materiel; and Law, Government, Regulation, and Administration Relating to Land Forces* (New York: D. Van Nostrand, 1864), pp. 461-62. Invalid pensions to soldiers disabled during Indian wars service, and to the dependents (widows and orphans) of soldiers killed in such service, were customarily extended by Congress under existing pension laws from the War of 1812 (Brigadier General William Henry Harrison's campaign against the Shawnees and affiliated tribes, for example) to the Civil War. Notably, they offered benefits the same as those for War of 1812 service to those combat casualties of Indian wars in Florida, Illinois, Iowa, Wisconsin, and elsewhere. The pension act of 1862 also included benefits to soldiers disabled in Indian conflicts and to surviving dependents. William Henry Glasson, *History of Military Pension Legislation in the United States* (New York: Columbia University Press, 1900), pp. 64-66; William H. Glasson, *Federal Military Pensions in the United States* (New York: Oxford University Press, 1918), p. 114. For the various early pension acts, see Robert Mayo and Ferdinand Moulton (comps.), *Army and Navy Pension Laws, and Bounty Land Laws of the United States, Including Sundry Resolutions of Congress, from 1776 to 1852* (Washington, D.C.: Jno. T. Towers, 1852); *Laws of the United States Governing the Granting of Army and Navy Pensions Together with the Regulations Relating Thereto* (Washington, D.C.: Government Printing Office, 1912), chapter 2, and *passim.* A less bureaucratically phrased account of early pensions into the 1880s, designed especially for informational purposes for soldiers and veterans, is in *The Soldier's Manual: A Hand Book of Useful and Reliable Information showing Who are Entitled to Pensions, Increase, Bounty, Pay, Etc.* (Washington, D.C.: Milo B. Stevens and Company, General War Claims Attorneys, 1888), *passim.*

[Sac and Fox] war, the Creek war, Cherokee disturbances and the Seminole war"). Amendments in 1902 and 1908 extended pension coverage to veterans whose service fell between 1817 and 1860. A 1908 amendment raised widows' pensions to $12 per month, while another in 1913 increased those for invalid veterans under the 1892 act to $20 per month. Surprisingly, at this late date a soldier's participation in Indian warfare between 1860 and 1891 was not yet recognized for attaining pensionable status.[6] In effect, disabled survivors of the Sioux and Apache troubles of the 1870s, 1880s, and 1890s went without pensions, even though the War Department had acknowledged their service with authorization of a campaign badge in 1907.

During the late nineteenth and early twentieth centuries, in efforts to come to grips with the pension question for Indian wars service, several regional groups organized to improve opportunities for those veterans. The Indian War Veterans of the North Pacific Coast organized by 1889 and commemorated the service of soldiers, mostly militia, during the Indian warfare in the Northwest during the 1840s-1850s. Likewise, the Utah Indian War Veterans Association, composed largely of former Mormon militia soldiers who had fought in that territory's Black Hawk War, organized at Springville, Utah, in 1893, to work for federal pension recognition for their service. In Kansas in the early 1920s, a regional group called the National Indian War Veterans sought to promote pension legislation, but in 1925 changed its name to the Cantonments of the National Indian War Veterans of the United States of America to differentiate from a larger body then-current called the National Indian War Veterans Association (see below).[7]

6   Glasson, *Federal Military Pensions,* p. 115; *Laws of the United States Governing the Granting of Army and Navy Pensions,* pp. 20-21, 22, 23, 184-85; *Winners of the West,* October 30, 1935; *Winners of the West,* September 30, 1937. Throughout the post-Civil War Indian wars period, the standard retirement for career enlisted men was thirty years, after which they were entitled to enter the Soldiers Home, Washington, D.C. Don Rickey, Jr., *Forty Miles a Day on Beans and Hay: The Enlisted Soldier Fighting the Indian Wars* (Norman: University of Oklahoma Press, 1963), pp. 29, 341.

7   "The Grand Encampment. Indian War Veterans of the North Pacific Coast," membership certificate dated July 16, 1889, in the editor's possession; Peter Gottfredson (comp., ed.), *History of Indian Depredations in Utah* (Salt Lake City: Skelton Publishing Company, 1919), pp. 332-35; Amendment to Charter of the Cantonements [sic] of the National Indian War Veterans of the United States of America, Wichita, Kansas, January 7, 1925, State of Kansas, Department of State, executed February 28, 1925. Original copy in the Scrapbooks of Albert Fensch, National Adjutant General, NIWV and UIWV, Scrapbook No. 1, editor's collection (hereafter cited as Fensch

While these regional groups fostered fraternal objectives, their primary focus lay in enhancing the well-being of their constituents. They lacked sufficient numbers and direction, however, to successfully accomplish that end, and remained largely fraternal in character until most of their members ultimately merged with a single unified national body.

The preeminent national association that coexisted with these regional bodies through much of their own histories was first called the National Indian War Veterans Organization when founded in Denver, Colorado, in April 1909 (it incorporated under the laws of Colorado on April 17, 1911).[8] Later its name changed to the National Indian War Veterans Association. The NIWV proved an activist body, chartered for the purpose of improving the lot of ex-soldiers whose service in the West and its attendant sacrifices had seemingly been forgotten by the government. More precisely, as the group evolved through ensuing years its stated mission became:

> to seek out veterans of the Regular Army eligible in either the "Indian Wars" or "Regular Establishment" [pension] class; and all State Troops eligible to pension in the Indian Wars class, and bind them together into one common fraternal brotherhood and comradeship, cooperating together for their common good, especially in the matter of obtaining just recognition from the Congress of the United States by the enactment of equitable pension laws.[9]

Scrapbooks). "National Indian War Veterans [Kansas], in *The Veteran,* 8 (November, 1925), p. 7. Luther Barker of Clay Center, Kansas, founded the Kansas organization. Authorization for badges for Indian wars service appears in General Orders No. 170, War Department, August 15, 1907, as cited in "Report of the Adjutant-General," October 17, 1907, in *War Department, U. S. A., Annual Reports, 1907* (Washington, D.C.: Government Printing Office, 1907), pp. 260-61.

8 *Winners of the West,* March 30, 1926; U. S. Congress, House, Subcommittee of the Committee on Pensions, [*Hearings Regarding*] *Pensions for Survivors of Certain Indian Wars,* 63rd Cong., 2d sess., March 7, 1914, p. 3; Certificate of Incorporation, National Indian War Veterans, State of Colorado Office of the Secretary of State (duplicate), April 17, 1911. Fensch Scrapbooks, Scrapbook No. 1.

9 *Winners of the West,* July 30, 1930. Pension benefits were administered by the Bureau of Pensions of the Department of the Interior until 1930, when the Veterans Administration was created. *VA History in Brief: What It Is, Was, and Does* (Washington, D.C.: Government Printing Office, 1983), pp. 1, 2, 4. Technically, membership was extended to "those who served in Indian wars

Many of these veterans, opined an exponent of the organization,

> spent the best years of their life [sic] protecting our frontier. Their
> gallantry and bravery, the endurance of . . . terrible hardships and
> fearlessness of the most horrible of deaths, made possible the
> opening and populating of the Great American Desert, which is
> now the backbone of the greatest and wealthiest nation on the face
> of the earth. Even though some of the men who enlisted for the
> Indian wars were not in actual combat, they helped to keep down
> uprisings among the savages and endured the terrible hardships of
> hunger and weather, which were [often] a great deal worse than the
> actual fighting, and were there ready and willing to fight when
> called upon. Many of them fell victims of disease, storms, hunger,
> and thirst, and of those who survived through sheer hardihood,
> many are cripples from frozen limbs or disease.[10]

Organization of the NIWV in Denver occurred under the leadership of
Charles R. Hauser, a Fifth Cavalry veteran who assembled local ex-solders
with Indian wars service to seek pension benefits. The seal of the
incorporated body read: "NIWV," encircled by "The Men Who Protected
the Frontier." Seeking to improve the pensionable status of members and
their families, the Denver leaders, together with those of camps established
in 1912 in San Francisco and St. Louis, campaigned to change existing laws
to include veterans with post-Civil War Indian campaign service in the West.
Over six years, the members of the Denver, St. Louis, and San Francisco
camps joined with those camps founded in Philadelphia, Washington, D. C.,
and Newark to promote new and more broadly encompassing legislation.

As a result of lobbying efforts by nearly 500 members of the NIWV and
collateral groups, a law enacted on March 4, 1917, extended previous
legislation regarding veterans of the early Indian wars, fixed age for pension
eligibility at 62, and for the first time specified campaigns between 1866 and
1891 for which service would be recognized for pension claims. Under
provisions of the Keating measure (named for Representative Edward

---

between Jan. 1, 1817, and Dec. 31, 1898, in accordance with the
classification given Indian war veterans by the United States pension office."
St. Joseph Gazette, September 13, 1927.

10 *Winners of the West,* December, 1923. An early undated roster, perhaps
from ca. 1917-18, lists the names and addresses of 407 members of the
"N-A-I-W-V" (National Association of Indian War Veterans). Original in the
Walter M. Camp Collection, Little Bighorn Battlefield National Monument,
Crow Agency, Montana.

Members of General Custer Camp No. 4, United Indian War Veterans, at their Los Angeles convention in 1929.

Keating of Colorado), pensions of $20 per month would be allotted to qualified ex-soldiers of the later Indian campaigns, while widows of such veterans might qualify to receive the standard $12 per month.[11]

The significant Keating law additionally provided for invalid pensions for qualifying individuals who served in specified state and territorial militia organizations that campaigned against Indians in Texas, Oregon, Idaho, California, Nevada, Utah, Minnesota, the Dakotas, Colorado, and Nebraska from 1859 to 1868. Further, as sanctioned by the War Department, pensionable Regular Army service was at last recognized in the following campaigns:

11 *Winners of the West,* December, 1923; *Winners of the West,* February, 1924; *Winners of the West,* December, 1924; *Winners of the West,* July, 1925; *Winners of the West,* March 30, 1926; *Winners of the West,* December 30, 1935; *Winners of the West,* September 30, 1937; *San Francisco Examiner,* December 22, 1912; Glasson, *Federal Military Pensions,* p. 115. (A table showing numbers of Indian wars pensioners and pension expenditures between 1893 and 1916 is in ibid.) For the act, see Public Law 400, *Statutes at Large,* 39, Part 1, pp. 1199-1201.

Campaign in southern Oregon and Idaho and northern parts of California and Nevada, 1865-1868.

Campaign against the Cheyennes, Arapahoes, Kiowas, and Comanches, in Kansas, Colorado, and the Indian Territory, 1867, 1868, and 1869, inclusive.

Modoc War in 1872 and 1873.

Campaign against the Apaches of Arizona in 1873.

Campaign against the Kiowas, Comanches, and Cheyennes, in Kansas, Colorado, Texas, Indian Territory, and New Mexico, 1874 and 1875.

Campaign against the Northern Cheyennes and Sioux, 1876-1877.

Nez Perce War, 1877.

Bannock War, 1878.

Campaign against the Northern Cheyennes, 1878 and 1879.

Campaign against the Ute Indians in Colorado and Utah, September, 1879, to November, 1880.

Campaign against Apache Indians in Arizona and New Mexico, 1885 and 1886.

Campaign against the Sioux Indians in South Dakota, November, 1890, to January, 1891.[12]

---

12 *Winners of the West,* January, 1924; General Orders No. 170, War Department, August 15, 1907, as cited in "Report of the Adjutant-General," October 17, 1907, pp. 260-61. Keating later wrote: "As originally drawn, the Keating bill was to pension all veterans of all Indian conflicts. The members of the committee on pensions of the House of Representatives took the position that only those who had participated actually in 'Indian campaigns' should be pensioned. That made it necessary to get a definition or designation of 'Indian campaigns' or 'Indian wars.' So we appealed to the War Department, and found that at various times the Secretary of War and his associates had designated certain 'campaigns' against the Indians as 'wars.' The committee on pensions took it for granted that the War Department knew what it was doing, and we wrote into the bill the official designation of every 'war' that the department certified to us. I am now [1923] convinced that there are a great many 'campaigns' or 'wars' which were omitted by the War

Despite the success of the Denver-based NIWV in pursuing pension benefits for Indians wars veterans, the organization headquarters in that city waned in the years after World War I. As Denver Camp No. 1 dissolved, the San Francisco chapter became increasingly active, soon assuming a national role in the organization and promoting the establishment of several smaller West Coast chapters of the group. Few further improvements to veterans' benefits occurred, however, until 1923. The revival of the national NIWV at that time was due to the dedication of George W. Webb of St. Joseph, Missouri. Webb had served with the Third Infantry during its 1870s campaigns on the southern plains, and he brought organizational talent to the languishing group (and in 1927-29 served as National Commander of the NIWV). He prepared a petition to Congress regarding Indian war veterans' pension needs and distributed it among seven thousand veterans and widows for signatures to be forwarded to Congress. His primary innovation, however, was to design, edit, and publish a monthly (briefly bi-monthly) newspaper entitled *Winners of the West*. The tabloid, which highlighted pension matters and kept its members abreast of related legislative developments, also offered members an outlet for writing about historical events from their service. *Winners of the West* was roundly applauded and contributed to the acceleration of NIWV membership nationwide.[13]

One of Webb's missions lay in convincing the smaller regional bodies of Indian wars veteran organizations to join together in the larger national group to create a unified lobby. The motto of the NIWV became "One for All, All for One." As Webb put it: "It behooves every comrade, every widow, and every friend of our cause to stand shoulder to shoulder and

---

Department, which should have been included in that bill." *Winners of the West,* December, 1923.

13 *Winners of the West*, December 30, 1935; *Winners of the West*, April, 1924; *Winners of the West*, December 28, 1944. Two other publications initiated by Webb were his compilation entitled, *Chronological List of Engagements between the Regular Army of the United States and Various Tribes of Hostile Indians which Occurred during the Years 1790 to 1898, Inclusive* (St. Joseph, Mo.: Wing Publishing and Printing Company, 1939; reprinted New York: AMS Press, Inc., 1976), and a commemorative booklet *First Account of the Custer Massacre published in the Tribune Extra, Bismarck, Dakota Territory, July 6, 1876. Republished for Distribution at Sixtieth Anniversary Commemoration of The Custer Battle, Custer Battlefield, June 25, 1936* (St. Joseph, Mo.: Winners of the West, 1936). *Winners of the West* was published twice monthly for a short time; it also changed its format and design several times during its run.

present a solid front of effort in their own behalf. Thousands of comrades have kept their names off of the rolls of all such organizations because they do not propose to be drawn into a scrap with their comrades because [of their] belonging to separate organizations. . . ." Webb especially targeted the Kansas group with its sizable membership. Both the NIWV and the Kansas organization held conventions in September, 1926, and Webb urged members of both groups to see the folly of their ways. "These two conventions . . . have it within their hands to put a stop to this foolishness forever. Elect only comrades to office who will be willing to co-operate to bury the differences which now separate them as organizations. . . . Let us . . . get together in one mighty effort before the last one of our aged veterans and widows are laid beneath the sod, beyond any possibility of earthly help." Webb's message was clear, but the Kansas veterans remained remote. The NIWV expanded in membership during the 1920s, and in 1931 the association obtained a perpetual charter from the State of Colorado.[14]

Through two decades up to 1944 following Webb's assumption of affairs, between twenty-two and forty-four camps variously operated in major cities throughout the country (although some appear to have been paper camps with few if any members; many became defunct within a few years). In 1928, membership was reported to be 1,300. In addition, there were designated departments at the state level operated by appointed commanders. Within departments, various camps bore such names as Gen. Nelson A. Miles Camp No. 32 (Boston), Gen. George A. Custer Camp No. 4 (San Francisco), and Gen. Philip H. Sheridan Camp No. 20 (Chicago). (Two in New York City, plus those in Boston, Chicago, Milwaukee, and Portland, Oregon, contained core membership and were designated "Big Six Camps.") Abraham Lincoln Camp No. 30, San Antonio, comprised enlisted veterans of the Ninth and Tenth cavalry and Twenty-fourth and Twenty-fifth infantry regiments—all-black units known to history as the "Buffalo Soldiers." St. Joseph became home for Winners of the West Camp No. 11, the so-called headquarters camp, to which members nationwide who were unaffiliated with municipal camps might belong (this camp in 1933 numbered 600 members). Additionally, during the 1930s four ladies' auxiliary camps existed, including Elizabeth B. Custer Camp No. 3, Los Angeles, and Lorena

14   *Winners of the West,* October, 1924 (first quote); *Winners of the West,* October, 1924; *Winners of the West,* June, 1925; *Winners of the West,* July 31, 1926 (second quote); *Winners of the West,* February, 1938. The constitution and by-laws of the NIWV appear in ibid.

Delegates' Convention of the National Indian War Veterans in St. Joseph, Missouri, 1927. George W. Webb is seated in front center, with cane. To his right is his wife and ladies' auxiliary national leader, Lorena Jane Webb. To his left is NIWV National Adjutant General Albert Fensch. Fensch was a leader in the walkout the next year that led to the founding of the United Indian War Veterans.

Jane Webb Camp No. 1, Stockton, California, the last named in honor of George Webb's wife.[15]

An average camp meeting consisted of a formulaic assembly of veterans, probably not unlike that held monthly by the Captain James H. Bradford Camp of San Antonio, Texas. "After the camp is called to order while all the members stand at attention, 'America' is sung and the

15 *Winners of the West,* September, 1940. The creation of the different camps is periodically discussed in various issues of *Winners of the West* between 1923 and 1944, its range of publication. Camp No. 11 evolved after disaffected members of the Kansas organization united against the Kansans' leadership to honor the spirit of the original Denver NIWV. *Winners of the West,* September, 1940. For a comprehensive list of the NIWV camps, see Jerome A. Greene, *Indian Wars Veteran Organizations* (Mattituck, New York, and Bryan, Texas: J.M. Carroll and Company, 1985), pp. 33-35.

Members of NIWV District of Columbia Camp No. 5 pose with President Calvin Coolidge on the White House lawn, 1928. Left to right, Evan D. Lewis, A. V. Dummel, G. A. Scheader, Jerome Lawler, Paul Schneider, C. W. Crawford, the President, J. J. Murphy, Henry McDonnell, and C. T. Edwards. *Editor's collection.*

invocation asked by the [camp's] chaplain. Then follow the salute of the colors, reading of minutes and [consideration of] applications for membership. Each candidate is required to repeat an 'Obligation of Candidates,' in which he pledges loyalty to his country and obedience to its laws, defense in time of danger and allegiance to his comrades of the Indian wars. After other business is attended to, the meeting closes with a patriotic song, the salute of the colors, and a benediction."[16]

Membership in the NIWV was "Active," "Associate," or "Honorary." Active members were veterans eligible for invalid pensions based on actual Indian wars service, while Associates were veterans and dependents deemed ineligible for Indian wars pension status. Associate members included Civil War, Spanish-American War, and World War veterans who nonetheless supported the ideals of the body. Similarly, Honorary members comprised interested non-veterans who aspired to the ideals of the association. Annual dues were $1.50 for men and $1.00 for women. (To help defray costs, the NIWV permitted dues to be paid in two semi-annual installments of half the total, i.e., 75 or 50 cents, respectively, every six months.) The command hierarchy consisted of both elected and appointed officers from Commander-in-Chief (National Commander) through Vice-Commander down to state and district commanders. There were also honorary positions, like National Chief of Staff, National Adjutant General, National Quartermaster General, and National Grand Marshall. National headquarters of the NIWV was at first located in the home city of the National Commander, although most administrative functions took place in St. Joseph under the guidance of Webb, who was appointed National Chief of Staff in 1925. Throughout most of its existence, the NIWV sponsored annual conventions, usually in the hometown of the National Commander. The assembly of 1924, for example, convened in San Francisco, presided

---

16 *Houston Post-Dispatch,* January 16, 1927. Minutes of Scranton Camp No. 22 on February 10, 1930, read as follows: "Meeting opened at 8:00 o'clock [p. m.]. Advance of colors, after which club sang three verses of 'America.' The camp was led in prayer by Chaplain Mrs. Jacob Goerlitz. Reading of last meeting's minutes. Reading of communications from Geo. W. Webb. A motion was passed and seconded that the Hawaiian Trio be non-paying members on the condition that they bring their instruments to each meeting. Refreshments were served. Meeting adjourned." "National Indian War Veterans, Scranton Camp No. 22" Minutes book, 1928-1931, in editor's possession.

over by National Commander J. F. W. Unfug. Eventually, St. Joseph, Missouri, became permanent National Headquarters City.[17]

The mother camp of all NIWV chapters remained that in Denver, which enjoyed resurgence in the early 1930s largely because of John F. Farley, who became Colorado state commander for the body in 1931. A former Third cavalryman who had been wounded by Apaches near Fort Bowie, Arizona, in 1871, Farley years later had served as Denver's chief of police. He single-handedly rejuvenated the membership in flagging Denver Camp No. 1, and served as state commander until his death in 1940.

Through the work of Farley, Webb, and others, the NIWV prospered, affording unity and therefore valuable assistance to veterans who had heretofore perceived their sacrifices as having gone unacknowledged by the federal government. Pension-related objectives of the body continued to lie in the solidarity of its members. Whereas congressional omnibus measures often included individual pension claims for Indian wars service, the NIWV promoted a community of support to seek legislation that would best serve all such veterans. "Congress will do nothing if it is bombarded by hundreds of different claims and appeals," opined Webb, "and it stands to reason [that] Congress will likely be disgusted and the waste basket is the depository of your writings."[18]

Although neither the NIWV nor its collateral bodies could ever boast large memberships, the NIWV nonetheless registered some worthy accomplishments in its lobbying before Congress. In 1924 the group enlisted the aid of former Lieutenant General Nelson A. Miles, then eighty-five years old and himself a past participant in notable western campaigns. Supporting

17 *Winners of the West,* July, 1925; *Winners of the West,* July 30, 1930; *Winners of the West,* October, 1924; *Winners of the West,* July, 1925; *Winners of the West,* September 30, 1937. The NIWV constitution and by-laws appear in *Winners of the West,* February, 1938.

18 *Winners of the West,* December, 1923; *San Francisco Examiner,* December 22, 1912; *National Tribune,* March 19, 1936; *Winners of the West,* December 30, 1931 (quote); *Winners of the West,* October, 1940. Farley's attempts to resurrect the Denver camp are mentioned in Webb to Farley, April 29, 1932, and May 31, 1932. Copies provided by Marcella Farley Dillon in the editor's collection. For more about Farley, see Mary M. Farley and Marcella E. Dillon (comps.), *The Farley Scrapbook: Biography of John F. Farley, 1849-1940, One of "The Winners of the West"* (Pueblo, Colo.: Privately printed, 1985). For a list of pension recipients in a single typical omnibus bill, see *Winners of the West,* April 30, 1926.

then-pending legislation on behalf of Indian war veterans, the retired commanding general wrote that these men:

> placed their lives between the . . . unprotected settlements and savage barbarians who were committing atrocities of the most cruel and savage character. They endured the severe and destructive heat of the extreme southern districts of our country, as well as the blizzards and the winter blasts of the extreme north, and by the exposure and hardship of the service the lives of many have been shortened.

Most bills advanced, however, never became law. Beyond the significant 1917 legislation, perhaps the major success to which the NIWV contributed occurred on March 3, 1927, when a measure co-sponsored by Representative Elmer O. Leatherwood and Senator Reed Smoot of Utah, and which superseded all previous Indian wars pension legislation, passed both houses of Congress.

The new law extended the period of requisite Indian wars service from 1817 to 1898 and insured that veterans received a minimum of $20 per month graduated upwards with advancing age to a maximum of $50 (still less, however, than that received by veterans of other wars). Moreover, fully disabled veterans might receive $20 to $50 more per month commensurate with their individual impairment. And for the first time, widows of Indian war veterans would receive $30 per month, besides an allowance of $6 per orphaned child up to age sixteen. Unlike earlier legislation, Leatherwood-Smoot did not enumerate specific Indian campaigns for which service pensions might be granted. Instead, it included provision for service "in the zone of any active Indian hostilities," wording that proved imprecise and confusing for many veterans.

In addition, the schedule accompanying the law was unduly complex and many veterans perceived inherent inequities in its application. While the act brought legislative success for Indian war veterans, it came only after a long drought following the 1917 Keating legislation. By 1927, many veterans had reached an age where its benefits would be minimal.

Nonetheless, passage of Leatherwood-Smoot produced an increase of around one thousand Indian wars pension claimants by 1930.[19]

Despite overall improvements to Indian war veterans' lot from the Leatherwood-Smoot measure, the NIWV continued to seek pension increases for its constituents on an equitable par with those granted veterans of other wars. During the 1930s, however, the fight ran counter to national circumstances during the Great Depression, and in March, 1933, while implementing his New Deal recovery program, President Franklin D. Roosevelt directed a 10% reduction in veterans' pensions for a period of one year. The NIWV vigorously protested the cuts as being unfair, as George Webb editorialized in *Winners of the West*. "When the Veteran of Indian Wars . . . witnesses the Civil War Veteran receiving a pension of $100 per month, the Spanish-American and World War Veteran considered eligible [for] various amounts even in excess of that paid to Civil War Veterans . . . he begins to question whether or not he is being dealt with by the Government

19 *St. Joseph Gazette,* October 11, 1928; *Winners of the West,* December, 1924 (Miles quote); *Winners of the West,* January 30, 1930; *Winners of the West,* October 30, 1935; *Winners of the West,* September 30, 1937. For details of a typical bill never enacted yet seeking apportioned increases in pensions based upon advancing age and disability, as well as extending increased benefits to widows with provision for orphaned children, see *Winners of the West,* June, 1924. Precursor of the Leatherwood-Smoot measure was various legislation introduced in 1925 and 1926 by Senator Selden P. Spencer (Missouri), Representative Addison T. Smith (Idaho), Senator Frank R. Gooding (Idaho), and Representative Leatherwood. *Winners of the West,* October, 1925; *Winners of the West,* December, 1925; *Winners of the West,* March 30, 1926. The Leatherwood-Smoot bill of 1927 passed Congress over the objections of Secretary of the Interior Hubert Work, who opposed the cost of the increase. *Winners of the West,* June 24, 1926. For an effort to publicize the act to appropriate veterans, see "Pension the Indian Fighters," *Frontier Times,* 4 (July, 1927), pp. 36-37. The 1898 addition accommodated service during the Chippewa uprising of October, 1898. For the act, see Public Law 723, Statutes at Large, 44, Part 2, pp. 1361-63. Later amendatory efforts did not succeed to provide for those who served during the 1906 expedition to capture Ute Indians (the "Absentee" Utes) who left their Utah reservation to take up residence at the Cheyenne River Sioux reservation in South Dakota. See U. S. Congress, House, Committee on Invalid Pensions, *Hearings . . . on . . . Bills to Liberalize the Now Existing Benefits with Reference to Veterans and Dependents of Veterans of the Indian Wars,* 76th Cong., 3d sess., January 22 and 23, 1940, *passim.*

Birthplace of the United Indian War Veterans at 901 Charles Street, St. Joseph, Missouri. Members who bolted the National Indian War Veterans convention in September, 1928, reconvened at this address to organize their own body. *Editor's collection.*

with any spirit of fairness. . . ." Webb's future successes were limited. In August, 1937, a new pension law increased by $5 (a "magnanimous sum," he remarked) the monthly stipend to all Indian war veterans, while allowing those totally disabled $72 per month.[20]

By late in the decade, only slightly more than 3,000 qualified Indian war veterans still lived (including, interestingly enough, 400 who were Indians—former scouts who had enlisted to serve against their kinsmen). Dependents of deceased veterans numbered approximately 4,500. Yet another pension act passed Congress in March, 1944, providing for graduated raises based upon age and disability, and at last accorded Indian war veterans (those with appropriate service in specified Indian wars or

20 *Winners of the West,* March 30, 1933; *Winners of the West,* February 28, 1934; *Winners of the West,* June 30, 1933 (quote); *Winners of the West,* September 30, 1937. Throughout the 1930s, many bills introduced in Congress sought to amend the 1927 law to raise pensions of the Indian wars class to a level equitable to those of other war veterans. Some proposed a single higher rate (as high as $75) for all Indian wars pensioners, yet none were enacted. See *Winners of the West,* January 30, 1931; *Winners of the West,* January 30, 1932; *Winners of the West,* December 30, 1933; *Winners of the West,* March, 1937; *Winners of the West,* May, 1939.

campaigns) certain parity with Civil War and Spanish-American War veterans. This legislation was the last supported by the NIWV as an identifiable body. By then the association had become an untenable enterprise with increasingly mounting deaths in its membership. George Webb had died in 1938, and continuation of *Winners of the West* rested with the volunteer efforts of interested non-veterans. Shortly after Webb's death, National Commander Edmund Graham resigned, and many camps with dwindling rolls disbanded altogether. In 1940 a brief revitalization attempt occurred led by the General O. O. Howard Camp in Chicago that resulted in the installation of a new slate of officers.

But the inexorable march of time, hastened by the sudden onset of World War II, ultimately insured the end of the NIWV. (During that conflict *Winners of the West* carried such incongruous headlines as "Veteran Who is Almost Blind . . . Would Enjoy Chance at Japs and Nazis with His Old Springfield," and "[He] Saw Geronimo Fall: Axis Next.") In 1941 only nine diminishing camps remained active, and three years later, with publication of the final issue of *Winners of the West*, the National Indian War Veterans Association ceased existence.[21]

The demise of the NIWV did not close the pension movement for Indian war veterans altogether. Since 1928, a successful rival organization had emerged with headquarters in California whose work paralleled that of the NIWV. Among numerous western camps, a simmering dispute had arisen over George Webb's domination of the organization as National Commander, and many opposed his re-election to that office.

In 1928, at the eighteenth annual NIWV convention in St. Joseph, Missouri, the rebels took issue with a motion by Webb supporters to dispense with the reading of the officers' reports because some contained criticism of Webb. On the afternoon of October 10, when the matter was put to a vote and the regulars won, the minority faction of delegates from six

21 *Winners of the West*, May 30, 1937; *Winners of the West*, March 28, 1944; *Winners of the West*, December, 1939; *Winners of the West*, January, 1940; *Winners of the West*, June, 1940; *Winners of the West*, April, 1941; *Winners of the West*, May 28, 1943; *Winners of the West*, June 28, 1943; Frank Ostlin, *What Every Veteran Should Know* (Chicago: Published by the author, 1945), pp. 100-01, 102-03, 108. Following Webb's death, the editor of the paper from 1938 to 1944 was Virginia Elizabeth Wing (Mrs. Frederick S. Bangerter) of St. Joseph. *Winners of the West*, June 28, 1942. The final issue, dated December 28, 1944, carried the following notice: "Due to existing conditions beyond our control, labor finances, and war-time constriction, we are forced to discontinue the publishing of *Winners of the West* at least for the duration of the war. This is our last issue."

Editor's collection

Attendees at the third annual convention of the United Indian War Veterans stand before the Yavapai County Building, Prescott, Arizona, September 14, 1931. Note the banner at right for the Gen. George Crook Camp No. 1, Los Angeles.

camps bolted the meeting to convene nearby where they drafted their own constitution and by-laws and elected officers. Horace B. Mulkey, who had been National Senior Vice President of the NIWV, became National Commander of the new United Indian War Veterans of the United States (UIWV).

Of the 1,300 NIWV members scattered in camps throughout the nation, UIWV leadership immediately claimed 542 members in camps in San Francisco; Chicago; Los Angeles; San Antonio; Billings, Montana; and Yountsville, California, and additionally announced that the three independent groups in Kansas, Utah, and Oregon would join with the new national body.

The organization eventually embraced thirteen departments across the country, each under a commander. The UIWV was incorporated under the laws of the State of California on November 5, 1928, and held its first annual convention in September, 1929, at the Disabled Veterans Hall in Los Angeles.[22] Oddly enough, by the 1928 rupture, the very unity that the Indian

22 Pertinent news clippings from the *St. Joseph News Press,* October 11, 1928, and the *St. Joseph Gazette,* October 11, 1928; State of California, Department of State, Articles of Incorporation of the United Indian War

war veterans as a relatively small group had long advocated, and that had been vital to fostering pension reform, became effectively lost as the two national groups, each with declining memberships based on attrition, individually competed for the same objectives.

Following the splintering off of the UIWV, the old San Francisco NIWV camp founded in 1912 became Gen. George A. Custer Camp No. 4, United Indian War Veterans, U. S. A., and became the nucleus around which the new organization evolved. The group's slogan, "There's Only a Few of Us Left," belied the state of the UIWV, which thrived for decades as the last of the Indian wars veteran groups. The primary objectives of the body were:

> To cultivate a spirit of harmony and comradeship amongst those whose services in our country were identical or similar in its nature, and to perpetuate the memory of such service in future generations of our descendants, and

---

Veterans of the United States, November 5, 1928. Original copy, along with cited clippings in Scrapbook No. 1, Fensch Scrapbooks; Program, *First Annual Convention, United Indian War Veterans, U. S. A.,* Sept. 15, 16, 17, 1929 (copy in editor's possession). The charges against Webb apparently centered on the belief "that the St. Joseph Camp No. 11 was exercising more power than it was entitled to have at the convention. As editor of the publication *Winners of the West,* Webb was alleged to be able to dominate the convention. "He has been president [National Commander] for two years." Clipping from an unidentified St. Joseph newspaper in Fensch Scrapbook No. 3. Another charge against Webb was "that he had sought to control the organization by enrolling distant veterans in St. Joseph Camp No. 11." Clipping from the *St. Joseph Gazette,* October 12, 1928, in ibid. Webb was re-elected commander of the NIWV following the walkout by the rebels, while St. Joseph was voted as the "permanent national headquarters" of the NIWV. Ibid. A prospectus for a history of the United Indian War Veterans in 1931enumerated and perhaps exaggerated the causes culminating in the breakaway from the NIWV as "the struggles against the exploitation, graft, racketeering methods for selfish gain, and maladministration into which it [the NIWV] had fallen prior to the 1928 . . . reorganization." Fensch Scrapbook No. 3. In the organization into UIWV departments, four camps of Utah Indian War Veterans joined the Department of Nevada and Utah under commander Brigham Jarvis, while the Kansas organization amalgamated into the Department of Kansas, Iowa, Nebraska, and Missouri, under Luther Barker. The Indian War Veterans of the North Pacific Coast merged into the Department of Oregon, Washington, Idaho, and Alaska, under William Murphy. *Prescott Evening Courier,* September 15, 1931; "Annual Convention, Encampment, and Reunion United Indian War Veterans, U. S. A. Our Old 'Winners of the West,'" *Yavapai Magazine,* 21 (August, 1931), p. 7.

OBSERVANCE OF

Sixtieth Anniversary

Custer Massacre

THURSDAY EVENING, JUNE 25, 1936

7:00 o'clock

at HOUSE of HOSPITALITY

CALIFORNIA PACIFIC INTERNATIONAL EXPOSITION

Balboa Park, San Diego, California

Program

1. "Star Spangled Banner" - Merkley's Musical Maids
Walter P. Reeves, Director

2. Introductory Remarks - - - Hon. Elwood T. Bailey
Vice President, California Pacific International Exposition

3. Selections: "The Girl I Left Behind Me" and "Garry Owen"*-
- - - Merkley's Musical Maids

4. Introduction of Distinguished Guests - -

5. "How My Husband Recovered Custer's Battle Flag" -
- - Mrs. Ora McClinton
Ladies' Corps, Gen. Geo. A. Custer Camp No. 4, San Francisco

6. Selection: "Indian Girl" - - Merkley's Musical Maids

7. Indian Specialty Act: "Fallen Leaf" - Singing Bird
Black Hawk Indian Whistling Artist

8. Awarding of Prizes for Essays on "The Life of General Custer"
- - - Col. Ralph Donath
National Commander, United Indian War Veterans, U. S. A.

9. Reading of Prize Essays by Winners of Contest - -

10. Address:"General George Armstrong Custer"-Hon. Thomas Whelan
District Attorney, San Diego County

11. Selection: "American Soldier" - Merkley's Musical Maids

Program Chairman: Viola Ransom Wood,
National Historian, United Indian War Veterans, U. S. A.

* On leaving Fort A. Lincoln for the last time "The Girl I Left Behind Me"
was played by the Seventh Cavalry Band as the regiment paraded around the
garrison. On leaving the garrison, the band played Custer's favorate tune,
"Garry Owen." Colonel Ralph Donath, Nation Commander, United Indian
War Veterans, U. S. A., is believed to be the only survivor of the men who, at
at that time, presented arms as the Custer Expedition left the fort on their ill-
fated journey.

Program for the United Indian War Veterans' observance of the sixtieth anniversary of the "Custer Massacre" on June 25, 1936, in Balboa Park, San Diego, California. During the exercises, Mrs. Ora McClinton offered a telling of "How My Husband Recovered Custer's Battle Flag" at the Little Bighorn. *Editor's collection.*

To use all and every proper means of bringing about recognition by our government, of such services equal to that accorded those who participated in other wars in which our country has been engaged, the results of which were not of greater value than those attained by our own struggles against its foes.

During ensuing years the UIWV proliferated along the West Coast with three camps and a like number of associated ladies' corps units. The bitterness with the NIWV continued, with UIWV National Adjutant General Albert Fensch privately branding Webb "the St. Jo bandit," and his paper the "Losers of the West." "I think the Webb outfit is gradually disintegrating," wrote Fensch in the early 1930s. "His 'convention' was a farce, so we heard, and his many 'strong' camps are all in his head and in his 'rag' of a paper."

As of 1931, the UIWV claimed twenty-four camps nationwide "of which only about 16 are really active," with total membership at "between 1400 and 1500." (It was estimated that of 17,000 then-surviving Indian war veterans—all of those who had served in the West, 1865-98—less than one-third were on the pension rolls.) [23]

Like the NIWV, which it survived by more than twenty years, the UIWV promoted pension legislation favorable to the Indian war veteran class while providing fellowship among its aging constituency. The organization also helped members prepare and file individual pension claims. Officers were elected annually at conventions held usually in Los Angeles or San Francisco, but occasionally at places like Prescott, Arizona, where in 1931 Governor George W. P. Hunt welcomed the body at its banquet and was made an honorary member. A resolution approved at the Arizona meeting sought to raise invalid pensions for "aged and infirm" Indian war veterans from $50 to $100 per month (claiming that disabled Spanish-American and World War veterans received as much as $157.50 per month).

23 *Winners of the West,* December 30, 1935; *Program, Eighteenth National Convention, United Indian War Veterans, U. S.A., and the Ladies Corps, San Francisco, California,* October 16-17, 1948. Excerpts of the constitution and by-laws of the UIWV appear in *Program, Twenty-fourth National Convention, United Indian War Veterans, U. S. A., San Francisco, California,* October 15-16, 1954; *Program, Twenty-ninth National Reunion, United Indian War Veterans, U. S. A., and the Ladies Corps, San Francisco, California,* October 13-14, 1960; Albert Fensch, "The Policies of the United Indian War Veterans," clipping in Scrapbook #2, Fensch Scrapbooks (quote); Fensch to Lieutenant Colonel Willis Metcalf, U. S. Army, ca. December, 1931 (quote regarding Webb). Transcribed copy in editor's collection; *Prescott Evening Courier,* September 15, 1931.

In 1937, the UIWV published a pamphlet of original poems to bring attention to their cause; they dedicated it to President Franklin D. Roosevelt and disseminated it to the congressional membership. In 1936, the camp in San Diego sponsored an observance of the sixtieth anniversary of the "Custer Massacre" at Balboa Park, the program including Seventh Cavalry band selections, the award of prizes for essays on Custer's life, and a "Black Hawk Indian Whistling Artist."

After World War II, with its membership falling, the UIWV focused more on fostering such social activities over improving pension benefits. During the 1950s, more than 300 surviving Indian war veterans, including many of the UIWV, were contacted for historical information about their service; questionnaires completed during the study are on file at the U. S. Army Military History Institute in Pennsylvania.

The UIWV sponsored its annual meetings into the 1960s, when three camps still functioned. Late in 1962, twenty-nine members assembled in San Francisco for their annual meeting, presided over by National Commander Edward Snider and Ladies Corps Commander Minnie Saunders, age 97. Six years later, only four veterans attended.[24]

24 *Prescott Evening Courier,* September 15, 1931; *Prescott Journal-Miner,* September 16, 1933; *Prescott Journal-Miner,* September 17, 1931; *Los Angeles City News,* February 11, 1937. Some UIWV camps were located in the East, for example, the Gen. Adna R. Chaffee Camp of Washington, D. C. Pension news was disseminated to UIWV members via a mimeographed paper entitled *The War-Path,* published initially in 1939. The pamphlet cited was *Rimes and Chimes of the Mountains and Plains* (Los Angeles: United Indian War Veterans, U. S. A., 1937). Broadside regarding the "Custer Massacre" observance, "Thursday evening, June 25, 1936" in Fensch Scrapbook No. 4. Historian Don G. Rickey conducted the survey mostly in 1954, and assembled a body of questionnaires, personal letters, and interview materials. See the Rickey Papers, Manuscript Archives, U. S. Army Military History Institute, Army War College, Carlisle, Pennsylvania. Based partly on this information, Rickey published *Forty Miles a Day on Beans and Hay.* The final UIWV assemblies are recounted in clippings from an unidentified San Francisco newspaper, circa October 10, 1962, and November 13, 1968, in Fensch Scrapbook No. 5. The last two surviving Indian war veterans were Reginald Bradley, 105, who joined the Fourth Cavalry at Fort Bowie, Arizona Territory, in 1889, and died February 5, 1971; and Fredrak W. Fraske, 101, of Chicago, who died June 18, 1973. *San Francisco Chronicle,* October 26, 1967; *Washington Post,* February 6, 1971. For three terms, Minnie Saunders served continuously as National Commander of the Ladies Corps from 1930 through 1962. Before UIWV was organized, she belonged to the NIWV.

The survival of the UIWV into the second half of the twentieth century was remarkable. By the 1940s, to say nothing of the 1960s, a veteran of frontier service was something of an anachronism. Unlike Civil War, Spanish-American War, and World War I veterans, those survivors of the Indian campaigns had no single chronological block on which to focus their service for commemorative purposes. Theirs was sandwiched between major wars, did not respond to any particular national emergency, and was generally characterized more by routine activity that spanned several decades of postwar development only sporadically infused with campaigning and combat. Unlike those veterans of the nation's larger conflicts, the survivors of the Indian wars found it difficult to assemble for purposes of camaraderie, to say nothing of uniting to seek government benefits. That they nonetheless succeeded to some degree in both was due to a tenacity of spirit perhaps acquired years earlier under arduous conditions in forbidding climates during far-flung service on the plains and in the mountains and deserts against the followers of Geronimo, Sitting Bull, Joseph, and Cochise. As one of the old veterans averred in a closing poetic reflection of his time in the West, "And some of these days, it won't be long, Our names will be called and we'll all be gone. But so long as it lasts, let us never forget, 'Tis an honor to be an Indian War vet."[25]

---

25 Albert Fensch, "By-Gone Days," in *Rimes and Chimes of the Mountains and Plains,* pp. 11-12.

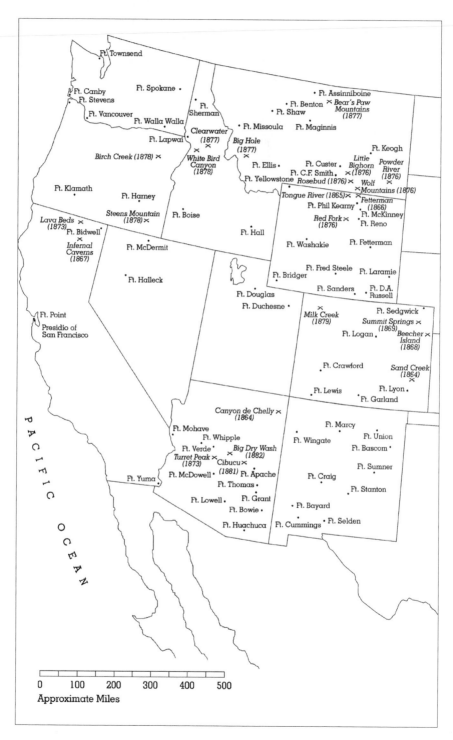

Ft. Townsend

Ft. Canby
Ft. Stevens
Ft. Vancouver

Ft. Spokane

Ft. Walla Walla

Ft. Sherman

Clearwater (1877)
Ft. Lapwai

White Bird Canyon (1878)

Birch Creek (1878) ✕

Ft. Missoula

Big Hole (1877)

Ft. Ellis

Ft. Yellowstone

Ft. Assinniboine

Ft. Benton
Ft. Shaw

Bear's Paw Mountains (1877)

Ft. Maginnis

Ft. Keogh

Ft. Custer

Little Bighorn (1876)

Powder River (1876)

Ft. C.F. Smith

Rosebud (1876) ✕

Wolf Mountains (1876)

Tongue River (1865) ✕

Ft. Phil Kearny (1866)

Red Fork (1876) ✕

Fetterman (1866)

Ft. McKinney

Ft. Reno

Ft. Klamath

Ft. Harney

Steens Mountain (1878) ✕

Ft. Boise

Ft. Hall

Ft. Washakie

Ft. Fetterman

Lava Beds (1873) ✕
Ft. Bidwell ✕
Infernal Caverns (1867)

Ft. McDermit

Ft. Fred Steele

Ft. Laramie

Ft. Halleck

Ft. Bridger

Ft. Sanders

Ft. D.A. Russell

Ft. Point
Presidio of San Francisco

Ft. Douglas

Ft. Duchesne

Milk Creek (1879) ✕

Ft. Sedgwick

Summit Springs (1869) ✕

Ft. Logan

Beecher Island (1868) ✕

Ft. Crawford

Sand Creek (1864) ✕

Ft. Lewis

Ft. Lyon

Ft. Garland

Canyon de Chelly (1864) ✕

Ft. Mohave

Ft. Whipple

Ft. Verde

Turret Peak (1873) ✕

Big Dry Wash (1882)

Cibucu ✕

Ft. Marcy

Ft. Wingate

Ft. Union

Ft. Bascom

Ft. McDowell

(1881) Ft. Apache

Ft. Thomas

Ft. Craig

Ft. Sumner

Ft. Stanton

Ft. Yuma

Ft. Lowell

Ft. Grant

Ft. Bowie

Ft. Bayard

Ft. Huachuca

Ft. Cummings

Ft. Selden

PACIFIC OCEAN

0   100   200   300   400   500

Approximate Miles

Major Forts and Encounter Sites, 1864-1898

Major Forts and Encounter Sites, 1864-1898

Part I:
Army Life in the West

Much of the army presence in the West during the post-Civil War period (1865-1898) was occasioned by activities other than campaigning. The troops variously conducted security patrols along established routes of travel; protected settlers and ranchers; aided law enforcement in the pursuit and arrest of criminals; helped out citizens during floods, insect invasions, and drought conditions; labored to improve roads and trails and to renovate, maintain, and rebuild (or build) forts, camps, and cantonments; maintained drill and target-shooting proficiency; encouraged business and economic development (many communities sprang up around army posts); guarded Indian camps and reservations; protected Indian lands against trespassers; oversaw treaty assemblies and civil elections; and otherwise acted as domestic overseers to settlement and progress. The pursuit of Indians occupied a relatively minor amount of the time of the average soldier stationed west of the Mississippi River. Indeed, most enlisted men passed the majority of their time under hard labor conditions and few experienced the rigors of campaign; fewer still took part in skirmishes or battles with Indians during their service.

In the passages that follow, Indian war veterans (the term here includes all of those who served in the West—the broadest possible zone for service to classify for such designation), and in one case a veteran's dependent, reminisce about their non-combat experiences on the frontier. Several describe the years of their enlistments, discussing the routine aspects of army life at posts spread across the Plains, the Northwest, and the Southwest in statements of duty in post and field that reflect the tedious reality of their service—a veritable kaleidoscope of military existence of the period. Included are incidents at a recruit depot, the army life of Buffalo Soldiers (members of one or another of four segregated black units—the Ninth and Tenth cavalry and Twenty-fourth and Twenty-fifth infantry regiments),

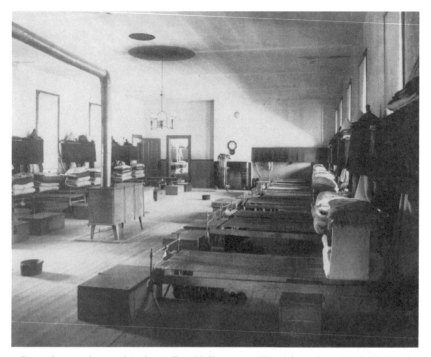

Barracks squad-room interior at Fort Yellowstone, Wyoming, circa. 1892. Note the iron bunks, footlockers, and heating stoves. An arms rack stands at the end of the room beneath the wall clock. *National Archives*

descriptions of the posts at which frontier soldiers served out their careers, and non-battle and campaign activities in which they took part. Among the special remembrances are a social dance at Fort Custer, Montana Territory, in 1885, a remarkable Christmas at Fort Robinson, Nebraska, in 1882, and accounts of the historic trek of the Eighth Cavalry in its transfer from West Texas to Dakota in 1888, an event often likened to a campaign experience in the annals of the regiment.

A Press Interview with Five Veterans

(From *Winners of the West*, July, 1940)

Last month Camp 36, [National Indian War Veterans,] Philadelphia, gained national interest anew. It all came about in this manner: a columnist of the *Philadelphia Inquirer* voluntarily commented upon the Indian War Veterans' rally held May 12 [1940] at the home of their State Commander, Ralph Edwards of Malvern, Pennsylvania. The comment, though brief, was

Privates of Company D, Twenty-fifth Infantry, at Fort Custer, Montana Territory. The man at lower right wears Grand Army of the Republic membership badges, besides his membership badge in the Regular Army and Navy Union. The man standing at right likewise wears his RA&NU badge, and also marksman and sharpshooter qualification pins. *Courtesy of James B. Dahlquist*

followed by a series of interviews which were published in the *Evening Bulletin*. These interviews included all of the veterans that the *Bulletin* could reach in and around Philadelphia. These interviews translated the veteran from a shadowy figure into a hero of valiant deeds worthy of attention. Following are some extracts from each of the interviews. Each interview has been cut down considerably as they were quite lengthy and accompanied by several pictures, as published originally in the *Evening Bulletin* of Philadelphia.

Extract of Interview with Comrade Harry Conver [on pursuing Geronimo, 1885]:

"I see where they've made a movie hero of old Geronimo," says Harry Conver, retired lieutenant of Philadelphia police. "And I saw a picture the other day of a monument the WPA has erected to his memory at Douglas, Arizona. I'd like to put my idea of a monument to the old buzzard. It would be a crowbar, like the one I saw in New Mexico. . . ." Conver, who lives now at 2048 Boston Ave., traded shots with Geronimo, and thinks he got the worst of the bargain. His left shoulder has a wound that still hurts occasionally, though the bullet has been out for fifty-five years. Conver was a lively youngster with a taste for trouble back in 1883. Grandson of two Pennsylvania preachers, grandnephew of Henry Ward Beecher, he too heard "a call," but his was the call of the Far West. And that's how it happened that he was at Fort Clark, Texas, on the Rio Grande, when the border, in 1885, got an electrifying message: "Geronimo has gone out!"

The wiliest, most bloodthirsty chief in American history had broken from the Apache reservation where he had been nursing his wounds for two years. With a band of ninety, he had celebrated his first day of freedom by wiping out an Arizona ranch family. And now he was heading for the border, murdering as he went. "There is no describing the savagery of the man," says Conver today. "His tribe, the Apaches, were the cruelest and most heartless of all the Indians. And Geronimo was feared and shunned even by his own people. Conver saw a sample of Geronimo's technique just after his troop reached Fairview, New Mexico, to take up the trail. A group were on scout duty when they heard shots a mile or two away. "We turned and raced to the spot," he says, "but flames were already destroying the ranch buildings. At the door we found the rancher and his family, horribly mutilated. A half-mile away we found five cowboys. They had been digging holes for a fence and their rifles were stacked against a post. They had been shot from ambush, then hacked to pieces. A little black dog at their feet had been shot more than fifty times. And one of the men, as an artistic touch, had been pinned to the earth with his own crowbar, plunged through his abdomen. . . . And that was the work of the man they're building monuments for!"

A bloody game of hide-and-seek followed that horror, as the Apache chieftain and his band dodged the troopers through canyons and desert wilds of Arizona, New Mexico, and Old Mexico. Conver's troop of the Eighth Cavalry tracked the savages across one 100-mile stretch of alkali desert in southern New Mexico that is still marked on maps as "El Journado del Muerto"—the "Journey of Death." And they nearly gave that desert new claim to its title when their canteens went dry. But they got through, and not long afterward they had Geronimo trapped—they thought! Scouts found the Apaches in a wild New Mexico canyon, and with utmost caution a circle was thrown around the spot. At a signal the troop closed in. But Geronimo's uncanny knowledge of the mountains saved him again. The troop, closing in, found that the warriors had escaped through a secret gap in the hills. Left in their camp were only a dozen squaws.

With George Morris [on the Crow Rebellion, 1887]:

Gnawing on a part of the roasted leg of an army mule, a young Englishman who was 5,000 miles from home sat on the frozen ground of the Big Horn Mountains and cursed his own folly. And today, fifty-three years later, George Morris, ex-burgess of Darby, and for twenty-nine years a fire insurance broker there, still remembers that blizzard. It was Wild West stories in London's penny-dreadfuls—stories of the Custer Massacre and Rain-in-the-Face—that lured young George Morris out of Victorian England to search for painted redskins. Four months later, Private Morris, Troop I, First U. S. Cavalry, was facing 3,000 hostiles at the Battle of Crow Agency, Montana, November 5, 1887.

They were the same warriors who had massacred Custer less than a dozen years before [sic—These were Crows, some of whom, in fact, had scouted for the army in 1876.]. On the warpath again, they had murdered the Indian agent and his staff at Crow Agency, burned the agency buildings, and stampeded off the reservation. "We went out from Camp Crook [Fort Custer]," says Morris, "and met them on the same battlefield where they had wiped out Custer's force [sic—The confrontation occurred about one to three miles north of the battlefield.]. Odd, wasn't it, coming all the way from England to find myself fighting on that very spot? And for a while it looked like fun, too. Three thousand Indians, a few hundred of us. But Brigadier General Thomas H. Ruger handled it like a master. He sent word to the

Indians that we would attack at noon. Indians who wanted to be our friends were to move their camp to the neighborhood of a certain tall birch. The rest would be considered hostiles, and destroyed.

"It was a tense morning as we watched the slow drift of the Indians toward that birch tree. Those who went there were disarmed, and a guard posted. But at noon there were still some 600 left in the hostile camp. General Ruger gave word for the attack. The cavalry charged, and took a volley from the Indian camp. At 200 yards we leaped from our horses and flattened out behind clumps of sagebrush. We traded shots for a while, until two Hotchkiss field guns on the hill began dumping two-inch shells into the Indian camp. That broke them."

With Comrade John R. Nixon [on Wounded Knee, 1890]:

He hadn't got the taste of Schuylkill water out of his mouth before he was up to his ears in painted Indians at Wounded Knee. That was in December, 1890—the month when Ghost Dancing burst into flames on every reservation in the Dakotas. The outbreak brought the Seventh Cavalry—Custer's old regiment—roaring up from Fort Riley, Kansas, on the double-quick. Private Nixon, of Troop I, was with them.

"Our job," he relates, "was to round up Big Foot and his gang of Oglala [Minneconjou] Sioux. We got word of them on the 28th and ran them down at Wounded Knee Creek, five miles from the Pine Ridge Indian Agency. There was a parley, and Big Foot surrendered—but he had his fingers crossed. They let us herd them into camp as peaceable as you please, but next day, when we started to disarm them, the fun began. With five troops stationed in a circle around the camp, the braves were ordered to pile their weapons in front of their tepees. They were sullen and painted up as if they were looking for trouble. They put down a few rusty guns, and said that was all they had. Then they stood around while the soldiers searched their tepees. From my post in the ring of guards, I watched the medicine man—a sour-puss old duck—standing with folded arms in front of his tepee.

"Then I saw him reach down and pick up a handful of dirt. I was trying to figure that out when he threw the dust high in the air. And that was the signal. In a split second all hell broke loose. Every Indian whipped a repeating rifle from beneath his blanket and cut loose. One shot went through my right side, though I hardly felt it at the time—I thought a pin was sticking me. Captain Wallace went down in the first thirty seconds. I turned just in time to see a Paiute bash his brains out with a war club. I let go one shot at the Paiute, and that emptied my carbine. Then I had troubles of my own. A Sioux with a face like a Mummer jumped me. He grabbed my revolver with his left hand. His right had a knife that looked two feet long, and he struck for my jugular. He missed, and I grabbed for his wrist. All I got was the blade of his knife—but right then I wasn't particular. I held on until I could get my revolver loose. And then—well, he turned into a good Indian mighty quick."

The battle went on for a half hour, until there was only one wounded Indian sniper left, hiding in a trooper's tent. He dropped four soldiers. Then came a Hotchkiss shell—and silence. That night the Seventh Cavalry returned to Pine Ridge with the bodies of twenty-four of its men. But behind, in a deep trench, it left the bodies of 128 Sioux. One of them was Big Foot.

With Richard F. Watson [on pursuing the Apache Kid, 1893-95]:

Geronimo wasn't the last of the Apaches. There was the Apache Kid, too. Richard F. Watson, book and novelty salesman now living in retirement at 1627 Summer Street, traded lead with the Kid for nearly three years back in the '90s. "And those who knew the Kid," he says, "say he could have given Geronimo cards and spades for sheer downright insane cruelty."

The Apache Kid was a renegade, never a chief, whose career in blood began abruptly at Fort Grant, Arizona, just a few years before Watson, a Camden boy from the White Horse Pike section, reached that post in 1893. The Kid had been a well-liked sergeant of scouts at the post until one day an Indian named Old Rip got to brooding over the fact that the Kid's uncle had stolen one of Old Rip's squaws—a little matter of forty years earlier. Old Rip decided on revenge, and killed the Kid's uncle. The Kid, in turn, brooded Apache-fashion for a month or two, and then killed Old Rip. His career of murder was on. Cavalrymen caught him, with ten followers, and he shot his way free. A few days later he needed a change of horses and wiped out a family of six whites to get them. He had a quaint conceit—when he had ridden a horse to exhaustion he would stab it to death in the left shoulder as a reward for its services. No squaw would stay with him willingly, so he captured new ones frequently, holding them by force and tying them to trees when he went on his raids. He was captured a few months after Watson reached Fort Grant and sentenced to death with five followers. But on the way to Yuma in custody of Sheriff Glenn Reynolds, of Phoenix, he caught the officers off guard.

Handcuffed, the Kid threw his arms over Sheriff Reynolds's head and pinioned his arms. His companions overpowered Deputy "Hunky-Dory"

Holmes. With the officers' guns, they shot Reynolds, Holmes, and the stagecoach driver, took the handcuff key from Reynolds's pocket, and fled. So the hunt was on again and for two years Watson and his troop followed a trail that was marked by the blood of ranchers and their families. Twice, Watson caught sight of the Kid and they exchanged shots across deep canyons in the Table and Superstition mountains. Twice, the troopers drove the Kid out of his favorite haunts in the Superstitions [and] far into the wilds of Old Mexico. But each time the Kid returned and announced his arrival with a succession of blood massacres. In the end, it was a miner named Wallapai Clark who ended the career of the only Apache the troopers couldn't bring in.

With Major Wilkinson [on the killing of Sitting Bull, 1890]:

Nearly fifty years after he had tossed the bullet-riddled body of Sitting Bull into an army dump cart, Major William G. Wilkinson, a soft-spoken ex-army man who now lives in Long Lane Court, Upper Darby, Pennsylvania, rode by automobile to Fort Yates, North Dakota. His car whirled past a tiny knoll in a moment, but for that moment Major Wilkinson's mind's eye saw once more a bright clear morning in September, 1888. Troop G, Eighth U. S. Cavalry, was completing probably the longest continuous march ever made by a body of troops. It had marched 2,200 miles in fifty-eight days, from Fort Davis on [near] the Rio Grande [sic]. And as the weary troopers swung through the gap in the hills, their destination only a few miles away, they found their road leading through a temporary Indian village where the Sioux had camped while drawing their semi-monthly government rations.

That very summer brought the "Messiah Craze." To the throb of tom-toms, Sitting Bull was proclaiming a holy war against all whites. He had talked with the Great Spirit. A divine leader was coming, marching at the head of an army of ghosts—the spirits of all the warriors who had died battling the Paleface! And in December, 1890, Sitting Bull was ready for his war of extermination. "From Lieutenant Bull Head, chief of the Indian police," says Major Wilkinson[, then an enlisted man], "came word that the old medicine man was about to give the signal for a break to the Black Hills. His arrest was ordered—a ticklish job and one that could only be handled, it was felt, by the Indian police. So a plan was worked out. Lieutenant Bull Head and his men moved secretly on Sitting Bull's village with orders to lie in wait until the ghost dancing stopped for the night. Then, it was thought, they could enter quietly, surprise Sitting Bull, and remove him without arousing the village.

"But when we reached Oak Creek, after a twenty-mile march through a blizzard, there was no sign of the police. We pushed on, and were only two miles from Sitting Bull's village when we met a courier. His message: 'All police dead.' Lieutenant Bull Head was still alive when I found him. He was terribly wounded, obviously dying, but he showed no sign of his agony, and while a doctor gave him opiates I held his head and he told me what had happened. The police had managed to enter Sitting Bull's house without disturbing the village and woke the old medicine man to tell him he was wanted. He consented at first to go with them, but he spoke in a loud voice that woke some squaws and Catch-the-Bear. In an instant, Catch-the-Bear was arousing the whole village. A few minutes after giving me this story, Lieutenant Bull Head passed away in my arms. Later, he and the other slain Indian police were buried with full military honors in the Fort Yates Cemetery. But there were no honors for Sitting Bull. His body was put into a dump cart, a hole dug in the ground in the military cemetery, and his body tossed into the hole. The ground was leveled over and no mark whatever was left to show where the body of Sitting Bull, last of the great Indian chiefs, rested.

A Typical Entry in *Winners of the West*, appearing March 30, 1928

I enlisted at Jefferson Barracks on August 24th, 1876, and was sent from there to Fort D. A. Russell, Wyoming. Was there for thirty days and then sent to Camp Robinson, Nebraska, where I was attached to Troop D, Fourth U. S. Cavalry, and fitted out for a winter campaign after the Northern Cheyennes.

Was in the Battle of Powder River in the Little Big Horn Mountains [sic], and from there we came back to Camp Robinson in the spring of 1877. Then ordered to Fort Sill where we stayed until the spring of 1878, then going to Fort Clark, Texas, then to Fort Duncan, and in the fall of 1879 to Fort Garland, Colorado. In the spring went out after the Utes but did not have much luck. Went to Fort Hays, Kansas, and in the spring of 1881 took the field again after the Utes, and this time we captured them. Was discharged as ranking sergeant on August 24, 1881. Am now getting a pension of $30.00 per month.

Wm. J. Murphy, St. Paul, Minn.

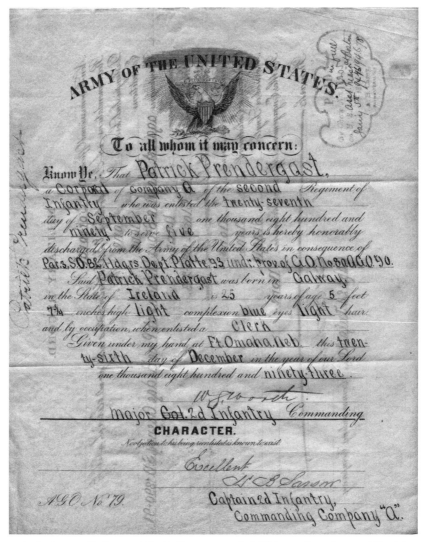

Typical army discharge of the Indian wars period. This one is to Corporal Patrick Prendergast, Company A, Second Infantry, at Fort Omaha, Nebraska, 1893. Prendergast's unit joined the army command at Pine Ridge Agency in 1890 and served against the Sioux Indians, but he was unsuccessful in seeking a pension for that duty. *Editor's Collection*

Finding the Right Drum Major, 1872 (By John Cox, formerly of
Company K, First U. S. Infantry. From *Winners of the West*, January 30, 1928)

The old Drum Major had died and a new one was to be chosen. This was
a very important matter, and seemingly every man, woman, and child at the
Recruiting Depot [at Newport Barracks, Kentucky] was interested in this
affair excepting the recruits. All of the officers and their families and the two
permanent companies were all agitated and anxious to know who would
wear the big fur hat and twirl the big silver-headed staff. I excepted the
rookies, 150 in number. One reason why they were not much interested was
because no one ever seemed to be interested in them. Then they expected to
be sent away soon, where they did not know or care. But there were two or
three candidates from the permanent companies and the time came when
these were to be tried out. Each had their friends who were trying to create
sentiment favorable to their man. They were to act as Drum Major at
"Retreat," one each day for three days.

At the first tryout the entire depot population was present to see the
show. The permanent people were plainly agitated while the 150 recruits
looked on listlessly. The band took its place, as did the two permanent
companies. The adjutant called Private Brown, of one of the permanent
companies. As Brown advanced to the adjutant to get the Drum Major's
staff, his friends applauded, but none of these were among the official class.
Brown was plainly agitated and ill at ease. He managed to start the band off
properly enough, but handled the staff clumsily. He looked like he was glad
when the agony was over.

The next morning Private Jones was called on to wield the big stick. He
had self confidence and assurance and started off promisingly, but
committed the unpardonable military sin of strutting past the officers out of
step. Even his backers did not have heart to applaud. The next evening the
depot people were present in full force. The official ladies were enthusiastic.
Even the recruits seemed to have roused some enthusiasm. It was felt that
both of the men who had been tried out had failed. Now it was up to the third
man to carry off the honors. But one thing sure, he must do much better than
the other two or the commander would never appoint him. When Corporal
Black of a permanent company was called, a roar went up from the
permanent companies and there was much handclapping among the official
class. It was plain that Corporal Black was a favorite with the officials,
especially with the ladies.

The corporal looked as if the had just stepped from a band box. He was every inch the perfect regular soldier. But he was deficient in size and in height; he was actually undersized. But it was evident though that the corporal felt that he was about the biggest man on the parade ground. His friends tried to forget his size and tried to create sentiment in his favor. The recruits eyed him critically and gave expression to opinions. "He's a little whippet," growled one. "The big bearskin hat would extinguish him," was the opinion of another. Some way the recruits were not favorable to the corporal's candidacy.

The corporal took his place at the head of the band. At the command, the review began. The corporal was doing nicely. He handled the big staff fairly well. He kept perfect step. If he had gone on through as he began, it would have been creditable, perhaps passable. But he thought to give the commanding officer a salute that would crown his efforts with glory. He tossed the staff high in the air, intending it to fall horizontal, and he would catch it in the middle and twirl some didoes. But he was too self confident to be careful. He glanced upwards and caught a glimpse of the staff coming down point first. He jumped to one side and made a grab at the staff and missed catching it. It banged on the ground at his feet.. The corporal was a passionate lad. He flew into a rage. In that awful instant, he knew that his name was Dennis, that he would never be Drum Major. In his disappointment and rage, he kicked the staff to one side and strode direct to his quarters. The only comments by anyone was made by the recruits, and they were not complimentary. The permanent companies felt humiliated, the officers were angry, and the ladies looked like they could cry.

The adjutant announced that there would be another trial the next evening by an unknown candidate. Then tongues wagged for twenty-four hours. Who was the unknown? It seemed that only the adjutant and the commander knew who he was and they would not talk. Just here let me describe one of our recruits. He was an Austrian of heroic build, tall and well proportioned. He was perhaps the most perfect man, physically, at the depot. He could talk but little English, but was always good tempered and accommodating, so that he was a favorite with the recruits. At the next "Retreat" we were all in place ready to see who the mystery man was. Even the recruits had awakened and were crowding close the side lines. Every eye caught a glimpse of a big recruit walking up to the adjutant, receive the staff, and take his stand at head of the band. "Who is he?" was the whispered query among the men of the companies and the official class.

Trumpeter George Lutz, of Troop C, Fifth Cavalry, ca. 1876. Lutz posed wearing his musicians uniform and holding his sword. His pistol and dress helmet sit on the stand next to him. *Editor's collection*

All of us recruits recognized the stranger as our big Austrian. But not a word was spoken. We were too much surprised to even whisper. Some seemed to almost cease to breathe. But we watched our man critically and anxiously. We saw him take his place as if he were an old hand at the business. We caught our breath when we saw him take a professional attitude, and then stand like a piece of statuary. At the command, "Forward March," our man with his staff started the march as gracefully as any man ever did it. On the march, he counter-marched his men, swung them at corners, beat perfect time, and never once "broke step." When he came to the commanding officer, [there] came the supreme test. So far he had acquitted himself perfectly. Without pausing, he tossed the staff horizontally fifteen feet into the air. Without a glance upward, or the slightest pause, the staff dropped into his right hand, was twirled wheel fashion and reversed under his right arm. He glanced respectfully at the commanding officer, at same time giving the officer a soldier's salute with his left hand. It was perfectly done, and everybody knew it.

The parade was dismissed and bedlam broke loose. The recruits then had their inning. They cheered and when the Austrian came back to his old quarters the recruits escorted him to our quarters. And be it said for the permanent men that they were game. They came to congratulate him on his promotion. These joyous exercises were interrupted by the appearance of the commanding officer's orderly with orders for our man to move his effects to the band quarters and then go to the tailor to be measured for his Drum Major's uniform. That evening our man visited us and told us some inside facts. He was a trained musician and a Drum Major of a military band of the Austrian army for years. He came to America and enlisted in the army and came to the depot as a recruit. During the contest, he told some of his experience to a friend, who at once notified the commanding officer. At once it was decided that if the corporal failed, the recruit would be given a chance. That is one time the recruits put it over on the permanent people.

But our joy was short lived. We proposed, when our man appeared in his dazzling uniform, finer than Solomon in all his glory ever wore, that we would celebrate appropriately. But within two days we were ordered to our regiments and companies, and so we never had the privilege of seeing him again. But we heard of him often, and it always pleased us to hear that he "made good." But we will never forget the victory the rookies won over the lordly permanent lads.

Ten Years a Buffalo Soldier (By Perry A. Hayman, formerly a sergeant in Troop M, Tenth U. S. Cavalry. From *Winners of the West*, March, 1925)

I enlisted on the 6th day of January, 1874, in Philadelphia, and was sent to the St. Louis barracks, and in February, 1874, was assigned to the Tenth Cavalry, arriving at Fort Sill, Indian Territory, on the 22nd day of February, and was assigned to Troop M under Captain Stephen T. Norvelle, Colonel Benjamin H. Grierson commanding the Tenth Cavalry. I was drilled from the 22nd day of February until the 8th of March. Troop M was then detailed on summer campaign, and went into camp at Camp Beaver, Texas, where we remained until about the middle of May, 1874. Prior to this time I did not use tobacco. During this time the supply train came in with rations. Of course we had to accept that which was issued. Well, about the middle of the month the boys ran out of their supply of tobacco, but as I did not use it, I still retained mine. Some of you old timers will agree with me when I say that a man was out of luck in those days when he was shy on tobacco. To make a long story short, I sold my tobacco at auction. I cut the plug in half, receiving $4.50 for one piece, and $4.00 for the other piece. This incident was the beginning of good times, as I thought, not knowing that reverse times were just around the corner, so to speak.

Now my first excitement as a soldier occurred in April, 1874, in this manner. A man and his son whose name we did not know came into camp with a wagon load of candies, cakes, and such things that would appeal to the taste of a soldier. There were two troops of us, C and M. A soldier by the name of Charles Holden of C Troop, thinking this peddler had whiskey, deliberately shot the son dead and mortally wounded the father in the attempt to rob them. We all heard the shots fired. Now, as a matter of fact, we were in a bad Indian country and naturally our captain, hearing a shot fired, at once started to investigate its origin. Finding no trace of hostile Indians, the captain at once reached the conclusion that the shot must have been fired by one of our men. On further investigation we discovered the dead and wounded men. Now the captain, after propping up the father against a stump, had the two troops formed in single file and marched past the wounded man for identification. Now right here, comrades, allow me to state that although I knew that I was innocent, I sure was a scared recruit, thinking he might mistake me for the guilty one. As each man marched by him, the injured man would shake his head in the negative until Holden confronted him. Though mortally wounded when he saw Holden, he tried to get up and get to him, thereby proving beyond a doubt that Charles Holden was the guilty one.

Holden was arrested, placed in double irons, and turned over to the civil authorities at Fort Smith, Texas. I have never heard of Holden since. The injured man did not live thirty minutes longer, after he identified Holden.

Early in May the Indians attacked a ranch about six miles from Camp Beaver. The rancher had two men and this fact the Indians were aware of, and they took advantage of the situation. The rancher managed in some way to dispatch a courier to the camp for help and M troop responded. This occurred about 11 o'clock in the forenoon. We took out after those Indians, who in [the] meantime had sighted us, and we chased them from 11 o'clock until about the edge of dark. I want to note that the larger number of us were recruits and in the saddle for the first time. Darkness caused our commander to abandon the chase and the recruits when they dismounted were unable to stand erect. We made a dry camp that night, and the next day we started back to Camp Beaver, and it took us three days to return, while during the chase we covered the distance in about six or seven hours. Several of the recruits were forced to go on sick report as a sequel to the outcome of that ride.

In the latter part of May we were ordered to Fort Sill, Indian Territory, and in October ordered on a general cooperating campaign with Colonel Nelson A. Miles. The troops represented were C, D, H, L, K, and M. We camped at the base of Mt. Scott preparatory to being inspected by Lieutenant General Philip H. Sheridan, prior to entering the campaign. First Sergeant Levi Hainer of Troop M detailed me on the greatest detail that ever befell me in my ten years of army career. He detailed me to act as mounted orderly to General Sheridan. Let me add that I was still a recruit. Some of you readers will remember about this period, October, 1874, when the Indians were mad sure enough, and to add to the deal Second Lieutenant Silas Pepoon on the first day in camp committed suicide about eight miles from Fort Sill. The next day we scouted the plains, and did so until the last of October. Now Colonel Miles's command had driven the Indians our way, and we ran into them at Goose Creek. We captured a band of 205 and 2,000 ponies. After a general roundup, we started for Fort Sill. On the night of October 28th, along about 8 o'clock, the whole herd of horses stampeded. Every horse got away but one, the trumpeter's horse [belonging to] Charles Hazzard. We recovered the horses the next day, and they gave me a log next day as a reward for my horse breaking his sidelines, and I carried that log two hours [as punishment]. I am still mad over the incident yet. This happened in 1874. . . . The next day we started for Fort Sill, arriving about the first week in November. The chief of the band we captured was Lone Wolf. He was sent to Atlanta, Georgia [sic—Fort Marion, Florida]. We came in off that campaign and remained until February, 1875. I had been in the army just three months when I was made a corporal.

My troop was detailed on detached service five days at Cheyenne Agency. We had no clothes with us except those we had on, and we stayed seventy-two days. The cooties had full possession of our backs, and that demanded the greater part of our attention for quite a while. Everything went all right until the 6th of April, 1875, when Chief Stone Calf's Indians came into the Cheyenne Agency with two white girls. Stone Calf's warriors had overtaken the family and after killing the father, mother, and son, made captives of the two girls. In the meantime, a courier had come in and told us that the Indians were there with the two girls. There were three troops of cavalry stationed at Cheyenne Agency at this time—D and M of the Tenth and M of the Sixth—and two companies of the Eleventh Infantry. We received orders to saddle up and rescue the girls, in which we were successful. While we were engaged in putting the brave that led the band in irons, a squaw ran out, waved a blanket, gave the war whoop, and "then the fun began." The Indians broke for cover and, by the time M Troop of the Tenth got there, the Indians had crossed the North Fork of the Canadian River.

As the first set of fours crossed the river, the Indians opened up on us, and Corporal George Berry was wounded. After we had crossed the river, Captain Stevens T. Norvelle of M Troop formed the line and gave the command to dismount to fight on foot. Captain Norvelle gave me the command to inform Captain Alexander S. B. Keyes of D, who was 300 yards to the right of our command, to form his troop at right angles in order to make an attack on three sides. Being dismounted, I had to run for it, the Indians shooting at me all the time. Having delivered the dispatch, I started on the hot foot back and reached my troop okay. I can venture to say truthfully that I believe there were a hundred shots fired at me in carrying that dispatch. The next was the order to charge. We charged them and dislodged them, our captain now giving the command to take cover. While under cover a rain came up that only lasted about five or ten minutes, just enough to wet the sand. While [I was] rolling around on the ground my rifle got some sand in the stock breech. I had to get a stick to clean it out, and in doing so I got in full view of the Indians. It was here that I got shot in the right side. I laid down behind a stump, and again those Indians fired a number of shots, but none of them hit me. Some came so close to me that they threw sand in my face as they would hit the ground. Laying as if I was dead, the Indians gave up shooting at me, as they no doubt thought that I was dead. This was between

11 and 12 o'clock in the day when the scrap started. I stayed there until dark and then I managed to crawl away from my hiding place. After dark the Indians forded the river and got away. The next morning the soldiers saddled up and took the trail. There was only one man killed, Clarke Young. I crawled out of my tent and wanted to saddle my horse, but the captain made me go to the hospital.

The troops followed those Indians for one month, overtook them at Medicine Lodge, and wiped them out. I was not in the Custer Massacre, but was stationed at Fort Stockton[, Texas]. When the news reached the fort, which was the end of the telegraph line, Private Paine and I were detailed to carry the dispatch to Fort Davis, seventy-five miles distant. We covered that seventy-five miles from 11:45 a.m. to 4 a.m. the next day. Twelve miles of this distance was through mountain passes, and I have never seen it rain harder, and lightning and thunder more terrific than it did on that occasion. I served ten years on the frontier, five being in cavalry and five in infantry.

Cavalry Duty in the Southwest in the 1870s (By George S. Raper, formerly of Troop B, Eighth U. S. Cavalry. From *Winners of the West*, November, 1925)

Fifty-five years ago, . . . at Louisville[, Kentucky,] I enlisted as a general mounted service recruit. First Lieutenant Lyster M. O'Brien was the officer in charge. After I put my name on the dotted line, the sergeant handed me a suit of blue that was made for a man twice my size, and the sergeant, being a good-natured sort of a cuss hating to put any unnecessary work on us, gathered up all of our citizen clothes and took them away and sold them. I have often wondered if it was just absent-mindedness that prevented him from "whacking up" with us. That evening we started for Fort Leavenworth, and after a month there we (about 150 of us) were fortunate enough to be assigned to the Eighth Cavalry, then in command of that splendid officer, Colonel John Irvin Gregg. We loaded into cars and started to New Mexico.

We got to Kit Carson, Colorado [Territory], and the first thing we saw the next morning were two fellows strung up under a railroad bridge where they had been hung the night before by a vigilance committee. . . . The monotony of the long trip across Kansas and part of Colorado was only broken by the thousands of buffalos. Six years afterward, when I was returning home, the buffalos were all gone and the country was almost a solid field of wheat across western Kansas. At Kit Carson we were given guns, and we picked up a bunch of "doughboys" headed for the Fifteenth Infantry. All of us were under command of Second Lieutenant Hampden S. Cottell, long since dead. There we started on our long march of nearly 1,200 [sic] miles to New Mexico.

Anyone now passing over the Atchison, Topeka, and the Santa Fe Railroad from Las Animas, Colorado, to San Marcial, New Mexico, probably would not appreciate what a God-forsaken country that hike took us through back in the fall of 1870. The first place we struck that told us we were still in the United States was the flag at Fort Lyon, then in command of Lieutenant Colonel John R. Brooke, Third Infantry. I have no recollection of Las Animas. Trinidad was just one street with a few scattering adobe shanties down near the river. We crossed the Raton Mountains at Dick Hooten's ranch, and found the Red River of the South, west of the foot of the mountains, only about ten feet wide. One place where we camped for a night there was a rancher living. It was said that at this house they had soda biscuits three times a day, 365 days in the year. I had a good many meals there and I never found any other kind of bread, so it must be so. At this place we saw our first Indians. They were Utes, and one of them had on a major general's dress uniform—coat, epaulettes, and all, which had been given him by General William T. Sherman. The old chief also had a letter from the general which he prized very highly. The letter advised the reader to watch the old fellow very close, that he would carry away anything he could get his hands on.

Cimmarron was about the only place we found that would lead one to believe that there had ever been anything but a Mexican in that country. Fort Union was the headquarters of the Eighth Cavalry. I was fortunate enough to be assigned to Troop B, with Captain William McCleave in command. He is long since dead, but I want to go on record as believing that there were very few officers that were his equal. At Fort Union we lost the men who were assigned to troops at that station, and also those for Fort Garland. After a few days' rest we again took up the weary march, and two days after we camped at Las Vegas, an old Mexican town. What is now East Las Vegas was not at that time even a hole in the ground. At Albuquerque we first saw the Rio Grande, and lost our comrades that were en route for Fort Wingate. At Fort Craig the fellows for Fort Selden and Fort Bayard kept on down the river, and we that were going to Fort Stanton crossed the river and hiked east through the sandy desert. The first of November we reached our long-looked-for "happy home."

We were not long in taking up the duties of soldiers, with foot and mounted drill nearly every day. We had a splendid drill master in Sergeant Patrick Golden, an old soldier of several years' service. A short time before we reached the post, the Apaches killed a member of our troop and also a member of Company I of the Fifteenth Infantry, within a few miles of the post. A scout was at once started after the murderers, who were followed so closely that in order to let the bucks get away the squaws got in the way of the charge going up a narrow canyon, knowing, as they did, that in order to get around them it would delay the charge. Several prisoners were taken, and we found them still in confinement at the post with a guard over them. That post was not very desirable. We enlisted at $16 a month, but Congress got funny and reduced our pay to $13. Of course, that did not set very good, and the result was the army lost many men by refusal to reenlist and by desertion. One of the latter was my bunky.

It would be hard for anyone who has not passed through the experience to realize the irksome sameness, or want of variety of a soldier's life in New Mexico, and especially at Fort Stanton, in the early 70s. The nearest point of anything that might be called civilization being Las Vegas, more than 150 miles away. Not a book or anything to read. Mail once a week and taking from four to five weeks for a letter from as far east as Ohio. Where one was fortunate enough to have a friend who sent them the home paper, it was read by every man in the troop until entirely worn out. There was nothing to attract one's attention except the same old round of soldier duty, an unending sequence of guard, stable police, kitchen police, and fatigue, and then back over the same thing. We cavalrymen had a little the best of the infantrymen. We got all the escort duty, scouting, and other things of that kind. For a few days we had a chance to lose sight of the old stone buildings of the post. We looked forward with delight to the afternoon that we were the old guard, as we then had the splendid duty of herding the horses for grazing. It certainly was fun to get the horses all excited in the corral (when there were no commissioned officers around), and then turn them loose and run them until they got their play out. We all felt as though we had lost our best friend when mounted drill was taken off.

All of the officers of the regiment above second lieutenant had seen service during the Civil War. Several of them had reached the rank of brigadier general. With us as we were making our tramp were four second lieutenants that had graduated with the class of 1870. I think only one of them is now [1925] living, Brigadier General Samuel W. Fountain, retired. Second Lieutenant Richard A. Williams only lived long enough to get his captain's commission. I have understood that Second Lieutenant Frederick E. Phelps lost a leg at Wounded Knee and was retired; Second Lieutenant Edward A. Godwin became a brigadier general, retired. Samuel B. M. Young was one of our original captains, appointed in 1866. He was, I think, the last one to die. Captain James F. Randlett was transferred to the regiment in 1870 and was a captain for sixteen [sic—nineteen] years.

This letter starts by saying "55 years ago I put on the blue." Now I close it by saying that fifty years ago First Lieutenant John H. Mahnken, regimental adjutant, handed me my discharge at Santa Fe, New Mexico, for expiration of term of service, signed by Colonel Gregg, and the major was kind enough to write the word "Excellent" under the black line.

Wyoming Service in the 1870s (By George F. Tinkham, formerly of Troop G, Third U. S. Cavalry. From *Winners of the West*, April 30, 1926)

In January, 1872, I noted in a Boston, Massachusetts, newspaper, "Wanted for the U. S. Cavalry, 200 able-bodied men for frontier service," giving the number of [the] recruiting office in Boston. I was then nineteen years, five months of age, and went to Boston, enlisting March 20, 1872. I was sent from Boston to New York City, and as they had smallpox at Carlisle [Pennsylvania], where the drilling was generally done before assigning to companies, I with other recruits was sent to Fort McPherson, Nebraska. From there I was sent to join Company G, Third U. S. Cavalry, stationed at Fort D. A. Russell, Wyoming [Territory]. In May, we were ordered to go into camp at Chugwater, near Fort Laramie, Wyoming, to watch and keep Indians on their reservation, escort wagon trains, and carry mail to and from Fort Laramie.

It was a busy summer of scouting and escorting, and following up Indian scares among the ranchmen, protecting the two cattle ranches of Cooney and Philip, which were located in that section of the territory. One night in September, I was put on picket duty, and the next day assigned to guard duty on a high bluff where I could see anyone or anything moving about the plains within my vision and could overlook the country. I also had to watch the movements of our horses, where they were grazing in the valley between my stand on the bluff and camp. About 2 p.m., there came up the river a hailstorm and wind and hit the horses so sudden that they stampeded and took a course up the valley toward Laramie Peak. Knowing that if I could reach the lead of that troop of horses I could lead them back to camp, I came down the pass and got into the race. I had almost reached the lead of the horses when my horse stepped into a prairie dog's hole and threw me into a bunch of cactus. I was thrown so heavy that it completely knocked my breath from me and the thorns were sticking into my body like a porcupine. My horse stood guard over me and in that way kept the running horses from trampling the life out of me.

That night there was a rumor of an Indian uprising, and some shots were heard and a few yells. We were called to "Boots and Saddles," and I was one of the first to respond. We rode fast until near morning, and when we reached Cooney's ranch we found the shooting and yelling had been done by some drunken cowboys. This did not stop us from going on a scout looking for stray Indians, and it began to rain and that night we camped on wet ground. By sleeping on the wet ground, I contracted a cold, but still I did not give up. A short time after that occurred, we were ordered into winter quarters and we returned to Fort Russell. We encountered heavy storms of wind and sand and a terrible march.

Soon after our return, our horses began to die off. They would apparently be well today, and tomorrow they would be dead. I was detailed to help the veterinary surgeon try to find the cause of the horses' dying. It was bitterly cold, snow on the ground, and when I went to the barracks both of my feet were frozen. I was taken to the hospital and there I remained nearly four months. My feet had gotten well, except the loss of the ends of the big toes. But I did not recover my strength and health, which caused the surgeons to give me an examination. They found that my heart was diseased and in bad shape caused by the fall and exposure. I was discharged May 20, 1874. . . .

Relocating with the Sixth U. S. Infantry (By William Fetter, formerly of Company M, Sixth U. S. Infantry. From *Winners of the West*, May, 1925)

In September, 1872, we were ordered to Camp Supply, I. T. The Junction City, Texas, and Galveston Railroad was ready then up to within seven miles of Fort Gibson, so we had a ride to Junction City, and then we went to Hays City, Kansas. From there we hoofed it 200 miles south to Camp Supply, I. T. From there, two companies of infantry and Troops L and M of the Tenth Cavalry went as escort with the surveyors of the Atchison, Topeka, and Santa Fe Railroad, besides escorting emigrant trains and mail coaches.

They had two relay stations between Camp Supply and Fort Dodge and seven men always had to stay a week. . . .

While at Camp Supply, the clouds grew dark in the north and in May the whole regiment was ordered to Dakota Territory. There were four companies in Camp Supply, two in Fort Lyon, Colorado [Territory], two in Fort Dodge, Kansas, and two in Fort Hays, Kansas. Orders were to be in Sioux City, Iowa, by the first of June. We started about the 7th of May and as all the officers from first lieutenants up had families and two men in each company had their families along, it took quite a string of wagons to transport all our property and provisions. We had thirty-six six-mule teams and I think three ambulances. They were for the women and children and the sick. We got along fine until we got to the Cimmaron River. On the 12th of May we went into camp about 10 o'clock p.m. on the north side of the river. It was too far to the next watering place so the teamsters unhooked for the day and watered their outfits and took them across the river to graze. Seven men were sent along as guards to watch the stock. Scouts had seen no Indians around, but we had hardly got the tents pitched when the Indians swept around a hill and under cover of the river bank, [and] with a couple of yells and a few shots they had the mules stampeded and off they went. We opened fire right away and the men on the other side had to duck for cover from our own and the Indians' bullets. A couple of Indians fell from their saddles, but were picked up and taken along. They got away with 136 head of mules and that sure left us stranded with our schooners. As the Indians fired in our camp from the rear, we could pay no attention to the mules, but had to turn and protect our own hides.

No matter how serious a situation is, something funny is sure to turn up. Our company cook was an old fellow named John Abbe who had been in the service over twenty-eight years. He paid not the slightest attention to the rumpus but had his soup kettles going until a bullet struck one of the kettles and the juice started running out on both sides. Then he got mad and with the exclamation, "Oh, the sons of_____," grabbed a rifle and blazed away. So he would not hit anyone, he held the gun nearly straight up.

We were forty miles from Camp Supply and after dark two scouts went back for more moving power. Uncle Sam was short, but a Mexican bull train accidentally arrived so a lot of greasers with their horned mules pulled us to Fort Dodge. It was slow going, but those fellows were in no hurry. After three days, we got within twelve miles of Fort Dodge and the ambulance drivers received orders to start right after breakfast for Fort Dodge. They left as we were striking tents. They were not gone a half mile when we saw Indians coming from the east and west, and firing commenced. Those ambulances sure made a quick right about face and did not object to our company from there on. Well, we finally got to Fort Hays and found the rest of the regiment there waiting for us with three railroad trains to take us. We got to Sioux City on time, and the two days on the train was all we saw of civilization during the five years of service. When we arrived at Sioux City, there were three steamboats waiting to take us on board. We left the trains and marched right on the boats and in a couple of hours we were on our way to the Dakota Territory. . . .

Battling in the Little Bighorn (By Alonzo Stringham, formerly of Troop I, Seventh U. S. Cavalry. From *Winners of the West*, June 30, 1934)

We of the Seventh U. S. Cavalry were ordered to take the field at Fort Abraham Lincoln, D. T., in May, 1877, and hit for the northwestern territory in Montana. We were soon encamped on the Musselshell, about eighty miles north of the Yellowstone and north[west] of the mouth of Tongue River. All of the field units were alert to discover any Indian trail or any sign that might lead to a contact with the hostiles.

In the midst of all of this activity came an order from Brigadier General Alfred H. Terry to [the] captain of I Troop to take his troop and repair to the Custer Battlefield and re-bury the remains of those who had fallen there with Custer. And to disinter the remains of Lieutenant Colonel George A. Custer, ten of his officers, and three civilians and prepare [them] for shipment, Colonel Custer having had a standing order that he should be buried at West Point. The battlefield was about as far south of the Yellowstone as we were north of it at the time the order came, about 160 miles.

When we came to the north bank of the Big Horn River and nearly opposite the mouth of the Little Horn, which was about eighteen miles north of the battlefield, we met our first real difficulty which was the crossing of the Big Horn, which was a tremendously swift and deep river and the water ice cold and about a half mile wide with a steep high bluff on the opposite side where we would have to make our landing. We had a bull boat made by stretching a green hide over a framework as nearly the shape of a small boat as possible, and our captain proposed placing five men in the boat, each man to lead a horse with a rope and other men detailed to row the boat. The boat was hauled upstream some distance above where the landing was desired to be made on the opposite bank, which was at the mouth of the Little Bighorn.

If a horse or man missed this landing they would strike a stone wall twelve to fifteen feet high.

Our crossing had been about half completed when an accident occurred which turned five horses loose in the river, and as they could not make the land and struck the high stone wall, they turned and swam back up the river to an island. Captain Henry J. Nowlan was in command of the embarkation of the horses and men, and Second Lieutenant Hugh L. Scott was in command of the receiving end on the opposite bank. Seeing that my horse was one of the five that had become loose in the river and swam back to the island, I determined to swim out and get him and also Sergeant John Goggin's horse and try to pilot them over to Lieutenant Scott's landing, which I succeeded in doing, but fearing my horse would not safely make the landing, I dismounted and while he went safely to shore, I was swept below. Fearful of being unable to swim back to the island, I went pounding down that bluff until I at length caught hold of some overhanging vines and drew myself up until I could get one arm above the cliff and there I hung until a searching party sent out by Lieutenant Scott came along above the cliff on their way back and I heard one of the boys say, "Poor Stringham. I guess he is gone for keeps this time." But I yelled at them, "No, he hasn't, just please give me the right hand of fellowship and I'll show you I am pretty much alive yet." Sergeant John W. Burkett had not spoken to me for a year until now. He was the first to run to me and shout, "Here, Stringham, I'll help you," and he and one of the other boys had me safely on top in a jiffy. I was chilled to the bone, but the boys wrapped me in a blanket and laid me out in the sun to get warm, and in a few moments I was all right again.

Lieutenant Scott came to me and said, "Stringham, one of those horses on that island belongs to Private William T. Higgins, and he has been asking me to let him swim over and get his horse, but I am afraid to let him try it. What do you think about letting him try it?" I raised my hand to salute and said, "Sir, don't let Higgins try it. He can never make it." The lieutenant replied, "That's just what I thought." He then said, "Do you think you can get those horses off of the island?" I looked him straight in the eye and replied, "Sir, I am not afraid to try it." The lieutenant replied, "Well, Stringham, I want you to understand I am not ordering you to do this, but if you think you can, you have my permission." With that I saluted, turned, and ran up stream about 200 yards where I found a cottonwood log extending straight out into the river. I ran out to the end of the log, leaped out into the stream as far as my strength would carry me. This was to give me as good a start on my long sweep as possible. But when opposite the landing, I found I was only about one-half the distance to the island. Then I swam. Oh, how I swam! I grew very tired and let down my feet to try to touch the bottom, but there was none within reach and I gave up trying that any more until I had made the very last stroke possible then I breathed a little prayer to God and let down my feet once more and found the water only hip deep.

I took a good rest and heard Lieutenant Scott shout, "Bravo." I soon caught the horses, led them as far up the shallow water at the head of the island until I struck the water too deep to wade, then turned toward the landing. I was riding Higgins's horse and just as soon as he struck the deep water he turned over backwards. I tried several times to guide the horses to the opposite bank, but while I found them willing to swim back towards Captain Nowlan's side, but across to Lieutenant Scott's landing, no siree. The lieutenant, seeing my predicament, waved his hand and shouted, "All right, take them wherever you can." And that was just what I was obliged to do.

Fourteen Years in the Army, 1881-1895 (By Ernst A. Selander, formerly of Troop C, Fifth U. S. Cavalry, and Troop F, Second U. S. Cavalry. From *Winners of the West*, October, 1925)

Two young men, the writer of this, Ernst A. Selander, and G. Wyman, left Omaha, Nebraska, in the spring of 1881 to seek their fortunes further out West, signing up as laborers for a railroad gang to obtain their transportation. When the train arrived at Sidney, Nebraska, we left it and in skirmishing around we observed the U. S. flag waving at Fort Sidney, in close proximity to the town. As we were about broke, Wyman suggested that we enlist. We enlisted on February 3, 1881, in Captain Emil Adams's Troop C, Fifth U. S. Cavalry. As ex-clothing clerks our first experience was rather strenuous. Besides the regular drill, horseback and otherwise, as rookies we were put to digging trenches for water pipes for a new water system, and shoveling coal from the railroad cars for our quarters, and hauling sand to fill in ground for new stables and the like, until our hands were blistered.

In December, 1882, we removed 500 Cheyenne Indians from Fort Sidney, Nebraska, overland to Pine Ridge Agency, South Dakota [sic—Dakota Territory]. This was a rather hard trip due to the inclement weather, from 20 to 30 below zero and the snow being at places two feet deep on the level. Fuel was scarce, only what little was taken along. No buffalo chips—everything snowed under. We had to shovel the snow away before we could put our Sibley tents up. These tents were just then issued to the cavalry, were in the shape of an Indian tepee, held twelve men, and had a sheet-iron stove in the center. After the stove had been burning a while, everything was mud and slush, and in the morning our gloves and boots were frozen. About the third day out from the post, a government teamster killed a papoose by accident. It fell off the wagon and he drove over it and crushed it. This put the redskins in an ugly mood. When we started out they seemed to possess only a few old Springfields, but after this accident happened, and at night in the camp, there were plenty of good Winchesters in evidence which had been hid in the squaws' blankets. That night a chain guard was put on by the captain, as the odds were too uneven, fifty-five soldiers to about 400 bucks. But the old story of the Indian, if he didn't have the advantage he didn't fight [pertained,] and in due time we reached Pine Ridge Agency, South Dakota, plus some frozen ears, fingers, and toes [sic].

In the summer of 1883, Troop C participated in an expedition against riot and labor troubles at Omaha, Nebraska. We, the regulars, had a good time and never any trouble, while on the other hand the state militia was despised. This was due to the fact that a militia soldier, being excited, had run his bayonet without provocation through an old inoffensive citizen. We actually had to guard the militia and take them to their meals by company. From July to November, I was escort to President Chester Arthur, Lieutenant General Phil Sheridan, and others through the Yellowstone National Park, the Switzerland of America. This was quite an outing, and Captain Edward M. Hayes with Company G went along as guard to the president. We employed three complete pack trains, a colored chef and assistant. A large 300-pound range was carried by a large pack mule. Last, but not least, two large mules were each carrying a large wicker basket on each side containing choice liquid refreshments. Among these was some hospital brandy bottled in 1865. The country was infested by quite a lot of rattlesnakes. Caught some with sixteen rattles.

In the fall of 1885 and 1886 I was on detached service in Oklahoma Territory, being then stationed at Fort Reno, Indian Territory, ejecting boomers over the line at Caldwell, Kansas, and over the line into Texas. Later I played cowboy for the government, herding and driving out cattle left by the cow barons. Indian Territory was at that time not open to settlers. I was discharged on February 2, 1886, from the post hospital at Fort Reno with character "Excellent," having had a severe fall from a horse six weeks previous to the expiration of my term of service. I left Fort Reno in February, 1886, for Caldwell, Kansas, nearest railroad terminal being 110 miles distant, in an open farm wagon, taking the place of the stage, drawn by four balky condemned government horses. After leaving the post, it started to snow, obliterating the few broken roads. We got stuck several times and had to pull the wagon, as well as the balky horses, out. The ice was not safe to cross on the Cimmaron River, as the water was of a brackish consistency and the ice full of air holes, so we had to draw the wagon across by hand, tying a rope to the tongue, and we led the horses over singly.

We got lost on the prairie in a snow storm about twenty miles out from Caldwell and had to camp in the open and the snow without any fire. There were three of us, namely, the driver, a soldier discharged for consumption, and myself. The soldier was going to his home in Wisconsin and there regain his health. We kept warm by tramping around the wagon in a circle and huddling together in the wagon alternately. As soon as we laid down, the coyotes sneaked up to our horses and tried to nip at their heels. I had my private .45 Colt, and as soon as I dropped some coyotes the live ones would devour their dead comrades. Next morning at daybreak, we found our bearings and arrived at Caldwell, Kansas, about 9 a.m., stiff as a poker and had to be lifted off the wagon. A good hot lemonade with a stick in it, and a good hot breakfast later on, made us forget our hardships. From Caldwell, Kansas, I left for Germany, the home of my parents, taking treatment with eminent surgeons for the injuries to my back received in the service. After one year's sojourn, I enlisted again at Baltimore, Maryland, and was upon request assigned to Troop F, Second Cavalry, under Captain Samuel M. Swigert. My old ailment asserted itself again and horseback riding got unbearable. I transferred in April, 1888, to the then-organized hospital corps at Fort Walla Walla, Washington [Territory]. After a few months as hospital attendant, I was detailed to drive the four-mule hospital ambulance on an expedition with the Fourth Cavalry and Fourteenth Infantry through the Cascade Mountains in Oregon. On this trip, for weeks we had nothing but rain, and our clothes were soaked and we slept in wet blankets. I used to sleep in the ambulance, and as the top leaked I used to ditch the one side and put gunnysacks on the top to keep dry.

On November 30, 1891, I was appointed acting hospital sergeant, Hospital Corps, U. S. A., and assigned to Fort Sherman, Idaho, where I was discharged at expiration of my term of service, February 29, 1892, with character "Excellent." I reenlisted March 1, 1892, and participated in an expedition against Coeur d'Alene mining outbreaks at Wardner, Wallace, Burke, Idaho, and other mining towns and camps from July 12th until November, 1892. Was again on detached service accompanying troops through northern Idaho guarding mines and railroad property during the miners' strike, from July 7, to September 19, 1894. As my old ailment was getting unbearable, I applied for my discharge February, 1895, and was granted same after three month's furlough, May 31, 1895, under General Order 80 of 1890.

Fifth Cavalry Service (By Charles M. Hildreth, formerly of Troop A, Fifth U. S. Cavalry. From *Winners of the West*, April, 1925)

I enlisted for cavalry service in New York City, February 7, 1882, and went by way of Jefferson Barracks, St. Louis, to join my regiment, Fifth U. S. Cavalry, with headquarters at Fort Sidney, Nebraska, and after four months was again moved to Fort Washakie, Wyoming [Territory], where we remained until May, 1885, when the Fifth was ordered from the Department of the Platte to the Department of the Missouri, with headquarters at Fort Riley, Kansas. Our stay there, however, was short, only about two weeks, and we were again moved to Indian Territory, as the Indians down there were getting restless, as the government had ordered the cattlemen to vacate in order to open up the country to settlement. After camping at different places, my troop took station at Camp Supply, I. T., where we remained until July, 1893, when our regiment was ordered to Texas, with headquarters at Fort Sam Houston, where I took my discharge May 6, 1895. Personally, I never really participated in any engagements with hostile Indians, although we were constantly in close touch with them on different reservations in Wyoming, Nebraska, Indian Territory, and Kansas. . . .

One day while guiding a government wagon across Wind River in upper Wyoming in January, 1884, my horse broke through the ice, and let me tell you I thought my time had surely come, as we both struggled out of the icy river and finally to the shore and to the camp. After I got a change of clothing and a hot cup of coffee, I seemed to be all right, but when I got back to the fort I was taken down with a fever which landed me in the hospital for six weeks. In June of that same year my horse fell with me under him, injuring my left leg so that I was obliged to hobble around on crutches for at least four weeks. Also, while stationed at Camp Supply, I. T., and while at pistol practice one morning, my horse slipped and fell with me under him of course. They picked me up and carried me to the hospital where I lay with a plaster cast on my leg for three weeks, and remained in the hospital for seven weeks.

While stationed at Fort Sam Houston, Texas, in 1894, I was again sent to the hospital and underwent three operations. The first was for fistula, second

An unidentified private of cavalry in full dress with saber, ca. 1886, probably at Fort Leavenworth, Kansas. Note helmet to his left with brass eagle, yellow horsehair plume, and cords. *Editor's collection*

for piles, and the third for another fistula, and [I] was carried on the sick report of my troop for 142 days. The above relates to some of the hardships common to soldiers of the regular army, and now I want to relate a little regarding some of the pleasant incidents we experienced.

While stationed at Fort Washakie, Wyoming, in the latter part of August, 1883, President Arthur and a party of officials, including Robert T. Lincoln, Secretary of War; Lieutenant General Phil H. Sheridan; Senator George G. Vest of Missouri; Colonel Michael V. Sheridan; [retired] Colonel Anson Stager, and other dignitaries whose names I cannot now recall, made a trip into that country on a fishing, hunting, and sightseeing trip, as well as of inspection. Two troops of the Fifth were detailed as escorts, and Troop A particularly established a courier line. The president's party was all mounted on cavalry horses, and camp equipage and supplies for men and animals was transported by pack mules, three trains of sixty mules for each train. Courier camps were established about every fifteen miles and placed in charge of a non-commissioned officer and three privates at each station.

Being a corporal at the time, I was placed in charge of a station on a small creek near a cattle ranch of a man by the name of Eugene Amoretti. The next camp from mine was fifteen miles away, called Camp Bishop, on Denoir Creek, a small branch of Wind River. At this camp the party tarried for three days as there was good hunting and fishing. I carried the first mail and dispatches that arrived at my camp for the presidential party, and made the trip in two hours, although the trail in some places was very rough and dangerous. That night Colonel Sheridan came over to our camp and wanted some of the boys to go over and entertain the president with songs and camp lore. What we gave them must have pleased the president, for he laughed and applauded us most heartily. I remember I concluded the entertainment with a comical song entitled, "When McCarthy Rules the State." The last refrain of that song stated, "We will paint the White House green, when McCarthy rules the state," and it seemed to please the president greatly, so much so that I was obliged to repeat the song. I returned to my station that night, and that was the last I ever saw of the president and his party, as they soon went on over into the Yellowstone region. . . .

An Incident at Fort Abraham Lincoln in 1884 (By Archibald Dickson, formerly of Company C, Third U. S. Infantry. From *Winners of the West*, April 30, 1935)

I enlisted in Philadelphia February 7th, 1882, and after three months as a recruit at David's Island, New York Harbor, was promoted to high private in the rear rank and sent with fifty others to Fort Ellis, Montana, and assigned to Captain James A. Snyder's Company C, Third U. S. Infantry. Next I was sent on detached service for one year (1884) to the Ordnance Department, Fort Abraham Lincoln, Dakota Territory.

I was detailed to carry the mail in the morning and to herd cattle in the foothills in the afternoon. I was supplied with a good horse, a Colt's revolver, and a web belt with fifty rounds of cartridges. On July 4th, 1884, I took the cattle out to the grazing grounds as usual and about 3 o'clock in the afternoon I noticed a cloud of dust arising in the distance, but as the weather was very dry I thought but little of it at first, but soon discovered it was a bunch of Indians running away from Standing Rock Agency, and I knew it was up to me to get my cattle and myself under cover as quickly as possible. There was a small path of timber near, and I had not more than made the woods when a band of about fifty Sioux, crazy with whiskey, which they must have got in some way in Bismarck, came riding by shooting and yelling like the wild men they were. It sure made me feel creepy, and after they were well out of sight I began to round up my cattle and found that one was missing.

I reported to Captain James A. Rockwell, then in charge of the Ordnance Department, and he complimented me on saving all of the cattle but one, and said it was better to lose one cow than my scalp. He telegraphed to the agency for them to take care of the Indians, and about a week later there was a band of bucks and squaws camped not far from the woods in which I had lost the cow, and this band had my cow cut up into jerked beef. They evidently had been scouting through the timber and found it.

I have always been glad that band of drunken Sioux did not see me that day, or I would not be here now to tell this story.

Reminiscences of an Eighth U. S. Cavalryman, 1883-1888 (By Frederick C. Kurz, formerly corporal, Troop E, Eighth U. S. Cavalry. From *Winners of the West*, March 30, April 30, and May 30, 1931)

I enlisted in the fall of 1883 in Milwaukee, and after being transported with a consignment of others to Jefferson Barracks, near St. Louis, went through the usual recruiting service of setting-up exercises, manual of arms, and bareback riding around a bull ring conducted by that cock-eyed drill sergeant you all perhaps remember, who used not very polite language whenever one of us accidentally fell off the horse, or dropped a gun while drilling. After about four weeks of this tormentation, a bunch of more than 100 were sent to San Antonio, Texas, which was the headquarters of the Eighth Cavalry. There were only a few troops of the Eighth actually stationed there, most of the other troops being distributed amongst the different forts along the Rio Grande, some at Ringgold, others at Fort McIntosh, near Laredo; Fort Brown, Camp Del Rio, and Fort Clark. The last mentioned was the headquarters of the Nineteenth Infantry and also contained four troops of the Eighth Cavalry, E, F, G, and L Troops, and later on Troop K was added.

The writer, with sixteen other recruits, was assigned to E Troop. Fort Clark was about 135 miles west of San Antonio and fifteen miles from the nearest Southern California Railroad, and about the same distance from the Rio Grande. During the first year of my service I had considerable malarial fever, also yellow jaundice, all no doubt due to the poor army rations, for we only had beans, black coffee, no milk at any time, nor any kind of vegetables or potatoes. However, we chipped in $2.00 every two months from our pay (which was $13.00 per month, less 12 ½ cents deducted by the government for the National Soldiers Home) towards a mess fund. With this we secured Irish potatoes, onions, and a few canned goods, which gave us a little variation from our everyday army grub. We had to do quite a lot of scouting and border duty along 1884 and 1885, and those dusty alkali trails and roads were hard on the eyes, as well as the throat and lungs, whenever we were ordered out to march and in camp. Our food on these trips was usually salt pork and hardtack. The salt pork was nothing like our present bacon, and the hardtack was full of little black bugs, a sort of weevil. We used to dip the hardtack in water first, so as to let the little fellows creep out before eating. The hardtack was of a grayish color, no doubt from age, and we often wondered if it was not [leftover] remnants of the War of the Rebellion.

The Indians, Mexicans, cattle and horse thieves, and general bad men in those times were very active in this party of the country, and we were kept on the march scouting along the border of the Rio Grande most of our time, also protecting the railroad to a certain extent, and there were no bridges of any sort, and we had to cross rivers the best way we could. Our trips used to take us west of the Pecos River toward El Paso and we had some camps at Meira Springs and Eagles Nest. During that time, Mrs. [Lily] Langtry, an actress, passed through Eagles Nest, which was a jerkwater station of the Southern California Railroad, and she admired the wild and rugged scenery around there during the time the train stopped, so the Southern Pacific named the place Langtry in her honor. The place consisted of an eating house, a water tank and section house, also a grocery store and Roy Bean's saloon. Our main camp was about 1,000 yards from this place on a bluff over the Rio Grande, and we had a sweeping view of the surrounding country. Whenever we alternated with some of the other troops after leaving Fort Clark, we had to cross the Devil's River and later on the Pecos River.

I will never forget the first time we had to do guard duty behind our six-mule teams in going down the canyon to the crossing of the Pecos. The road was hewn in solid rock, more of a trail, and down about 600 feet deep—very steep—and I was often fearful, with my heart almost in my throat when I saw the wheels of our wagon within a few inches of the rim of the trail, almost ready to topple over. The driver was in those times riding the left mule next to the wagon, the other four mules ahead being guided by him with a jerk line. This line consisted of a single broad belt leading to the front mules two abreast. By certain pulls and jerks, these leaders knew and were guided where to go. Of course, these mules were broke and trained and were generally very sure-footed.

Game in those times was plentiful and easy to get. I remember one time in the winter we had about fifteen deer hung up in our cooking tent and we ate deer meat for breakfast, dinner, and supper for weeks. We also had wild turkey, as well as wild hogs, buffalo fish, as we called them, from the Devil's River, and fine big catfish from the Rio Grande. Roy Bean, who ran the saloon at Langtry, was a character of the wild and woolly West. He was about fifty years old, full beard, and stout of build. He was justice of the peace and the law west of the Pecos, and nobody dared to dispute him in that, for he was equally fast on the trigger. The cowboys used to come in about every so often and help to dispose of Roy Bean's wet and dry goods in good quantities, and there were many scraps and shooting up and around the saloon, also many bloody fights.

While the Southern Pacific Railroad was building a new bridge across the Pecos one day, a fellow fell off and was killed. Roy Bean ordered one of the Mexicans to bring the body in and, as he acted as coroner, rendered a verdict of accidental death. Somebody turned the body over and found a six-shooter and $40 on the dead man. At once Roy Bean reopened the inquest, found the dead man guilty of carrying concealed weapons, confiscated the gun for the deputy, fined the dead man $25 and $15 court costs, and so the law west of the Pecos collected the whole $40. That's how the dead man paid his fine. At another time while our troop was in camp at Langtry, a cowboy shot and killed one of the Chinamen who worked in one of the construction camps near Langtry for the Southern Pacific Railroad.

Roy Bean arrested the cowboy and in short order had him up for trial back of his saloon. We all crowded in and around the "courtroom" to see and hear the trial, and the final verdict, which was as follows, as near as I can remember: "I, Roy Bean, as judge of all laws west of the Pecos, have duly searched all my law books, heard all the evidence of the killing, and find that in this state when a man kills another he must be hung by his neck till dead, but in all my books of law I cannot find a single item in which the law so applies or even mentions a Chinaman. I therefore discharge the prisoner." We all had a drink or smoke on the prisoner at Roy's place, after which Roy handed the cowboy his hardware and the other cowboys brought the ex-prisoner's horse. The ex-prisoner jumped on, Roy Bean fired a shot in the air and yelled: "Yonder is the setting sun. Now get!" and away flew the ex-prisoner and his bunch of cowboys amidst a cloud of dust. That's how the law applied to a Chinaman, who was buried right along the railroad track at Langtry.

These were a few of the incidents while we were in the neighborhood of Langtry, from which place we did considerable scouting up and down the Rio Grande and along the Southern Pacific Railroad. One of the other troops from Fort Clark alternately relieved us on these scouting trips. The Southern Pacific Railroad in those times ran a morning and an evening train along this line, and these trains made a stop at Langtry for about twenty minutes to take on water and coal, also to give the travelers a chance for a bite to eat and to stretch their legs by a short walk on the platform. We used to hang around the station when off duty and so did the cowboys, just to watch the travelers. One day on the evening train from the east a man stepped off the train and asked a lot of questions about the country. Finally, he wanted to know what they really raised besides cattle out there. "Well," said a cowboy, "we raise cactus, rattlesnakes, and hell." I guess he told the easterner about the truth, for during my soldiering down there we often were kept busy picking one another's cactus thorns out of the seat of our pants and legs, and we killed more rattlers, especially in those rocky canyons and ravines along the Rio Grande, than in any other part of the country.

Fort Clark itself was built on a very rocky formation, and had good quarters, as well as good stables and fairly good water supply from a spring below the fort and between there and the nearby town of Brackettville, which was a typical cowboy town, wild and woolly, having one-half dozen saloons and gambling halls, dance halls, and a few general stores, and mostly adobe houses or sheds. The roulette wheels were spinning day and night, and faro games, studhorse, and poker games ran continuously by Mexicans as well as white men and half-breeds. The cowboys and soldiers were the main support of the town, and we saw many shootings and stabbings, also several public hangings, while stationed there. Close to Fort Clark was also a Seminole Indian camp of about 300 or 400 Seminole Indians, who had about as many dogs as women and children. Once every two or three weeks these Indians held their Saturday night celebration, which lasted well on till 2 or 3 o'clock in the morning, by dancing, whooping, and howling and being very hilarious. Usually on these occasions they roasted or cooked some of their dogs, which was considered the proper festival food (Indians do not eat turkey, as they are very superstitious about that bird). These Indians were kept there by the U. S. Government and went often with us as scouts on special occasion and expeditions when going on the road or march, and they were very trustworthy.

In those times the soldiers had neither mattress nor a pillow, but a bed sack made of white canvas. This had to be washed and scrubbed every four weeks for monthly inspection, and we usually filled it once a month at the quartermaster's corral. Before filling our bed sack, we usually took a pitchfork and shook the snakes and cactus out of the hay, for the Mexicans who supplied us with hay were not any too particular what it contained, so long as the weight was in it, as they got paid so much per hundred by the U. S. Government. Our horses were a mixture of Mexican broncho and American, but made pretty good mounts and stood hard riding after being broken in.

In the early summer of 1885 we received orders from Washington to pack up and draw rations for the Indian campaign, as the Apaches under Geronimo were on the warpath in Arizona, also some of the Cheyenne and Comanches in Indian Territory. Part of our outfit was sent to Arizona, the rest of the troops from Fort Clark, including my troop, in heavy marching order, proceeded the same night to the nearest railroad station where a train was all ready waiting for us, and we put our horses in the cattle cars, also our rations, and piled into day coaches and were shipped to the extreme western part of Indian Territory, on the Kansas border. General Nelson A. Miles, who was brigadier general at that time, was there in person and had charge of that campaign. There were lots of other soldiers from different regiments strung all along the border, and the Indians on the warpath had a poor chance of breaking through the line and making raids on the settlers of western Kansas, as we had them all surrounded. Their object was to unite with the Apaches and start a general war on settlers [sic].

We were there during the better part of the summer and after General Miles held a big review of all outfits, we got orders to march through Indian Territory and gather up all hostile renegades. It was hot and dusty during that drive and we kept the Indians constantly on the move, and finally landed with a lot of them in Fort Reno, and later on in Fort Sill, where this campaign ended, as all Cheyennes and Comanches had been driven back to their respective reservations after being disarmed.

We proceeded on our march and eventually crossed the Red River, when everybody took a much-needed bath and washed his underwear, and while waiting for them to dry we laid in the sand, mostly naked, and nearly everybody got a dose of poison ivy, which caused a lot of discomfort. We crossed the Staked Plains in Texas and finally reached Fort Clark again, but stayed there only a short time, as some of the Apaches from Arizona, who were still on the warpath, had been seen in the extreme western part of Texas, and all the settlers and ranches were asking the government for protection. It was now late in the fall and we were ordered out again, and after taking on supplies marched to the extreme western part of Texas and border of Arizona, guarding ranches along our scouting trips and doing general border duty to deep away the Indians from coming across the Rio Grande. We were out all winter and part of the spring, when some other troops from the Eighth relieved us and we marched back to Fort Clark, for about that time the hostiles in Arizona had been driven over into Mexico and General Miles was negotiating with Geronimo, who was about to surrender, and this about ended the Geronimo Campaign. This was about September, 1886.

After being stationed at Fort Clark for a short time, we received orders to pack up and march to Fort Duncan, near Eagle Pass, for border duty. Arriving at that old fort, which was a remnant of the Mexican War, we first proceeded to clean out some of the old quarters, which were occupied by thousands of large bats. The bat manure was about a foot deep on the floors and for weeks these animals flew not only at night, but sometimes during the day, and finally we began to smoke them out so we could move in. Meantime, we made a camp on the old parade grounds. This also had been overgrown with cactus and mesquite shrubs and formed a regular jungle, and in some rocky places rattlesnakes were comfortably housed. These we cleaned out with our sabers. The quarters and stables in this place were all built of adobe (a sun-dried mud brick), but made a fairly good place to live in, but the nauseating odor from the bats hung for a long while. As there was no available water supply at Camp Eagle Pass, which name the place received after we took possession of it, we had to ride our horses down to the Rio Grande twice daily over a high bluff to water them. Our drinking water we hauled in a water wagon from the nearby water tank of Eagle Pass on the railroad track.

During the winter of 1887, or rather toward spring, one day lightning struck one of the quarters which we used as a storage place for hay or grain for our horses, and set the hay on fire. The fire, which was very stubborn and right in the center of the building, made us pitch most of the hay out in the rain, and we tried to bail up some rain water from the gulley and ditches with the old-fashioned leather fire buckets, which were no doubt remnants of the Mexican War, but the fire and rain caused most of the hay to be a total loss. From this place, part of the outfit had to do scouting along the Rio Grande toward Laredo to keep the Mexican smugglers and cattle and horse thieves as much down as was possible in that open country right on the border. We did have several scraps with the cut-throats, but mostly came out ahead, for those outlaws would rather fight than eat, but had all respect for the boys in blue, and usually made a fast getaway by jumping in and swimming the river for the Mexican side where the mountainous country soon swallowed them up.

In the spring of 1888, being relieved by a troop of the Third Cavalry, we received orders from Washington to march to Fort Concho, there to concentrate with the rest of the other troops of the Eighth Cavalry, and from there to march to North Dakota [Dakota Territory], overland, to change stations with the Seventh Cavalry. We packed our horse feed in a six-mule wagon and our own food, as well as tents and camping outfit, in another. Our overcoats, tents, and spare blankets, as well as lariats and other equipment, we always carried on our saddles in heavy marching order, even our sabers were strapped to the saddle. These cavalry ornaments often came in handy in cutting down grass, chopping wood, digging out tarantulas, and knocking the heads off rattlers and water moccasin snakes, of which there were plenty along part of that God-forsaken country in Texas. We left on the 15th of May and marched to Fort Clark, and from there due northwest till we reached Fort Concho.

Because our troop came from the farthest place on the lower Rio Grande, most of the other troops had arrived there before we did. Consequently, we only had a few days' rest and time to draw feed and rations before we started on the long march to North Dakota under Lieutenant Colonel John K. Mizner in command. I was corporal at that time and carried our troop's guidon (flag) most of the way to Fort Riley, Kansas, and as we headed north through the staked plains and Texas Panhandle country we often had to build our campfire with buffalo chips because wood was rather scarce in that part of the country, especially for twelve troops. We came to the Brazos River, which stream happened to be high water, and we camped there several days before we could safely cross, and when we did cross, or rather swim part ways, everybody was wet from head to foot, for one could only see our heads and those of our horses sticking out of the water. While camping on the shores of the Brazos, we found the whole place covered with white sand, and this held, or was infested with, hundreds of tarantulas' nests (a big poison black spider) whose bite is often fatal. These nests we dug out with our sabers before spreading our blankets.

Lieutenant Colonel Mizner was rather fond of regimental drilling along that march, and he had us often strung for miles in skirmish drill, trotting, galloping, and even charging over the wild plains, where roads were unknown, and only buffalo trails could be followed, also where prairie dog holes by the thousand were a constant menace of getting a sudden spill if a horse's foot got caught in one of the holes. Arriving at the Red River, we found that stream in fairly good condition and did not have much trouble fording it, although the water reached over our saddles. We did not mind that, however, for by that time we were fairly used to getting wet. We were now in Indian Territory (now called Oklahoma) and reached the fork of the Canadian River without any mishap, which we crossed safely and made camp about 7 p.m. Everybody was waiting for our six-mule teams to arrive, when finally a guard rode into the camp and reported quite a few of the wagons, including ours, were stuck in the quicksand of the Canadian River. I was corporal of the guard that evening and was detailed with about fifteen men to ride ten miles back and help get our wagons out by unloading. We were in the river till about 11 o'clock that night up to our necks, unloading horse feed as well as our heavier pieces in the cook's wagon. After unloading the wagons and hitching a dozen mules onto them, we finally pulled them out, loaded them again, and got into camp after midnight. Along toward 1 a.m. we had our supper—a cup of black coffee, a slice of sow belly, and one-half dozen of those aged gray hardtack, the first bite since breakfast.

In those times we marched all day and made no stops for lunch. Everybody had a canteen full of water and a few hardtack, just to keep the stomach from growling. On reaching Fort Sill, we got a few days' rest, also fresh meat and real bread and some vegetables, which the troops stationed there kindly supplied us, and certainly were gratefully received by us. After drawing rations there, we started out again for Fort Reno, where we also had the same courtesy extended us as before at Fort Sill. We ran into quite a number of rainstorms toward the Kansas border and the mud was terrible in some places. Often the wind and rain would blow our Sibley tents down during the night (each troop had about three large Sibley tents besides some

A private of the Sixth Cavalry stands in full dress uniform with chin strap employed, at Fort Logan, Colorado, in the early 1890s. *Editor's collection*

wall and A tents). A Sibley tent would hold about sixteen men. It is a round tent and looks like an Indian tepee.

Our march through Kansas was rather hot and dusty. It was now late July and good camping ground was rather hard to find for a whole regiment. In many places we nearly drank the creeks and wells of settlers dry, and after crossing the Smoky [Hill] River we reached the bottom land, near Fort Riley, Kansas, safe and sound, where part of the Seventh Cavalry was also encamped. This was early in August, and we camped and rested there several weeks. Our troops received some new horses, for quite a few of the older ones were completely worn out, and many had sore backs caused from the heat and perspiration, and a number of the plugs were inspected and condemned. Several dozen soldiers, including myself, whose time of enlistment was about to expire, were now assigned to some of the troops of the Seventh Cavalry at Fort Riley because we could not be taken along on the road with the regiment and perhaps be discharged in the open prairie, so after the regiment drew new rations, clothing for men, and fresh equipment, we bade our comrades farewell. The Eighth Cavalry finally reached Fort Meade, [Dakota Territory,] in September, and my troop, which had come from one of the hottest parts of Texas, was sent to Fort Buford, up near the Canadian border—a change from the Mexican to the Canadian line.

I may state here that from the original seventeen recruits assigned to my troop in 1883, just three returned after serving their full five years' enlistment in August, 1888, including myself. Some died of fever, some were wounded or injured and sent to the Soldiers Home in Washington, [D. C.,] and some were killed; a few deserted. During the campaign in 1885-86 while in Arizona after the Apaches, some troops of our regiment were ambushed by Geronimo and lost quite heavily in killed and wounded. Among those killed was our Dr. Thomas J. C. Maddox, who had been stationed with us at Fort Clark, Texas, up to 1885. He was the doctor who brought me through when I had malarial fever . . . and the government certainly lost a fine man. Dr. Leonard Wood was at that time just a contract doctor (citizen doctor enrolled by the government) and got his start in that campaign, when he in later years with Theodore Roosevelt became a colonel of the Rough Riders [First U. S. Volunteer Cavalry], and later on governor of the Philippine Islands. All in all, I think the Eighth Cavalry did as well as any other regiment of the U. S., and that march from Texas to South Dakota certainly was the longest one any U. S. regiment ever made, and that without any serious mishaps. It was an experiment by the War Department and proved what could be done if it became necessary.

In conclusion, I may state that I was only a youngster of seventeen and one-half years when I enlisted, but easily passed for twenty-one, and my memory always becomes wide-awake when I recall the five years of service in the Eighth Cavalry. We generally carried forty rounds of ammunition in our web belts and one extra one in our pocket, this last one saved for ourselves should fate so design it. I received my discharge at Fort Riley, Kansas, in the latter part of 1888, signed by Lieutenant Colonel Samuel M. Whitside, Seventh Cavalry. [I received a notation of] excellent character and recommendation for re-enlistment. . . .

Twelve Years in the Eighteenth Infantry (By Phillip Schreiber, formerly of Company H, Eighteenth U. S. Infantry. From *Winners of the West*, August 30, 1937)

I enlisted at Chicago, Illinois, April 18, 1884, and was sent to Columbus, Ohio. The first sergeant, having found out that I was a barber, asked me to start a shop in the company. He then took me to Sergeant Bowser, the chief bugler, and asked him to make a bugler out of me as he intended to keep me at the Columbus Barracks for a year. After the year was up I was assigned to Company H, Eighteenth U. S. Infantry, as they were in need of a combination bugler and barber. I was sent as part of an escort to take a batch of prisoners to Fort Leavenworth, Kansas. There I was attached to Company G, Eleventh U. S. Infantry, to await the arrival of my regiment, which at that time exchanged stations with the Twentieth U. S. Infantry. They arrived June 13, 1885. I joined my outfit, Company H, and was given the nickname of "Kid," which stuck to me throughout my service.

Companies G, H, and K got orders to go by rail to Caldwell, Kansas, and from there to hike 110 miles to Fort Reno, Indian Territory. On our third day out we were joined by Company F, Twenty-second U. S. Infantry. They brought word of the Cheyenne and Arapaho uprising at the Darlington Agency, near Fort Reno. We made the trip as fast as we could over the desolate roadless country. On the evening of the sixth day, a trainmaster with an escort from the Ninth U. S. Cavalry arrived with enough transportation to haul us to the post. They also brought a few cases of ammunition. Each man was issued forty rounds. Next morning we piled into the wagons, adjusted the covers, and off we went. But, oh how it did rain. We drove right through the Indian villages and at last my boyhood wish to see real Indians was amply fulfilled. I'll never forget how a few young bucks rode from wagon to wagon pulling back the canvas flaps to take inventory of everything inside.

When we finally reached the post we were lined up on the parade ground and, not minding the downpour, were inspected by the post commander, Major Edwin V. Sumner of the Fifth U. S. Cavalry. When we finally got under roof, we all looked like drowned kittens. Brigadier General Nelson A. Miles came the next day and two days later Lieutenant General Philip H. Sheridan arrived. It didn't take them long to bring the redskins to terms and within two weeks all the tepees from around the post disappeared. It was during this time that all the troops that were gathered around the reservation were crowded on the parade ground for the memorial services of ex-President U. S. Grant [who had died on July 23, 1885].

Two months later, our three companies were ordered to Fort Riley, Kansas, headquarters of the Fifth U. S. Cavalry. In 1887, they left Fort Riley and were replaced by the Seventh U. S. Cavalry. The following year our three companies were split up. G and K were sent to Fort Logan, Colorado, while Company H went to our headquarters at Fort Hays, Kansas. It seemed that my captain had a grudge against me for he took the bugle away from me and decorated me with corporal stripes, which gave me a raise of two dollars per month. The following spring I finished my first five years, reenlisted in the same company as a bugler, which I considered best to run a barbershop. In the same year, Fort Hays was abandoned and the whole regiment went to Fort Clark, Texas, where we doubled up with three troops of the Third Cavalry. This surely was very exciting with two colonels, two adjutants, two sergeants major, and two bands. The adjutants mounted guard alternately.

In 1891, my company was ordered to Eagle Pass for duty, while the regular cavalry troop chased Garcia [sic—Catarino E. Garza and his followers] along the Rio Grande. During the winter of 1892, I was with a mixed detachment at Camp Langtry, Texas, where I got an attack of sciatica so bad that I had to be sent to the Army and Navy Hospital at Hot Springs[, Arkansas]. In 1894, our regiment was split up again and my company with three more established headquarters at new Fort Bliss. We were the first troops to occupy that post, where I received my second discharge. I enlisted for the third time and in 1896 I took my discharge on the twelve-year veteran act. I always liked the service, especially the first enlistment when as a young soldier I came in constant contact with veterans of the Civil War, where nearly all the sergeants and officers from captains up and a good many first lieutenants were Civil War veterans. I had a great respect for them and was always ready to take their advice. But one of my happiest days was back in 1887, when Colonel Charles E. Compton called me to his quarters to shave the Commander-in-Chief of the Army, General Philip Sheridan.

Private Howard Easton, Seventh Infantry, Fort Logan, Colorado, stands in field dress with the newly issued Krag-Jorgensen rifle, ca. 1896. *Editor's collection*

Cemeteries at Fort Laramie (By Michael M. O'Sullivan, formerly corporal, Company F, Seventh U. S. Infantry. From *Winners of the West*, May 30, 1927)

I enlisted at Springfield, Massachusetts, December 22, 1887, and was sent for training to David's Island, now better known as Fort Slocum; and on April 2, 1888, joined Company F, Seventh U. S. Infantry, at Fort Laramie, Wyoming Territory. This fort, frequently spoken of in writings of Charles King, was first established as a trading station by the Hudson Bay Fur Company in 1844. It stood in a basin of considerable area, encircled by low lying hills and plateaus, was ninety-eight miles north[east] of Cheyenne, sixty-five miles east of Laramie Peak, and three-quarters of a mile from the confluence of the North Platte with the Laramie River. So dreary and desolate was the country by which it was surrounded, that in any direction but few habitations would be encountered within a radius of thirty miles. Aside from the yearly visit of a Roman Catholic priest, the appearance of a distant squatter or cowboy, the sight of a white man, except the soldier in uniform, was indeed so rare a thing that he was absolutely looked on as a novelty.

At the time of the station being established, as well as for several decades after, this locality was thickly infested with marauding and hostile Indians, and believing the station untenable, and the lives of those connected with it constantly in danger, the company appealed to the federal government for protection. The appeal being taken into consideration and granted, it was made a military post and remained as such until finally abandoned in the month of October, 1889. This fort in those times served a very useful purpose in that lawless and God-forsaken region. It enabled settlers in the Chug[water] Valley, the distant cottonwoods and north and south along the Platte River, to do business and live with a considerable degree of security. It kept bandits on their good behavior, and was a popular rendezvous for gold seekers in the Black Hills.

Upon gold being discovered there, Fort Laramie became a rallying point for prospectors heading in that direction. There they would remain until they were of sufficient number to start off with no little feeling of safety. But if within a reasonable time the desired number was not at hand, a troop of cavalry would escort them for half the distance, where they would be taken in hand by a troop from the other direction and conveyed to the end of the journey. In those days also, parties traveling under escort usually got through with a fairly good degree of success, but it not unfrequently happened that when traveling under different conditions the effort would end in disaster, a fact which in the opinion of many made certain places along the trail all but veritable graveyards. To the uninitiated this may seem a rather sweeping statement, but what will be said when convincing evidence to that effect was even brought to light within the limits of the garrison [sic].

In the spring of 1889 it was decided to construct a drain from the hospital, for a distance of about 700 yards, to the Laramie River. The direction of the ditch as marked out was close up to and parallel with the hospital veranda. The first day of the digging, about two in the afternoon, a human skeleton was unearthed, and the matter reported to the commanding officer, who upon arriving at the scene ordered the bones picked up and buried and the diggers to go on with the ditch. About ten o'clock the morning following, another skeleton was exposed. This was decidedly the skeleton of a young woman, because of a neatly done up ball of blonde hair which was yet in place on the skull. That was enough. The commanding officer, at a loss to account for their being, except as the result of one of the aforementioned massacres, countermanded the digging and ordered the ditch filled in.

There were two cemeteries at Fort Laramie, one that of the soldiers daintily laid out and enclosed in a well-kept picket fence and on a hill spur eastward and about a half a mile from the barracks. The other was on a side hill, directly north of these same barracks, and at a distance of about 600 yards. Unlike the former, it had no adornments, fence, outline, or uniformity. Instead, the graves were scattered toward every point of the compass. This, dear readers, was the final resting place of victims of foul play, some of whose bodies were formerly discovered by soldiers out on a fishing or hunting trip. Nobody from Adam down knew who they were or whence they came. The result being that every grave marker not already rotted away carried the stencil and indeed impressive information that the unlucky occupant of said grave was "unknown."

Such was the West of those days, and such the tragic and untimely end of those unfortunates, who not only died in, but were actually buried in, their boots. And who will say that even at this late day, but that for some the light is still kept burning, sustained by the hope of again meeting the loved ones whom they are destined not to meet this side of eternity.

Yet from the foregoing it would be a mistake to infer that Fort Laramie was nothing but a citadel of gloom. Indeed, the reverse might be said to have been the case. For what of its varied talents? What of its interesting rifle competitions? What of its games, socials, and dances? What of the lectures and comedy? What of the pranks and laughter of children? What of the enlivening and inspiring strains of the band? What of the innumerable calls on the bugle? And what of Old Glory waving compliments to its defenders, and defiance to its enemies, from the masthead?

Life as a Rookie (By John T. Stokes, formerly of Troop K, First U. S. Cavalry. From *Winners of the West*, December, 1939)

I enlisted at Des Moines, Iowa, in March, 1892. I saw a pretty sign on East 5th Street, telling of all the good things in the Army, so I took on. Sergeant George W. Batson took about ten of us to Fort Grant, Arizona. We went from Willcox in quartermaster wagons. On coming in sight of the fort, the driver showed us the hog ranch. Well, we thought that was where the soldiers got their pork. Some of you old First Cavalry men know all about the pork.

We got to the fort about 1 p.m. Dinner was over, but they had saved us some slum. One rookie asked about butter and was told to go ask the first sergeant for "butter money" and as it was only the 8th of the month there would be about $1.50 coming. That was a lot of money. Well after we had our slum and coffee, we went strolling into the quarters and we had our leader go for his butter money. Into the orderly room he went, never stopping to knock, and asked for his butter money. . . . And the way he came out! Well, the rest of us did not want the butter money. The first sergeant wanted to know who sent him in. All soldiers look alike to a rookie, so it was never known who sent him in.

Next day I was [on] stable police. One man told me to ask for a star and club. I saw a lot of stars when I asked and got the club or something bigger! Then came the bull ring drill, riding a horse with a blanket. We rode the horse from one end to the other. After a few days [of] bull ring drill we had no use for a chair. After we got all the drill learned, we were sent on duty as a real soldier. The first duty was guard. Bughouse Brown [either First Lieutenant William C. Brown or First Lieutenant Oscar J. Brown] was officer of the day. I surely had one grand time trying to make believe I knew the general orders. It was down by K Troop stables. I surely would have liked to have thrown him into the water tank one time when a bunch of rookies came in. Hal Winslow of K Troop took his big U. S. belt buckle, daubed it with red ink and branded a big U. S. on his [own] hip and then told the rookies that they were to be branded with a hot iron. He then slipped his trousers down and showed them his brand. Two of that bunch of rookies were never seen after that evening. Well, it is a good man that lives through his rookieism to tell about it.

A Boyhood at Tongue River Cantonment and Fort Keogh,

1877-1882 (By Dominick J. O'Malley, a Second Cavalryman's dependent. From *Winners of the West*, May 28, 1943)

Early in the summer of 1877, Colonel Albert G. Brackett of the Second U. S. Cavalry at Fort Sanders, Wyoming [Territory], received orders from the War Department at Washington to transfer his regiment from Wyoming to Montana. Orders were sent by him to the various forts and camps in Wyoming that were garrisoned by the Second for the troops to mobilize at Medicine Bow from which point the march would begin early in September. The first troops to arrive at Medicine Bow were troops A, B, D, and E, along with the regimental band from Fort Sanders. In a few days other troops came in from Fort Fred Steele, Camp Stambaugh, Fort Laramie, and other stations, and by August 26 the entire regiment, with the exception of two troops that were already serving in Montana at Fort Ellis, were at Medicine Bow awaiting orders to begin the march into the Indian country. There were a great many children in the camp, many of the officers and enlisted men being married and their families were traveling with them to the new country. To the children, the camp was a scene of never-ending interest.

Immediately after breakfast, September 2, a trumpeter sounded the call to break camp, and everyone sprang into action. Tents began to fall and were rolled and tied; camp property was put into shape and loaded. I cannot recall the different places at which we camped, but the first sign of habitation was Fort Fetterman on the Platte River. This fort was situated on a high hill close to the river and commanded a view of the surrounding country. Here the command met its first trouble. The Platte is a treacherous stream full of quicksand and holes. We were nearly all day fording it. Two teams were drowned, as was one of the soldiers who became entangled in the chains and harness of the drowning mules. We stayed in camp all the next day and the drowned soldier was buried at the fort. The two wagons were recovered from the river and put in shape again. One six-mule team was obtained from the quartermaster at Fetterman. The other wagon was left at the fort. After leaving Fetterman, orders were issued that only one move a day would be made and camp was usually made around 2 p.m.

As soon as a place was found suitable for a camp, the picket guard was placed, two or three soldiers in a place on the highest ground within a mile of the camp. I remember one afternoon about four days out from Fetterman, all stock had been brought in. Cavalry horses were tied to the company picket line. Mules were tied at their wagons. Numerous children were playing in front of the tents, when all of a sudden they heard the trumpeter at the guard tent sound that significant call, "Boots and Saddles." Instantly the camp was a scene of excitement. The soldiers sprang from their tents to their horses. The women and children were hurried to the center of the camp where the heavy wagons were always parked in a hollow square for their protection. Then "Assembly" sounded. A troop surrounded the square where the women and children were and the rest formed in line and advanced toward where the picket had reported a body of horsemen. We could see the troop halt and then two troops advanced in a skirmish line. The skirmish line had gotten about 600 yards in advance of the main body of troops, when up on a little ridge where the picket had been stationed who gave the alarms, rode a bunch of twenty-five horsemen. One of our guard said, loud enough so some heard him, "There they come all right," and then added quickly, "Say, they've got a guidon. It's soldiers," and it was. It was a detachment of mounted infantry from Fetterman who had been sent after us with some orders for the colonel of our command. The orders had been delayed and had not reached Fetterman until three days after we departed.

Before the command reached Wind River, signs of Indians were noticed and skirmish lines were thrown out twice, but no live Indians put in their appearance. Once, three dead bodies were found on scaffolds built in the branches of cottonwoods. On investigation, it was found they were Sioux and had not been dead long. Double pickets were put out and double guards placed at night. About eight miles from Wind River we crossed a fresh trail which evidently had been made by a large band of Indians who appeared to be traveling in the same direction we were. The command was ordered into camp as soon as we reached water, and a troop of cavalry (I think it was K Troop) was sent to follow the trail and report any signs of Indians. They followed the trail for ten miles when it swung to the northwest. They found no Indians except a dead one in a tree. The scout with the troop said he thought the trail was at least three days old. We found out after we reached Fort Keogh that a bunch of about 400 Sioux had made that trail and had been engaged by troops from Fort Ellis and captured.

The next camp of any note that I remember was at old Fort Phil Kearny on the Piney. This fort had been harassed by Red Cloud and his fighting

Sioux about [1866 and] 1867 until it was abandoned by the government and the troops were barely out of sight of the fort when the Indians had every building burning. It was at or near Kearny that Captain Fetterman and his command were killed by the Sioux in 1867 [1866]. We camped just below the old fort. The charred remnants of a good many of the old buildings could be plainly seen. The fort was built of logs, and much of the old charred logs were used by our command for their kitchen fires. We stayed in the camp two days, as there was plenty of wood and water and grass for the stock. The afternoon of the first day, one of the soldiers of C Troop who was on herd guard came near causing mutiny in the regiment and also among the teamsters. While the horses were on water, he got off his horse to get himself a drink and noticed in a gravel riffle quite a quantity of what he thought was gold dust. He managed to secure about a teaspoonful of it, which he put in a tin tobacco box, and when he got to camp he showed it to some of the troops and told them the creek was full of it. The news soon spread over the camp and it was with difficulty the soldiers were restrained from going in a body to get the gold. It took a show of arms to hold them, and several of the soldiers who had had experience in placer mining convinced the gold-eager men that the stuff was mica, or as it was commonly called, "Fool's Gold," and was not worth a dollar a ton.

A few days after the command had left Kearny, more excitement was caused in camp, this time by two boys, myself being one of them, the other a boy named Will Aughey, whose father was in Troop B. The command was making noon camp on Cherry Creek. Chokecherries were abundant around camp, and women and children were busy picking them, Aughey and I among them. We noticed a clump of cherry bushes just outside the guard line. We had not gathered many before we saw—a little way up the creek—another patch where the fruit seemed still larger than what we were picking, and as we were out of sight of the guard, it was not hard to get to this patch. By this time we had forgotten about camp lines, Indians, or anything else except big cherries, and we kept on discovering better (in our estimation) and bigger cherries, each patch being a little bigger farther from camp. Suddenly, Will said, "Wasn't that a bugle call? Maybe camp is going to move and we had better get back quick." We started to return and realized that camp was not in sight anywhere. We didn't really know which way to go, but, by good luck, we started down the branch which we thought was the one the camp was on. After going what we thought was at least ten miles, we found our creek emptying into another one and we stopped. We could not remember having seen this creek before. We were at a loss as to which way to return, when we saw a line of horsemen come in sight along a little ridge to our right and we recognized them as soldiers. Pretty soon the line seemed to show up a mile long. Then we showed ourselves and the trumpet sounded "Rally." It was Troop B in a skirmish line looking for us. When we were missed at camp, our absence was reported at once and "Boots and Saddles" was sounded. That was the call that Will had heard that brought us to realization that we were lost.

A few days after the cherry episode, we made camp on Goose Creek and here occurred the second fatality of the trip. It was found that there was plenty of fish in Goose Creek, and permission was given the troops to catch some. One party of soldiers made a makeshift seine out of gunny sacks and was meeting with fair success. While they were dragging the seine in a bend of the creek where the water was deep, one of the soldiers stepped into a deep hole and went out of sight. He failed to come to the surface and the others attempted to find him. He was found in ten minutes, about twenty-five feet below where he had disappeared and was caught in the roots of some old drift logs beneath the surface. He was dead. I do not remember his name, but I remember he was a trooper of K Troop. This cast a gloom over the camp. From Goose Creek, we moved to Prairie Dog Creek and went into camp for a couple of days, and we could see that some new arrangements were being made and it was found that the command would move in two parts when we left. Part of the troops and transportation were to go to Fort Custer and part to [Fort] Keogh. The balance of the regiment, with the band, went to Fort Custer, which was to be the headquarters of the Second Cavalry, Fort Keogh being the headquarters of the Fifth Infantry.

The troops for Custer began their journey the third morning after we had pitched camp on Prairie Dog, and the Keogh contingent were to leave the following morning. That night it was found that the wife of a trumpeter of Troop E was in no condition to move for possibly a week and a new problem faced our commanding officer. It was decided to leave our doctor and a detachment of soldiers at that camp while the command went to Keogh from where an ambulance and other transportation were to be sent back for them. The commanding officer called for a volunteer from among the women to stay with the sick woman and though there were about twenty-five married women in our camp, my mother was the only one who volunteered to stay. A detachment of twenty-five men under command of my stepfather, Charles White, was left to guard camp. It was with misgivings that the little group watched the rest leave. We were alone in a wild country overrun with hostile Indians and no one knew when a war party would show up. Mrs. John

An infantry sergeant and his wife sit for the cameraman at an unidentified post, ca. 1880s. *Editor's collection*

Clancy's baby was born that night. White divided his small command into two guards. One guarded camp during the day and one at night. It seemed to me as though he (White) was on guard all the time. He seemed to be up at all times of the day and night.

The third day after the troops left our camp [we] experienced the worst scare of the whole trip, and for a time everyone thought we were due for an

Indian attack. My mother sent me to the creek, not over twenty yards away, for a bucket of water. The creek was guarded on both sides. I went to the water hole to fill my pail when I thought another water hole a short distance below looked better (the same as the cherry patches had a short time before). When I got to this hole, I noticed a trail which seemed to lead to a thick clump of trees. My curiosity got the best of me, and leaving my pail, I went up the trail. When I got to the top of the bank, I was petrified with fright. There in a little opening in the trees and in plain sight stood an Indian tepee. For a few seconds, I seemed paralyzed, then I ducked back and gained the creek bed again. I grabbed my pail and hurried back to camp. I sought my stepfather and told him what I had seen. He immediately got the men together and by some signal notified those who were on guard of danger. A hurried council of war was held. I told him again what I had seen and where I had gone up the bank. White finally decided he would investigate. [He] gave orders to the men and started alone the way I had gone. The rest stood ready around the tents. The women had not been told what was going on, the only intimation they had was to keep the children inside the tents. It seemed ages before anything was seen or heard of White, when suddenly he appeared from the timber and came on into camp. The tepee was an old one and had been deserted for at least a year. I came in for questioning then, as to why I went so far from camp to get the water. The timber was over three-quarters of a mile from camp. I got an emphatic promise from White that I would suffer if I ever did such a trick again. Everyone wondered why it was that the tepee hadn't been seen before, as the whole command had been in that camp three days before it split up. No one, it seemed, had gone near that bunch of trees until I blundered into it. Vigilance around our little camp was redoubled for some thought this place might have been a regular camping place for the Indians, as numerous signs were found of old camps. The children, of whom there were six, four of Clancy's, my sister, and myself, were not allowed to go farther than fifty feet from the tents, and that in front of the tents.

The evening of the sixth day after the troops had left us, we heard the sound of a military trumpet from down the creek sound, "Halt." White, who was at the tents, ordered Clancy to sound "Advance," and the entire camp was alive. In a minute or so, from across the creek came a body of horsemen followed by a Red Cross ambulance and two four-mule jerk-line teams. It was a detachment of soldiers from Keogh who had come for us. One of the fort doctors, Rosten G. Redd, was with them, and they had medicine for the sick. Camp was lively that evening. We children had a fine time with the new soldiers, who were from the Fifth Infantry. They were mounted on captured

Indian horses. Two of them were of our own troops, who had been sent with them as guides. Dr. Redd found that Mrs. Clancy was in condition to be moved and the next day we started for Fort Keogh. Mother went in the ambulance with Mrs. Clancy, while we children were placed in the wagons carrying camp equipment. We moved a lot faster now than we did with the main command. After we struck Tongue River, the country was smoother and the cavalry and all the wagons that had preceded us were kept on a trot whenever practical.

About 2 o'clock p.m., October 5, 1877, we came in sight of Fort Keogh, our future home. We surely were an excited band of boys and girls. We made all sorts of conjectures as to where we were going to live and what we were going to do, and could hardly wait for the mules (who now seemed to us to be creeping along) to get us to the fort. We went directly to the new fort, which was not yet entirely built, and the tents for the two laundresses of Troop E, my mother, and Mrs. Clancy were pitched about 200 yards east of the troop quarters. We stayed in tents all winter, as no quarters had been built for the enlisted men's wives as yet. But all the fine double frame buildings for the officers and their families were about completed. Each married soldier had two 10 x 14 wall tents to live in. These were pitched, one directly in front of the other, and both topped by a large government tarpaulin. They proved to be comfortable, and we lived in ours until the following spring, when log houses were built apart from the fort and were laid out in regular formation. The houses were about fifty feet apart with a back yard of 100 feet. A sort of street sixty feet wide separated the line of dwellings. There were about sixty-five of these dwellings in this section of Fort Keogh, which was known to the soldiers as Tub Town, and Sudsville, because most of the women who lived there were regular company laundresses.

Fort Keogh, when the Second Cavalry arrived, was a busy place. Colonel Nelson A. Miles, in command of the Fifth Infantry, the year before had built a cantonment at the junction of the Yellowstone and Tongue rivers and, as soon as men and material could be obtained, began building Fort Keogh. The cantonment was about two miles east of the new fort. As I have said, the new fort was a busy place when we arrived. There was a small army of civilians there, carpenters, bricklayers, and the like, a great many quartermaster employees, packers, and teamsters. Teams were coming and going all day hauling from the boat landing on the Yellowstone and from the cantonment, moving troops up as fast as quarters were finished. There were fourteen companies of soldiers stationed there, the entire regiment of the Fifth Infantry and four troops of the Second Cavalry. Detachments of troops with either a string of pack mules or several wagons could be seen almost any day, either leaving the fort in pursuit of some raiding band of Indians or coming into the fort with a bunch of captives who were put in camp just west of the fort.

Indians were roaming everywhere to see what they could pick up or what they could beg to eat. One thing I never saw among all the Indians there—and there were nearly 4,000 of them in 1881—and that was an Indian who would refuse to eat. They were always hungry. When we came to Keogh, I thought every Indian I saw was ready to scalp me, and it was at least two weeks before I would venture 100 yards from our tent. One time mother sent me to the store just after guardmount about 9 a.m. [p.m.?] The store was on the southeast corner of the fort, nearly three-fourths of a mile from our tent. I made the trip and got back safely just before retreat at sundown. I dodged Indians all day. Another time shortly after, I went out of our tent and ran squarely into three Indians. One of them said, "How, John." I immediately had urgent business in our back or bed tent and whatever it was I was looking for was under the bed and I hunted for it faithfully. Pretty soon I heard my sister laughing and got bold enough to peep out and I saw she was playing with an Indian baby or papoose. My three ferocious warriors were three squaws who were enjoying themselves eating bread and potatoes. There were so many Indians and I couldn't hear of anyone being scalped by them at the fort, so the fear of them wore off, and I soon became acquainted with a great many, all chiefs, if you would take their word for it.

Among those whom I got to know and with whom I became fast friends were Two Moon, Wolf Voice, High Walking, Fire Crow, Sand Stone, and Stump Horn, of the Cheyennes. I also knew quite a few of the Sioux—Hump, Two Roads, American Horse, Spotted Elk, and many others. I remember Rain-in-the-Face well. He was a sullen, morose fellow, hardly ever spoke, and was always on a horse. He was crippled from a gunshot wound, and one leg was shorter than the other so he rarely walked. During 1878 and 1879, the troops had quite a few brushes with the Indians and lost a number of men. I remember two of the soldiers who were killed were from the troop to which my stepfather belonged. Their names were Leo Baader and Milton F. Douglas. Douglas had only thirty-two days to serve to finish his five-year enlistment when he was detailed to go after some Indians and met his death. The detachment which Douglas was with was under command of Sergeant Thad [Thomas B.] Glover of Troop B, Second Cavalry. One Indian was killed and one wounded. One soldier (Douglas) was killed, and one trooper (Corporal Charles W. Gurnsey) was wounded. Seven Indians were captured and brought in to Fort Keogh. Captain Andrew S. Bennett of Company B, Fifth Infantry, was killed in a fight with Bannock Indians in 1879 [1878]. Quite a few other soldiers whose names I cannot now recall were killed by the Sioux. First Lieutenant William Philo Clark, in command of E Troop of the Second Cavalry and some of B and I troops of [the] same regiment in 1880 [1879] had a fight with a band of Cheyennes under Little Wolf on the head of Custer Creek and captured the entire band, about 175 men, women, and children, and 300 head of ponies, without the loss of a single soldier. Seven were wounded, but none seriously. The Indians lost twenty-five of their number. This was about the last engagement between the army and the Indians of the Sioux War. [sic—There was no engagement at the time Little Wolf yielded his people to Lieutenant Clark on March 25, 1879. The troops involved consisted of Troops E and I besides a body of Indian scouts.]

One incident that occurred at Fort Keogh will live in my memory all during life. One day in the fall of 1879, a large number of the soldiers' children were playing on a level flat between the military stables and the married soldiers' dwellings. I was with a number of the boys playing baseball. Suddenly one of the boys said, "What is that man doing on that hill? There aren't any pickets out now." We looked in the direction he indicated, and on the top of one of the countless little buttes about two miles south of the fort we could see the figures of a man and horse. While we looked wonderingly, the horseman moved and began riding around on the top of the butte in a circle. We children all knew that this was a signal to his companions, whoever they might be. Some of the children became frightened and started running to their houses. Just at this time, the sentry, who was on post at the stables, came around the corner, and we called his attention to the horseman who was again riding in a circle. The sentry stopped and gave out the call, "Corporal of the Guard—Post No. 5." In about a minute's time he repeated the call and discharged his rifle in the air. About that time, I heard another sentry give out his call (I don't remember the number of his post or beat) followed by the report of his rifle. In about two minutes, we heard the bugle sound "Boots and Saddles" from the trumpeter on guard duty, and then every trumpeter in the fort was out sounding that significant bugle call. By this time, all was excitement around the laundresses' village—women running here and there looking for their children—married soldiers who were at their homes hurrying as fast as they could to their respective company quarters or to their stables carrying their rifles or carbines, with their ammunition belts and six shooters buckled around them. All thought that an attack on the fort by Indians was imminent. In a very short space of time we heard the trumpet sound "Forward March," and around the northwest corner of the stables came a column of three troops of cavalry, A, E, and I, under command of Captain Eli L. Huggins of Troop E. The mysterious rider by this time had dismounted and was lying on the ground. The troops advanced and when about a half mile distant from the fort we heard the trumpet sound "Load Pieces." Then the call, "Deploy," and the three troops swung into a skirmish line formation. Then came the call, "Trot," and at a trot they advanced toward the man on the butte who, by this time, was on his horse again and was apparently watching the advancing soldiers. When the troops reached the first line of buttes, the rider rode two or three times around in a circle, then disappeared from sight. We at the fort could see the long line of soldiers enter the rough stretch of land, and soon could see the soldiers on the hills still advancing. About four hours afterward, we saw them returning in column formation. No trace of the rider could be found. A camp of seven hunters was found about five miles from the hill the rider had disappeared from. They were on their way to the Musselshell [River] to trap. They said they had seen no one at all, and an inspection of their horses indicated none of them had been ridden that day. No one else could be found by the troops. The seven trappers camped close to the fort that night and left early next morning. Who the man on the hill was, or what his object was in being there was never found out. Most of the people who saw him agreed that it was not an Indian. A picket guard was placed around the fort for several nights, but no sign of any danger was seen. To this day, the identity of that rider has never been found, nor could anyone figure out what he was on the butte for, giving the U. S. danger signal of a picket guard.

One morning in the early part of June, 1881, Major Guido Ilges, who was then in command at Keogh, sent one of the government scouts whose name was John Bruguier to the Indian camp with a message to the Indians to break camp and move to a point one and one-half miles east of the fort, and put up their camp there where they would embark on the steamboat for Standing Rock. The Indians had grown to be a bit arrogant and sent back word that if the white chief wanted their tepees down to send some soldiers to take them down. Major Ilges ordered "Boots and Saddles" to be sounded, and in less than twenty-five minutes every soldier in the fort was in the saddle awaiting orders. Trumpets sounded and the troops advanced toward the Indian camp and formed a battle line across the flat in front of the camp. Three pieces of artillery—two revolving Hotchkiss guns and one Rodman, which shot an exploding cartridge and was called by the Indians "shoot today, kill tomorrow"—were placed in position. My stepfather was in charge of the Rodman, and a member of H Company, Fifth Infantry, named Private John McHugh had one of the Hotchkiss guns. The third man I cannot recall. Again, Bruguier was sent to the camp to tell the Indians to have their tepees down and be ready to move within an hour or they would open fire on the camp. A good many of the soldiers said afterward that the Indians had the tepees down and were ready to move with twenty minutes to spare.

The troops escorted the Indians to the new camp site and two troops were left on guard. Soon all the tepees were up and all was in readiness for the coming of the boats. There were to be five of them to take nearly 3,000 Indians aboard. If I remember rightly, the five boats were the *Fanny Bachelor, General Rucker, Katie P. Kountz, Nellie Peck,* and *Far West.* Within four days, four of the boats were at the landing, but the *Far West* had not put in its appearance. The troops waited four days and the commander became anxious, as the water in the Yellowstone was falling and should it get much lower the boats would not be able to make the trip. On the morning of the fifth day, the *Far West* came in sight. Engine trouble had delayed her just after she had entered the Yellowstone. As soon as possible the loading began. For awhile, pandemonium seemed to reign. Every Indian in camp—men, women, and children—were talking and shouting and it was a task to get them on board properly. A great many from the fort had come to see the Indians aboard, and many squaws were running hither and yon, shaking hands with the white squaws whom they knew. As fast as the boat got its load, it would start down the river, and loading another would begin. I remember one laughable incident: one of the boats had gotten well out in midstream, and every Indian was talking and shouting, when we saw an Indian jump off the boat out in the river and swim ashore. He was looking for his family, and found after he got to shore that they were all on the boat he jumped from. He was put on the next one, and I don't believe he got to his family until he got to Standing Rock. The Indians' horses were driven overland in charge of Captain Ezra P. Ewers of E Company, Fifth Infantry.

This was the last act in the Great Sioux War, and many a person who saw the last boat leave the bank of the Yellowstone that day in June breathed a deep sigh and said, "Thank God, Montana is done with the Indians." After the Indians were sent from Keogh, its importance as a military protection began to wane. Soon troops were sent to different posts and it was not many years till merely a handful of soldiers were left to guard it. Today [1943], the big flat where it stood and which was often the scene of military maneuvers is a big farm and what is left of the old fort is a remount station for the government.

The happiest days of my life were spent at Fort Keogh, and I often sit and think of the old times and scenes there, and in my mind's eye I can see many well-known men of the days of 1877-1882. Among them, Colonel Nelson A. Miles (I went to school with his two children, Celia and Sherman), "Yellowstone" (Luther S.) Kelly, John Bruguier, Bill LaCross, all scouts; Captain Thomas B. DeWees, Captain James T. Peale, and Captain Huggins of the Second Cavalry; and many others. I sit for a while and think of the old home and then come back to earth and say, "Never again. Keogh, Miles, all of you . . . goodbye."

The Border-to-Border March of the Eighth Cavalry, 1888 (By William G. Wilkinson, formerly of Troop G, Eighth U. S. Cavalry. From *Winners of the West*, October, 1938)

In May, 1888, the Eighth U. S. Cavalry, then stationed in western Texas, received orders to march to Dakota and take the stations occupied by the Seventh Cavalry. The Seventh Cavalry was to take stations in Kansas and Indian Territory (now Oklahoma), and the Third Cavalry was to occupy the stations vacated by the Eighth Cavalry in Texas. The headquarters of the Eighth Cavalry was at Fort Davis, Texas, located in the Davis Mountains, in the western part of the state, and not far from Marfa. Marfa at that time consisted of a freight shed and six or seven adobe shacks. The regiment was scattered over the western part of the state, in the following posts: Fort Davis, Fort Concho, Fort Hancock, and Camp Pena Colorado (near Marathon). The orders were for the regiment to concentrate at Fort Concho, located in the central western part of the state and on the edge of the town of San Angelo, which at that time was wild and woolly, but has now [1938] grown to be a good sized modern city and the largest wool and mohair buying market in the state. The new headquarters of the regiment was to be at Fort Meade, Dakota Territory, which is situated at the foot of the Black Hills and about twelve miles northeast of Deadwood.

The regiment as a whole marched approximately 1,700 miles, from Fort Concho to Fort Meade, but some of the troops, notably L and G, marched an additional 500 miles, or a total of 2,200 miles, in going to the concentration point and then to their new stations beyond Fort Meade. The hardships endured in a march of this description in those early days cannot be visualized by the present generation, because they are accustomed to travel in luxurious trains, fast airplanes, and high-powered motor cars over good roads, where there are good, comfortable sleeping berths, fine hotels, or good tourist camps, so that they may enjoy a good, comfortable bed, first-class meals, and scarcely ever out of sight of a town.

Our equipment was crude and very limited; our rations were hardtack, bacon, and black coffee, except when we reached a post like Fort Reno, Fort Riley, or Fort Sidney, then we would get some fresh beef and real bread, and that was a real treat. Railroads were few and far apart; in fact, we did not touch a railroad after we left Marathon, which was our starting point, until we reached Fort Reno in the Indian Territory, 600 or 700 miles distant. The two things which caused most of the hardship and suffering which we had to endure were the intense heat and lack of water. After getting out of Texas our troubles, so far as water was concerned, were at an end, as from there on we had an abundance of water, not always of the best, but it was water.

Troop G, Eighth Cavalry, of which the writer was a member, was stationed at a small, one-company post called Camp Pena Colorado. This post was situated in what is known as the Big Bend country of Texas. It derives its name from the great bend made by the Rio Grande River, and at the time of which this article was written it was one of the wildest and least traveled sections of Texas. Game in this section was very plentiful. There were black tail deer, bear, mountain lion, herds of antelope, lobo wolves, and a great number of coyotes.

On May 20, 1888, the troop moved out from the post and the long march was started. As it was mid-afternoon when we started, we marched only three or four miles, to Marathon, a freight shed on the Southern Pacific Railroad, and made our first camp. The second day we marched about thirty-five miles, and as it was very hot and having had very little water except that which we had in our canteens when we broke camp in the morning, it was rather a hard day. Everybody was pretty sore and very tired when we went into camp, and to make matters worse we had to make a dry camp—that is there was no water. As soon as we halted and dismounted, Captain Edmond G. Fechet, the troop commander, gave orders to have all of the canteens collected and placed under guard, so that whatever water there was in them could be used in making coffee for supper and breakfast. The horses and mules had to go without water until we found some the next day. No one can appreciate the value of water until one has marched all day in the hot sun, over dusty, stony ground, without it. In those early days the only means that troops on the march had for carrying water was the men's canteens and sometimes a small keg slung under a wagon. Marching across Texas in those days was always a severe hardship, as there were very few streams of water, and the water in many of them was so full of alkali as to make it unpalatable. Of course, we found a few springs of good water, some pools that had been formed by previous rains, in which cattle had stood, and some small pockets of water in among the rocks. In many cases this was covered with a green scum, which we skimmed off and then scooped out with a spoon, then put in some vinegar to kill the taste; after all, it was water, and many days we went without it.

The only stream that we crossed between our starting point and Fort Concho, a distance of over 200 miles, was the Pecos River. We were traveling over almost barren grounds, in an almost uninhabited district, following a wagon trail, not over well-paved roads, but across country nearly as the crow flies. About the third or fourth day we arrived at old Fort Stockton and the town of Stockton. Here was a splendid spring of water, but not a living thing was in sight. The fort and the town had been abandoned. When the fort was built it was in the heart of the Comanche Indian country, but as the Indians had since been moved up into the Indian Territory, there was no further use for troops in that section and they had been moved to other stations and the fort abandoned. As the town was almost wholly dependent on the troops for its existence, when the troops were moved [and] their means of livelihood gone, there was nothing for the people to do but move also, which they did, abandoning the buildings, taking only that which was easily moved. The fort buildings were constructed of stone and adobe, surrounded by a wall with loopholes every few feet so that the troops could repel an Indian attack without exposing themselves. Some of the buildings in the town were good and substantial, especially a stone store building that had been occupied by a man named Friedlander. His large sign was still on the building. Fort Stockton today [1938] is a town of about 3,000 inhabitants.

Leaving Fort Stockton the next morning, we continued our march. Two days later we crossed the Pecos River. This river gave us no trouble, as it is not very wide and only about waist deep, so that it was very easily forded, but crossing it down near where it empties into the Rio Grande, which we did a year previously, is not only very difficult but dangerous, as it was necessary to float the wagons and swim the horses and mules across. About one week later we arrived at Fort Concho, the concentration point. The next day, L Troop arrived from Fort Hancock under command of Captain Morris. The whole regiment being now assembled, we remained there a couple of days while the organization was being completed and details worked out for the long march ahead. San Angelo, which adjoined Fort Concho, was wide open; its principal industry was saloons and gambling joints. The boast of The White Elephant was that it was never closed, that it had no front to close. The writer himself was lucky enough to make a small stake playing poker in The White Elephant before leaving. A trumpeter from one of the troops had been around town all day borrowing the price of a drink wherever he could, but could not make connection often enough to get drunk. Late that night he was pestering one of the bartenders in The White Elephant, until finally the bartender said, "Here, I'll give you a drink." Then he put a large tumbler on the bar and filled it with whiskey and said, "Now, damn you, drink that and get out of here." The man looked at it and it almost sobered him, for the quantity really scared him momentarily, but he finally drank it like so much water. Taken so much at one drink, it is a wonder that it did not kill him. Some time later he was lying up against a building, completely unconscious, but he was all right the next day and apparently suffering no ill effects.

In a couple of days, the organization and complete details having been worked out, the march was started. The regiment was composed of twelve troops of sixty-five men each, a band of about twenty-five men, and the headquarters staff. There was a total force of about 900 officers and enlisted men, and about 110 animals. Colonel Elmer Otis, the regimental commander, being in poor health and unable to take command, went on sick leave and Lieutenant Colonel John K. Mizner took command, First Lieutenant Charles M. O'Connor was regimental adjutant, First Lieutenant Quincy O. Gillmore regimental quartermaster. The regiment was divided into three battalions of four troops each, Major John A. Wilcox in command of the First Battalion, Major Reuben F. Bernard in command of the Second Battalion, and Captain Louis T. Morris acting as a major in command of the Third Battalion. The arrangement of troops and the order in which they marched was the best and fairest for everyone that could have been devised, and was as follows: the ranking captain and his troops was first troop, first battalion, the next ranking captain and his troop was first troop, second battalion, the third ranking captain and troop was first troop, third battalion, and the others arranged in the battalions according to their rank, but on the march their position was changed daily. On the first day, G Troop was first troop, first battalion, or the head of the line; the second day the first battalion dropped back to third position and G Troop was the last troop in the line; on the third day the first battalion was in second position and G Troop in third place within the battalion. Each day saw the same kind of change, so that every twelfth day each troop had its turn to lead the line. The importance of this arrangement can be appreciated when one remembers that the road might be ankle deep in dust, or the same with mud, and the troop lucky enough to be in the lead escaped the worst of it.

The daily routine was: 4:45 a.m., reveille and stable call; 5:00 a.m., mess call; 5:30, the general call. No tents were allowed to be taken down until the general call sounded. At the first note of the trumpet, all canvas was dropped almost as one tent. Each man had an allotted task; each man had already rolled his bedding, carried it to the wagon and laid it on the ground; two men were in each wagon (each troop had two six-mule wagons) to pack the equipment, rations, and forage as it was handed to them. As the tents dropped, one man took the poles, two others folded and rolled the tent. The other men had taken all of the horses off of the picket line and were holding them, so that the picket line could be put into the wagon in its proper place, for it was a nice job to pack the equipment of a troop of sixty-five men, together with ten days' rations and forage for the horses and mules, in two wagons and do it in fifteen minutes. At 5:45 "Boots and Saddles" sounded. The men loading the wagons had their horses saddled for them by some of the other men. At 5:55 the order to "Fall In" was given, and after counting fours, the order "prepare to mount, mount," and on the dot of 6:00 a.m., regardless of weather conditions, the orderly trumpeter sounded "Forward, March," and the column moved out. Everyone was given to understand that excuses for not being ready to move promptly at 6:00 a.m. would not be accepted, and as a matter of fact none were necessary during that long, hard march.

Leaving Fort Concho, we marched northeast, passing through Buffalo Gap, Abilene, Fort Griffin, Albany, and Henrietta, all of which were very small villages. In the meantime, we had crossed the Colorado River, the south fork of the Brazos and the main Brazos. Of all the rivers that we crossed during the whole march, none were so dangerous or gave us so much trouble as the Brazos. We reached it late in the afternoon. It was then in flood, and crossing that day was out of the question. By morning it had subsided considerably. After breaking camp, two men succeeded in getting across and carried a line across with them, finally getting a heavy picket line across and fastening the end to a tree, the other end being fastened to a tree on the opposite side. Then two troops were ordered to cross, keeping on the upper side of the rope so that in case a horse went down the man could grab the rope and save himself. The water was not over five feet deep but was running like a race horse. After the two troops crossed, the writer being a member of one of them, the men stripped and went back into the river, holding on to the rope for support. Then a six-mule team and wagon was driven into the river, a line was hooked on to the lead mules and the men in the water pulled the team across. Once the team was in the water, they had to be gotten across quickly, as the bottom of the river was quicksand and had the team been allowed to stop they would have quickly sunk in the sand. We succeeded in getting across with only the loss of a small two-horse wagon on which the officers had some supplies. It took all of one day to make the crossing. In addition to the Brazos, Pecos, and Colorado, during the march we crossed the Trinity, Red River, Ouachita, Canadian, Cimarron, Blue, South and North Forks of the Platte, main Platte, Niobrara, White, South and North Forks of the Cheyenne, Belle Fourche, Moreau, and Grand Rivers.

One of the lessons to be learned in marching across a section like western Texas was how to conserve the water supply. If we were lucky enough to have camped alongside of a stream of good water, we could start out with full canteens, but there was no assurance that we would get any more that day and it behooved each man to drink very sparingly of his small supply. The old soldier had learned how to do this from past experience, but the recruit on his first march would not heed the advice of the older men and had to learn through bitter experience. The older men, if they did not chew tobacco, would put a small pebble in their mouths, which kept their mouths moist. Occasionally they would rinse their mouths out and take a very small swallow of the water, and regardless of how hot and dusty the day, they would still have plenty of water in their canteens when we went into camp that night. But not so with the recruit. He had drunk all of his water in about two hours after starting, and then had to suffer the rest of the day, for the older men would not give them any from their meager supply. But after a day or two of this the recruit learned his lesson.

The heat was intense, and both men and horses suffered greatly at times. We lost seventeen horses in one day from exhaustion through lack of water and the heat. After crossing the Red River into Indian Territory, our troubles so far as water was concerned were at an end, as we had plenty from there on. Upon entering the Territory the whole character of the country changed. Through Texas there was little vegetation other than cactus, chaparral, and mesquite, the grass being short and sparse, the ground being stony or sandy, with few trees except a few cottonwoods along the streams. Here in the Territory the soil was a black loam, the grass as high as a man's head, and plenty of timber, mostly oak. Through Texas we had had no rain, in the Territory we had frequent showers. One afternoon after making camp, we witnessed the spectacle of two storms meeting. It was a wonderful sight to see the lightning shooting from the black clouds into the blue sky until the clouds came together. Then the rain came down in torrents; the thunder and lightning was terrific. What a wonderful change has taken place in that section since we crossed it. Then, the country was practically in its virgin state, just as it had been created, and we little dreamed of the fabulous wealth that was under us as we rolled up in our blankets at night and lay asleep on the ground. Today, there are fine farms, modern cities, and untold wealth has been taken from the ground over which we marched and camped. One evening we camped near a Kiowa Indian village, and one grizzled old fellow who visited our camp made a rather grotesque figure. He was dressed in moccasins, breechclout, blanket, and high silk hat. We rested one day at Fort Sill and another day at Fort Reno, both of which we thoroughly enjoyed. Our trip through the Territory was the easiest part of our whole journey.

Crossing the border into Kansas, we made our first camp at Arkansas City. Here we had our first experience with prohibition, for Kansas even at that early day was dry. Shortly after we had camped, word was passed that a livery stable close by had some extraordinarily good water, and from the number of soldiers that constantly passed in and out of that stable, and judging from their queer actions after coming out, the water certainly possessed extraordinary qualities. As our route lay through the farming section of Kansas, we were able to buy some butter, eggs, and fresh vegetables from the farmers. This made a very welcome change from hardtack and bacon. All the way across the state, each day after making camp we continued to find the same extraordinary water; some of it actually foamed when put into glasses. The roads through the state were terrible. They were either ankle deep in dust or the same in mud, and what made marching more difficult was the fact that on both sides of the road hawthorn hedges grew to a height of ten or twelve feet, making almost a solid wall, so that the dust kicked up by the horses almost suffocated us and covered us with a thick coat of black dirt.

After leaving Arkansas City, the most important towns were Winfield, Wichita, Newton, Abilene, and Junction City. Here we crossed the Republican River, over the first bridge we had met so far, and entered Fort Riley and remained four days. Here we met the Seventh Cavalry and exchanged transportation with them. These four days gave the horses a much needed rest and helped to heal the sores on their backs caused by the saddles. Those having the worst backs were turned over to the post quartermaster and left behind. Leaving Fort Riley, which was the half-way point, our first camp

Men of Company E, Fifth Infantry, possibly at Fort Bliss, Texas, in 1888-91. *Editor's collection*

was at a little town called Morganville. Our camp was pitched in a wheat stubble field along the main highway. The people in the town evidently knew that we were coming, for the churches had combined for the purpose of holding an ice cream and strawberry festival, and had erected booths along the roadway fronting the camp, expecting of course that the girls would be able to do a big business selling ice cream and strawberries to the soldiers. We had been paid while in Fort Riley; in those days pay day came only once every two months.

At stable call we mounted our horses (bareback) to go down to the Republican River to water the horses. The river was some distance from camp. While we were down at the river one of those terrific thunderstorms, for which Kansas was noted, suddenly broke over us and everybody made a wild rush for camp. By the time we had reached there, all our tents had blown down, we were soaked to the skin, our boots were full of water, there was not a dry stitch in camp, and the camp was a sea of black mud ankle deep. Of course, the festival fell flat, although they did transfer it to an empty store, but the affair was not the success that had been expected. The men were wet and had lost their desire for ice cream. Those who did go to the festival left a trail of water behind them.

As everything we had was wet, it was useless to erect the tents again, so we lay down in the soft mud without them. The mud made rather soft beds. As it was very warm, being wet did not do us any harm. The next morning at 6:00 a.m. sharp, as usual, "Forward, March" was sounded and again we were on our way, and for four days it rained so that there was no chance for us to get dried out, nor could we take off our boots. Had we done so it would have been very difficult to have gotten them on again. Nobody seemed to suffer any ill effects from the four days' soaking, as there was practically no sickness in the command.

Before proceeding, I want to relate an incident that occurred back at Wichita. After we had pitched camp, which was on an open common on the edge of town, a man came into camp and ordered us to move off as he did not want the troops to camp on his ground. Colonel Mizner tried to reason with him, explaining that he had had an officer in the town for several hours before our arrival looking for the owner of the ground so that arrangements could be made for the camp, that he had been unable to find him, that the troops would do the ground no harm, no refuse would be left behind, and besides, it was an open common, and no "No Trespassing" signs were visible, therefore he had a right to camp there if he so desired; but the owner of the ground would not listen to reason and insisted that we vacate immediately. Finally, the colonel called for a member of the guard and instructed him to escort the man off the ground and to see that he did not return. Of course, we camped there for the night.

As my horse was one of those left at Fort Riley, and as there were not a sufficient number of extra horses to give every man whose horse had been left behind another horse, it fell to my lot to ride a little black mule, which the troop had captured from Geronimo's band of Indians in New Mexico, and I believe that all the contrariness of the mule family was concentrated in her makeup. As we marched in column of twos, whenever that mule felt like leaving the line to graze on the side of the road, she just went. Orders governing the march meant nothing to her. She would continue grazing until she felt like moving on, then she would trot along until we overtook the troop and took our regular place in line. Of course, both the captain and first sergeant would jump me for leaving the line without permission. When we passed through towns, I usually came in for a lot of guying, being the only one mounted on a mule, and such a small one, we no doubt did make a rather ludicrous appearance.

When we reached Clay Center some of the fellows got a keg of alcohol from an undertaker's establishment and brought it into camp, and soon sugar and hot water were in big demand for making alcohol toddies. In a short time there was a pretty wild bunch in camp. The next day there was a pretty sick bunch on the march, and it seemed as though we would never reach camp. All of our camps in Kansas and Nebraska drew crowds of people for miles around. The principal attraction, aside from the usual sights of an army camp, was the band, as every night, weather permitting, the band played a concert. This, or course, was quite a treat to the people, as there were very few civilian bands in that territory in those days. The band leader, John Klein, was a wonderful cornetist, and it was worth going a long distance to hear him. They did not carry their instruments with them during the day, but packed them on their wagons.

Continuing on, we crossed the state line into Nebraska, passing through Superior and Hastings. We crossed the Platte River at Kearney, then turned west following the river and Union Pacific Railroad on through North Platte City (the home of Buffalo Bill). We re-crossed the Platte and followed the South Fork to Julesburg, Colorado, also called the Denver Junction. Here we were stuck in the mud for four days. The soil is a blue clay, about the consistency of putty. The wheels of the wagons cut into it until the bodies of the wagons rested on the ground. Moving was out of the question until the rain was over and we had a chance to dig the wagons out and build a corduroy road. By this time, we were pretty well used to sleeping in puddles of water, fording streams, and marching in wet clothes, but it apparently had no ill effects upon us. Regardless of weather and road conditions, there was an unwritten rule that the wagons containing the food supplies must get through to camp on time. The other wagons might be stuck in the mud and be delayed, sometimes for a couple of days, as happened at Julesburg, but not the chuck wagon. We could sleep without blankets or tents, but we had to eat. Give a soldier plenty to eat and he will put up with almost any other hardship without complaint. Immediately upon getting into camp, it was the custom in the troop of which the writer was a member, to have a couple of men take buckets and get some water, while others got some wood. A fire was started and in a short time each man was given a cup of good, strong, black coffee. It was surprising how quickly they recovered from the fatigue of a hard day's march after getting their coffee.

Following the railroad and river west to Sidney, Nebraska, we again turned north on the old Deadwood Trail. This is the road over which supplies were hauled by wagon trains between Sidney and Deadwood in the Black Hills during the gold rush days. Many a bloody battle took place on this old trail. Sometimes it was the Indians attacking a wagon train or stagecoach, or bandits that attempted a holdup. In the gold rush days a trip over this trail either to or from the Black Hills was fraught with great danger, and those who got through without being attacked were very fortunate. Following the trail up through Buffalo Gap and Rapid City, mining villages, we finally arrived at Fort Meade, where the new headquarters was to be. At this point, as far as the regiment as a unit was concerned, the march was at an end, and the troops were again to be scattered over a wide territory. While the march was officially ended, six troops still had a long march ahead of them before they reached their final destination. E and K Troops went to Fort Buford, Dakota, H and L Troops to Fort Keogh, Montana, and F and G troops to Fort Yates, Dakota. Before the troops separated, Lieutenant Colonel Mizner, who was in command on the march, had an order read commending the troops for their obedience to orders and the fine manner in which they had conducted themselves on the march, as he had not received a single serious complaint during the whole march.

Those of us who had to continue to other stations were very loath to go, for it meant the breaking up of friendships that had been formed during that long and hard journey, and in most cases it really meant goodbye forever, and friendships formed under such circumstances are not lightly broken. There was many a moist eye as the final handshake was made and goodbye was waved. Leaving Fort Meade, F and G Troops turned northeastward, crossing the Cheyenne and Belle Fourche rivers. On the bank of the Belle Fourche stood a tree known as the hangman's tree, as seven men had been hanged from it for various crimes. The tree was excellently situated and shaped for the purpose, as it had a limb that grew straight out from the trunk of the tree about ten feet from the ground and overhung the river, which was about fifteen feet below. The method was to seat the man on a horse close to the edge of the bank, tie the end of the rope well out on the limb, put the noose around the man's neck, and then start the horse, and as the man was pulled out of the saddle the body swung out over the river.

After several days, we crossed Grand River and entered the Standing Rock Indian Reservation, the home of Sitting Bull's tribe of the Sioux Indians. We did not go through his village, although we did pass through several others. Our last camp was at Fire Steel Creek, nine miles from Fort Yates. Near the camp a curious sight met our gaze. Close by was a large tree with five large bundles up in the branches, which we learned were the bodies of Indians that had died, the method of burial among the Sioux being to wrap the body tightly in blankets, strap it to two poles, and place the poles across the branches of the tree. On the morning of September 18th, 1888, coming through a gap in the hills out on a wide plain, we had our first glimpse of Fort Yates, a few miles distant, and the end of the long trail. Before reaching the post, we passed through a good-sized temporary Indian village, and as we learned afterward, this was one of the many temporary villages that were made every two weeks as the Indians gathered near the agency from all over the reservation to draw their bi-weekly rations, which were issued to them by the government. Standing along the road near this village [and] watching us march by was the famous chief, Sitting Bull (Ta tonka u tonka). He stood with his arms folded, as immobile as a statue, little thinking as he watched us that in two short years we would have a hand in his death. In a short time we had reached the post where the final command to halt and dismount was given, and after unsaddling our horses a rush was made for the quarters to make our selection for the position of our bunks, the fastest runners having the first choice.

Thus ended what was, so far as the writer has been able to learn, the longest continuous march by a body of troops on record, a total distance of 2,200 miles in two days less than four months. While we endured many hardships on that long, hard, tiresome march, yet, when it was ended the men were sorry, because it meant a return to the tiresome routine of garrison duty. On the march there is a certain routine that must be followed, of course, but the picture is constantly changing and was not as monotonous as the daily routine followed in one isolated army post in those old days. The most remarkable feature of that long march was that both men and horses were in better physical condition than when we started.

Sidelights of the Eighth Cavalry's Historic March

(By Soren P. Jepson, formerly of Troop L, Eighth U. S. Cavalry. From *Winners of the West*, March 30, 1932)

On July 17, 1888, we left Fort Riley, Kansas, and kept on plodding through the mud until we got to Kearney, Nebraska, on the 3rd of August. We struck west from there on the 5th and made Willows Island on the 7th. Here we got stuck in the mud, the river having overflowed and almost drowned us. We stayed there three days, standing in water up to our knees. At night we would pile up to a wagon wheel and sleep that way, standing up. That was some experience. If it hadn't been in the summer time, we would all have frozen to death. At the end of three days we finally worked our way out of there by the men taking ropes and helping the mules to take the wagons to dry land three miles away. But we were a sight, covered with mud. In that condition, we arrived at Fort Sidney, Nebraska, on the 19th of August.

We stayed there one day to get rid of some of the mud. From there, we struck north on the 21st and got to Clark's Bridge on the 22nd. This was a toll bridge over the North Platte River. The bridge keeper thought when he saw us coming that here was a chance to make a killing, so he slapped a padlock on a big boom across the bridge and demanded $1000.00 to let us across. Major Morris stroked his moustache a while; finally he said, "And how much do you want to let our wagons across?" "Two hundred dollars," says the man. The major turned to the adjutant and told him to draw a warrant for $200.00. Then he says to me, "Ride down along the command and order up all the farriers. (If anyone does not know what a farrier is, he is a horseshoer, among other things, and carries a bag of tools.) There was one in each troop, and by the time we got back, the last of the wagons was driving on the bridge and the man was ready with his boom and locked it. The major grinned at him and says, "I suppose you are wondering how I am going to get the men across. I will show you in a few minutes." Now the bridge was fenced in for two miles along on either side with a high wire fence. Then the farriers were ordered to pull all staples in the fence for a distance of 200 feet and lay the fence down. Then the major ordered "Forward, march!" and we all went into the river and was all across in no time. The river was supposed to be all quicksand at the place, but the major figured that as we all came from Texas and had crossed lots of rivers with quicksand in them we could cross the North Platte. We made camp on the other side of the river and we had a good laugh over it.

On August 26th, we got to Fort Robinson, Nebraska. Here we were surprised to meet four troops of the colored cavalry who came out to meet us and you talk about soldiers—those soldiers were all dressed in their best and surely presented a beautiful sight. Everything about them shone like the sun, even their horses hoofs were shined all black. We stayed there two days and arrived at Fort Meade, [Dakota Territory,] on September 4th, as this fort was going to be our headquarters. The regiment was split up. Troops A, B, C, D, I, and M were left here. Troops F and G went to Fort Yates, [Dakota,] Troops H and L to Fort Keogh, Montana [Territory], Troops E and K to Fort Buford, [Dakota.] I being in Troop L, of course, went to Fort Keogh, where we arrived on September 17, 1888, and we could then say that we had made practically 2,500 miles in four months and a half. You may wonder how I can supply dates, but the fact is I made a list of the camps in my notebook and can tell every camp we made all the way with dates. I had a hunch it would come in handy some day. . . .

Memories of Old Fort Cummings, New Mexico Territory (By Wolsey A. Sloan, formerly of Troop H, Fourth U. S. Cavalry. From *Winners of the West*, July 30, 1935)

In the spring of the year 1880, Troop H, Fourth Cavalry, stationed at Fort Reno, on the north fork of the Canadian River in the Indian Territory, received orders to go to New Mexico to help quell a cattle war near Fort Stanton in which the notorious Billy the Kid was a leader against law and order. Before we arrived, however, the trouble ended. Some of our regiment were left at Fort Stanton, while Troops A, G, and H continued on our way to Fort Cummings. First Lieutenant James Parker of A Troop was the senior officer in command. We camped on a side hill just above a rock-enclosed spring, and during the night we were washed out of our beds by a torrential rain.

This old fort is some forty miles west of the Rio Grande and about twenty miles north of where Deming, New Mexico, is now located in the foothills on the eastern slope of the Los Mimbres Mountains, a spur of the Black Range. Near this little spring four centuries ago Spanish treasure hunters pitched camp on their historic trip into the northern wilds, resulting in the foundation of Santa Fe. In after years, Spanish soldiers camped here while on forays to capture Indians to build churches and cathedrals for their Catholic majesties of Spain. This is attested by the fact that a Spanish spear head was found near the spring imbedded in the soil, and leg irons of Spanish make. Then it became a rendezvous for freebooters who laid in wait to attack unwary travelers and supply trains.

At last in desperation, the Spaniards built a fort to protect their treasure trains. It was patterned after the medieval style of Spanish architecture: each wall about 500 feet long, twenty feet high, and two feet thick, made of adobe bricks. The corners projected in bastion style to protect the walls from escalading parties, while in the center of the southern wall an immense sally port provided entrance to the plaza. Eight men could easily ride abreast through its portal. At night, or when attacked, an enormous portcullis of heavy timbers was lowered giving perfect protection to the garrison. Surrounding the plaza were the quarters of the officers, men-at-arms, slaves, and stock corral. After the Mexican War, the United States secured possession of it through the Gadsden Purchase. Shortly after it became part of the United States occurred the California gold excitement, and American soldiers were sent to this old weather-beaten fort under the command of Major Joseph Cummings, for whom the fort was later named, to render aid and protection to those seeking the new El Dorado over the Mexican national highway, now known as the Santa Fe Trail.

This was a dangerous and hazardous road, the hardiest travelers finding only terrible hardships and suffering, and very often death in its most agonizing forms by Indian torture or thirst. Those taking the trail west of the Rio Grande had to go through a deep gorge or box canyon, the walls of which rise perpendicularly over a thousand feet, and in places are less than thirty feet apart, while it is several miles in length, strewn with rocks and boulders, making travel slow and difficult. Gazing upward, stars may be seen in broad daylight shining in the blue vault of the heavens. Along this trail on the heights above, hidden in the rocks, lurking Apaches awaited the oncoming of unwary travelers, upon whom they hurled rocks and boulders until no living thing was left, while those taking the trail east of the Rio Grande had to pass through the *Journado Estacado El Muerto* (Journey through the Valley of Death). This valley is about 150 miles in length. Deep arroyos, rocky clefts, and fissures impassable for man or beast prevent access to the Rio Grande, while mountains of white sand confronted the weary, thirst-crazed victims of the lust for gold on the east. Water on the *Journado* being unobtainable, many died of thirst, as the bleached human bones gathered by soldiers readily testify. So for many years, the old fort served well its purpose as a haven of refuge for the courageous men wearied and harrowed in their attempt to cross this desert of sand and cacti while running the gauntlet of murderous bands of Apaches.

During the time of my service with H Troop in Fort Cummings, it was in a dilapidated state. The walls and bastions were crumbled to dust again, the portcullis was gone, while the commander's quarters was used as a guard house and an armory and the officers' quarters to house the mules of the Quartermaster Department. When I gazed upon this crumbling ruin of a past age, with the ravages of time upon its grim walls, it seemed like a warrior of old, defiant of the destroying elements of wind and rain. Its broken and defaced walls seemed to say, "I am wounded most mortally, my strength is gone. No longer can I aid in civilizing this wilderness." Surrounding the old fort are low lying hills sparsely covered with gramma grass, sagebrush, greasewood, cacti, and many other thorny plants, while sunning themselves on the burning sands or jutting rocks may be seen many varieties of creeping, crawling insects and lizards and venomous snakes. Among these freaks of nature of a bygone age are salamanders, gila monsters, chameleons, horned toads [lizards], tarantulas, scorpions, copperheads, and rattlesnakes.

Some nine miles as the crow flies, west by north, rises Cook's Peak, loftiest mountain in the Black Range. It is a fitting landmark to overlook this sun-baked inhospitable region, exemplifying for all time by its gruesome aspect of a tragedy that it is typical of the fact that torture and murder is rampant. Permit me to illustrate. Imagine a man of titanic size, his body encased in the enduring rocks, his head the Peak, his face turned to Heaven, so that his profile clearly shows a brow of classic mould, nose indicating power and character, a firm mouth and chin indicating tenacity of purpose, all clearly cut in the rocky contour of the Peak, in ideal proportions, each feature about a mile long. As you study this wonderful face, you realize that nature has committed torture and murder. For where the eye should have been, a cavernous hole appears, and the ear hangs pendant from the lobe as though severed from the head, while scraggly cedars form a fringe of hair at the back of his head and the top is bald as though scalped. Then you see that his throat has a gash in it half a mile wide and fully as deep. On the northern slope of the Peak in an old mine working were found leg irons and a piece of a bastinado, used undoubtedly by early Spanish conquistadors, while several hundred feet below the mine parts of several human skeletons were found.

Gazing southward from the chin of this titan may be seen all that is left of the village of Mimbres, where tragedy stalked in the trail of the Mescalero Apaches, who raided it and killed every human being. Babes had their brains dashed out against the adobe walls, men and women had stakes driven into their bodies and set against the adobe walls, or staked over ant hills to die of slow torture. In Black Canyon, about two miles west of the old fort, the son of Victoria Nana and six other renegade Mescalero Apaches were killed while on a murder raid . . . [I] tried to get the boy's body (he was only fifteen years old) to articulate the skeleton, but desisted when several Yuma Indian scouts showed their displeasure. Later it was taken to Silver City and the skeleton was kept in a glass case in a saloon there.

At one time during the campaign against Victoria Nana and his band of Mescalero Apaches, there were over a thousand soldiers in this old fort, as I remember there was six troops of the Ninth Cavalry, three troops of the Fourth Cavalry, eight companies of the Sixteenth Infantry, and six companies of the Thirteenth Infantry, 100 Yuma Apache scouts, and about 150 civilian packers, teamsters, and other employees. Guard mount was the most thrilling feature of our daily life, there being at one time as many as twenty-two posts, so upwards of seventy-five men were in the guardmount line, many of them seeking the honor of being orderly for the commanding officer or officer of the day. Guard mount took place in front of the old sally port on what had been the highway, but now used as a parade ground. Across the parade ground from the sallyport was the adjutant's headquarters, and on either side were the officers' quarters, all made by the troops from adobe. The Ninth Cavalry were camped west of the old fort, while the infantry were on the east side, and the three troops of the Fourth Cavalry were camped east of the officers' quarters, with the corral between. After Victoria Nana's activities were stopped, hunting parties often came back loaded with the spoils of the chase. During the winter of 1882 and 1883, many turkeys, several deer and antelope, two yearling bears, and a mountain lion hung from the sides of our mess hall, the result of one ten-day trip. The troops were all housed in Sibley tents with a Sibley stove in the center, six men to a tent. In summer they were hotter than hell, while in winter they were like the outside of an Eskimo igloo. Of course, they were far superior to the dog tents we used during the first year and a half, when we certainly became familiar with soil in the shape of dust as well as mud, for we slept in it, ate it, traveled in it, and were usually covered with it. My troop probably had as fine a lot of noncommissioned officers as were ever gathered together in one command—First Sergeant Gately (succeeded by one of the squarest Scotchmen I ever knew, Sergeant Joseph S. Hopely), Sergeant Louis B. French, Casey Cummings [George Cumming?], Durr, Rankin, and others whose names I cannot now recall, any one of them capable of maneuvering the troop if called upon in an emergency.

The Fort Custer Dance (By Maurice J. O'Leary, formerly of Troop K, First U. S. Cavalry. From *Winners of the West*, October 30, 1930)

Did you ever hear of the biggest dance ever given by soldiers at any army post in Montana? No? Well, it was given at old Fort Custer. I can tell you the names of some of the old-timers that were at that dance. There was old man Dana, a big livestock man; Jim McNutt, a contractor; Paul McCormick, of Billings; Theodore Borup, who later was with the old *Pioneer Press* for years; and old Liver-Eating Johnston. Those are just a few of the prominent ones I recall. There is only one other man besides myself living [1930] in Helena who was at that dance. That is an old Regular Army

Broadside for an outdoor performance by the Second Cavalry Band at Fort Custer, Montana Territory, in 1883. Such concerts provided entertainment relief for troops and their families at frontier garrisons throughout the West. *Editor's collection* man—he was with our outfit—Billy Spinning. He's got a ranch down by the gas works. I don't see Billy very often any more. He don't come up to town very often now.

Well, we soldiers gave that dance at Fort Custer in 1885 and it cost us $500. We were getting $13 a month then—so just figure it out for yourself. One hundred of us gave $5 each. I will tell you how this thing came up. At the fort there was a nice hall and a stage, with some scenery. But under the chaplain in charge then it was always used as a chapel. Then we organized a kind of a temperance society, enrolling all the girls and women at the fort—there were about seventy-five of them—and since none of the soldiers, or very very few of them joined, it was mighty lonesome for the buck private and some of the officers. He would not let us use the hall for a dance. Well, there was a switch in commanding officers, and some of the boys got at him first and the commanding officer said the building was to be used by all of the boys at the garrison, and that we could go ahead and give a dance if we wanted to.

We got together and organized what was known as the Rounders' Club. It cost five bucks to join, and to belong there were several qualifications that would not please Mr. Volsted now. We raised our $500 and bought turkey, and ordered lemons, oranges, grapes, and other fruits from St. Paul. The dance was to be given on the evening of St. Patrick's Day. We sent an escort wagon over to the Junction, which was nothing but a cowtown, and that day it got mighty cold. The men built a large fire and threw in a lot of good-sized rocks. In the morning, when the fire cooled, they fished the hot rocks out, put them in the escort wagon, and packed in the fruit and covered it all up with a tarp. It arrived at the fort all okay.

Well, the big night arrived. We had supper in the schoolroom, back of the stage. There were babies tied in chairs and lying on blankets all over the stage. Folks came for [from] miles around. The officers and their ladies cast aside all formality. There was not enough room to seat them all at midnight, so the officers' wives and the laundresses, and nursemaids, and visiting ladies all sat down to the same table and had a good time. Later the men followed suit. The old Cavalry Band played and the orchestra was made up of bandsmen who could also play stringed instruments. The orchestra played a lot of old Irish airs. Then Captain Frank D. Garrity of the Seventeenth Infantry rose to his feet. He expressed a great desire to dance one of the old Irish reels, if he could only find an Irish girl from the old country who could dance it with him. Gosh, I wish I could remember her name. I believe she is still living down in eastern Montana. And how that Irish girl could dance!

Well, they danced two or three Irish reels and the fun was on. Colonel Nathan A. M. Dudley of the First Cavalry was commanding officer. And I am sure Mr. Dana was there, as Second Lieutenant James B. Aleshire, who later became Quartermaster General of the U. S. A., was then keeping company with Dana's daughter.

Well, we appointed a committee to check up the finances. We had $17 left in the treasury. We bought $17 worth of beer, closed the books, and the Rounders disbanded. And, oh heck, the next morning was just as it always is the morning after.

Christmas at Fort Robinson, 1882 (By Martin J. Weber, formerly first sergeant, Troop H, Fifth U. S. Cavalry. From *Winners of the West*, June 30, 1934)

I am reminded of one Christmas especially which is a sample of our experience in those never to be forgotten days out in the Sioux country. Troops H, M, and F of the Fifth U. S. Cavalry and Company C of the Fourth U. S. Infantry were quartered at Fort Robinson, [Nebraska,] at the time of this story. Little children of the army were just as anxious for the advent of Santa Claus as the somewhat more highly favored little ones in the midst of the civilized East. [In December, 1882, I was] . . . a corporal in Troop H, Fifth Cavalry. I was ordered on detached service by the commanding officer. My orders were to report to the Quartermaster at Fort Sidney, the nearest railroad point, to get the Christmas goods for the fort. A driver and a six-mule team were detailed for the purpose.

We started about December 10 [on] a six days' journey. The weather was ideal, clear, sunny days, and we arrived at Fort Sidney on time but were delayed two days owing to the non-arrival of the goods that were coming over the Union Pacific Railroad. They finally arrived the morning of the 18th. We loaded our wagon at once and pulled out for Fort Robinson 125 miles to the north. The weather had turned cold and frost began to fly through the air indicating a storm. We made good time that first afternoon, camping just before dark.

The next morning the storm broke in all its fury, a regular blizzard raging. We had to face or head into the storm. We made Camp Clark, where the Sidney-Black Hills Trail crossed the Platte River, a toll bridge, general store, and post office being kept at this point. Here we obtained shelter for ourselves, mules, and horses. The lady had a hot breakfast and coffee ready for us about daybreak. The storm had increased during the night. I mailed a report of the storm and that we would try and make the fort if possible to the commanding officer. The bridge tender and his wife advised us to stay until the storm should pass, as they did not think we could travel in such a blizzard. As much as we disliked to leave the snug quarters and hot meals (we were to enjoy for the next three days only a ration of frozen bread and bacon), we bid them goodbye and headed into the storm. Without shelter or fire [for] three days and two nights, when we thought each day would be our last, we traveled over an open country for about fifty miles and had to break trail all the way, it being 30 to 40 degrees below zero. The mules were going home. [That] was the only reason we were able to make them face the blizzard. We had plenty of corn and oats for mules and the horses, and at night we tied them so the wagon would act as a wind break and [we] covered them with blanket-lined covers. We would spread our tent on the snow, roll out our bed, and pull part of the tent over us and let the storm howl.

We got to the stage station on the Running Water after dark the night of the 23rd. Here we had hay for the mules and horses and a good fire and warm place to cook our supper. How good that hot coffee tasted. The stage for the Black Hills and Deadwood arrived about 3 a.m., the first in three days. The stock tender awakened us at 4 a.m. and had the coffee hot. It gave us new life and courage for the last twenty miles of our journey. The stage had broke the trail to the top of Breakneck Hill, the storm had passed, the sky cleared, the sun shown bright, and the Valley of the White River lay before us. The fort was only five miles away. We got safely down the Breakneck, crossed White Clay Creek, and broke trail across the valley, arriving at the fort about 2 o'clock the afternoon of the 24th.

I rode ahead to report to the commanding officer. When I passed the officers quarters the kiddies were all out running up and down the walks for the first time in five days, having been housed up on account of the storm. When they saw me they began to shout, "The Christmas Wagon has come." The officers and men hearing them came out and asked if it was true. They could hardly believe it until the teamster drove his six weary mules up and we began to unload the Christmas goods. Even the officers were willing to help.

Major Edwin V. Sumner was post commander at Fort Robinson. The teamster who drove the mule team was a man by the name of Fry. The youngster who got the rocking horse was Conrad Babcock, son of Captain John B. Babcock, in command of Troop M, Fifth U. S. Cavalry at that time. Captain John M. Hamilton was in command of Troop H, Captain John Scott

Payne of Troop F of the Fifth, and Captain Alfred Morton of Company C of [the] Fourth [sic—Ninth] U. S. Infantry. One year later I was promoted to first sergeant of Troop H.

Incidents of Army Life at Fort Wingate, 1892-1893 (By

Frederick H. Krause, formerly of Troop A, Second U. S. Cavalry. From *Winners of the West*, December, 1938)

[On] February 27, 1888, I was enlisted for the Second U. S. Cavalry at Fort Walla Walla, Washington. During my service at this post we were under orders occasionally for the suppression of Indian hostilities. On one occasion we were ordered to report to the Umatilla Indian Reservation, near Pendleton, Oregon, on a forced march for forty-eight hours without food or water through an alkali country. The white settlers near the Umatilla Indian Reservation suffered the loss of some of their livestock such as horses, cattle, and sheep, etc. And their homes were threatened with entire destruction by the Indians. Through the supreme generalship and an expert interpreter of the Second U. S. Cavalry, we succeeded in restoring the stolen property to its rightful owners without bloodshed or even firing one shot.

We camped there for ten days before returning to our headquarters at Fort Walla Walla, Washington. Previously, before being stationed at Fort Walla Walla, Washington, the Second U. S. Cavalry was stationed at Fort Custer, Montana. During the time since the Custer Massacre, the Second U. S. Cavalry had succeeded in providing the proper protection for the white people against the depredations of the Sioux and Cheyenne Indians without firing a shot. On account of the supreme record that the Second Cavalry had attained to establish peace among the different tribes of Indians throughout that territory, the Second Cavalry was ordered by the Secretary of War to change stations from Fort Walla Walla, Washington, to the station at Fort Lowell, Arizona. During the fore part of the year of 1890, before being located at Fort Lowell, Arizona, the Fourth U. S. Cavalry near the San Carlos Indian Reservation suffered much loss as a result of a massacre of a portion of the troops by the Apache Indians [sic—this "massacre" of members of the Fourth Cavalry did not happen]. During my time at Fort Lowell, Arizona, the Second Cavalry succeeded in making arrests among the Apache Indians and settled all disputes among the white people without the loss of a trooper. On account of the excellent record of the Second Cavalry, and the buildings being condemned as being unfit for occupation, we were ordered to change stations from Fort Lowell, Arizona, to the station at Fort Wingate, New Mexico.

During the latter part of the year of 1891, the Moqui [or Hopi] Indians were creating hostilities among the white people throughout that territory, stealing horses, cattle, sheep, and threatening destruction of the white people's homes. The Second U. S. Cavalry received orders from the governor of New Mexico to report to the Moqui Indian Reservation for the purpose of suppressing all hostilities and to restore all stolen property to its rightful owners. I, myself, served under First Lieutenant Lloyd M. Brett. He is very cool headed and fearless. When we arrived at the Moqui Indian Reservation, Lieutenant Brett leaned up against a ledge of rock and carefully rolled up a cigarette. He did not realize the dangerous position he was in, half way up the mountainside. Just two or three minutes before the Moqui Indian chief gave the final signal, which was a swing of his long knife over his head, for his tribe to open fire on Lieutenant Brett and his detachment, our expert interpreter conveyed the information to the Moqui chief, that if he and his tribe killed Lieutenant Brett and his soldiers, Captain Colon Augur was in the rear with another strong detachment at the foot of the mountain and all might be killed. Through this information, the Moqui Indian chief and his tribe surrendered.

As a result, Lieutenant Brett and our detachment proceeded to the top of the mountain and with Captain Augur and his detachment in the rear, succeeded in making arrests of nine Moqui Indians without firing a shot. The nine Moqui Indians were taken to Fort Wingate, New Mexico, and confined in the guard house. During each day, these Moqui Indian prisoners were released from the guard house and under heavy guard were put to work in keeping the grounds clean around the post. These Moqui Indian prisoners appeared to be contented and therefore the guard did not fear for their escape. However, these prisoners were secretly formulating a plan to escape to the mountains near the saw and planing mill. The guard being in sight, though at a considerable distance, did not realize their plans for escape. At a given signal, these nine Moqui Indian prisoners made a dash for liberty and succeeded in being hidden from view of the guard. They were in perfect seclusion before any reinforcements could be notified.

An Indian can outrun any white man and never tire. In that country, Indians have been known to run very many miles without a stop and when they get into the mountains you might as well hunt for a needle in a haystack. After their escape they were never recaptured during my time of service in that country. Fort Wingate, New Mexico, is surrounded by several Indian

Members of Company H, Tenth U. S. Infantry arrayed in fatigue dress against an adobe building at Fort Union, New Mexico Territory, 1891.

Editor's collection

reservations, consisting of the Navajos, Pimas, Moquis, Apaches, and several other tribes. During the latter part of the summer of 1892, a Navajo squaw and her grandson came to the rear of our quarters at the mess hall and demanded some food, and if her appeal could not be granted she would make it known to the chief of her tribe, who had 18,000 Navajo warriors organized for the purpose to wipe the post of Fort Wingate, New Mexico, off the map.

I happened to be on duty at the mess hall and I told the chef what this squaw said concerning the destruction of Fort Wingate, New Mexico. Upon this information, the chef with my assistance took her gunny sacks and filled them full of food which consisted of the leftovers from the day before. This Navajo and her grandson promised that no harm would be done to the post. Although doubting her story, the Second U. S. Cavalry and two companies of the Tenth U. S. Infantry were being prepared for the attack. Through an interpreter, it was made known to the Navajo chief and his warriors that we were ready for battle. We had Hotchkiss guns stationed all around the post. These preparations at the post were made known to the Navajo chief by the interpreter. As a result of this information, the Navajo chief and his 18,000 [sic—an overestimate] warriors backed down. All the Indian tribes in that country dread the Hotchkiss guns worse than death because a shell discharged from a Hotchkiss gun always results in complete destruction at long distance. During the latter part of the summer of 1893, I had a narrow escape from death as a result of a midnight attack on Fort Wingate, New Mexico, by several different tribes of Indians between 10 p.m. and 12 midnight. Being a moonless night, it was very dark.

During those days there was a canteen in operation at all posts. When Indians became intoxicated, trouble is inevitable. Shortly after supper one summer's evening, several Indians and soldiers congregated at the canteen. My comrade, Mr. Shattuck, the drum major of the band, was standing with his hands in his pockets about thirty feet from the canteen. All of a sudden pieces of bricks, rocks, and empty beer bottles were flying around and my comrade Shattuck's cadet cap was knocked off his head without the slightest injury. Finally, the interpreter was successful in restoring peace and the Indians agreed to return to their reservations. That evening shortly after 10 p.m., I was awakened by rifle shots all around the post and in the rear of our quarters bullets penetrated through the panels of the back doors and through the windows and the roof. One of my comrades ran from his bed through the front door in his shirt. He ran so fast that his shirttail flew out straight behind him about two feet. The Officer of the Day ordered every man to arms. A carbine was thrown on my bed with plenty of ammunition. The firing of the

Indians did not last long. The night being pitch dark, we were at odds. We could hear the bullets whistle, but fortunately I was not hit. The two companies of the Tenth U. S. Infantry, being stationed there with the Second Cavalry, made a charge in the rear of our quarters where forms of Indians were running back and forth.

I ran out with my carbine and back of the chapel building. I saw Indians cross a narrow gulch or ravine near the base of the mountains. It was such a dark night that much risk was taken for our proper defense. I was close in the rear of the Indians crossing this narrow gulch. Suddenly, I heard a shot close by. I kept advancing until I got across the gulch. When I got to the other side I stepped against something soft. I lighted a match and saw the face of one of our army Indian scouts. He was dead with a ghastly bullet hole through his head in the left eye. Soon after, I was stunned with a blow on my head, and was unconscious for some time. After I regained consciousness, I managed to crawl back to my quarters. There I saw one of my comrades hidden under his bed trembling from fear. I called him a coward. His carbine was on top of his bed, which he had failed to use. This night attack lasted nearly to midnight. . . .

Part II:
Battles and Campaigns

A. Northern Plains and Prairies

The most constant and lengthy Indian campaigns involving the largest Indian tribes took place on the Northern Plains and prairies between the 1850s and the 1890s after whites were drawn there seeking economic advantage. The soldiers who served in this region, spanning Minnesota on the east to western Montana on the west, and from the Canadian border on the north to Kansas and Colorado on the south, had to contend with extremes in temperature during the summers and winters, besides native foes of extraordinary endurance and pronounced fighting abilities. Among the army campaigns prosecuted by the government in this region, those here registered in the memory bank of veterans include elements of the so-called Red Cloud War of 1866-68, the Yellowstone Expeditions of 1872 and 1873, the Great Sioux War of 1876-77 (including the Battle of the Little Bighorn), the Cheyenne Campaign, 1878-79, the Pine Ridge Campaign of 1890-91 (including the Wounded Knee Massacre), and the Chippewa Insurrection of 1898. In addition, there are accounts of various isolated incidents and actions involving Indians operating in the vicinity of military posts (e. g., the Bates Fight of 1874), as well as of events tangential yet bearing on particular army campaigns (e. g., the death of Sitting Bull prior to Wounded Knee in 1890).

The Fetterman Tragedy, 1866 (By Timothy O'Brien, formerly of Company E, Eighteenth U. S. Infantry. From *Winners of the West*, March 30, 1933)

On March 29, 1866, in New York City, I enlisted in Company E of the Eighteenth U. S. Infantry and shortly thereafter our command was ordered to [Wyoming and] Montana, going by way of St. Louis, Missouri, Leavenworth, Kansas, and then on to [Wyoming and] Montana [territories], arriving there about May of 1866. At that time the Indians were making raids on different white settlements, stealing horses, cattle, and terrorizing the settlers. Upon our arrival in Montana [sic—northern Wyoming], we built a fort at Phil Kearny using the native pine and spruce trees then growing in the Rocky Mountains. The Indians became jealous of our presence and continually watched our work, constructions, and movements. Colonel Henry B. Carrington was in command of the fort with four companies of about sixty-six men to each company. In building the stockade at the fort, each day we sent out a train of seventeen wagons to the mountains to load and bring in the logs with which to construct the stockade. It frequently happened that the wood train would be attacked by the Indians and some hard fighting was required to drive the Indians off.

At that time it seemed that the whole country was infested with the various and sundry tribes of Comanches, Kiowas, Sioux, Apaches, Cheyennes, Snakes, and other tribes. It appeared that Chief Red Cloud, who always wore a red blanket about his head and shoulders, was a leader of all the tribes, and was chief of the Sioux. Red Cloud was a very brave man and always exercised good judgment in his attacks and skirmishes. I remember to have shot at him several times, but always in a running fight and from which he successfully managed to escape.

I will try to tell something of the massacre of Captain Fetterman and his command. On the morning of December 21, 1866, a detachment was ordered out with the wood train to bring in more timber and logs to construct the stockade at Fort Phil Kearney. Seventeen wagons went out with a citizen driver for each wagon and one soldier for each wagon well armed with rifle and ammunition. I was in wagon No. 2. We were about one mile out from the fort on our way to the mountains to get our load of logs when we were attacked by the Indians, about fifty or sixty of them. Corporal Albion C. Segrow of Philadelphia was in command of our wood train, and after repulsing the Indians we held a consultation and decided to go on to the mountains for our load of logs. Hearing the fire of our rifles back at the fort,

Colonel Carrington decided to send a relief to assist us, and this was the occasion of Fetterman being sent out with about eighty men to our rescue. (We of course knew nothing at that time of Fetterman being dispatched to the rescue of our wood train.) Bringing our wood train to the mountains, we hurriedly pulled logs down the mountain sides through the deep snow, and after loading our wagons we started for the fort. Upon arriving at the fort, I met Colonel Carrington at the entrance to the stockade. He asked me, "Were any of your men killed?" I replied, "No, Colonel, none of our men have been killed."

Colonel Carrington then related that he had sent out Captain Fetterman with eighty odd men to relieve our wood train, and that evidently Fetterman and his men had all been killed by the Indians. It was then immediately decided to take every available man at the fort and go out in search of Fetterman and his men. Second Lieutenant Winfield S. Matson being placed in command of our searching party, we started out toward Lodge Trail Ridge taking a twelve-pound Howitzer and six wagons. After crossing the creek at the same place where Fetterman and his men had crossed, we came to the crest of the ridge. At this point, Lieutenant Matson took out his glasses and began to search in all directions for some evidence of Fetterman's command. Far out to the north, Lieutenant Matson was able to see the bodies of Fetterman's men lying dead upon the ground. The wagons were ordered to advance to rescue the bodies of the dead. We took up the mangled bodies of our comrades, all of whom had been scalped by the Indians, save one man, Private Frank P. Sullivan, company clerk. For some reason, the Indians had spread a buffalo robe over his head.

I remember that my comrade and buddy Jimmie Filnain [sic—probably Private Timothy Cullinane] (who was born in Cork, Ireland) was not only scalped, but had both hands cut off at the wrists. This must have been done by the Indians in retaliation for the deadly fire and good mark of Jimmie's rifle. It was desperately cold, and after loading our dead we started back to the fort. In coming down the steep mountain side, one of the wagons overturned, throwing the bodies out into the deep snow. Loading them again, we brought them into the fort. A heavy guard was immediately placed about the fort in expectation of an attack from the Indians, and preparations went forward for the burial of the dead heroes. The cold, frozen ground made it a desperately difficult undertaking to dig the graves, but all hands worked with courage and fidelity to accomplish the task. And thus, there within the grounds of the stockade was laid to rest the bodies of our brave men.

Unidentified infantry first sergeant wearing uniform of the pattern used from before the Civil War through the early 1870s. *Editor's collection*

Note on the Fetterman Fight (By Alexander Brown, formerly sergeant, Troop D, Second U. S. Cavalry. From *Winners of the West*, February 28, 1927)

I enlisted in June, 1865, sent to Lookout Mountain, Tennessee, where I was assigned to the Twenty-seventh U. S. Infantry, and we were sent out on the plains, wintering at Old Fort Kearney on the Platte River in Nebraska. In the spring of 1866, we went up in Dakota [later Wyoming Territory] and established Fort Phil Kearny. The fight took place in December and I was one of the detachment to handle the artillery and we certainly shelled those Indians. I was standing alongside of Colonel Carrington on that fatal day of December 21, 1866, when he told Colonel Fetterman to take the men that was not on duty and go and relieve the wood train, but not to proceed or pursue the Indians over Lodge Trail Ridge. He disobeyed orders and consequently he and his command were wiped out. The following day we brought in the bodies and they were horribly mutilated. This is a true version of that terrible and tragic Fetterman disaster.

The Relief of Fort Phil Kearny and Fort C. F. Smith, 1866 (By Bartholomew Fitzpatrick, formerly sergeant, Company B, Eighteenth U. S. Infantry. From *Winners of the West*, February 28, 1927)

After the arrival of Portugee Phillips at Fort Laramie, the commanding officer at that post ordered Major James Van Voast to take Companies A, B, C, E, and G of the Eighteenth U. S. Infantry and to proceed by forced marches to Fort Phil Kearny to reinforce Colonel Henry B. Carrington, who was in command there. This march of 236 miles took place in the winter of 1866, and it was said to be the severest winter known to the oldest trappers who worked for the American Fur Company.

We arrived at Fort Phil Kearny and our company, B, was sent out to help bring in the bodies of the soldiers of Fetterman's command. After that, we put in the winter by doing all kinds of dangerous escort duty. I had the pleasure of being detailed to take charge of a mail escort with Portugee Phillips as mail agent and escort it back on the old Bozeman Trail to Fort Laramie. We had two engagements with the Indians while en route to Fort Laramie, and one returning to Fort Phil Kearny. It was rumored at that time that the troops at Fort [C. F.] Smith on the Big Horn River, Montana [Territory], a hundred miles away, had all been massacred by the Indians. Two brave first sergeants, Joseph Grant of Company C, and Joseph Graham of Company G, were dispatched to Fort C. F. Smith to find out the true condition of things. When nearing Fort Phil Kearny on their return, Grant's horse was shot from under him. Although badly frozen, he managed to climb on Graham's horse and they reached the fort in safety, reporting that the soldiers at Fort Smith were well except that they were sadly in need of supplies.

Major Van Voast was ordered to take the five companies of the Eighteenth U. S. Infantry and two companies of the Second U. S. Cavalry, with the famous scout, Jim Bridger, as guide, and convoy a supply train of wagons to Fort Smith. When the command returned to Fort Phil Kearny, the cavalry was ordered on to Fort Laramie. They reached there, however, on foot, as the Indians stampeded and stole their horses. Lieutenant Colonel Henry W. Wessells, the post commander, ordered Major Van Voast to send a detail of men out six miles to where the government wood cutters were employed, and I was put in charge of the detail. After arriving at the camp, we found a lot of wagon boxes strewn in a circular direction, which we remodeled and improved by throwing in more ox yokes and wood into them. All this took place a few weeks before the Wagon Box Fight. I was about sixty miles away at Fort Reno on the Powder River, when the valiant battle of the Wagon Boxes was fought. . . .

Guarding the Union Pacific (By Lauren W. Aldrich, formerly sergeant, Company A, Thirtieth U. S. Infantry, and Company H, Fourth U. S. Infantry. From *Winners of the West*, September, 1924)

I will briefly sketch some of my own experience. During the years of 1867, 1868, 1869, and 1870, I served in the Regular Army in the West. Some 800 of us were entrained at Newport, Kentucky, with Wyoming our place of destination. About 75% of the recruits had served in the Civil War and knew something of discipline. We detrained about September 1, 1867, about forty miles west of Omaha, and started at once on foot on a forced march from dawn to nearly dark every day over what seemed an endless desert, in face of hot winds and blistering hot sun, suffering daily for the lack of water, each carrying his personal effects averaging about thirty pounds. Even many of our mules succumbed to the hardships and died on the way. Thus we continued making an average of twenty-five miles a day until we arrived at a point some 150 miles west of the present site of Rawlins, Wyoming. Here we were assigned to various locations along the Union Pacific Railroad, which was then being constructed.

About fifty of us were assigned to Company A, Thirtieth Infantry, to be stationed at Fort Kearney, to which point we started about December 1, encountering all kinds of weather, including blizzards, etc. . . . At Fort Kearney we were drilled from 4 to 6 hours each day in manual, evolution, and target practice. We had occasional skirmishes with the Indians in small detachments.

On the 22nd of February, [1868,] I was made deaf in my left ear by the firing of national salute with brass cannon. In the early spring of '68 we were divided up into small detachments and stationed along the Union Pacific Railroad to prevent depredations of Sioux and Cheyennes, which were sometimes appalling. I was put in charge of a detachment of ten men at Plum Creek where we had some thrilling experiences. We were kept moving westward to those points where trouble was most expected, but as the U. P. was now completed, our movements were mostly by train and not so irksome. In the late fall of '68 we built Fort Fred Steele where the U. P. crosses the north fork of Platte River. While hauling logs from Elk Mountain our wagon train was attacked by Indians who captured about eighty of our mules. About fifty of us were mounted and recaptured nearly all the mules and thirty-six ponies besides, after a chase of fifty miles. Later on two men were killed and their bodies terribly mutilated near [present] Rawlins. In charge of a detachment of twenty mounted men, I chased thirty-five Indians about ten miles in a running fight, receiving two wounds and my horse three, but fortunately none was serious.

While yet at Fort Steele in the spring of '69, my company was transferred to Company H, Fourth Infantry, at the time of consolidation of the regular army. We went to Fort D. A. Russell, near Cheyenne, in July, '69, where I received a knife wound while arresting an undesirable citizen at a gambling hall in Cheyenne. About September 1, a detachment of us were sent to build a fort afterwards named Fort Fetterman. After the fort was finished in the severe winter of '69 and '70, I was put in charge of a detail of twenty mounted men to carry the mail half the distance between Forts Fetterman and Laramie. Owing to exposure to rigid weather, lack of vegetables in our diet, and other contributory agencies, a number of our men contracted scurvy and scrofula. It was my misfortune to develop the latter in the spring of '70, which grew worse until my discharge at Fort Fetterman, September 15, 1870. . . .

A Reality of Warfare (By Samuel H. Bently, formerly of Troop I, Fifth U. S. Cavalry. From *Winners of the West*, February, 1925)

I saw two years of hard service, enlisting at Carlisle, Pennsylvania, on January 25, 1870, to serve five years in the Regular Army. I was discharged at Fort D. A. Russell, Wyoming, on February 19, 1872, for disabilities. I served in Troop I, Fifth Cavalry, being with Colonel [sic] William F. Cody, known as "Buffalo Bill," for two long years. Our fights were chiefly with the Sioux Indians, although the Pawnees gave us a good deal of trouble. On one of our campaigns I saw a cottonwood stump, seven feet in height, where the Indians had tied a soldier and burnt him up. I saw his head, and picked up some buttons that came off of his blouse, showing that he was a soldier. We always put one cartridge where we could get it, for if we were captured by the Indians we knew what our fate would be, and rather than this we would far rather shoot ourselves.

A Skirmish at Heart River, Dakota, 1872 (By John W. Jenkins, formerly first sergeant, Company G, Sixth U. S. Infantry. From *Winners of the West*, May, 1925)

In 1872, several companies of the Eighth, Ninth, Seventeenth, Twentieth, and Twenty-second U. S. infantry was sent as an escort to the surveyors of the Northern Pacific Railway from St. Paul to Puget Sound. We left Fort Rice, Dakota Territory, early in July, 1872, under command of Brevet Major General David S. Stanley, Colonel of the Twenty-second, and went as far as the mouth of the Powder River. Little of note occurred going out, but coming back was different. We practically fought our way back.

In the afternoon during our first days camp on the Powder River, Colonel Stanley ordered a shot from our 6[-pounder] Napoleon field gun as a signal for Major Eugene Baker, who with a battalion of the Second U. S. Cavalry was intending to connect with us at this point. The shot did not bother Major Baker, but it did excite a band of redskins that was secreted in a cottonwood grove into which Stanley's 6-pound shell found its way, and spread abroad amongst the bushes. In a few minutes, more Indians had piled out of that grove than we could shake a stick at, and [they] headed for the open country where they could see whether any more iron works were coming their way.

That shot opened the ball. From that [point] on until our return to Fort Rice, we were annoyed with the red pests. Actual engagements were frequent. Rosebud, Powder River, O'Fallon's Creek, Little Heart Butte, and Heart River, and the latter will be remembered by those who were there until their dying day. Companies C and F, Seventeenth Infantry, under command of Major Robert E. A. Crofton, were dispatched homeward a week in advance of the main command in order to conserve the supplies which were running low, and incidentally to sweep the path of the red pests. [Scout] Charley Reynolds, with half a dozen Santee Indian scouts, accompanied us. These were in advance of us and were waiting for us when we came up to Heart River for the night camp. It was an ideal camp for wood, water, and grass, but a natural death trap, a basin entirely surrounded by tall bluffs through which the river cut from northwest to southeast, and narrow gorges along the river.

A few minutes after entering camp, several deer were seen to emerge from the northeast gorge, and First Lieutenant Eben Crosby, Seventeenth Infantry, my company commander (who left one of his arms on the battlefield of Chancellorsville), a famous marksman and idolized by all his men, approached the major for permission to go and get some of those deer. The major refused his request on the grounds that he (Crosby) had been detailed for officer of the day. Crosby turned away grieved and downhearted and the major called him back and said, "Mr. Crosby, if you still desire to go in pursuit of deer I will take your place as officer of the day, and you may go." Crosby brightened up, thanked his superior, and with a smile started off at a trot. The last we ever saw of our beloved officer alive was when he disappeared through the gorge following the course of the deer that had preceded him.

Eight o'clock came that night, but Crosby did not. A trumpeter was sent to the top of the bluffs to sound all the familiar calls, but no response came. A fire was kindled, but poor Crosby came not to its welcome light. Breakfast was ordered ready by daylight, that a detail might go in search of the officer. As we ate our breakfast between daylight and sunrise, we heard several shots and our men cheered and exclaimed, "There's Crosby. We will have venison for supper." Some ran out of their tents to look, and behold, the rim of the bluffs as far as the eye could reach was covered with the red hell hounds, howling and yelling, riding back and forth like mad. The major ordered the men not to shoot, that it might be a friendly hunting party, that there were no hostiles in the vicinity.

After the Indians had settled themselves for grim work, one of them signaled for a talkfest. The major called the interpreter and told him to meet the gentleman of copper tint and find out what his wishes were, whether for peace or war, suggesting he could have his choice. The interpreter returned with the wishes of the red gent, which were that we evacuate the camp immediately, leaving everything just as it was, to take nothing away but one day's rations. No guns, ammunition, or extra clothing. We were then sixty miles from Fort Rice. The major smiled and remarked, "Generous, wasn't he? We'll leave him something, however, some bones of his braves to bleach on those hills. Here, bugler, sound the call to arms."

The words had hardly lost their sound until the Springfields were barking, and the red skunks on the bluffs were beginning to show signs of being disturbed. Here was a soldier. Every inch of that six feet was game to the core. I went to the cook fire to get a cup of coffee. Emanuel Gearing was our second cook and was measuring out coffee. A sniper among the Indians sent a bullet through the visor of his forage cap as he poured out my coffee, and it dropped into the camp kettle. He dropped the dipper and disappeared immediately. I looked around to see what went with him as I thought he had been hit. I saw the broad soles of his government shoes sticking out of his tent door. He had dived headlong into the tent and lay prone on the ground and seemed to be so well satisfied with his position that no amount of coaxing could get him to come out. And there he remained until the Indians were gone.

There was an overhanging bluff opposite camp that afforded shelter from the enemy fire. Charley Reynolds made for that, and Sergeant Johnson with about twenty men of Company C ran across the river and followed him, zig-zagging the bluff until within a couple of rods of the crest, when they halted for a fresh supply of wind. The reds discovered them and such a yell and such scampering would be hard to describe. In less time than it would require to tell it there wasn't an Indian to be seen. Reynolds and Johnson went "over the top" but there was little to be seen when they got there. Away toward sunset could be seen some black specks bobbing up and down. The squaws were far behind, screaming, howling, and lambasting their ponies, their travois bounding up and dropping off a dead buck and then was pandemonium let loose. The scene was so pitiful that the boys refrained from shooting into them. Now that the war was over, our attention was again turned to the search for Lieutenant Crosby. Sergeant John Massena and a detail of six men were sent out. In about two hours they returned with the mutilated body of the lieutenant. The law forbids that I use the necessary words to describe the condition of his person. The work was done principally with knives, and occurred too near our camp to burn him. They knew where we were. . . .

The Yellowstone Expedition of 1873 (By William Foster Norris, formerly second lieutenant, Company E, Ninth U. S. Infantry. From *Winners of the West*, September, 1938)

I was commissioned a second lieutenant of infantry in the Regular Army in June, 1872. I joined my regiment in the fall of that year at Omaha

Barracks, since known as Fort Omaha. It long ago lost its military character, being superseded by Fort Crook, which became and still is [1938] the headquarters of the department. I was fortunate in my regiment and its commanding officer, as well as [in] the company to which I was assigned. Brevet Major General John H. King[, colonel Ninth Infantry,] was a fine specimen of the old-time army officer. I can see him now, as with stately tread he walks from the adjutant's office, after guard mount, to [the] commanding officer's quarters situated at the center of the row of officers' quarters. The regimental adjutant, First Lieutenant Leonard Hay, an officer worthy of his chief, was a calm, quiet, reticent man, with whom few, if any, would be on intimate terms, but by whom all who knew him, highly respected. As I remember them both, he closely resembled his famous brother[, John Hay], then known as a literary celebrity, but who since acquired wider fame as one of the authors of the *Life of Abraham Lincoln* and a distinguished diplomat. The captain of the company, Captain Edwin Pollock, was an energetic, ambitious officer, thoroughly devoted to his profession. I wish I could meet him again to tell him of my appreciation of his courtesy and consideration, but he was killed by an untimely accident after my retirement from the service. The first lieutenant subsequently became colonel of a regiment, was wounded during the Boxer Rebellion, and subsequently was stationed in Manila, where he died shortly before he would have retired from active military service.

My first active military service was during the winter of 1872 at Omaha Barracks. It was a pleasant winter; the duties were light, there being no work at that time excepting the routine work of the garrison, such as serving in turn as officer of the guard or officer of the day. The young officers spent much of their leisure time in Omaha where we were so fortunate as to enjoy the society of the Nebraska metropolis. . . . In the spring of 1873, an expedition was sent to protect a party of engineers engaged in making a survey of a projected route of the Northern Pacific Railroad from the Missouri to a point on the Yellowstone River. Such protection was necessary as the route lay over the plains infested by hostile Indians, principally Sioux and Northern Cheyennes. Several companies from the Barracks, including my own, were sent to join the expedition, which was to assemble at a point on the Missouri River. I think it was Fort [Abraham] Lincoln, one of the frontier posts in what is now the state of North Dakota.

Our command marched from the Barracks to the Missouri River, where we embarked on the Steamer *Josephine*, which was to convey us safely up the river to Fort Lincoln. It seemed a hard task for the little steamer to force its way upstream against the current of the mighty river. Every now and then we would run on a sand bar or against a snag, at which times the nigger would be called upon to lift us off the sandbar or over it, as the case might be. The nigger appeared to be a little engine which did its work admirably and successfully, as we arrived safely at our destination despite sandbars and snags.

At Fort Lincoln, the entire force was consolidated, consisting of the railroad engineering party under [former] General Thomas Rosser, an ex-Confederate officer. The Seventh Cavalry, or part thereof, was under Brevet Major General Custer, lieutenant colonel. The entire command was under Colonel David S. Stanley. The expeditionary force was quite large for those days, numbering some fifteen hundred men, infantry and cavalry. There was a long baggage train of six-mule teams loaded with supplies for the command, as it was necessary to take our food with us. This consisted largely of boxes of hardtack, as the meat supply, consisting of several hundred beef cattle, marched along in rear of the column. We had an oversupply of hardtack, part of which may have afforded nourishment to our foes, as a large number of boxes were taken from the wagons during the expedition and piled snugly away in a sequestered place, but not so concealed as to be safe from the eyes of the red men who were very fond of this particular brand of bread.

Shortly after disembarking, we set out on our march to the distant Yellowstone. The gentle, undulating plains presented but little serious obstacles to our progress. It was a trackless route, I suppose never before traversed by a wagon train. Occasionally we came to the dry bed of a stream which caused some trouble in descending the steep bank on one side and ascending on the other. Sometimes a wagon would upset or have to be unloaded, but as a rule the column marched on and on day after day, with but little interruption from such mishaps and none at all from our Indian antagonists. I recall one of the mule drivers who gained my lasting respect, which has continued for the half century to the present day. I saw him drive his six mules without an oath or ejaculation unless it was an encouraging word to his team, who were pulling with all their might and all together the heavily loaded wagon up the side of one of the dry beds. I well remember his asking the soldiers who stood on each side not to shout at the mules, and silently, without whip, or more than gently urging, this well-trained team did its duty to the utmost. This humble mule driver taught a much needed lesson by his example to all observing officers as well as soldiers and more than all to his fellow teamsters.

It was a weary, dreary, monotonous march over the dry and arid plains. As the season advanced, the days became intensely hot. The plains lent themselves to heat. There was no carpet of green grass beneath our feet, no trees, no running streams, no cooling breeze. The ground in places was white with alkali, the grass dry and scant. Instead of trees and familiar bushes, there were acres and acres of sagebrush, which was in complete harmony with its environment.... One of the discomforts of our long march arose from lack of water. The canteen with which the men went out in the morning would be emptied long before making camp at the close of the day's march. It was hard on the men but much harder on the poor animals, especially when we went into a dry camp at night. On these occasions, which very rarely happened, the camp was not literally dry, but the water was so impregnated with alkali as to be undrinkable by man or beast. It was pathetic to hear the animals eagerly give voice in their different ways as they saw the pool of water ahead where we were to camp, but it was still more pathetic to hear them express their disappointment when upon plunging their heads into it, they were unable to drink. It was distressing to hear the mournful lowing of the cattle, the braying of the mules, the neighing of the horses—a chorus of discordant protest from the unfortunate animals who, after traveling all day without water, were denied a drink at night.

Officers and soldiers were prohibited from wandering from the marching column as no man's life was safe outside of military protection. One day two civil employees went to the Yellowstone River, evidently tempted by the attractions of abundant water and shelter under the trees fringing the stream. Their bodies were found transfixed with arrows, showing how they met with their death. Such were existing conditions when we were astonished to see approaching in the distance a wagon drawn by one horse. As it drew nearer, it proved to be a covered wagon surmounted by a cross. In the vehicle was a single driver arrayed in a black robe. He came up to the command which was halted, descended and conversed a while with the higher officers, re-ascended to his seat and drove on out into the plains in the midst of the hostile Indians with as little concern as he would have driven along the streets of St. Paul or Minneapolis. I mention these cities, as I remember he was a Jesuit priest from Minnesota.

As we watched this lonely man drive away over the plains in the midst of hostile savages, unarmed and unprotected except by the symbol surmounting his carriage and his own reputation and clerical garb, I thought it one of the most notable examples of heroism that I ever saw. This was three years before the Sitting Bull War, during which occurred the battle known as the Custer

Massacre. Fifty years takes us far back in the history of the northwestern plains, but early as it was we were too late to see the vast herds of buffalo that formerly fed upon the nutritious grass that bears their name. The buffalo grass was there, but few of the noble animals were left. Grim mementos were strewn over the plains, as the massive skulls of the slaughtered animals were long in decomposing. We saw only one herd, but what a shadow was the few scattered animals we beheld at a distance of the vast herds that a few years before shook the earth with their multitudinous tread, extending in every direction as far as the eye could reach. [See the recollection below of William D. Nugent.]

The disintegrating skulls of the noble animals were left just where the wolves and coyotes had gnawed the last shred of flesh from them. What a feast the remorseless buffalo slayers spread for these ravenous beasts of prey. I wonder if even their insatiable appetite could devour the superabundance of meat. What must have been the reflections of the Sioux and Cheyennes as they beheld their herds of cattle turned over to the wolves and coyotes. I will never forget my first view of the river toward which we were marching. We felt relieved to see it, for somewhere, at some point of its course, our march would end. But in itself it was a picture of loveliness. I don't know that the river where it flows over the plains possesses any peculiar attraction, nor that the cottonwood ranks high as to timber value or beauty, but to the men plodding along their weary way, the green trees and the clear water was a most attractive as well as tantalizing spectacle, for though we might look we could not drink from this elysian stream flowing through an elysian region.

I would like to see the Yellowstone now from the same point of view, which cannot be, because I do not know just where we were at the time the rapturous view burst upon our vision, and viewed from a seat in a Pullman car it would present quite a different aspect than when seen from one marching through the heat and dust over an alkaline plain with several hundred men all like himself, weary and thirsty and longing for green trees and clear water. The return march from the Yellowstone to the Missouri was neither wearisome, monotonous, nor dangerous. We had no fear of Indians. We were going home. The days were not so warm and the nights quite cool. I still remember with what a sense of comfort we would spread our blankets or buffalo robe in a clump of bushes or thick weeds and snuggle down in this natural shelter and sleep soundly till the bugle call would rouse us at early dawn. The *Josephine* was waiting for us. We pushed off and started downstream—not up, but down, which meant a good deal on the Missouri. The current carried us down, aiding, instead of opposing our advance. The nigger was seldom, if ever, called to our aid. The trip was soon ended and we were soon reinstated in our comfortable quarters for the winter of 1873-74, to again enjoy the pleasure of the delightful society of Omaha. . . .

Notes on the Yellowstone Expedition (By John Walsh, formerly of Troop M, Seventh U. S. Cavalry. From *Winners of the West*, August, 1924)

[The recent article by William F. Norris of Great Falls, Montana, called] attention to the killing of Veterinary Surgeon John Honsinger of the Seventh U. S. Cavalry and of the death of the sutler [August Baliran] who accompanied the Yellowstone Expedition of 1873. [The author]. . . makes no mention of Private John H. Ball, who was also killed the same day. Ball was leading an extra horse of his captain's and was riding some distance off from the command.

After having been missed, a search was made with no success, but on our return a search was made and [we] found his bones, picked clean. All this on the 5th day of August, 1873. Norris says the horse doctor and sutler were buried and the mules allowed to tramp over their graves. Nothing of the kind. They were buried underneath where the 7th U. S. Cavalry band horses were tied to the picket line and I am the soldier that walked post over those horses that night. No tramping over their graves but the band horses. He makes no mention of the engagement at the mouth of the Big Horn, August 11, 1873.

I never knew anything of Norris on that expedition, but I knew Charley Reynolds, a famous scout who was afterwards killed with Custer in '76, 25th of June. In the engagement on the 11th of August, '73, Custer had a horse shot from under him, his orderly, Private John H. Tuttle was shot through the head and Second Lieutenant Charles Braden was shot through the thigh. The Seventh had to draw him along by hand, 250 miles.

A Buffalo Stampede during the Northern Pacific Survey Expedition, 1873 (By William D. Nugent, formerly of Troop A, Seventh U. S. Cavalry. From *Winners of the West*, March 15, 1926)

I will relate . . . the story of my greatest scare in all of my army life. This occurred on one of the hottest days in September, 1873, after we had completed the survey of the Northern Pacific Railroad at the Musselshell River at the point where the survey met the one from the west. We turned back to cross the divide on our long trail for Fort [Abraham] Lincoln, [Dakota Territory]. As we had [had] two engagements with Indians in passing through this country previous to this, we expected trouble with them again, as soon as we entered the lane. Rumors had increased the number from a few thousand to twenty thousand warriors. Marching o'er the prairies, we saw many animals. We saw wild horses, buffalos, deer, elk, wolves, coyotes, and other animals that frequented that region. On this day we were on a high table land and could see as far as the eye could distinguish an object to the east, south, and west. Our view to the north was limited because it was broken country, rolling hills and plains. We saw a large wagon train, consisting of nearly four hundred [wagons], treading over the plains. It was being driven eight wagons abreast, with ten companies of infantry on the left flank and ten on the right. Six companies of cavalry were in the advance, and two companies were acting as rear guard, with two companies deployed as flankers. It could easily be seen that the commanding officer was on the alert for danger, as every precaution was being used for safety in a country infested with the wily and treacherous Sioux.

I was aroused from the monotony of our march by seeing our advance halting. I saw that something of much interest was taking place as all who had halted were intently looking to the north. Suddenly there came a dull roar to our ears, and everyone was startled and apparently at a loss to account for the sound. Many like myself were just young fellows, and very few knew anything of the plains. Some had had experience in campaigning before, but they were inclined to exaggerate and it was their delight to raise the hair on the recruit's head. Every second increased the volume of sound. Some thought it was an earthquake, others that it was the end of the world, and still others that it was Sitting Bull and his twenty thousand warriors. In the north, a cloud of dust was rolling high and coming on at express speed. The line of dust seemed to come from all directions, and as it came near we found it was composed of many different sounds, the rattle and clatter of chains and cooking utensils. We now had the solution and all understood what this awful menace was: buffalos by the millions were coming like a cloud before the wind, as far as the eye could see. In that fear-driven, crazy mass of animals was a force as irresistible as a snow slide or an avalanche.

It looked like sure death, as we were in danger of being gored and punctured by the horns of the buffalos and then to be trampled into a shapeless form under their hoofs. Our worn horses could not outdistance this onrushing death for even one mile. Oh, mama, I was sure sick at the stomach. I was like the old owl "that lived in the oak, the more he saw, the less he spoke," and I sure saw enough. I wished that my brother was there and I was at home. I never told any of my comrades how scared I was, and was sure glad afterwards that they did not know that I closed my teeth together to keep them from chattering.

I saw Colonel Custer with some twenty men advance to possibly one hundred yards in the direction of the oncoming menace, but no thought entered my mind that any efforts that could be put forth by anyone could save us. When the buffalos had approached within one hundred yards of this small bunch of men, the soldiers shot one volley after another in[to] the herd and wonder or wonders happened. The buffalos split, part passing to the right and the rest to the left, passing like a mighty power of destruction and death. This left me surprised, relieved, and happy, but oh how weak. After this, at various times I saw many herds of buffalos, but none that would equal this one great stampede. It hardly seems possible that today they seem to have almost all disappeared, when a few years back the prairies were covered with them. Many a recruit will remember their first buffalo stampede as well as I, although very few will confess that they were as badly scared, and I have waited many years to confess. . . .

Bates's Fight in the Owl Range, 1874 (By James H. Rhymer, formerly corporal, Troop B, Second U. S. Cavalry. From *Winners of the West*, March, 1925)

I desire to give you the following account of the Battle of Owl Range, Wyoming Territory, fought by Company B, Second U. S. Cavalry, under command of Captain Alfred E. Bates and Second Lieutenant Frank U. Robinson, with Dr. Thomas McGee as medical officer, on July 4, 1874. We left Camp Brown the night of July 1, 1874, with eight pack mules, but when we arrived at Hot Springs, which is three and one-half miles from Camp Brown, we were ordered to take four of the mules back to the post by Lieutenant General Philip H. Sheridan. We were accompanied by a frontiersman by the name of O'Neil, and also 300 Shoshoni Indians under the command of Washakie, the chief, and Little Humpy, the war chief. Little Humpy had discovered the village of the hostiles [Arapahos], who had been preying upon the settlers in the Wind River Valley, and who had killed Mrs. Hall and Mrs. Richardson the year before.

We traveled all that night, and at the break of day we camped at the head of the Big Wind River, where we laid over, not even building a fire to boil coffee over. The next night we traveled and reached the Little Muddy, where we were treated to a buffalo hunt by the Shoshone Indians. They brought a buffalo near our camp and killed it with arrows, so as not to fire any guns and make any alarm. My bunky, Private James M. Walker, awakened me near morning and said that we were going to strike the Indians about daylight. He had heard Little Humpy tell Captain Bates. He also told me that he was not coming out of that battle alive, which later proved to be the case as he was the first man shot and killed.

We again traveled all night and just at the break of day we were at a point overlooking the village, which was shaped like a large L and which we judged contained about 105 tepees. Our Indians made a noise in getting prepared for battle and thus alarmed the hostiles. We dismounted and number four [i. e., each fourth man] held the horses while our small command of sixty-four men in all attacked the large body of Indians. One great help to us was the friendly Indians under Second Lieutenant Robert H. Young of the Fourth Infantry who ran off the herd. Lieutenant Young was shot through the leg. We charged down to the village using our carbines and revolvers, and the slaughter for a time was great. The Indians now rallied, and we had to retreat back from the village leaving the bodies of Walker and Private Peter F. Engall where they had fallen in the skirmish. The Indians, in the meantime, had captured our mules and medicine and we had to bind up the wounds of our wounded the best we could and retreat. We had six men wounded and two killed. Lieutenant Young was severely wounded.

After being two days and two nights in the saddle and fighting the Indians, we reached Wind River, where we met Company D of the Second U. S. Cavalry, who [sic] had made a forced march, as the report had been circulated that we had been massacred. We finally reached Camp Brown badly exhausted, and I am safe to say if it had not been for the Indians capturing the herd so as to prevent the hostiles from following us, none of us would have escaped. [In 1875,] Captain Alfred E. Bates was made major [and] paymaster, and afterwards [1899] made General Paymaster of the United States Army.

I consider this one of the greatest battles fought in the West, as the Indians went back to their agency and reported that we had attacked them on their hunting trip and had killed and wounded about 140 Indians [estimated twenty-five killed and perhaps 100 wounded]. It had been this band that had been operating against the settlers and I never saw a village better provided with everything and [in] a better location than the one we had attacked. . . . We were known as the "Buckskin Company" on account of our dress.

Service at Red Cloud Agency, Nebraska, 1874-1875 (By Lines P. Wasson, formerly of Company K, Ninth U. S. Infantry. From *Winners of the West*, February, 1925)

I enlisted in Company K, Ninth U. S. Infantry, on December 13, 1870, and served until December, 1875. While in the army I got the pitiful sum of $13 per month. While we were not in any actual engagements with the Indians, we were constantly on the lookout, expecting every moment to be attacked, especially the last eighteen months of my service. We were stationed at Chief Red Cloud's agency [Red Cloud Agency], which is [in] South Dakota [sic—Nebraska]. . . . We were placed here to see that the Indians stayed on the reservation, and that all miners and settlers stayed off the reservation. At that time the gold excitement in the Black Hills was at high pitch, so the miners and settlers were flocking in there by the hundreds. The government was under obligation to the Indians to keep all miners and settlers off the reservation, consequently we had to keep on the go all the time, winter and summer, rain or snow.

I made two trips from Camp Sheridan. One with Captain Anson Mills in command, and the other trip I cannot at present recall the name of the officer in command. Talk about hardships. We sure saw plenty on those trips. In the spring of '75 we made a trip that was certainly hard on us. Always plenty of snow, and we had to dig away the snow to get a place for our beds, as we had no tents. We could not make a fire to fry bacon on, for the fear of being spotted by the Indians. Raw bacon and hardtack was all we had, but we thought it pretty good at that time. . . .

With the Third Cavalry in 1876 (By Oliver C. C. Pollock, formerly of Troop M, Third U. S. Cavalry. From *Winners of the West*, November 30, 1926)

I thought I would give an account of one year's experience of a buck soldier's life, a high private in the rear ranks of Company M, Third U. S. Cavalry, from January 9, 1876, to November 20, 1880. I enlisted in Pittsburgh, Pennsylvania, on Saturday morning, November 20, 1875, under the name of John E. Douglass. Was sent to Jefferson Barracks and from there with many other recruits was sent to Fort D. A. Russell [Wyoming Territory]. On January 9, 1876, we were assigned to various companies of the Third Cavalry.

An unidentified corporal of Company K, Ninth Infantry, had this image made at Omaha. He likely saw duty at Camp Robinson, Nebraska, through most of 1876 during the period of principal campaigning of the Great Sioux War. *Editor's collection*

On the 20th day of February we left Fort D. A. Russell for a winter's campaign against Sioux Indians, and arrived at Fort Fetterman on February 28th. The next morning we left for a twenty-six days' march, the average cold being 26 degrees below zero. We made a forced march that day and night to make a surprise attack upon a band of Indians who were foraging in that country. Early the next morning [March 17, 1876] we attacked the Indian village, which the scouts had discovered, and fought nearly all day, finally destroying the village of 110 tepees. We captured 300 ponies, but unfortunately they were stampeded and we lost two men who were given a soldier's burial. We returned to Fort D. A. Russell on April 7th.

Then in early May we started on the noted campaign of 1876, in which the government intended to break up the marauding of the Sioux Indians under the capable leadership of Sitting Bull and Crazy Horse, supposed to be in the vicinity of the Big Horn Mountains. Brigadier General Alfred H. Terry and his troops were to attack from the north, and Brigadier General George Crook and his troops from the Department of the Platte, from the south. This narrative has to do with the Crook campaign. We were attacked by roving bands of Indian scouts on June 9th, and from then to the time we established our supply camp on head of Powder River, at foot of Big Horn Mountains, we were harassed, our supply of cattle stampeded and lost, the grass around our camps set on fire at night, and thus we got little sleep.

On June 15th, the scouts under Buffalo Bill [sic—Frank Grouard] reported they had found the Indian villages of Sitting Bull and Crazy Horse located at the mouth of Dead Man's Canyon. We made a forced march of forty-five miles the next day. Then another day, and we marched about ten miles to the head of the canyon. We picketed our horses to graze and expected to make a night attack and surprise the Indians. However, very shortly in came the Crow and Shoshone Indian scouts shouting, "Heap come Sioux." The hills became a mass of humanity, and the great fight, known as the Battle of the Rosebud, began June 17, 1876. In that fight we lost nine killed and twenty-seven wounded. Among those wounded were Corporal John A. Kirkwood and Bugler [Trumpeter] Elmer A. Snow of Company M, Third Cavalry, Snow being shot through both wrists. General Crook decided to attack the stronghold and ordered about one-half of the command under Captain Mills of M Company to proceed down the valley under the leadership of a scout named Frank Grouard. Grouard remarked, "General, I am no coward, nor yet am I [a] fool. I will take your command to where they can go into the village, but I will not go in nor stick my head in where I know I cannot get it out again." We started down this valley, which proved to be a veritable death trap. Very shortly the firing on the hill ceased, and General Crook believing an ambuscade was being planned, had retreat sounded for the soldiers in the valley, and we gladly obeyed. To this day I have felt that this recall saved a portion of Crook's command from the fate that Custer met. We now

General Crook's troops bivouacking in the Black Hills during the Sioux Campaign of 1876. *Courtesy of Little Bighorn Battlefield National Monument*

returned to our supply camp on account of lack of ammunition, and here in July we received the dreadful news of the Custer Massacre.

We started on August 5th with fifteen days rations to avenge Custer's death. We traveled for five days and arrived at the point where the Powder River enters the Yellowstone. Here we found a mass of burning corn and oats, destroyed rations, also what was left of the Seventh U. S. Cavalry and General Terry's command. The next day we saw Buffalo Bill and his black horse leave on the supply boat. He was sore because Frank Grouard proved he knew the country better than Bill, and Grouard's advice was taken. We decided to strike out for the Black Hills on half rations rather than to go to Fort [Abraham] Lincoln for full rations. We soon found ourselves in the badlands of Dakota, and it rained twenty-one days out of the first twenty-four days we were out. We often stood up at nights, for to lay down we had to do so in the mud and water. From August 11th to September 9th, we partook of raw horseflesh, partially for substance and partly to quench our thirst. It was decided after a consultation of officers, to ask for volunteers of 150 men with the best horses, under the command of Captain Anson Mills, who had volunteered to take charge, and with Grouard, to make a forced march and find rations in the Black Hills for the rest of the command. They left and on the night of the 8th a scout reported that they discovered an Indian camp, and for the command to hurry forward.

On the morning of the 9th, we attacked and destroyed an Indian village of 125 [actually thirty-seven] tepees, losing one [two] soldier[s] . . . and a scout, Will Moore, called Buffalo Chips [sic—Jonathan White]. We captured a large amount of dried buffalo meat here, and then pushed on, and on September 15th reached the Belle Fourche River, and here we received a supply of rations [that] our volunteers brought out to us from Crook City. Here, as usual, that enemy of the buck soldier, strong drink, was brought out in about three wagons from the mining camp. Fortunately, it was discovered to be such instead of food and was soon destroyed by the boys, and the men who brought the same panhandled until the officers interfered. In October, we left the Black Hills and Company M was assigned to guard the Spotted Tail Agency at Camp Sheridan, Wyoming [Nebraska], where we wintered. Crook was in the field again and chased Sitting Bull into Canada [sic]. Crazy Horse came to the Spotted Tail Agency, but with a band undertook to go back to the plains. He was captured and returned to Red Cloud Agency at Camp Robinson, where he met his death resisting being confined in the white man's guard house.

I served under the name John E. Douglass, being a corporal in Company M, Third U. S. Cavalry, under Captains Anson Mills and Deane Monahan and Second Lieutenants Frederick Schwatka and George K. Hunter. . . .

Fighting at Powder River and Rosebud Creek, 1876 (By Phineas S. Towne, formerly of Troop F, Third U. S. Cavalry. From *Winners of the West*, February 15, 1926)

I enlisted on November 8, 1875, at Boston, Massachusetts, and with seventeen other recruits was sent to New York City where we remained a short time. Then I was sent to St. Louis, which was a general recruiting depot. Here I remained a few weeks and with other recruits was sent to Fort D. A. Russell, Wyoming [Territory], which was the headquarters of the Third U. S. Cavalry. I was assigned to Troop F, commanded by Captain Alexander Moore, known as "Rocky" Moore. I had been in the troop but a short while when we went out on a winter campaign known as the "Crazy Horse Expedition of 1876." It certainly was a cold expedition. We went up into the Big Horn Mountain country, located the camp of Crazy Horse, and destroyed it on March 17, 1876. A few days previous to our capturing the village of Crazy Horse [sic], we camped at old Fort Phil Kearny, where ten years previous the massacre of Colonel Carrington's troops occurred. On this expedition I rode four extra horses and one Indian pony, besides the horse which had been issued to me at Fort Russell when the expedition started out. These horses were completely played out and had to be killed as they were too weak to travel because we had used up all of our forage and there was no grazing for them on account of the deep snow. The troops themselves had nearly run out of rations. First we were put on half rations and then on quarter rations and we were very fortunate to get back to Fort Russell before running out of rations entirely.

Then came on the summer expedition against the Sioux Nation, which was on the war path and in which Lt. Col. George A. Custer and his troops of the Seventh Cavalry met defeat and death on that fatal 25th of June. Eight days before this, or on June 17th at the Battle of the Rosebud, I was severely wounded and captured by the Indians, tied with a lariat to a pony and hurriedly dragged over the ground in their haste to carry me away, but I was taken from them by the men of my troop. I had been on the skirmish line. Had I not been taken from them and the Indians had gotten away with me, well, I guess that the pension office would not have to pay me a pension now. . . .

Attacking the Cheyennes at Powder River in 1876 (By John Lang, formerly of Troop E, Second U. S. Cavalry. From *Winners of the West*, February, 1925)

[I saw] service from the fall of 1874 to the spring of 1877, being discharged for disability on account of a gunshot wound received in action. It was early in 1876 that General Crook fired the opening gun in a campaign which was destined to end for all time trouble with the Sioux Indians. After a strenuous march we reached a point on the Tongue River on the evening of

March 16, 1876. It was cold, so we missed our usual hot coffee, as fires were forbidden. We were not allowed to strike a match for fear of being located by the enemy. After eating a few [pieces of] hardtack and raw bacon, we started on a night march for Powder River, where at the mouth of Lodgepole Creek Crazy Horse with his warriors had made camp [sic—It was a village of Northern Cheyennes under Old Bear]. His camp had been located by our chief of scouts Frank Grouard. The suffering we endured during the night cannot be described. The temperature dropped to 45 below zero by one o'clock a.m. We were forced to stop, dismount, and run the bullring to get our blood to circulate. We reached a point overlooking the valley at daybreak.

The village was plainly discernable, but we kept out of sight until three companies led by Captain James Egan of K Company, Second U. S. Cavalry, had descended into the valley and had charged through the village. The balance of our troops then charged down the hillside and met the Indians as they fled toward the hills for shelter. The village was destroyed, and toward evening we moved down the river some distance and made camp. I, with other wounded, received such aid as was available, and [was] made as comfortable as a campfire, blood-soaked blanket, and hot coffee would afford. Thus ended March 17, 1876.

Next day we moved on down [up] the river, as it was necessary to get the wounded to a hospital as soon as possible. I entered the hospital at Fort [D. A.] Russell, Wyoming [Territory], on April 8th, being twenty-one days on the road after the fight. I was discharged eleven months later, able to walk with the help of crutches. This was then the beginning of a campaign that furnished many casualties, chiefly the Custer Massacre, but which finally ended in subduing those bloodthirsty demons.

A Sioux War Diary (Kept by George S. Howard, of Troop E, Second U. S. Cavalry. From *Winners of the West*, February, 1937)

March 16, 1876—We had two night marches, one from Crazy Woman Fork to Clear Creek, one from the head of Mizpah River to Powder River, about 35 miles each. The one from Mizpah River being the night of Monday the 16th, the night before the Crazy Horse fight of March 17th, 1876. This was a fight lasting five hours in which we lost four killed and seven wounded. Indians loss—104 lodges burned, 700 ponies captured by U. S. troops. During the trip there were four night alarms. We traveled with pack

An infantry corporal of the 1870s-80s here sports a tailored fatigue blouse and a black campaign hat of the pattern issued to soldiers in the mid-1870s. *Editor's collection*

mules from the 17th to the 22nd, making some 340 miles from Crazy Woman Fork to Tongue River, to creek running toward Mizpah, then over to Powder, up Powder to old Fort Reno. One herder shot and the beef stolen the second night out from Fort Fetterman. Camped on the South Cheyenne.

May 26th—Camped on Platte River about six miles below Bulls Bend. Two graves here, one Narcissia Givens, 1854, and the other Ripley, 1862.

May 27th, 1876—Marched to Fort Fetterman. Companies "C" and "G" of the 3rd left for a scout toward the head waters of the Powder River. Here ready for the Expedition were Co's A, B, C, D, E, F, G, I, M, L, of the 3rd Cavalry, A, B, D, E, I, and K, 2nd Cavalry and six companies of the 4th and 9th Infantry.

June 2nd—Left camp at Antelope Springs at 7:15, marched down dry fork of Powder River, 12 miles then over the ridge to the Powder, striking the river opposite the ruins of Fort Reno abandoned in 1868. No trouble yet with Indians.

June 5th—Left camp on Clear Creek at 7:30. Marched to old Fort Phil Kearny.

June 6th—Left camp at old Fort Phil Kearny at 7:30 a.m. and marched past the scene of the massacre of November 28, 1867 [sic—December 21, 1866].

June 8th—Lay over in Camp on Tongue River. "I" Co. 2nd Cav. captured one pony and killed two buffalo. Buried a man of "B" Co. 3rd Cav. here named Tiernay [Private Francis Tierney].

June 9th—Lay over in camp. The Indians gave us a little performance this evening. Some 50 or 60 came on the bluffs on the other side of the river in hopes to draw out a small party to follow them. They were finally driven away by four Co's of the 3rd Cav. Some spent bullets came near my tent, one horse and one mule were shot.

June 17th—Three months today since the Powder River fight with Crazy Horses band. We started early this morning went down the Rosebud Creek six or seven miles, then halted for a while on account of the scouts having seen some Indians hunting buffalo and soon another performance began. The Shoshones commenced the scrimmage, or rather the Sioux commenced on them, the first shot breaking a Shoshones leg. We were unsaddled at the time and were nearly an hour saddling up, but then we had a hot fight with some 2600 well mounted Indians, our command consisting of 15 companies of cavalry and five of Infantry. The result as near as I can learn are 20 enlisted men and one officer (Capt. [Guy V.] Henry of the No. 3rd Cav. shot through the face) wounded, and nine enlisted men and one Shoshone scout killed. The bodies were all recovered more or less mangled, except one who was so badly cut up he could not be brought away. Our company not being engaged in the close fighting and having a careful company commander had no losses. It is know for certain we killed 19 Indians. After fighting for some time we charged down the Canyon to find the village but the Gulch was so favorable for an ambush we came back. Saw the Indians five or six miles away going toward the Little Big Horn but ammunition being nearly expended and only two days rations more we gave up the pursuit.

June 20th—Camped on Goose Creek, wounded all doing well.

June 21st—Wagon train and wounded left today for Fort Fetterman. The rumor is they are bringing more troops and some artillery.

June 23rd—Lying over, Courier from Fort Fetterman with dispatch which says; eight companies of 5th Cav. at Laramie under Col. [Eugene A.] Carr coming out here. Signs of Indians today. General Terry had fight crossing the Yellowstone, about 100 killed on the two sides and about equally divided [rumor].

June 24th—On picket duty. Scouts report large village of the enemy to the north. Smoke of several large fires seen toward the north, thought to be Col. [John] Gibbons of [Fort] Ellis, Montana.

July 1st—B Co's scouts saw two of the enemy.

July 4th—Courier from Fetterman says train will not be here for 12 or 14 days yet. Orders consolidation with Terry sometime, probably after arrival of train.

July 9th—One pack mule and one horse stolen by Indians. The Infantry fired on them. [Second] Lieut. [Frederick W.] Sibley's party came in today. They were attacked by Indians some 100 miles from here and had to leave their horses. They were found by a party of hunters this morning and food and horses were sent out to them. Cornwall [Sergeant Oscar R. Cornwell], of Co. D, became insane from fright and suffering.

July 10th—We had quite a battle last night, making ten so far this summer. The Indians accomplished nothing except firing the prairie which caused us some trouble. The Indians lost one man and one pony. Today we heard of the last terrible fight of Gen. Custer.

July 11th—Went out this morning with Co's E and B and scouted through the foothills but found no Indians. Reached [site of Fort Phil] Kearney [Kearny] at 12:20.

July 12th—Marched back toward camp but the train couldn't make it so camped near a spring in the foot hills.

July 13th—Courier from Terry in, confirming the death of Custer's party, 256 men killed, 213 Shoshones came in to act as scouts.

July 14th—Grand parade of Shoshones in full war dress.

July 20th—Dispatch from Gen. Terry, contents unknown. Indians say the Little Big Horn is lined with Sioux dead from the Custer fight.

July 22nd—It is thought the enemy is on the Big Horn mountains northeast of here.

July 24th—We are now within 65 miles of a large body of the enemy, so the scouts say, but we have got to wait for ammunition and reenforcements. The story is that eight companies of the 5th Cav. accompanied by the four companies of Infantry are on the road to join us. Rumor says we leave here for a fight the 30th.

July 25th—Shoshones report large body of warriors in the mountains, two or three miles from here.

July 26th—Col. Carr expected today but has not arrived. Shoshones have all gone out to provoke a fight.

August 1st—The Indians came in from down the creek fishing and told so wild a tale that all the horses were taken in and tied to the picket line and it surely looked like a fight.

August 2nd—The fifth Cav. expected tomorrow.

August 3rd—The fifth are somewhere but no one knows where.

August 4th—Orders to start tomorrow for fifteen days with four days rations on the saddle. Storm brewing in two ways.

August 6th—Marched down Tongue River through nice bottoms and again camped on Tongue. Crossed the river seventeen times.

August 7th—Went from Tongue River over the divide to the Rosebud, 29 miles. Reached the Rosebud some thirteen or fourteen miles below the battlefield of June 17th. Sioux reported fourteen dead just above here killed in our fight or in General Custers.

August 8th—Started again this p.m. at 6 o'clock and marched down the Rosebud, 17 miles. Signs of large Indian village all the way down the creek with plenty of evidence that the party camping here were in the Custer fight.

August 10th—Still marching down the Rosebud, went past several quite fresh Indian graves and the remains of a large "shade" where a sun dance had been held. There were six buffalo heads in the ring and a war pole in the center smeared with blood. Met General Terry's command consisting of remnants of the 7th Cav. and the fifteen companies of Infantry belonging to the fifth, 18th and 22nd. Drew rations from Terry's wagon train. His train was 200 wagons and they are using seven steamers on the Yellowstone to bring up their "needfuls."

August 11th—Marched over to Tongue River. Found skeleton of white man who had been shot in the back and scalped.

These Fifth Cavalry privates gathered for this picture in October, 1876, in the Black Hills near the close of General Crook's summer campaign. They are identified as, standing, left to right, Richard Davis, John Jones, and Lewis Boone, and seated, August Schneider and Musician Frederick Sutcliffe. Sutcliffe alone remained in the army until 1902, following which he removed with his family to St. Paul, Minnesota, where he died in 1916. *Editor's collection.*

August 12th—Found out two of my friends were killed with Custer.

August 17th—Today is Indian Day. Started down river crossed and went up on table land, 11 by 8 miles. Lots of Indian Trails going East. It looks like a big squaw trail they having wounded on Trevois [travois].

August 28th—Camped at Sentinel Buttes. General Terrys train should meet us here with ten or twelve days rations.

September 5th—Party of soldiers camped on other side of the river. Couriers went in tonight. Half rations.

September 6th—First day on half rations, marched 33 miles.

September 7th—Marched 33 miles south today. Capt. Mills 3rd Cav. started with 160 men and part of the pack train for Deadwood settlement, Black Hills, to obtain rations for the command. Clothing and blankets wringing wet.

September 8th—Marched south. Issued for rations one-half coffee, one-half hard bread and horse meat.

September 9th—Rained all night. Had marched about 15 miles when news was received that Capt. Mills had had a fight, a portion of the command was hurried forward and by the time we arrived they had captured a village of 36 Tepees, 150 ponies, and best of all some 2 ½ tons of dried meat. This was a God-send. We picketed the horses and went to the village. Besides the meat the Indians had immense quantities of dried berries and plums put up in bags for transportation. We found a great many articles used in civilization among the collection. Almost every article used by the housewife and a great many things recognized as belonging to the 7th Cav. showing that these Indians had been in that fight. A few of the Indians had taken refuge in a heavily wooded ravine. From there they had killed one and wounded two of our men. (Buffalo Chips [Scout Jonathan White] killed). The Indians came on again in the evening and wounded two men of the 5th Cavalry one of whom died before morning.

September 10th—Pickets fired occasionally all night and the Indians came around this morning. The 5th Cavalry laid for them and killed nine besides wounded others. We are getting horse meat to eat using the horses that are playing out, one-half pound dried meat per day.

September 18th—Moved up past Crook City onto the Centennial grounds of Black Hills fame. Crook City, a town of about 1000, Indians bother them quite a little coming almost into town and stealing stock. Water a long way off, wood the same but plenty.

September 19th—Moved up Deadwood Creek taking the road to Custer City. Made 26 miles and at Box Elder (Mountain Meadow) met "I" company of 4th artillery with supples for us. They had come some 200 miles 7 days nearly, hearing we were starving.

September 21st—Moved south to Rapid Creek, 13 miles, stopped at Camp Crook, so named in 1875 by Col. [Richard I.] Dodges expedition. Met. Capt. Egan and detachment of Co. K, 2nd Cav. with empty wagons for our wounded, they having left supplies at Custer City for us. They had no news except the 4th Cav. is at Red Cloud and some of the 4th Art.

September 23rd—Marched to Custer City on French Creek. A large mining city partly deserted. They are houses enough for 3000 inhabitants. Another train up from Red Cloud.

September 25th—Moved up French Creek 2 miles. Rumor is that 600 Indians had been disarmed at the Agency, the rest gone on the warpath. They say our train left Fort Laramie yesterday for here. Wild Bill [James Butler Hickok] was killed some 20 days ago at Deadwood City.

September 26th—Rumor is Indians want peace. One man of "B" Co. 2nd Cav. died today in hospital.

October 1st—Went out looking for new camp on Red Cloud road. We have made 752 miles since leaving wagon train the 5th of August.

Arrived at Fort Saunders [Sanders] Nov. 5th after being out 8 months and 19 days, and in the saddle 2600 miles, a pretty fair summer campaign.

Combatting Cheyennes at Powder River and the Red Fork, 1876 (By James N. Connely, formerly of Troop K, Second U. S. Cavalry. From *Winners of the West*, July 30, 1928)

I first enlisted in 1866 in the Fourth U. S. Infantry and served three years, then in 1869 I enlisted in Troop K, Second U. S. Cavalry under Captain James Egan at Omaha, Nebraska. My first experience in Indian warfare was shortly after my enlistment in Troop K. It seems that a large war party of Sioux Indians had attacked the Pawnee Indian Agency on the Loup River in Nebraska and my troop was ordered out to capture the Sioux and defend the Pawnees. It was an intensively hot day and after riding rapidly for more than twenty miles, many of our horses were overheated and died. We did not catch any of the Sioux, but we protected the Pawnees.

From Pawnee Agency we went to Fort Laramie, Wyoming Territory, in 1872, where our chief duties were escorting a wagon train out to Laramie Peak after timber for government use at the post, a distance of forty-five miles. We generally had an escort of thirty-five men under the command of a commissioned officer. On one of these trips, [on February 9, 1874,] First Lieutenant Levi H. Robinson [Fourteenth U. S. Infantry] and Corporal John C. Coleman [Company K, Second U. S. Cavalry] took a short cut from the wood camp to the post and were ambushed by a large war party of Sioux Indians and both killed. The wagon train and escort under the charge of Sergeant Charles Dahlgreen saw many an Indian but were not attacked by them. We camped at Cottonwood Springs that night about twenty-five miles from Fort Laramie, thinking the Indians would attack us in the morning. I volunteered to ride to the fort for reinforcements and left the camp at nine o'clock at night on a good horse and had not gone far when I ran into the Indian camp, but by making a detour I managed to escape the Indians and reach the post. I returned to Cottonwood Springs that same night with reinforcements and we went out to find the bodies of Lieutenant Robinson and Corporal Coleman. There were fourteen arrows in the lieutenant's body but neither of them were badly mutilated.

During the summer of 1874 gold was discovered in the Black Hills in the Sioux Indian Reservation which was held by the Indians as sacred ground. Consequently, the Indians made strong resistance against any invasion on their ground and many prospectors and others were killed. The government took the matter up and made a treaty with the Indians for relinquishment of the Black Hills, and my Troop K and Troop I of the Second U. S. Cavalry were detailed an escort for this commission. A peace conference was held with the Indians on the White River about ten miles below the Red Cloud Agency, where about 15,000 Sioux Indians were in attendance, all mounted and most armed with repeating rifles. The young warriors were violently opposed to relinquishing any of their land and only for the great influence of Chief Spotted Tail and other chiefs, the commission and the troops would all have been massacred. The outcome of this treaty was that many of the sub-chiefs and their tribes left the reservation and went on the warpath against the whites, which ended in the Custer massacre on the banks of the Little Big Horn River in June, 1876.

During the winter of 1875 and '76 my troop and Troop I of the Second U. S. Cavalry joined the Third U. S. Cavalry under Colonel Joseph J. Reynolds at Fort Fetterman the first of December and scouted the upper Powder River around old Fort Phil Kearny and in March we found the village of Chief Crazy Horse [sic—the village was that of the Northern Cheyenne chief, Old Bear] at the mouth of Powder River. My troop and Troop I were ordered to charge the village at daylight. The Indians were taken completely by surprise. Captain James Egan led the charge with Troop

K, and Troop I was to capture the Indian ponies. Troop K, numbering about sixty men, charged down through the Indian village about a half mile long through a dense growth of cottonwood trees and rallied at a point just below the village, reformed and all of the number fours remained mounted. The Indians, thinking there was only a file of soldiers, came out of their tepees like mad hornets, most of them armed with repeating rifles, their first volley killed or wounded all of our number fours and one trumpeter. Many of the cottonwood trees had fallen down, which made an excellent protection to the men on foot, otherwise they would all have been wiped out.

Captain Egan and Troop K got high praise for the brave manner for which they charged the village and stood off the Indians until reinforcements came up. The Third Cavalry that was to bring up the line had difficulty in crossing a deep ravine. The Indians numbering over a thousand were completely routed. The location of the Indian village was in the bend of the river running against a high bluff that was covered densely by pine trees, which made an excellent hideout for the redskins. The troops burned up all of the tepees, dried meats, buffalo robes, and took about 15,000 Indian ponies, leaving the Indians without food, shelter, or means of transportation. On our return to Fort Fetterman, the buck Indians followed the troops for four days and succeeded in re-capturing many of their ponies and would have gotten them all only that the colonel [Reynolds] ordered them shot.

We arrived at Fort Laramie about May 1st and did scout duty from Fort Laramie to Deadwood City in the Black Hills during the summer of 1876 where we saw many pilgrims that had been killed by the Indians. In November, 1876, my troop was detailed as a body guard of General Crook, who was commanding an expedition against the hostile Sioux under the leadership of Chief Dull Knife on the headwaters of Tongue [Powder] River near where Fort McHenry [McKinney] now stands. This expedition was made up of the Fourth U. S. Cavalry under command of Colonel Ranald S. Mackenzie. The Indians were located and [the village was] captured [on November 25, 1876.] [In] the latter part of January, 1877 [sic—December, 1876] . . . the expedition returned to Fort Fetterman and disbanded.

These two campaigns against hostile Indians were waged in the midst of much cold weather and under the endurance of much hunger. Hardtack and bacon was the only ration and much of the time but little of that. Many of the men had their fingers and toes frozen and it was no unusual thing for horses to be frozen stiff while tied to the picket line. During the summer of 1877, I served with my troop at Omaha in the midst of the railroad riot that was causing so much destruction of property at that time. From the scene of these riots, our whole regiment of the Second Cavalry under command of Lieutenant Colonel Albert G. Brackett was ordered to take charge of Fort Custer, Montana, located on the banks of the Big Horn River, just east of the [present] city of Hardin, Montana. Was discharged from the army in the fall of 1879, taking my residence in civil life at Coulson, Montana, on the Yellowstone River near where the city of Billings now stands. . . .

Campaigning with the Seventh Infantry in 1876 (By George C. Berry, formerly of Company E, Seventh U. S. Infantry. From *Winners of the West*, September 28, 1942)

All of the Seventh Infantry was stationed in Montana in 1876—six companies at Fort Shaw, one company at Fort Benton, one company at Fort Ellis, and two companies at Camp Baker. The latter post was renamed Fort Logan later after Captain William A. Logan, who was killed at the Battle of the Big Hole in 1877 by Nez Perces under Chief Joseph. Colonel John Gibbon was in command of the regiment at this time, and early in 1876 six companies of his regiment started down the Yellowstone River. Company E left Camp Baker about the middle of March and I know that the first [day?] out we shoveled fully two feet of snow off the ground to put up our tent, which was of the common "A" type and supposed to hold four men, but we had lots of bedding as my bunkie was an old campaigner and knew what to expect. Our route at this time was across the Belt Mountains to the Missouri River, which we crossed the next day at the Edmundson Ferry, and then up the river to Fort Ellis, which was near Bozeman. At Fort Ellis our company met a wagon train that was loaded for the Crow agency, and [we] escorted it to its destination. The agency at that time was on a little creek on the south side of the Yellowstone River and quite a way back from that stream. As it seems to me now, we made at least one camp after crossing the Yellowstone before we reached the agency. (Agency then located southwest of Columbus at present site of Absarokee.) When we did get to the agency, we camped just outside of the stockade by the main gate, and as there was a large empty building that was also outside, we used it for a cookhouse. Our company was to stay at the agency until the rest of the Montana troops caught up.

Someone brought us a load of cordwood, and shortly afterwards a couple of young Crow squaws going past asked for a couple of axes and soon had the wood ready for the cook stove a lot quicker than we would have done it ourselves. We offered to pay them for the work, but they only asked for

Recruit David L. Brainard joined the army in the fall of 1876 to fight the Sioux and Cheyennes who had defeated Custer at the Little Bighorn. As a Second Cavalryman, Brainard took part in Colonel Nelson A. Miles's engagement with Chief Lame Deer's Minneconjous at Muddy Creek, Montana, in May, 1877. Later commissioned in the army, he became a noted polar explorer. *Editor's collection*

some soap which we supplied them with. While the squaws were chopping and splitting this wood, one of the agency employees went by and spoke to one of them in English and said: "Why, Em, what are you doing here?" And she replied in the same language: "We are just cutting this wood for these soldiers." This was the same woman who lived with Major Reed at Reed's Fort near where Lewistown stands. She was a French halfbreed, but the Indian predominated in her so much that anyone could be mistaken in her—that is, take her for an Indian. She afterwards sat beside me in the stockade that surrounds the buildings of the agency and interpreted a speech that Chief Iron Bull was making to the Indians there assembled for one of their dances.

This Chief Iron Bull was a big man and a sensible one, too, and was recognized by the government as chief of the Crows. He had been to Washington. His talk as Emma Shane gave it to me was along the line of taking up ranches—that is, he advised the Indians to do that, and said that he expected to locate one that summer and turn farmer, do as the white men were doing. Of course, all of these doings were inside of the stockade and were mostly for the benefit of the white men and women of the agency, as we were given to understand that the Indians engaged in this dance had been to other places and gone through the same performance. One of the things I remember quite well was the invitation by our company cooks to Iron Bull and squaw to have dinner at our cook house on a certain day. Well, about noon on the day set, he and his squaw showed up, and from somewhere she produced a table cloth and spread it on the cook house floor and both seated themselves by it and as their dinner was all ready it was served to them, but they never touched a thing until one of the cooks handed them knives and forks. Now the soldiers engaged in serving this dinner would never think of the table cloth for Indians, but these two did.

We were at the agency about two weeks as I recollect now, when one morning some of our regiment appeared and told us that the rest of the command was down on the Yellowstone, so in a day or two we struck camp and moved down to them and found that Colonel Gibbon had added the four companies of cavalry that were stationed at Fort Ellis to his command. The wagon train that we escorted to the agency had the supplies which the expedition was to use until we met the steamboats that were to meet us later, and a change in plans was the cause of our going to the agency at all, as the stuff we had stored there was moved to our new camp right away and taken down the river with us. Colonel Gibbon also engaged a number of the Crow Indians to act as scouts, and among that number was Emma Shane with several other squaws. The next time we made a camp to stay any length of time was at Fort Pease, which is nearly opposite the mouth of the Big Horn River, we of course being on the north side of the Yellowstone. This Fort Pease it seems hadn't been built very long, and was used mostly as a wolfer's camp—that is, the inhabitants had killed buffalos and other game and inoculated the carcasses with strychnine and left these bodies around on the prairie. After a time, they skinned up the wolves and other varmints that had eaten of this bait. But the Indians got so bad the winter before at this place that the men sent one or two of their number up to Fort Ellis for help, and when the troops got down there the outfit packed up and went back to civilization with them. We found, too, four or five newly made graves at this post which no doubt were made for the bodies of men killed by the Indians.

Before we got to Pease we had forded the Yellowstone on account of rough hills and country ahead of us. Now we had three pieces of artillery with us—two Gatling guns and a twelve-pounder. There was one of the boys, a young fellow of German extraction, who was just learning to talk English, who sat next to me when we had just forded the river to the south side, and as most of our men were over, the teamsters were starting to bring our artillery and the wagons across. Now a Gatling gun doesn't stand very high, and as the first one went under the water my German friend exclaimed, "Himmel, der gose the doodlesock." On another occasion, this young fellow was found asleep on the picket line, and when told that Sitting Bull might catch him that way some time, wanted to know "who that sucking Bull" was, anyway.

In fording streams like the Yellowstone, Colonel Gibbon usually sent part of the cavalry ahead and had one of the cavalrymen lead about three horses back, so that in that way we infantrymen got over dry shod. Of course, the river was low at this time of the year, but we always crossed at a good ford and I think it was mostly on account of the supplies in the wagons. As soon as we passed the hills and rough country on the north side of the river, we crossed again. Will say, too, that Colonel Gibbon on his way down the Yellowstone took along with him four companies of the Second Cavalry under Major [James S.] Brisbin that were stationed at Fort Ellis, so that his command consisted of the cavalry, six companies of the Seventh U. S. Infantry, and the Crow Indians. I don't remember where we picked up the white men scouts we had along, of whom there were several, but Muggins Taylor, George Herendeen, and Mitch Boyer are the only ones whose names I can now recall. We also had some packers along, but I will tell you of them later, and we had Matt Carroll along with some of the teams that I think still belonged to the Diamond R outfit, which at that time was the biggest freighting outfit in the then territory. This Matt Carroll is the same that the town of Carroll is named after, which town was situated on the Missouri River, the company to which he belonged at that time having built a road from Helena by way of White Sulphur Springs and the Judith Basin to the Missouri River. [First] Lieutenant [James H.] Bradley was in charge of the scouts. We also found at Fort Pease some rowboats that the men who were there the fall and winter before had left there, and it fell to the lot of the company to which I belonged to take them on down the river. We were supposed to camp with the command every night and keep them in fresh meat as game was more plentiful along the river than it was back a ways, so we took it slowly in the morning and I don't recall but one night that we camped away from the main outfit.

Our next permanent camp was on the north side of the river, and as near as I can say now was above the Rosebud, which comes in from the south. One thing that I do remember, though, was that on the last of May or the first of June it snowed all day, but it was a soft wet snow that melted as fast as it fell. But one of the boys had a letter from Camp Baker shortly after this and the writer stated that some of the boys went sleighing at that place in two feet of snow. This was the camp, too, that our scouts [traveled from and] found the big camp of Indians on the Little Big Horn River that afterwards did up the Custer command. It was the camp, too, where a hunting party was killed by the Indians. It was made up of two soldiers of the Second Cavalry and one civilian, and if I remember rightly, the latter was one of the teamsters of the Diamond R. Anyhow, it was in the morning and I have an idea that the Indians were laying for our herd, but this hunting party walked into them. Our camp herd at that time contained most of the cavalry horses and all of the freight mules, besides quite a number of others, and would have made quite a haul for the hostiles if they could have gotten them across the river. But I have serious doubt of that, as Colonel Gibbon tried that when the scouts first found their camp, but the American horses of the cavalry drowned too easily.

It was shortly after this that the steamboat *Far West* put in an appearance, and so did General Terry and the Seventh Cavalry, but the latter regiment was below us and on the south side of the Yellowstone, so we didn't get to see them until after the battle. Things moved pretty fast from this on. General Terry, Colonel Gibbon, and Colonel Custer met and formed a plan of battle, but I do know that we gave at least five of our scouts to Custer and they were George Herendeen, Mitch Boyer, Curley, Half Yellow Face, and Fighting Lion. This last Indian is not mentioned in any of the histories I have read of this battle, at least not by that name, but I speak of him as I knew him for the further reason that he was wounded in the charge down the river with Major Marcus A. Reno. Our command went back up the river to the mouth of the Big Horn, and General Terry accompanied us. He was a brigadier general at this time, and in command of the Department of Dakota, which at that time included Minnesota, Dakota, Wyoming, and Montana. We camped on the north side of the Yellowstone if I remember right, the first night, and it was the next morning that I saw our packers at work for the first time, as we were to change and use a pack outfit from here up the Big Horn River. The mules used were the same ones that had so far hauled our wagons, and as most of them had never had a pack on, most anyone can imagine what a time the packers had. It was fun for everyone but the packers and, of course, the mules, but Jack Bean, who was head packer, understood his business and made a better job of breaking these mules to pack than seemed possible. One of the infantry companies was left in charge of our camp on the Yellowstone, as all of the wagons, harness, and a good deal of camp equipment was left behind, but I don't remember now which company it was.

After we got ready and the mules had quit trying to buck their packs off, the steamer *Far West* ferried us across the Yellowstone, as all the streams in this part of the country were very high by now. On the way up the Big Horn River we suddenly came across our Crow Indian scouts, and they told us that they had just been talking to Curley, who appeared to them on the west back of the Big Horn, and they, with our outfit, were on the east. Of course, their talk was by the sign language and he advised them not to go on as Custer and his men were all killed, and the hostiles were without number. This was the last we saw of our Indian scouts for a couple of weeks or more, excepting two that we found with Reno's men, and I will tell more of them later. This was in the forenoon of June 26, and about noon, or a little later, we forded the Little Horn, and I want to tell you the water was cold and nearly up to our necks although a good many of the soldiers thought it was close to one hundred in the shade that day.

It was during this afternoon that the command reached some high ground and saw some smoke ahead on the Little [Big] Horn River, one of whom, as I remember, was Lieutenant Woodruff, who shouted, "I think Custer has got them and the smoke we see is where he is trying to smoke some of them out." We, of course, did not believe what Curley had told the other Crows from across the Big Horn that morning, but we did know that we were nearing the camp of the hostiles, as members of the cavalry were sent out to the flanks of the outfit mostly on the higher hills, as the command kept right up the river bottom, it being easier walking for the infantry. These cavalrymen were instructed to ride in a circle whenever they saw anything suspicious, and, too, I noticed they took to the highest ground that they could find in order, I suppose, to see over the country better. Some of the hostile Indians were pretty late in leaving their camp, as our flankers soon began to ride in circles, but it was getting late in the evening and we did not know what was ahead of us, so we camped just before dark. The infantry camped in form of a hollow square, and nobody took any clothes off. Each man slept with his rifle beside him, and each one had a belt full of cartridges. This was on the 26th of June, and I had served just four years, leaving me one more year of a five-year enlistment and, of course, I remembered this date.

Our officers knew by this time that something had gone wrong, as according to the talk among the soldiers this was the date we were to have met Custer and all hands were to tackle the Indian village together, but Custer, it seems, had ideas of his own on that matter, and I don't believe that he thought that enough Indians could be brought together to whip his regiment—that is with himself in command. We soldiers thought that Custer could not be beaten. I thought, too, that the officers of our regiment were disappointed in the turn affairs had taken, as they were a fighting bunch and most of them had risen from the ranks during the War of the Rebellion, especially the captains.

We were astir at daylight next morning and after breakfast started on our way up the river. Very soon after we started we came in sight of the Custer command on a side hill to our left as we went up the river—every man laying where he fell, and as this is the only sight I had of this battleground, I won't say much about it, only that it was three-fourths of a mile off our road and no one went to it as I remember now. Another thing that I remember was that stragglers from the hostile camp had disappeared altogether. We next went through the Indian campground, and it surely looked as though they left in a hurry, and lots of their camp equipage was left behind. I saw lodge poles, buffalo robes, pots and pans galore, and in one place I saw a stack of new milk pans which no doubt had been taken from some settler, as gold had been found in the Black Hills and a rush in there had been started a year or so before '76. One of the last things we passed in the village was two complete tepees, covers on and all which I was told afterward contained the bodies of seven Indians who had been killed in the battle, and their favorite ponies had been slain and were laying on the outside of these tepees. These Indians we were told were petty chiefs. After passing the Indian camp we soon came to the ground that Major Reno and his command fought over, and wherever we saw a batch of feathered arrows sticking up, we knew that there the body of a trooper lay, especially those who had life in them after they had fallen, and were told that this was work of squaws and young bucks that weren't old enough to go on the firing line.

We did not see anyone that we knew at this time, as decomposition had already set in; the weather, too, had been very warm. A first lieutenant named Donald McIntosh was lying on his face directly in our line of march, and he had on a buckskin shirt with his name written or printed on it. A captain of our command who was on horseback was riding near me when we passed this body, and said that he knew McIntosh in life, and that the lieutenant was a part Delaware [sic—Mohawk] Indian himself. The captain who made these remarks was killed a year or so later at the Battle of the Big Hole by the Nez Perce Indians, and the name of Camp Baker was changed to Fort Logan in his honor. As soon as we got in sight of Reno's camp on the hills where he retreated and intrenched his command, we camped as usual about as near to them as we could get. It happened that on this particular day our company was in the lead, and on account of the bluffs and timber we were out of sight of his camp until we came just opposite to it, it being on the other side of the river. A man we called Reddy Stevenson [Thomas W. Stevenson, Company G, Seventh Cavalry], whose time had expired the fall before this expedition, and who was not a good walker, had gone East and reenlisted for the cavalry, and for this trip he was assigned to that regiment. We had hardly begun our camp preparations before five or six of the men on the hill came down to our camp, and among them was Reddy. They told us how glad they were to find that we were not Indians, as they at first thought, owing to the dust we kicked up on our line of march, and too, they asked if we knew what had become of Custer and his command. After we told them of the men we had seen lying to our left, and told them also about Curley's going down the Big Horn River and the talk he made to the other Crows across that river, they came to the conclusion that it was Custer's command, and that Curley the Crow scout was right and so far as learned he was the only one to escape. One of the men then turned loose on Custer and seemed to blame him for the outcome of the battle, but none of the men I heard speak of the matter had anything but praise for Captain Frederick W. Benteen, who, according to their story, managed things after they got together on the hills.

General Terry had, so I was told, an investigation of that battle shortly after we got there, but as we did not hear anything more of the matter, [we concluded that he?] came to the conclusion that everyone had done their best and that there were too many Indians for Custer's outfit. The first chore we did that morning was to bury the dead and haul off the horses that lay on the ground where we were camped, as we were camped on the ground that Reno fought over. Part of the cavalry went to bury the Custer men and part of them followed the Indian trail that leads away from the battle ground. The Indians, according to these men's story, went west, then south, then east, and kept breaking up into small parties so that no one could follow. They said, too, that a good many bloody rags were scattered over their trail. I next found the Crow scouts that Colonel Gibbon had loaned to Custer, that is, those that fought with Reno. I found Half Yellow Face and Fighting Lion both together in a sort of tepee. Lion was trying to string some beads with one hand, as he had been wounded in the other arm and was putting the beads on his sore arm, while Half Yellow Face was outside of the tepee rounding up some ponies that he had captured.

George Herendeen, whom I met later, had a plan of battle of his own which I thought visionary, since his idea was to capture Indian ponies first and then go after the camp, but as there were more Indians than the troops could handle, anyway, it seemed to me that the plan followed was the best. I asked him how many ponies he thought there were, and he said about 10,000. I also asked him what was the cause of the Indians pulling out in so much of a hurry when they found our command so close, and he said he thought they were out of ammunition. As I remember now, all of the camp equipage left by the Indians was piled together and burned, at least we were told so, and none of it was in sight when we passed that way on our road out with Reno's wounded, of which he had about fifty. Our first attempt at this chore was by hand litter. These litters were made of green quaking aspen poles, with the hide of the wounded horses that had to be killed, cut in strips and wound around these poles so as to carry a man. Now the weather was pretty warm and clear, and it was planned to pack out the wounded only after sundown. Two men were supposed to carry one wounded man, and the infantry were assigned to this job. My partner said he weighed 125 pounds and I didn't weigh much more at that time.

We were given to carry the first night a man who said that when he was well he weighed 185 pounds. He was badly wounded, too, as he was shot in the small of the back and didn't want to be put on the ground any oftener than could be avoided, but we had to set him down pretty often in order to rest, as there was no road, and after dark we kept tripping over weeds and sagebrush. Pretty soon the cavalry were dismounted and told to help with the litter, four carrying and four resting. Even then we made but three miles the first night. However, a change was made the next day, while we were lying in camp, and mules and horses were used instead of men to carry the litters—that is, one horse or mule was put in front and one behind, and in that way the outfit moved more rapidly; in fact, we made about seventeen miles that night, and reached the steamboat which Captain [Grant] Marsh had run up the Big Horn River somewhere near where the Little Horn runs into that stream. It was between two and three o'clock in the morning when we arrived at the steamboat, and was daylight shortly after that, and if my memory serves me right the boat pulled out as soon as it got good daylight for Fort Abraham Lincoln, Dakota, which was at that time the headquarters of the Seventh Cavalry.

I nearly forgot to mention that one of the men who came down off the hill with Reddy Stephenson the morning we camped on Reno's battleground had two bullet marks on one side of his face and one on the other. That is, that the bullets had gone close to his head to plow marks as described. That, I thought, was one fellow that had luck. Many of the soldiers that came down from the hill were without shoes, some using gunnysacks to cover their feet. Their clothes were torn. They had been a long time on the march. They were a sorry looking lot.

Memories of the Little Bighorn, 1876 (By Jacob Hetler, formerly of Troop D, Seventh U. S. Cavalry. From *Winners of the West*, November 30, 1935)

I enlisted in Chicago after the big fire, on February 30, 1872. I was immediately transferred to Jefferson Barracks, St. Louis. Later I was transferred to D Company [Seventh U. S. Cavalry,] at Chester, South Carolina, where our duties were gathering up Ku Klux Klan and destroying illicit distilleries. We then moved to Opalica, Alabama, where we remained until September. I was then transferred to Montgomery, Alabama, to put down an election disturbance. We were there six weeks before returning to Opalica. We then moved to Memphis, and from there up the river to Cairo, Illinois, and by rail to Fort Snelling, Minnesota. In June [1873] we were sent to the end of the Northern Pacific Railroad, which was at Breckenridge, by rail.

We marched seventy miles to Fargo, North Dakota (then called the Dakota Territory) and a week later marched thirty miles to Fort Assinniboine [sic—Abercrombie?] and on to Fort Pemberton [Pembina], which was seventy miles further. We landed there the 25th of June for the purpose of guarding the government surveyors against unfriendly Indians. Our territory was a large one, running from the Lake of the Woods to Chief Mountain Lake, a distance of 500 miles. We spent two winters here with headquarters at Fort Totten. I was then sent to Fort Abraham Lincoln and remained there the years of '75 and '76, and it was in June [May] of the latter year that we started the Sioux Campaign which ended so tragically for Colonel Custer and his men.

On the morning of June 22nd, 1876, we started a hurried march toward the Little Bighorn. We had nothing but a pack train and our most valuable bit of equipment was four demijohns of whiskey, which was taken along for officers only—although I did get a little of it while I was in a hospital tent. On the evening of that day we made camp off the banks of the Yellowstone, and the following morning we began a forced march with a pack [train] and one piece of field artillery, a small cannon known as [a] Rodman gun [Gatling gun]. We carried this until we came to a chain of bluffs where we had to take it apart and carry it through in pieces. Colonel Custer thought this took too much valuable time and it was his order which left the cannon behind, an order which many believe may have cost him his life, for if we had taken the cannon with us, we might have held the Indians at bay and saved Custer the last march which led to his death.

On this march we slept in our saddles and ate one meal. We arrived at the Little Bighorn on June 25, 1876, at 11:00 a.m. When we arrived [with Captain Benteen's battalion], Major Reno had already had an engagement with the Indians and had been repulsed on the bluffs, and [we were] just in time to save six men who had been cut off from their detachment during the melee. We gave the tired, thirsty soldiers water from our canteens—the first they had had in hours. I saw six videttes (signal men) stationed on a bluff, and next I saw Custer and a group of men going out of sight over the hills. This was the last time I ever saw my leader alive. For an hour and a half after that, Captain Thomas B. Weir of my company asked Major Reno for permission to go after Custer, and this was granted. We had heard firing and knew there was trouble and we hoped to arrive in time to aid Custer, but as the world knows now, we were too late. We were badly outnumbered when we finally came in sight of the scene of the massacre, and were fortunate to find a way to retreat back to the main company [command]. Only one man was lost on that march. Three of us were sent out for water, and as we got to the top of the ridge two of us were shot by Indians from ambush. I was sent to the hospital tent for medical aid.

The next morning, June 26th, while I was out getting fresh air, I heard a sergeant yell for more men, and I grabbed a gun and ran toward the ridge where he was stationed. But no sooner had I reached his side than I was again shot in the back. Until noon, the Indians tried to break in on us from three different points of attack. We held them until 4 o'clock in the afternoon when

Artist A. R. Waud's depiction of Custer's last stand at the Battle of the Little Bighorn, 1876. The event came to symbolize the Indian wars for most Americans. *Editor's collection*

General Terry and his forces loomed up on the horizon and the Indians retreated in short order. We were hours without water, and kept bits of stone and gravel in our mouths to keep from getting thirsty. When we finally reached water on the eve of the 27th [26th], we had been two full days without water. On June 28th there was a quiet but dramatic interlude when we buried Colonel Custer and piled brush over his slain soldiers, weighting it down with dirt. Sadly and quietly we marched back to Fort Benton [Buford?] on the

Missouri River, where many of the warring Sioux [eventually] came and gave up their ponies and guns. We herded 2,500 ponies up [down] the river to Fort Abraham Lincoln. When our company marched back to Fort Rice, I received an honorable discharge.

Some Thoughts about the Battle of the Little Bighorn (By Theodore W. Goldin, formerly of Troop G, Seventh U. S. Cavalry. From *Winners of the West*, August, 1924)

By way of introduction, I will say that I was a member of Troop G, Seventh Cavalry, in 1876, and took part in the fight at the Little Bighorn on June 25th and 26th, and later was awarded the Congressional Medal of Honor for the small part I played in that great tragedy. Prior to the start of the expedition, I was on extra duty as clerk at regimental headquarters and on the campaign served as one of the headquarters orderlies, leaving Custer's column probably a little over an hour before he was hemmed in on the bluffs and massacred. This statement will possibly serve to connect me with that fatal engagement.

It is not my purpose to write anew the story of that day, but rather to state a few facts . . . [about the battle.] A few words as to Curley. Curley the Crow *was* with Lt. Colonel Custer when I left the column; he [was] with Mitch Boyer and several other Crows, only one of whom is living today and whom I saw on a visit to the battlefield on the forty-eighth anniversary in June last [1924]. I also saw Curley after the fight and heard his story, in fact several of them. There has always been a doubt in the minds of officers and men who were in the battle as to just when Curley left Custer. However, in no statement ever made by Curley did he claim to have covered himself with a Sioux blanket and lain down on the field as if dead. Dozens of imaginative reporters from time to time have written of Curley, evidently allowing their imagination full rein regardless of facts. . . . Curley did say that he made use of a Sioux blanket to disguise himself and aid him in making his escape. He told in his original story things that happened after Custer was driven to the ridge where he fell, that were after corroborated by Gall and other leaders of the hostiles, but I believe the later and more general impression is that he saw the most of that final struggle while hiding in the immediate vicinity of the ridge awaiting an opportunity to complete his escape, yet near enough to easily see the things he told. So much for Curley.

The horse "Comanche" was a claybank gelding about twelve years old at the time of the fight. He was a troop horse belonging to Troop I, and for several years had been ridden by Captain Myles W. Keogh of that troop. When found he had been wounded in *six* or *seven* places (there has always been a doubt as to one wound as to whether it was a separate wound, or whether caused by a bullet passing entirely through his neck. The wounds were plainly visible at the time and the scars were later found by Professor Lewis L. Dyche of the University of Kanas, who later mounted the skeleton). Practically all the wounds were flesh wounds.

"Comanche" was ridden many times after his recovery. Brigadier General (then Captain) Edward S. Godfrey of the Seventh, in an article published in the *Century Magazine* in 1891, says: "After his restoration he was in great demand for a ladies' riding horse. The rivalry among the young ladies of the garrison at Fort Lincoln as to whom should be awarded the privilege of riding him on several occasions when riding parties went out from the post caused some heart burnings."

The colonel [Samuel D. Sturgis], to solve the vexatious problem, ordered that "Comanche" be retired from active service and be no longer ridden; that when the troop was paraded he should be led with the troop. This is further corroborated by Colonel Ezra B. Fuller (retired), formerly of the Seventh, in a letter to the curator of the Kansas University Museum, where the mounted remains have been for many years. I have frequently seen the horse in parades of the troop, *always fully equipped with bridle and saddle* and draped in mourning. Colonel Fuller says this continued as long as he remained with the regiment.

Now just a few words with reference to the disposition of troops on the 25th. About two in the morning the regiment crossed the divide between the Rosebud and the Little Bighorn, halted for some time, then advanced several miles to a point afterward ascertained to be about fifteen miles from where the Indian village was afterward located, where another halt was made to cook coffee, but the water was so strongly alkaline we could not drink the stuff.

It was at this point that Colonel Custer divided his command into really four columns. Benteen, with three troops—D, H, and K—, was ordered to proceed to the left or southwest, attacking anything he might run across. Major Reno, with Troops A, G, and M, was ordered to follow the Indian trail which here led down the valley of a small creek, with orders to attack the village if found; Captain Thomas B. McDougall with B was to act as rear guard and escort to the pack train which was in the charge of Lieutenant

Edward G. Mathey while Custer retained under his immediate command the remaining five troops—C, E, F, I, and L. These orders were carried out as given. Custer's column following in the same general direction as Reno's for some distance, in fact until within about two miles of the river when he turned sharply to the right or northwest, passing down a canon a short distance in rear of the bluffs bordering the river. Custer himself soon after this change of direction, left the column and rode to the top of the bluffs, where he was seen by Reno's men who were just engaging the Indians. Custer's column continued on down the canon a distance of some three or four miles, finally entering the valley some distance from the lower end of the village, from which point he was soon driven back to the ridge where the final struggle took place.

Reno, finding his position untenable, owing to the large force of Indians attacking him and failing to receive the support he had been led to expect, retreated across the river to the high bluffs, losing three officers and a number of men in effecting this retreat. Here he was soon joined by Benteen's column and a short time later by McDougall and the ammunition train. Soon after this, Captain Weir with D Troop, supported by the rest of the command, sought to find Custer, but by that time the Indians had finished him up and began to mass back on Reno, nearly cutting Weir off. Reno fell back some little distance, finally making his stand and continuing the fight until late in the afternoon of the 26th, when the Indians withdrew on the approach of General Terry's column.

These, in brief, are the facts, shown by official records. I give them only in the interest of accuracy, as somewhere there may be some of the old bunch who "rode the trail" in those exciting days, who, like myself, are interested in seeing only the real facts in print.

With the Water Carriers at the Little Bighorn (By William D. Nugent, formerly of Troop A, Seventh U. S. Cavalry. From *Winners of the West,* June 24, 1926)

Two days without water, the sun almost blistering hot and the ground like an oven. The wounded tortured with severe pain, their tongues in many cases swelled until it was impossible to close their mouths. Water, water, was the agonizing cry of all the sufferers.

On June 26, 1876, near 4 p.m., permission was given to go for water. To get to the river we had to cross a place that was open and would give the Indians the best chance in the world to shoot us. Very few cared to commit suicide by crossing over at that time. When I reached safety in a gulch leading to the river, I found four others, George W. Hammon of Troop F, and John T. Easley, Samuel Johnson, Howard H. Weaver, and myself of Troop A, Seventh U. S. Cavalry. Between ourselves and the river were many crooks and gulches opening into the one we had to follow to reach the river. Our expectations were to find Indians concealed in such places, but happily for us our expectations did not materialize, and we reached the river safely.

We paused before stepping out on the bank to take a general observation of the lay of things. On the other side of the river were between fifty and one hundred mounted Indian bucks awaiting our appearance on the bank. They were nearly 500 yards from the river but looked much less. We laid aside our guns, prepared ourselves for the rush for water by uncorking our canteens and shortening our hold on the straps, that all might be submerged at the same time. For some time I knew nothing of the others as I fell into the water and drank until suffocation broke my hold on that river. I guess my comrades were occupied in like manner. After resting and gaining sufficient breath, I would return to my interrupted drinking. In lowering my head to continue, I received a rap on my head accompanied by a deluge of water. I carefully examined my belfry and found out I was not dead, had not suffered the loss of any blood, and was not even shot by a bullet, and was sure glad that I was mistaken.

We returned to the place where we had left our guns and took a few shots at the Indians, but were deceived in the distance and did not hit any of the redskins. We made more trips to the river by turns, and our most useful vessel for carrying water was our camp kettle, until a playful Indian put a bullet through it. We raised our sights to 500 yards and once more turned loose on the Indians. This time our shooting was effective and the Indians started on the run. I had a real grouch against them, and when I saw one cut away from the rest, and he would have to ride about a thousand yards before he could get out of range, I made that Indian do some tall riding. Every time a chunk of lead passed him, he wig-wagged a signal back that he disliked such close shooting. Before he went over the hill, I had sent about a dozen shots after him, and I felt that I was at least even with one Indian for the grief they had dealt me at various times.

We filled our canteens, returned to the barricade on the bluffs, and the water was then given to the wounded. Never was there four braver or more loyal comrades than those who were with me. Hammon I never met with again. He had a brother in Troop L of the Seventh who was killed with Custer on the hill. [This was Private John E. Hammon of Troop G. He was not killed in the battle.] I was informed Hammon failed to identify his body as so many were badly mutilated that identification was impossible. Easley in his deportment was a perfect gentleman. Johnson was a man as near without fear as any man I have ever known. He proved it at different times, and was given the nickname of Swede. Howard Weaver was our historian and encyclopedian, and all disputes and arguments were referred to him for a decision. He was the only one of my comrades whose given name was known by me. Sure his was a heart of gold. I will never forget these four true blue comrades of mine, and will always remember them as heroes. The world may never know them, there will be no medals or citations, but in the heart of one old comrade their names will always occupy the front seat. . . .

Fought with Reno on the Bluffs (By Henry M. Brinkerhoff, formerly of Troop G, Seventh U. S. Cavalry. From *The Veteran*, June, 1926)

I was a participator of that engagement with Major Marcus A. Reno from the first shot until the last. . . . I'm the first man to know that Custer and his command was wiped out, as I encountered some of the Custer dead on my way to General Terry, and I found the horse old Comanche that Captain Myles Keogh rode in the fight where I crossed the Little Bighorn River, the only survivor of the Custer portion [except for the Indians].

On the afternoon of the 25th of June, '76, after we got up on the hill, Reno asked me to serve as his personal orderly, as his adjutant, orderly, and bugler had been killed. I stayed near him all the time and delivered all his orders to the troop commanders until the afternoon of June 26th, when Second Lieutenant George D. Wallace, of G Troop of the Seventh, was appointed adjutant by Reno. . . .

Mutilation of Custer's Dead (By William D. Nugent, formerly of Troop A, Seventh U. S. Cavalry. From *Winners of the West*, February 28, 1927)

In a recent issue . . . I see mention made of a headless body being dug up in some excavation, supposed to be one of Major Reno's men, but one of the unknown dead. I believe that I can give some information on this subject.

One of Company A was killed and beheaded in the bottoms. Later his headless body was buried near where he fell. Afterwards the head was found at the opposite end of the Indian village on a pole where one of their dances had been held on the night of the 25th. The name of this soldier was Armstrong—John, I think, Company A, Seventh U. S. Cavalry, and can easily be verified.

I also see in another statement that there was very little, if any, mutilation of the dead of Custer's men. It would be very difficult to convince one of the burial details that there could have been more mutilation perpetrated. Unfortunately, I was one of that number and will give the names of a detail, and if any of that number are living, I feel assured they will corroborate my statements. Sergeant Samuel Alcott, and four privates: Samuel Johnson, David W. Harris, Charles Aller, and William Nugent, all of Company A, composed one of the details. All of the bodies we heaped mounds of earth over were mutilated more or less, mostly more. Will give a description of the first we buried: first he was scalped; the skull was bare to the ears, the crown of the head chopped out, his cap put into the cavity. The body was nude between the waist and throat. There were twelve or fifteen places where no doubt a spear or knife had been thrust to the hollow. Blunt arrows were driven in and left in the wounds.

I saw others cut and maimed in ways that I would not care to name in private, much less in print. I see no good reason for smoothing the horrible details of the deeds of the bloodthirsty savages that the boys of the old Indian wars had to meet in the most unequal manner that soldiers ever had to meet in this country or any other.

News of the Custer Battle Reaches Fort Randall, Dakota (By John E. Cox, formerly of Company K, First U. S. Infantry. From *Winners of the West*, November 30, 1926)

On the 5th of July, 1876, four or five soldiers drove from Fort Randall, Dakota Territory, a distance of forty-five miles to Springfield, D. T. After caring for our team at a livery stable, we went to a hotel and registered. After a square meal, I walked up the street. As I was passing a small shack, I was startled by hearing a man's voice within the shack crying, "Come in here, Sergeant, quick." I sprang through the open door and found myself in a telegraph office. The lone operator evidently was greatly agitated. "Can you write fast?" was his query. I sat down at a table and grasped a pencil and a sheet of paper. "I will read and you write," he whispered hoarsely.

The dispatch was dated at Cheyenne, Wyoming, and stated that a messenger had brought the news of the battle ten days before, and that Custer and his command were wiped out. I got that far, dropped my pencil, and dashed from the telegraph office, ran to the hotel and hunted my comrades. After a moment's conference, we were agreed that we must get back to Randall as quickly as possible for two reasons. First, when we left the fort the telegraph wire was not in order, and the command there should know the news just as quickly as possible. Second, we feared if they did hear of it they might start at once for the fighting locality and leave us behind. As soon as our ponies could travel we started and made the best speed possible, reaching the fort up in the morning. We found a dispatch had gotten through and two or three companies were packing up to start for the fighting zone, my company being one of them. From that time until discharged next year, we were campaigning. . . .

The Skirmish at Warbonnet Creek, 1876 (By Chris Madsen, formerly of Troop A, Fifth U. S. Cavalry, and who decades later helped locate the site of the Warbonnet, or Hat, Creek action. From *Winners of the West*, November 30, 1934, and December 30, 1934)

Recently two monuments were unveiled at Montrose, Nebraska, where on July 17, 1876, seven troops of the Fifth United States Cavalry, commanded by Colonel Wesley Merritt, one of Sheridan's famous cavalry leaders during the Civil War, defeated and drove back on their reservations, 800 Sioux and Cheyenne warriors who were on their way to join Sitting Bull and other hostiles in the field, and where William F. Cody ("Buffalo Bill"), in single combat, killed the Indian subchief, Yellow Hand (or Hair), and secured the first scalp for Custer, who less than a month before had met his death at the hands of the Sitting Bull Indians on the banks of the Little Bighorn, Montana.

One of the monuments is erected as a token of gratitude for the swift and successful work of the officers and men of the regiment in stopping a raid, which, if it had been carried out as intended, would have caused the death of hundreds of peaceful citizens and the destruction of the improvements which they had labored so hard to erect for themselves and their families, who had no protection for life and property, except that rendered by the roaming squadrons of cavalry that were patrolling the outskirts of civilization by day and night—summer and winter—regardless of heat or cold.

The other monument is dedicated to one of the most famous frontier scouts and Indian fighters who had at various times served as chief of scouts for the Fifth Cavalry, but on the way to waylay the Indians, led the command to a place where it was known the Indians would attempt to cross Hat Creek, about six miles south of the Dakota line, and about twenty miles south from the Black Hills, where a natural place for concealment enabled the command to keep out of sight until such time as the troops be unmasked, much to the surprise and sorrow for the Indian marauders. . . .

[By way of background,] the discovery of gold in the Black Hills caused an influx of adventurers into the northwestern territories where the Indian agencies were located. The Indians objected, and when their protests met with scant attention they took to the warpath, and one squad after another left their reservations and joined Sitting Bull, the acknowledged leader of the hostiles. The young bucks, always thirsting for blood, swept over the sparsely settled country, killing and ravaging friend and foe alike. Brigadier General Crook, commanding the Department of the Platte, and Brigadier General Alfred H. Terry, commanding the Department of Dakota, with all the available forces under their commands, were in the field early in the spring (1876), but met with little success in subduing the hostiles.

On June 4, the Fifth Cavalry received orders to proceed without delay to the war zone. Special trains were provided for the troops and the tracks cleared for those trains. On June 7, eight troops of the regiment unloaded at Cheyenne, Wyoming [Territory], and as soon as provided with transportation for their equipment and feed for the animals, the troops started for the country used by the Indians as a highway for their travel between the agencies and the hostiles in the field.

At Cheyenne, William F. Cody ("Buffalo Bill"), who had been appointed chief of scouts for the regiment, reported for duty. At the urgent request of Lieutenant General Philip H. Sheridan, he had canceled his theatrical engagements in the East, where he had been playing to full houses. It was told that when he received Sheridan's request to join the army, he was dressed to go on the stage, but that instead of entering the play he stepped to the front of the platform and announced that he was through playing war and was going to where real war was going on. The announcement at first was taken as part of the play, but when backed up by the manager of the theater, Cody received an ovation from the audience such as had never been accorded him before. . . . When Cody arrived in Cheyenne he was dressed in his theatrical toggery, which he had not taken time to change, and in the velvet suit studded with silver and gilt buttons he looked more like a Spanish toreador than like a frontier scout.

During the latter part of June and up to July 12, the regiment was engaged in patrolling the borders of the Indians reservations at Red Cloud and Spotted Tail agencies. A few skirmishes of no great importance took place when the Indians either returned to get more rations or when they were trying to leave to join their hostile brothers in the field. In other parts of the war zone things, however, happened which made the War Department take notice. Crook met Crazy Horse and his band of Indians on the Rosebud, but was outnumbered, outmaneuvered, and outfought, and was forced to retreat to his wagon camp at the head of the Tongue River to reorganize his forces and wait for reinforcements. Custer, with five troops of the Seventh Cavalry, had been slaughtered by Sitting Bull's people on the slopes of the Little Bighorn River, June 25, a week after Crook's defeat on the Rosebud, and only for the timely arrival of General Terry, with his part of the command, the other seven troops of the regiment would have met a like fate.

On July 12, orders were received for the Fifth Cavalry to proceed by forced marches to the relief of Crook, who was still encamped on the Tongue River, more than 500 miles away. On the 14th, the command reached Rawhide Creek, twenty miles from Fort Laramie, where a courier from Fort [Camp] Robinson arrived with a dispatch from the commanding officer at Fort Robinson, notifying Merritt that as soon as the troops had left the reservation the Indians had commenced to prepare for a dash to the war zone. Merritt sent the fire-eating paymaster, Major Thaddeus H. Stanton, who had thrown his money bags away and joined the command as a volunteer scout, to ascertain the correct situation. He returned at noon on the 15th and reported that the Indians were all preparing to leave on the 15th. What should Merritt do? If he proceeded on his way as ordered and left the Indians to join the hostiles in the field, and on their way kill and ravish the few scattered homesteaders and the wayfarers, he would probably be court martialed. If he disobeyed the orders to join Crook without delay and did not succeed in stopping the Indians, he would be subjected either to severe censure or court martial. What should Merritt do?

If Merritt hesitated one minute, not even his closest advisors knew it. Hardly had he received the news when "Boots and Saddles" sounded and the men were in the saddle taking the trail back to where it was supposed the Indians would attempt to cross Hat Creek, about six miles south of the Dakota line. To reach that place unobserved by the Indians, the troops would have to march eighty-five miles while the Indians were making twenty-five. However, at 8 o'clock on the evening of the sixteenth the command reached the spot where a natural place in the creek bottom and behind two large

William F. ("Buffalo Bill") Cody scouted for the army in 1876, and during the engagement at Warbonnet Creek, Nebraska, fought and killed a young Cheyenne warrior, Yellow Hair. *Courtesy of Little Bighorn Battlefield National Monument*

buttes completely concealed them from the Indians until they would be too close to avoid an encounter.

The night was dark as night could be. No fires were allowed in camp, and no trumpet calls were sounded. Having been assigned to duty as signal man, I was sent to the top of the nearby butte with my flag and torch in order that the observation by the pickets posted at the front could be quickly communicated to headquarters. During the night nothing happened, but about daybreak Cody came in from the direction where it was supposed the Indians were encamped. He came directly to my post and told me to notify the command that he had been close enough to the Indian camp to see them preparing to move. However, he hastened to camp, and before the signal man in camp had time to make the report he was at Merritt's headquarters and made his report personally. In a few minutes the camp was alive and the horses saddled. The men were not feasted neither at supper time nor in the morning, for our provision wagons were miles behind.

As soon as the troops were ready, the orders were given to move to a point below the buttes where they would be completely concealed from any parties coming from the direction where the Indians were reported to be. Merritt and his staff soon arrived at the butte just below my station. What they said I could not hear, but from their movements I knew they were watching for the Indians to appear. Several of the company officers were nearly ready to carry out such orders as the chief would issue. Cody was near Merritt, and as some few Indians appeared about a mile to the southeast the troopers were quietly ordered to remain in the saddles with carbines loaded and ready for action.

The peculiar action of the few Indians who were coming down a ravine, where they could be seen plainly at times by the officers and pickets, seemed to puzzle Merritt until two couriers were seen coming across the prairie toward the place where the command had been camped during the night. The stage coach for the Black Hills, or some other covered conveyance, was also moving along on the road, and it soon became plain that the Indians were unaware of the presence of the soldiers but were bent on making a raid on the unsuspecting travelers. What Merritt told Cody I could not hear, but just as the Indians were near the mouth of the ravine Cody and a small party of scouts and soldiers dashed away to cut them off. Cody was some distance ahead of the other members of the party, and at the same time the Indians emerged from the ravine and were coming out in the open [where] Cody came face to face with them.

The reports and stories about the Indian chief and Cody challenging one another to single combat may be good stuff for dime novels, but did not happen. There was no time for talk on an occasion of this kind, where victory or death depended on who could pull the trigger first, and the two first shots fired by Cody and the Indian sounded as if only one gun had been fired. Cody's bullet had gone through the Indian's leg and killed his horse, a small pinto pony. Cody's horse had stepped into a prairie dog hole and stumbled, and Cody was either thrown from the horse or jumped away from the animal when it fell. Cody then took deliberate aim and the Indian's spirit was started on its way to the happy hunting grounds. Two shots fired by the Indian did no harm, and the battle was over before the scouts or soldiers had time to draw their guns. Several times afterward when I met Cody, he would discuss the affair with me, and when we did not agree on particulars would always acknowledge that at the time he was rather too busy to notice the details, while I, an observer out of harm's way, had time and leisure to take in the show.

As soon as the others recovered from their surprise, a general fusillade started, but as the seven troops came charging around the butte the Indians turned about and did not even look back. Eight hundred bold warriors, who were supported by a still larger party that never reached the front, found that a peaceful life on the reservation, where Uncle Sam supported them with plenty of rations, was, after all, a better place to spend their time in idleness than a life in the wilds where they would have to hunt for their food. As soon as the Indians fled, Cody went to the fallen warrior and removed his scalp. There is no mistake about that, although Brigadier General Samuel S. Sumner and Brigadier General Charles King, both company officers at that time and present near where the combat took place, say they did not see it. Perhaps they did not. They had their troops to look after and were not there as observers. And perhaps they felt that officers and gentlemen should not witness such a barbaric act without making a protest. But I, a common soldier, trained to see the effects of war on foreign battlefields, and having in mind that at some future time perhaps my topknot would be dangling from a warrior's belt, felt no regret or scruples about being a witness to an act which the savages in whose school Yellow Hair had been trained, had so skillfully employed themselves less than a month before when Custer and his command lay bleeding on the banks of the Little Bighorn.

Sergeant John Hamilton of Captain Sumner's troop, who later was retired as ordnance sergeant, in a statement made to [retired] Brigadier General William C. Brown, says that he saw Cody shoot Yellow Hand (or Hair), and that when the troops made the charge on the Indians he [Hamilton] had to stop at the place where the Indian was lying in order to help fix the saddle on a pack animal; that he found that the Indian's scalp had been removed; that he was lying on his stomach on bended arms, wrapped partly in an American flag, and had with him a scalplock of a yellow-haired young white woman; also tin bracelets on his arms, a charm, a wampum belt, and war feathers. When the man who had been detailed to bring my horse to me finally found me, and I was ordered to go to the extreme left flank with my signal outfit, I passed by the Indian and saw that his scalp had been removed, but did not take time to make any examination of the equipment.

I did not play any part of a hero in the drama, but by reading the many reports of the number of Indians killed, both by those who actually were present and by others who were miles away, I am forced to believe that I am the only man who did not kill at least one Indian in that "battle." And I was all primed to slay the whole bunch if I had been given a chance, but the guns issued to the army at that time did not throw a bullet five miles. That was about as near as I came to any of them after the scrap between Cody and Yellow Hair. So I must content myself with telling what others did, and for that part I am perhaps better qualified than those who did the real work, for the place where, by chance, I had been posted, gave me a better opportunity to see what was going on than was enjoyed by those actually engaged in the skirmish. I believe I have the upper hand of some of the writers who have filled magazines and pamphlets with stories of the "great" fight.

As for Cody scalping the Indian, I want to state that after we reached the reservation and the pursuit of the Indians ceased, the skirmishers were called in, and before I could find my company I met Cody and traveled with him for a short distance. We met two Indians apparently attempting to leave the reservation. Cody asked them where they were going and one of them replied, "To join Sitting Bull." They knew they were safe on the reservation and wanted to show their bravery where there was no danger. Cody pulled Yellow Hair's scalp from his saddle pocket and held it up for the Indians to look at, at the same time telling them that if they left the reservation something like what happened to Yellow Hair would happen to them in short order. They gazed at the scalp for a moment then let out a grunt and turned homeward.

The fight itself was of small magnitude, but the fact that the Indians had been outwitted, and that 800 who had actually left their reservations to reinforce the hostiles in the field, and that probably 2,000 more who turned back at the first news of the defeat of the other 800, had likewise been convinced that they were no match for seasoned troops commanded by expert officers, had probably more to do with settling that war than a greater battle would have accomplished. John F. Finerty, war correspondent in

1876, and later member of Congress from a Chicago district, in his report of the fight said: "Buffalo Bill was in the van, and reaped the brightest laurels of his adventurous life that morning by slaying Yellow Hand, the Indian leader, in single combat. . . . The savages taken totally by surprise were driven back upon the agency in wild disorder. They thought that Merritt must have dropped from the clouds." Eastern people, knowing little or nothing of life on the frontiers, condemned Cody for scalping the Indian. Why? They did not know that fire is best fought by fire on the open plains, and that fighting the Indian his own way had more effect than petting and handling him with soft gloves.

About midnight, my outfit reached Camp Robinson after passing through some of the camps and witnessing the Indians in their hideous make-ups dancing around fires and singing their death songs. It was easy to read in their manners what they would have done to us had they been masters of the situation. As it was, their weird songs and unearthly yells almost chilled the blood in a man's veins. As Custer once said, "One who had witnessed one of those witch-like performances would never forget it." The next day we took up the march to join General Crook, and joined his command at the head of Goose Creek in Montana [Wyoming] on the third day of August. Cody remained as chief of scouts until we reached the Yellowstone River, when he quit to rejoin his theatrical company. . . .

Witness to Cody at Warbonnet Creek (Diary entries by James B. Frew, formerly of Troop D, Fifth U. S. Cavalry. From *Winners of the West*, April 30, 1936)

Comrade James B. Frew, late Troop D. Fifth U. S. Cavalry, sends . . . a photostatic copy of a page of a diary which he kept day by day while serving in the army. Under date of July 17, 1876, the copy of his diary states, "Indians reported by the pickets. Command ordered to secrete in the ravines, but two couriers arriving from agency being in danger, Cody fired on them, killing the chief, Yellow Hand. The rest (Indians) tried to rescue him but we charged, killing six. Followed them into the agency 40 miles."

The entries preceding this one and Mr. Frew's explanation of the affair reveal that his detachment, which had been stationed at Fort Laramie in Wyoming had been sent on a scouting expedition. When the Indians were reported, he said, the order to conceal themselves was given the soldiers with an idea of taking the Indians by surprise. However, when the couriers arrived and were pursued by Yellow Hand and his band, original plans were revised.

Mr Frew said that Yellow Hand streaked out ahead of his band and Buffalo Bill, . . . who was riding ahead of the troops, spurred forward to meet him. As soon as Buffalo Bill was within range he fired at the red-skinned chief. The first shot, he said, wounded the Indian in one leg, but it killed his horse. As Yellow Hand extricated himself, Colonel Cody fired again, the bullet striking Yellow Hand in the body and dropping him.

Mr. Frew said he was riding not more than fifty feet behind Buffalo Bill when Yellow Hand fell. He said it was possible that Colonel Cody might have dismounted long enough to plunge a knife into the Indian to make certain of killing him, but he is certain that if anything as spectacular as the reputed knife duel had occurred he would have seen it and would have noted it in his diary.

Surrounding Red Cloud and Red Leaf (By Luther North, formerly of the Battalion of Pawnee Scouts. From *Winners of the West*, July 30, 1933)

We had a very good time [during a 1933 visit to the Nebraska Sand Hill country] and I met many old timers that I hadn't seen for more than forty years. . . . At Chadron we were met by a delegation of Sioux Indians. Some of the old bucks were in the Red Cloud village when Colonel Ranald S. Mackenzie surrounded and captured him on October 23rd, 1876. My brother and myself with forty of our Pawnee scouts were with Mackenzie.

We made a long night ride and reached Chadron Creek before daylight. We found the Indians in two camps about two miles apart. Red Cloud was in one village and Red Leaf and Swift Bear were the leading chiefs of the other village. Colonel Mackenzie divided his force, taking about 200 cavalry and twenty of our Pawnee scouts, under command of my brother, Major Frank North. He went to Red Cloud's village. Major George A. Gordon with about the same number of cavalrymen and twenty Pawnee scouts under my command went to the Red Leaf village.

The part the Pawnees were to take was to dash through the village and capture the horses. Then the soldiers were to surround the village and compel the Indians to move their camp to their reservation at Camp Robinson, about twenty-five miles away. We had strict orders not to fire a shot unless we were fired upon by the Indians. They made no resistance, so there was not a shot fired. We, with the Pawnee scouts, rounded up the horses. Colonel

Mackenzie told Red Cloud what he must do. Then he let the Indians have enough horses to move their camp to Camp Robinson, where the horses were again taken from them and turned over to Major Frank North with instructions to take them to Fort Laramie and turn them over to the quartermaster there. This was done, and Frank got a receipt from the quartermaster for 722 horses. A few days later, most of these horses were sold at auction by the government.

The Indians that met us a few days ago [1933] at Chadron took us out to the creek a few miles from town and pointed out to us where the Red Cloud and Red Leaf villages were located, with the object of having markers put up there. One of the old Indians, when telling me about the rounding up of their horses, said, "Tell him (pointing to me) that they never would have gotten our horses if they had not had the Pawnees with them." . . . .

Battle of the Red Fork, 1876 (By James S. McClellan, formerly first sergeant, Troop H, Third U. S. Cavalry. From *Winners of the West*, May 30, 1930)

On the morning of November 25, 1876, I was first sergeant of Troop H, Third U. S. Cavalry, in command of first platoon, with Colonel Ranald S. Mackenzie at the fight with Dull Knife's and Little Wolf's band of Northern Cheyennes on the Red Fork of Powder River, Wyoming Territory, then known to us as the North Fork. We went into the engagement on the north side of the village, and just after First Lieutenant John A. McKinney was shot and his company checked, Captain Henry W. Wessells, Jr., gave the command, "Dismount and fight on foot!" Troop H at once engaged the Indians.

Deploying, we followed up the washout which gave them cover, and as we advanced toward the foot of the mountain an Indian leaped out of a hole on my right front, and I was on the right front of the skirmish line. He fired point blank at me, but missed and did not have time to re-load, as I shot from the hip and quickly to put end to his career. I took from this Indian, whose name was Bull Head, a Sharps carbine and also a cartridge belt full of .50 caliber cartridges. On this belt was a silver belt plate with the name Little Wolf stamped thereon; also, in an old-fashioned army cap box studded with brass nails was a steel used for striking fire and a flint stone. The belt plate and the steel are the identical relics taken by me that morning from Bull Head, a half brother of Little Wolf, who in the rush had grabbed and fought with Little

Wolf's equipment. When the Indians surrendered at Camp Robinson the following spring, we learned that Little Wolf was the real owner of the outfit.

These articles have been in my possession since I took them off the dead body of Bull Head on the morning of the fight, but I regret very much that I have lost the rifle and cartridge belt. In those days we had hard work to keep alive, without loading ourselves down with souvenirs of the battle.

Dismounting and Disarming the Agency Sioux along the Missouri River (By Theodore W. Goldin, formerly of Troop G, Seventh U. S. Cavalry. Typescript in Folder 16, Philip G. Cole Collection, Thomas Gilcrease Institute of American History and Art, Tulsa, Oklahoma)

At the breaking up of the 1876 campaign the remnant of the Seventh Cavalry returned to its home station at Fort Abraham Lincoln in what is now North Dakota, expecting there to split up and return to the various posts where they were usually stationed, but instead of that the entire command went into camp on the flats below the post. It was already early in November [1876], the weather was cold but fortunately we as yet had no snow and managed to keep fairly comfortable in our tent homes. There was a rumor that there was a move of some sort in prospect, but where to and for what purpose no one seemed to know. Hardly were we well settled until a train load of some five hundred recruits arrived to fill our sadly depleted ranks, and a cosmopolitan bunch they were—English, Irish, Scotch, Italians, and French, with a goodly share of Americans. All ages from sixteen to forty and from all parts of the country, from farms, mines, cities, and towns, not one with the slightest idea of army life. There they were dumped down, out there on the frontier at the beginning of a hard winter, with but a meager supply of blankets and none too much clothing. They were at once assigned to the various troops and officers, noncommissioned officers, and the best of the older well-drilled men, and we started the task of making soldiers of them. I doubt whether a third of them had ever ridden a horse.

Poor fellows, we really felt sorry for them. As we were still in the field, our rations, so far as bread was concerned, consisted of hardtack about the size of an old fashioned soda cracker and made of a mixture of coarse flour, peas, beans, and other cereals, all ground together and baked hard. While it did not seem so, there was really much nourishment in them and fifteen usually comprised a day's rations, together with a slice of bacon, or boiled beef, with a weekly feed of baked beans. We older men had learned that five of these hardtack fried in bacon grease made a good meal with the addition of the bacon and huge tin cups of coffee, but the poor recruits had not yet learned this and we often found them eating all their hardtack at a single meal, often eating their bacon raw as they as yet had no frying pans in which to cook their food, and the result was that for a time many of them went hungry to bed, and, by the way, these beds consisted of piles of hay thrown on the ground and covered with their meager supply of blankets, overcoats, or anything else they could get hold of. Out of a real sympathy for them we tried to teach them as best we could and ere long they improved very much.

Hardly were we half through with their preliminary drill when a trainload or two or horses and mules arrived, the horses for the soldiers, the mules for the wagon train. Neither horses or mules were broken, and it was right there the fun began, breaking those horses and trying to teach the poor homesick recruits to ride them gave us both plenty of work and amusement. Day after day the training went on, with many a spill on the part of the poor recruits, but finally our work began to tell, although there was no cessation of the daily grind. Over in the quartermaster's corral hardy mule drivers were having their troubles with those green mules, but they, too, began to win out and the mules were soon in harness and getting accustomed to their new life. From day to day there were rumors afloat of a coming move of some sort, but nothing definite could be learned. Huge mountains of supplies were piling up in the warehouses and, finally satisfied that something was going to happen, we oldtimers began to prepare for it. We first drew a supply of heavy winter underwear and shirts, then a few of us joined in the purchase of light buckskin from the Indians out of which we had suits made that were almost wind proof, and, as there were no regulations as to what clothing we wore in the field, we had a second suit made from the many colored Indian blankets for which we had traded or bought. These suits were made in one piece, like the present-day union suits or coveralls, and were warm and in connection with the light suits of buckskin made the need of overcoats unnecessary. To these we added blanket caps with an attachment that came down around our faces and necks leaving only holes for the eyes, mouth, and nose. These with heavy woolen mittens completed an outfit that would enable us to withstand almost anything in the way of weather. For our feet and lower limbs we bought heavy fleece-lined socks and leggins combined, over which we wore a light overshoe to prevent the ice and frozen snow from cutting the foot covering. It was true the outfit was not very military looking, but they were mighty warm and comfortable and we felt prepared for any sort of weather.

The recruits drew extra blankets and otherwise prepared themselves for a winter campaign as best they could.

Additional rumors were in the air every day. The wagons were loaded with rations and forage, but still no orders reached us. But finally, late one afternoon six troops under command of our colonel [Samuel D. Sturgis], who had recently joined from detached service, broke camp, loaded their tents and cooking utensils, and moved across the Missouri River on the ice and went into camp. The remaining six troops under Major Marcus A. Reno still remained in camp, but orders were issued that men must not leave camp for any purpose. Where the troops on the other side of the river were headed no one seemed to know. Late one afternoon, after retreat roll call, we were notified that we were to break camp early the following morning and move out on the Black Hills trail, but under sealed orders that were not to be opened until we reached the vicinity of the Cannonball River. Three o'clock the following morning we were routed out, had a hurried breakfast, saddled up, and at five o'clock we swung into saddle and were off. It was a bright cold morning and, followed by our heavily loaded wagon train, we moved at a fast walk, striking the Black Hills trail a mile or so from camp.

It was early in the forenoon when we struck the valley of the Cannonball, where we halted. Officers Call was sounded and the officers gathered about Major Reno, who opened his sealed orders and we soon learned that our destination was Standing Rock Agency, where we were to cooperate with the infantry in taking the ponies and so far as possible the arms of the Cheyennes [sic—Sioux], many of whom had been out on the warpath the preceding summer. Losing no time, we struck out across the country directly for the agency. We were a long ways off the usually traveled trail, leaving that and Fort Rice far to the east of us. Leaving our wagon train under a small escort to follow us as best they could, we pushed forward at a rapid pace, halting occasionally to allow our horses a breathing spell. We saw no Indians, in fact did not expect to. It was well along in the afternoon when we were still some fifteen or more miles from the agency when a scout from the agency rode in to us with the news that in some way the Indians had learned of our approach and were taking their ponies and guns and hurrying away to the hills. It was afterward learned that the Indian wife of the post trader had in some way learned of our destination and had dispatched an Indian runner to warn her people. It was afterward reported that the guard at Fort Rice had seen this runner far out on the prairie, out of range from the fort as he passed. I might say that these runners were warriors of wonderful strength, fast of foot and keeping up their rapid pace mile after mile, hour after hour, even moving faster than a mounted column.

On receipt of the news from the agency, we at once moved forward at a trot, varied occasionally by short periods of walking. Finally we began to catch a glimpse of distant dust clouds and later could see the fleeing Indians. The trot now gave way to the gallop as we strung out in a long slim line seeking to surround the agency and if possible head off the Indians, but they had a good start on us and we soon found that most of them were beyond our reach, but we continued the movement to surround the agency and as much of the adjacent country as possible. Our recruits, unused to packing their saddles, soon began losing nosebags, lariats, sidelines, currycombs, and brushes, and even the heavy, clumsy buffalo overshoes many of them had drawn. There was no stopping for them now. In the rear of each troop rode a veteran sergeant with orders to allow no straggling, and every time one of the recruits would rein out of the line the sergeant, with drawn revolver, would charge down on him and send him scurrying back into his place. Most of the poor fellows, unaccustomed to riding, soon found themselves chafed and sore, but there was no rest for them and on we went, finally swinging around in a wide circle and putting off any further retreat of the Indians. Then with our right resting on or near the river, we began slowly to narrow our circle, heading off and turning back whatever Indians we encountered.

I happened to be with a bunch over near the river and in the heavy cottonwood timber, much of which had been cut to be sawed into green lumber for the construction of the buildings at the post. Making our way through the underbrush as best we could was slow work, and giving one of the men my bridle rein I climbed up on a huge log to try and find a better road out of the timber. The tree had been stripped of its limbs so that I was able to walk it without difficulty. Reaching the butt of the tree, I found a mass of brush and limbs piled up and jumped down on it, when to my amazement I heard a grunt from underneath the pile. Calling to the men to clear the pile away, we came on an Indian who with two fine ponies had been hidden under the brush heap, his ponies lying close to the ground. Seeing that he was outnumbered, he held up his hands in token of surrender. Prodding around in the mass of tree limbs, one of the men discovered an almost new Winchester rifle and an old .50 caliber Sharps carbine of the pattern formerly used by the army, with a well-filled belt of ammunition for the Winchester. We took possession of the ponies and the guns and belt and told the Indian he was at liberty to go where he pleased. He walked along with us a short distance, begging in broken English for his ponies, or even one of them, but getting no satisfaction he turned away and was lost to sight in the timber. We made our way through the woods to the open ground near the new military post where we found our command unsaddling and going into camp. We turned the ponies into the large corral near the post and the guns to the storehouse. We learned that about 900 ponies had been rounded up, and perhaps fifty or seventy-five rifles, most of them old fashioned ones, a few being muzzleloaders. It was quite late when our wagons finally rolled in and we were able to pitch our tents and get something to eat, of which we were sure in need, not having eaten anything since early morning. It was sure a tired bunch that crawled in under their blankets that night, tired, lame, and sore from their unaccustomed long hard ride.

The following day, after a conference between the Indian agent, Major Reno, and the commander of the post, the agent sent out couriers calling on the Indians to bring in their ponies and arms by a certain date, some three days ahead. We had nothing to do save sit around camp and wait. We did not have much hope that the Indians would comply with the agent's orders, but now and then during the two days that followed a small drove of ponies would be driven in and turned into the corral, but it was easy to be seen that few if any of their best war ponies were among them. It was reported on the last day of the limit set by the agent that we had about fifteen hundred ponies in the corral. It was announced at the agency that two days from that time we were going to leave with the ponies for Fort Lincoln where we would meet the other six troops whom we learned had been on an errand similar to our own at Cheyenne [River] Agency, some distance further down the river. That afternoon we learned that the time set for our departure had been set to deceive the Indians and that as a matter of fact we were to leave at midnight that very night, with a view of putting as much distance between us and the Indians as possible before they discovered our departure. After a hearty supper and as soon as it was dark, our tents were taken down, loaded into the wagons, which with an escort of infantry were to follow us the following day. The corral where the ponies were confined was near the military post and nearly a half mile from the agency and the Indian village. Quietly we saddled up and moved over to the corral, where the ponies were released and we herded them out on the trail. It was a cold moonless night, threats of a storm were in the air, and we pushed forward as rapidly as possible and by early morning were many miles on our homeward journey.

Even from the time we broke camp there was every indication of a storm. The wind from the northwest was cold and piercing and as daylight came on heavy gray clouds could be seen in the north and northwest and occasional dashes of sharp, biting snow struck us in the faces and there was every indication of a blizzard, but we pressed on driving our pony herd as fast as possible, but even at that we were moving slowly as the ponies were hard to drive, all the time trying to break through the circling line of mounted men and take the backward trail. The wind grew stronger, bringing with it occasional flurries of hard, icy snow, the sure forerunner of the dreaded blizzard, and about noon it swept down on us in blinding, biting snow which every moment grew worse and soon began to interfere with our progress. And as we were facing it the task of driving the ponies became more and more difficult and the storm began to tell on men and horses. On leaving the corral in the night, I with some twenty other older men were ordered to bring up the rear, guarding against any attempt of the Indians to recapture the herd. The ponies, grass fed, soon began to weaken and many of them fell behind and after many efforts to keep them up with the herd orders came back for us to shoot such as were unable to keep up. It was a thankless, pitiable task, but there was no help for it and more than a hundred were killed. The howling storm was seriously affecting our men, particularly the poor recruits, most of them used to a much warmer climate. Often when they dismounted they were so chilled that they could not remount, and all around in front of us we could see men beating them with the heavy leather sling belts to try and arouse circulation enough in their poor chilled bodies to enable them to continue the march. Even this failed in many cases, and they were picked up and thrown across their saddles and utterly helpless and in some cases hands, feet, and faces badly frozen. It was here that the suits some of us had secured showed their full value as we were not suffering as were so many of the men. More and more ponies dropped behind and were shot.

About two o'clock we abandoned every attempt to keep up the march and the column, herd and all, left the open prairie, turned sharply to the left and drifted down into the timber along the low ground near the river. Here we managed to escape the full force of the blinding storm, which now swept over our heads. Horses and ponies, with drooping heads and heaving sides turned their tails to the storm and stood just where they happened to be. The men who were able to do anything were busy gathering broken limbs and piling them up against the many downed trees around us and it was not long until we succeeded in starting huge fires in a dozen or more places, around which the half frozen men gathered, their backs to the storm, keeping moving in order to retain circulation. We had with us three or four pack mules on which were packed some camp kettles, hard bread, coffee, and bacon, and Major Reno ordered them unpacked. Snow was melted in the kettles and soon came the welcome smell of boiling coffee. Again and again the kettles were filled with snow and were emptied by the men as soon as the coffee had a chance to boil. All night long the cooking continued and the men almost fought for the cups of steaming coffee. About three in the morning the storm blew itself out, the snow ceased to fall, but it was still intensely cold. Such first aid as was possible under the conditions was given the men who were suffering from frozen hands, feet, and faces. Everything possible was done for them, but it was but mighty poor aid we were able to give them.

Daybreak came at last, the wind had died down, and while the snow was still deep enough to impede our progress we began preparations for a forward movement. We soon discovered that we were only about four miles below Fort Rice and three of the well-clothed men who had suffered nothing save exhaustion from the storm mounted and made their way to the post with orders to turn out ambulances, wagons, or anything to be found and get them down to our bivouac to carry the frozen, injured men to the hospital and to have a meal prepared for the entire command. We succeeded in securing a couple of ambulances and some half dozen six-mule teams, which we dispatched to the command, while all the infantry cooks in the garrison began preparing food for the entire outfit. The few mounted men at the post and some of the infantry in the wagons went with the relief party under our escort, but it was nearly noon before they returned with the frozen men, hurried them to the hospital where the one doctor in the post, with the assistant surgeon who was with us and all the hospital employees went to work on them. Many of them were badly frozen. One man had to lose a foot, another—two in fact—had to lose a hand. Our hurried meal was soon dispatched, all the men unable to continue the march were left at Rice and the rest of us, with the sadly depleted pony herd, took the trail for Fort Lincoln, about twenty-five miles up the river. It was still bitterly cold and the heavy drifted snow impeded our march, but just at dusk we marched into the post, corralled the pony herd, put our weary horses in the stables, and hurried to the comfortable shelter of the vacant quarters, where we soon had huge fires blazing in the fireplaces and finally managed to get thawed out and that night had a comfortable resting place.

We did not hear from the rest of the regiment for a couple of days, when they, too, came marching in with another herd of some two thousand ponies, but very few arms. From them we learned that the blizzard struck them while they were still in camp at Cheyenne Agency and that they made no effort to move until the storm was over, thus escaping the hardships and suffering we endured on that never-to-be-forgotten march. A rest of several days and Troops C and F, whose stations were many miles to the east of us, took the pony herd, driving them through to St. Paul, where they were later sold at auction, and the two troops returned to their winter stations and our winter expedition was ended.

Scouting with Lieutenant Baldwin in Montana, 1876 (By Joseph Culbertson, former U. S. Army scout. From *Winners of the West*, November 30, 1933)

I left my old home at Fort Benton with my father, Alexander Culbertson, in the year of 1872, and went to Fort Browning, which was located at the mouth of Poplar Creek, just south of where the town of Dodson stands on the Milk River. Browning was the only agency between Fort Buford . . . [Dakota Territory] and Fort Benton. It was the agency for all the Sioux and Lower Assiniboin Indians. Jack Simmons was the Indian agent for the Fort Peck reservation at that time, and James Stuart, the brother of Granville Stuart, was subagent. In 1873 Browning was abandoned and moved to Fort Peck, a trading post located at the mouth of the Big Dry on the north side of the Missouri River twenty miles south of Glasgow. In that year, a delegation of twenty-five Sioux Indians and the agent and my father, including myself, went to Washington to visit General Grant, then president of the United States. After visiting all of the principal cities of the United States [in the East], we returned by way of Salt Lake to Helena and then down to Fort Peck. A month was consumed in making the trip.

After the Custer fight [in] June 1876, Sitting Bull left the mouth of Powder River in the month of December, headed for Canada with about 150 lodges. Colonel Nelson A. Miles and First Lieutenant Frank D. Baldwin, [Fifth Infantry], were soon on the red chief's trail with their command of infantry and cavalry. Colonel Miles came down the Big Dry to old Fort Peck, but the old chief, getting on to Miles's move, beat it back to the head of the Redwater, leaving fifty or seventy-five of his men to watch Miles's movements while he was getting into winter camp. Miles split his command, taking all of the scouts, including his chief scout, "Yellowstone" Kelly. They went up Crow Creek and then back to old Fort Keogh [then Tongue River Cantonment]. Baldwin had no scouts and, sending for me, asked me how I would like a job as scout under the command of Colonel Miles. I was only 19 years old and didn't know whether to take the job or not. My father told me I had better go.

I took the job about the eighth of December, the soldiers giving me the nickname, "boy scout," which I still go by. We pulled out of old Fort Peck

Troops on the march in a typical plains blizzard. From *Our Wild Indians: Thirty-three Years' Personal Experience Among the Red Men of the Great West* by Colonel Richard Irving Dodge (1882).

for the mouth of the Little Porcupine. The first fight we had was just below the mouth of the Milk River. Our next fight was at the mouth of the Little Porcupine on our way back to Fort Peck. We captured ten lodges of hostile Indians under the leadership of Charging Thunder, Sitting Bull's right hand scout, who is still living [1933] on the Standing Rock Reservation. After returning to Fort Peck, Lieutenant (now General) Baldwin sent for me and said: "Joe, cross the river, going up the Redwater to its head and then to Fort Keogh." I replied that I didn't know much about the country on the south side of the Missouri, but that I would do my best. The general's reply was, "Joe, you have done fine work, and although you are a young man I put a great deal of confidence in you."

We left Wolf Point about December 11th and camped at the head of Wolf Creek, which empties into the Redwater. After striking the Redwater, we took our time. About the fifth day out I began to see signs of Indians but said nothing. After camping about where the town of Circle now stands, Lieutenant Baldwin sent for me and said, "Joe, the command will lay over here and rest the mules, and I want you to make a scout to see if you can see any fresh Indian trails leading toward the Yellowstone." I was a little bit shaky, as I was not much on the fight, but said nothing. I had one of the best horses in the country and an excellent pair of field glasses, and I felt just as foxy as any Indian that ever ran the badlands of Montana.

The winter of 1876 was a severe, open winter with not much snow. On the morning of the 18th [17th], I started out alone on my scouting trip, which gained for me the confidence of old Indian fighters in eastern Montana. It was a fine morning but snowing a little when I pulled out from the command. About ten miles out from camp, on Timber Creek that runs into the Redwater, I noticed two buffalo running. I got out of sight and pulled my field glasses out and kept a watch on them. I noticed a horseman on the trail of the buffalo and thought some of going back to the command. My feet began to get cold and I thought of home. But I went farther up the creek to where Timber Creek heads into the badlands just east of the Sheep Mountains. Here I spied old Sitting Bull's winter camp. He had gone into camp thinking he was safe for the winter. After locating the country and satisfying myself as to the number of Indians there were, I hit the back trail for the command and I sure made time. As I rode into camp, Baldwin, with one of his officers, met me and shook my hand and said, "Joe, what luck?" "Too many Indians for your command," I replied.

We lay there that night and about five the next morning pulled out. I was in the lead with Baldwin when at about two o'clock in the afternoon we had almost got to within a mile of the Indian camp before the command was discovered by the Indians. As soon as the alarm was given, one could see Indians coming from all directions. There were about four Indians to one white man. The Indian camp was well sheltered along the creek, with plenty of timber on each side of the camp. The fight was a hot one, and for a while the bucks held the troopers back while the squaws and papooses were making their getaway. Baldwin gave the command to charge, and the whole camp was captured with six hundred head of horses, two or three hundred robes, and their winter supply of dried meat. The next morning we pulled out for Fort Keogh, but before reaching the fort we had another fight on Custer Creek. We fought Sitting Bull's men four times that winter, but he made his way into Canada.

In the spring of 1877, Sitting Bull crossed the Missouri above the mouth of Hill Creek and camped on one of the points on the north bank of the Missouri. Here high water overtook him and he lost much of his camp outfit. He then pulled down Larb Creek and crossed the Milk River at the Big Bend, north of Saco, and returned [went?] into Canada. The winter of 1876-77 put an end to Sitting Bull's fighting.

After we had returned to Fort Keogh, on Christmas eve, Colonel Miles sent for me again and asked if I would take a dispatch back to Fort Peck, a distance of 150 miles, to which I assented with pleasure. I pulled out that night and the following morning was beating down the Redwater. I made the trip in one night and two days. I remained in the service for twenty long years and have thirty-two honorable discharges and a medal presented to me by the government for services rendered to the United States Army.

Fighting Crazy Horse in the Wolf Mountains, 1877 (By Luther Barker, formerly of Company D, Fifth U. S. Infantry. From *The Oregon Veteran*, August, 1922)

Chief Crazy Horse was one of the principal actors in the . . . Custer disaster on the Little Big Horn in Montana, June 25, 1876. Crazy Horse was the principal chief of the Northern Cheyennes [sic—Oglala Lakotas] and was noted for his hatred toward the white race. No mercy was ever shown to any who were so unfortunate as to fall into his hands in those days of Indian warfare. Tongue River, being well timbered and abounding in game, made an ideal place for a winter camp. So Crazy Horse selected a fine location some eighty miles up the river from the [Tongue River] Cantonment and as Colonel Nelson A. Miles had been fully occupied driving Sitting Bull out of Montana into Canada during the fall and early winter of 1876, Crazy Horse felt quite secure. As there was an order from the department that no Indian camp should be allowed within 150 miles of the cantonment, the Fifth U. S. Infantry was kept pretty busy in those days. This great camp of hostiles had been located by a scout about the time we returned from our last campaign after Sitting Bull just before Christmas time. The order was to make ready for another thirty days' scout up Tongue River, but owing to the frozen condition of the men, as the weather had been very severe during the last campaign and as Christmas was very near, the general decided to let the men doctor up their frozen feet and hands and spend Christmas at the cantonment.

This was a Christmas that will never be forgotten by the men who served at the cantonment on Tongue River, Montana, [in] December, 1876. When the men had had their Christmas feast and had in a measure recovered from the frostbites and the hard service of the past two months, we were ready to go after Chief Crazy Horse. The evening of December 26 found us in camp some distance from the log fort, up Tongue River. We recruits who had joined the regiment the first of October and were anxious for a campaign looked upon this trip in snow nearly a foot deep as being very prosaic.

Fifth Infantry soldiers at Fort Keogh, Montana Territory, ca. 1880, wearing buffalo overcoats, with Springfield rifles and fixed bayonets. Troops so attired campaigned through the winter of 1876-77 and fought Crazy Horse's warriors at Wolf Mountains.
Courtesy of Little Bighorn Battlefield National Monument

As E and F companies of the Twenty-second Infantry had not been out on the previous campaigns, they were taken on this campaign. Out of over 600 men at the cantonment, there were only 350 that were able to go after Crazy Horse with a large camp and more than 900 warriors. During the few days that we had been permitted to remain at the log fort, there had been a blizzard and the weather was very cold. Mercury ranged around 30 to 40 below zero. With this kind of weather and the snow growing deeper, as we would experience a snow storm every few days, would it not make an amateur wonder how much of this can a man stand? There was one consoling feature, that while we stayed on Tongue River we would have plenty of fuel and water.

We took with us on this march an extra supply of forage drawn by ox teams in the Diamond R trail wagons. When the country became too rough to longer handle this ox train, the wagons were parked and the oxen were driven along to serve the command as beeves. We experienced much difficulty in crossing some rough ranges with our mile wagon train. The teams would often have to be taken from the wagons and a company of soldiers would have to lower the wagons by ropes, then a company on the opposite side of the gorge would draw them up. In passing some sidling place, where the wagons were likely to upset, a rope would be fastened on the lower side of the wagon and thrown over the top of the wagon and a number of men would pull on the rope and keep the wagon from upsetting. This was very laborious and when added to our tramping all day in the snow and being on picket guard quite often, with other duties incidental to campaign work, we truly felt that we were earning our $13 a month. One of our many difficulties was that the wagons would often break through the ice and would have to be drawn out by the men. These mountain streams were treacherous. Sometimes only a few steps to one side from where the wagon train had crossed in safety a man on foot would break through and go down to his shoulders in ice water. In order to prevent men from almost perishing with cold at such times, the advance guard was instructed to build fires wherever the river was to be crossed.

In marching 140 miles, Tongue River was crossed 120 times. When we arrived at Crazy Horse's late camp the fires were still smoldering, as the Indians had only been gone a day or so. The camp extended about two miles in length along the river, denoting many hundreds of Indians. Their trail led up the river, as they craved its shelter and fuel as well as we. The following day, after passing their abandoned camp, the scouts ran into a party of Indians acting as rear guard and the way they dashed out over the hills it seemed that they were greatly surprised. So this party fell in our rear the rest of this trip, and to get even with us for disturbing their little band the evening before they killed a mounted man by the name of William H. Batty of Company C, Fifth Infantry, while acting as rear guard. This brought the command to a halt for a time. A grave was dug and Batty was buried in the wilderness. The men who were with him said Batty was game, as he was pulling the trigger when the Indians fired a volley. One ball passed through his right wrist and penetrated his temple; another struck his horse in the forehead. Both fell dead, the horse on top of the man. As we were now entering the Wolf Mountains, the snow became deeper and the trail more difficult, but still we trudged on. Crazy Horse's aim was to draw us as far from the cantonment as possible and when we were much exhausted, and in the place of his choosing, he intended to annihilate the whole command.

On the 7th of January we were entering a stretch of narrow valley with high hills on each side of the river. The farther we advanced the narrower the river valley became. About 3 p.m., while making a narrow pass on a side hill, a wagon broke down, which blocked further progress for some time. When we were ready to move forward again the sun was getting low, so Colonel Miles directed the quartermaster to park the wagon train in a large body of

Engraving of Colonel Nelson A. Miles's battle with the Lakotas and Northern Cheyennes at Wolf Mountains, Montana Territory, January 8, 1877. *Frank Leslie's Illustrated Newspaper*, May 5, 1877

cottonwood trees, a fine camping ground with a high bank running in a circle which sheltered our camp and stock. We were scarcely settled in camp when heavy firing was heard west of the river out in the hills. It proved to be an attack of a small band of Indians who were trying to release some squaws and children that the scouts had captured. While the mounted infantry held the Indians in check, Liver-Eating Johnston, the famous old scout, aided by some Crow Indians, brought the captives into camp.

The Indians were soon routed, but orders were passed to company commanders to prepare for a five-day scout in light marching order, as it had been decided to leave the wagon train at this camp and go with pack mules up into the Big Horn Mountains after Crazy Horse. We had been cheerful, although much fatigued, but this started a murmur all around the camp. E Company, Fifth Infantry, was to be left as train guard with the supplies that were to carry us back to the fort. We reasoned that if E Company was wiped out, our chance of ever getting back to the cantonment was very slim.

We believed the Indians would attack us in the morning and we prayed that they would. The pickets were firing all night and it sounded good. We ate breakfast at four the next morning and were packing our mules for the one-blanket start when all at once there came such a yell from every hill on both sides of the river. The valley up the river was alive with Indians. The big mound where our wagon had broken down the evening before was black with redskins. In fact, we were surrounded by not less than 900 braves, with hundreds of old men and boys and squaws to join in on the finish if they should succeed. While matters looked a little blue for a time, we went at it with a will and by noon, January 8, 1877, we had Crazy Horse and his braves on the run and the day was won. The 12-pounder field piece we had with us was a factor in our favor, as the hills were shelled and at one place a shell killed nine Indians. The Indians fired much ammunition, but usually overshot us. Crazy Horse was very optimistic, telling his warriors that the soldiers would never eat another breakfast. A heavy snowstorm set in about noon and covered up the gruesome sights, as a battle in the snow leaves a very unwelcome sight. Many of our 45-70s found their mark and more than 100 [sic] braves went to the happy hunting grounds. We lost a number of men killed and wounded. Some died of wounds, as they could not stand forty below zero weather.

This was Crazy Horse's last battle. He surrendered the following spring at Camp Bradley on the Little Missouri River [sic—Crazy Horse surrendered at Camp Robinson, Nebraska]. Later he tried to start another uprising and while resisting arrest was bayoneted by a sentry and died.

We found the return trip much harder, owing to the increased depth of snow. The old trail was drifted full and was of no help to us. We were now standing picket guard every other night, and by the time we had crossed our wagon train back over the rugged ranges our reserve strength was exhausted. We halted and took Batty up. He had not been disturbed. The last few days of this return trip we could only make a few miles a day . . . . The post band came out some distance to welcome our return. We cared little for that, but when we turned a point of timber and saw Old Glory flying, we cheered. I remember Sergeant Thomas Gray had prepared D Company a good dinner, but we would rather sleep than eat. When our first sergeant called out, "General Miles orders these men excused from duty for three days," my Irish bunky said, "Bless Paddy Miles."

The Surrender of Chief Dull Knife (Morning Star), 1878 (By Louis DeWitt, former U. S. Army scout. From *Winners of the West*, May 30, 1930)

It is with a fervent spirit of keen memory [that] I desire to express my own experience in the occurrence of 1878 with the band of Cheyennes under Dull Knife's command, which broke away from the Indian Territory assignment abode. I was in Rapid City, South Dakota [Dakota Territory], attending United States Federal Court when the United States Seventh Cavalry arrived. I was employed as scout and interpreter. My first order was to scout for the Cheyenne war party's movement. I went through the Badlands country across the Cheyenne River over to the head of Bad River [and] down to White River and Wounded Knee Creek, where I overtook the army after a three-days' scouting. We established headquarters at Camp Sheridan for the Seventh Cavalry from where the scouting parties were sent out. Word was received at Camp Sheridan that Dull Knife and his band had been captured; they were in dugouts in a heavy timber. A misunderstanding of their interpreter as to surrender caused Major Caleb H. Carlton of [the] Third Cavalry to send to Major Joseph G. Tilford of the Seventh Cavalry for aid in the use of a cannon and an interpreter to interview Dull Knife as to his intentions.

First Lieutenant and adjutant Ernest A. Garlington was detailed to take a detachment of soldiers, cannon, and the interpreter (myself), who arrived at Colonel Carlton's tent about midnight. He informed me to try to gain a meeting with Dull Knife. With their interpreter, I called to the Indians in dugouts, and after some parleying was admitted into their camp where I remained the rest of the night, hearing the[ir] repeated appeals not to return to the assigned territory, repulsive in climate and habits. In the morning, Adjutant Garlington took me to Colonel Carlton's camp, who upon hearing my reported interview commanded me to get Dull Knife and three of his men to talk to them. As a result of my untiring efforts with the Indians through the night in my repeated explanations to avoid bloodshed, which seemed imminent at any moment, [and] to look forward to the future development of their succeeding generations. I gained some assurance, which ended in Colonel Carlton giving them a half hour to surrender or fight, which meant being shelled out.

I explained to the colonel [that] Indians have no knowledge of clock time, hence I returned with Dull Knife to his dugout, who told his warriors of the order to which they agreed to surrender and be taken to Camp Robinson without fighting. I gave the signal answer, which immediately started the lineup of the men marching. I assisted in loading the women and children in wagons, seeing them start off peaceably.

At my present age of seventy-five years it gives me humble satisfaction that I take pleasure in stating these words of Brigadier General Garlington's (retired) letter of 1917 to me: "I have always felt that it was entirely due to your influence with the Cheyenne band who had dug themselves in the banks of Chadron Creek, that they consented to go without a fight, in performing the valuable duty of your interpretation of that night's service."

An Incident of the Fort Robinson Outbreak, 1879 (By James E. Snepp, formerly of Troop A, Third U. S. Cavalry. From *Winners of the West*, July, 1939)

[Here is my recollection of] the heroic deed of a buddy of mine. His name was Johnnie Hauck. In order to explain, we had about 250 [sic—130] Cheyenne prisoners held in a company quarters, and it all started by the outbreak, the Indians shooting the three men walking post at Fort Robinson, Nebraska, January 10 [sic—9], 1879. There was a heavy snow at this time. We killed and wounded more than 100 [sic] Indians the night of the outbreak. We followed their trail for several days, always losing several men whenever we located them in the mountains. On the 15th or 16th [sic-January 10th], my company was on the trail, and there were several details scouting through the timbers. The details were dismounted, on either side of the ravine where a trail led, and the men could walk on the crust of the snow. Corporal Henry P. Orr, who was in charge of one detail, was shot dead and fell on the crust of the heavy snow. It was sure death to try to recover the body, as some Indians, only a few yards away nestled in some rocks, had the body well covered.

The company commander, Second Lieutenant George F. Chase, left three men [with] Sergeant Gottlieb Bigalsky to recover the body at nightfall. When it was dark, the sergeant asked if any of the men would volunteer to undertake the job. Johnnie Hauck volunteered, if he could do it his way. No one objected. So he measured the distance in his mind from where they were under cover to where the body lay. He then cut a hole in the crusted snow and tunneled under the crust of the snow to where he thought the body was laying. Fortunately, the body was nearby. He cut the crust under it and it dropped into the tunnel. He then pulled and drug it to the entrance, unobserved. They tied the body on a horse and brought it to Fort Robinson.

For this heroic deed, my company, Company A, Third U. S. Cavalry, several months later was ordered on parade in full dress, and Johnnie Hauck was ordered to take thirty paces to the front where he halted, and the post commanding officer, Major Andrew W. Evans, advanced from the opposite side of the parade grounds and pinned a gold medal on Johnnie Hauck. The medal was issued by the secretary of war using a ceremony I do not recall. Johnnie Hauck's act was surely one of much bravery. We finally finished the job, which we started, on January 22, having killed most of the Indians who broke out of the quarters. My old comrades of Company A, "The Gray Horse [Troop]," will remember the above if any are still alive.

An Encounter with the Cree Indians near the Canadian Line,

1881 (By Lawrence Lea, formerly of Troop H, Second U. S. Cavalry. From
Winners of the West, September 30, 1931)

In October, 1881, the Crees [Indians from Canada] invaded northern
Montana, where their destination is supposed to have been the beautiful
Milk River Valley with its numerous abandoned log huts. In order to reach
the Milk River and have good camping ground with abundant wood and
water all the time, they could proceed down any of the wooded ravines or
valleys of the Milk River tributaries coming from the north, as the Woody
Island Creek, Cottonwood Creek, and others. The distance from Fort
Assinniboine to the first named of these creeks varies from about 70 to 100
miles.

When authorities at Washington, D. C., were apprised of this
encroachment on United States territory, the troops at Fort Assinniboine were
ordered out to drive the Indians back across the line. Accordingly, on October
8th the post commander, Captain Jacob Kline, left the fort with six companies
of the Eighteenth Infantry, two troops of the Second Cavalry, and a battery of
improvised artillery made up of infantrymen. About seven or ten miles
northeast from Fort Assinniboine the column crossed the Milk River,
whereupon the march was continued in an easterly direction on the north side
of the said river. The first three days out the weather was mild, but then a snow
storm came on and the temperature fell to 32 degrees below zero, Fahrenheit.
In the afternoon of the third day the expedition encamped in a somewhat
sheltered place near the river about forty-five miles from Fort Assinniboine,
and the next morning a detachment was sent back one day's march to [the
Indian agency of Fort] Belknap, presumably to be on the lookout for Indians in
that quarter, while scouts were scouring the country in other directions. The
Indians were soon located on a tributary of the Woody Island Creek, and the
detachment of Fort Belknap of which I was a member was recalled. On
rejoining the command, it appeared that on the previous day the main column
had been on the tributary and compelled the Indians encamped there to go
back across the line. . . . In the course of the night, however, scouts came in and
reported a large village on the Woody Island Creek.

The following day, the command started for the Indian village. The
weather had moderated somewhat, but there was a considerable amount of
snow on the ground, and every now and then while trotting or galloping,
hard lumps of snow or ice would detach themselves from under the horses
hoofs and hit the breast or face of the trooper behind. The trail led in a

northerly direction upward through a narrow valley known as the Lone Tree Coulee. While marching up this coulee we had advance guards, as well as flank guards, out. A soldier by the name of John Clark and myself were on the right flank with orders to keep at a distance of from half a mile to a mile from the head of the column. Presently, a fall of snow hid the column from view. About this time the trail having become warmer, the column had taken a trot and turned to the left and northward. As our horses evinced a disposition to turn in the same direction, we gave them the reins and they rapidly brought us within sight of the column. By this time we had emerged from the coulee and found ourselves on a wide plateau where could be seen various smaller parties of Indians, whom we quickly disarmed. All these parties seemed to be moving in the direction of the ravine or valley through which flows the Woody Island Creek. In the meantime, the infantry and artillery had been sent out to the right, while Troop H, who [sic] had marched in columns of twos, responding to the command, "left front into line," found themselves at the top of the declivity forming the right or near side of the valley. We then had before us the ravine with the creek and everywhere on the slopes to the left and in the bottom of the valley [stood] the tepees of an Indian camp or village estimated at 700 lodges, or approximately 4000 Indians. Along the banks of the creek there was considerable brushwood, and there was great activity in the village. The bottom of the valley lay presumably 100-150 feet lower than the prairie above, and its opposite side at this point was a perpendicular reddish brown earthen wall appearing as fresh as if the prairie had just sunk down to the present level of the bottom of the valley. On our side of the ravine the earthen wall had caved in, forming a slope of 45 degrees.

With loaded carbines, we immediately descended the slope, the horses fairly sliding down on their hindquarters. The Indians, who were mounted, were then rapidly forming a line of battle across the valley in such a manner as to have their village behind them. Less than 100 yards from the Indian warriors, Troop H formed a corresponding line of battle parallel to that of the Indians. It was an interesting situation, resembling that of General Hancock in the spring of 1867 in Kansas. After a brief space of time, during which the Indians were receiving constant accessions to their numbers, Captain Martin E. O'Brien of Troop H, which was that day on the right front, with an interpreter and scout, rode zigzag about halfway across the space intervening between the lines, where he was met by one or more of the Indian chiefs, whereupon a conference took place. The Indians agreed to return to their precincts in British North America and, if I remember rightly, to surrender two malefactors. It seemed that the Indians had made arrangements to stay; they had put up their tents and were well armed. But with winter at the door and confronted by a considerable armed force of the United States, on whose territory they had no right to stay, they found it prudent to yield. Accordingly, the warriors withdrew to the village, throughout which their heralds presently were heard loudly proclaiming the result of the conference.

The troops thereafter went into camp on the left bank of the creek, with the Indian village extending to its opposite bank. In the course of the evening and night, most of the command came in from the prairie, Captain Randolph Norwood of Troop L between one and three o'clock in the morning, and encamped in the valley. Nearly the whole command was on guard that night, one-half walking post at a time while the other half were sleeping with their clothes on and their loaded guns by their sides. The next morning, both the Indians and the troops broke camp. The former were accompanied to the border by a strong military guard, while the main column continued reconnoitering and eventually returned to Fort Assinniboine after an absence of twenty days.

In regard to dates and the strength of the Indians, there may be a little uncertainty, but the incident on Woody Island Creek must have taken place on or about the 13th or 14th of October. In regard to the number of Indians, [NIWV] Comrade August Teahl at Lincoln, Washington, states that there were 1600 lodges in all. My recollection is to the effect that the Indian village in the valley of the Woody Island Creek was estimated at about 700 lodges, but the valley made a bend, and part of the village may have been hidden from view. How big the village on the tributary may have been I have never heard. If these two villages combined contained 1600 lodges, the number of Indians present in them must have been about 8000 or four-fifths of the present strength of the Cree nation. . . .

On Patrol in Montana and Sitting Bull's Surrender in 1881

(By John C. Delemont, formerly of Company K, Fifth U. S. Infantry. From *Winners of the West*, September 30, 1930)

I enlisted under the name of John C. Grasser on October 2, 1880, and was sent with a transport of recruits to Fort Keogh, Montana Territory, arriving there December 24, 1880, and was picked out by Sergeant Major Ewert to act as clerk in the Adjutant's Office. On January 1, 1881, was appointed corporal in my Company K, Fifth U. S. Infantry, and on the 2nd was ordered to Fort Buford, Dakota Territory, and detailed on arrival there as company clerk, and after a stay of a few weeks my company was ordered back to Fort Keogh, M. T. When leaving Fort Keogh on January 2, 1881, a California broncho named "Baldy" was assigned to me. I mounted my broncho and had proceeded about five yards when he raised himself up full height and everything on his back slid down to the ground—saddle, rifle, and myself. I fell on my spine and hurt myself badly, but, nevertheless, mounted again and followed up my company, about five miles ahead.

At Fort Buford we performed garrison duty for about four months, guarding also some Nez Perce, Gros Ventres, and Blackfeet Indians, and then we returned to Fort Keogh. Soon thereafter, we were ordered to Camp Powder River to look for renegade Sioux. We performed patrol duty and then went to Tongue River. In charge of three men, we went to Camp Rosebud, M. T., for fresh buffalo and deer meat. We spotted a fat buffalo calf and shot it, but while we were going to load it up on our pack mule a bunch of Indians, no doubt attracted by our shots, appeared before us, claiming the dead calf, and more Indians appeared, and so I gave the command, "Mount," and off we were at a dead lope back to our camp, leaving the carcass behind.

We later returned to Fort Buford to guard the Sioux to be transferred by steamer to Standing Rock Indian Agency, Fort Yankton [Yates], Dakota Territory. Chief Rain-in-the-Face, of the Sioux, and their medicine man, Sitting Bull, were among the tribe. The married daughter of Sitting Bull lost her papoose by its falling from the steamboat into the river. She jumped immediately after it and saved it, and both were pulled aboard by deck hands. The troops were standing on both sides of the gangplank at charge bayonet during the drive of the Indians on board. After the Sioux had been placed on board ship, we returned to Fort Keogh, having been in the field in 1881 for about eight and one-half months.

In 1882 I was promoted to first sergeant and we saw service for several months at Camp Poplar Creek, and then at Fort Custer. I was recommended for examination for appointment to second lieutenant, but my old mother wrote me, asking me to come home to Bavaria to help her out of her difficulties. [I] applied for a discharge, which was granted me, with character "excellent." On my arrival in Bavaria, I found my mother very ill, and death soon relieved her. In 1886 I returned to the United States and enlisted in Company B, Battalion of Engineers, under the name of Delemont, and on my arrival at Willets Point, New York, was detailed as post schoolteacher. Was promoted first class private, corporal, and sergeant, and kept this place until I received a special discharge, character "excellent". . . .

An unidentified infantry sergeant and spouse pose before a studio setting at Fort Yates, Dakota Territory, during the late 1880s. *Editor's collection*

The Killing of Sitting Bull, 1890 (Account of James Connelly,
formerly private, Troop G, Eighth U. S. Cavalry, as related to George Grimes.
From *Winners of the West*, August, 1924)

[James Connelly was at the scene of the capture and death of the Lakota leader, Sitting Bull, December 15, 1890.] He helped pick up the bullet-ridden body of the medicine man and chief, and convey it, accompanied by two of his wailing wives, to Fort Yates for burial. Mr. Connelly was a member of the crack "Flying Squadron" of the Eighth United States Cavalry at that [time], in the dead of winter in 1890, and served in the smart troop, commanded by young First Lieutenant Enoch H. Crowder. . . .

The government, then as now, issued rations to its Indian wards every other Saturday. In October, 1890, Major James McLaughlin, Indian agent at Standing Rock [Agency], reported that Sitting Bull would not come in, but sent members of his family instead. At the same time, there came strange reports of new religious frenzies among the Indians—of a new dance, the "ghost" dance, and of new preachings. Indian police working for McLaughlin reported that Sitting Bull was foretelling the day soon to come when the whites would be driven forth.

At Fort Yates, James Connelly and his comrades of the Eighth Cavalry saw to it that their saddle trappings were strong, their horses in good condition, and their guns well oiled. The "Messiah" craze swept the reservations. The Indians left their log houses, and, surrounding the home of Sitting Bull, raised tepees and joined in the ghost dances. Sitting Bull proclaimed himself a high priest and made promises to his followers that their dead ancestors would be restored, that their old Indian customs of living would be returned, that the whites would be driven forth and that the white man's bullet would not have the power to kill.

Soon about 500 Indians were gathered around his home on the upper Grand River, about sixty-five miles from Fort Yates. "Eugene G. Fechet, captain, commanded the cavalry there," says Mr. Connelly. "The post was under Lieutenant Colonel William F. Drum, commanding the Twelfth Infantry. In August, Sitting Bull started the war dances and Major McLaughlin sent word to Washington and to Major General Nelson A. Miles, now commanding the Military Division of the Missouri.

"The Indians began to kill cattle and dry the beef and the squaw men, whites who had married Indian women, came into the agency, fearful of staying among the reds. Early in November, W. F. Cody ('Buffalo Bill'), Sitting Bull's friend, came to Fort Yates. After four days there he started for

Sitting Bull's camp, hoping to persuade him to give himself up, but at Oak Creek, thirty-five miles from the fort, he was recalled, after the commanding officer had telegraphed Miles that they were capable of handling the situation without the aid of a private citizen.

"Sitting Bull had his chiefs come in for a powwow and sent spies to watch the whites. Daily the strain became greater and for six weeks before the capture we kept everything in readiness for action." McLaughlin and Drum, fearing the effects of delay as the ghost dances kept up, finally were authorized by headquarters to arrest Sitting Bull. It was decided to filter Indian police into Sitting Bull's camp, and to arrest the chief and bring him in.

"On the night of December 14, 1890," Mr. Connelly recalls, "the Flying Squadron was ordered to saddle horses and be ready. At 11 p.m., a hot supper was served us and at a quarter before midnight the troopers moved out. Our destination was not announced, but we knew where we were going. On the 13th, the Indian agent had sent fifty of his policemen into Sitting Bull's camp. They were to kidnap him and leave his camp with him at midnight to meet us at Oak Creek.

"We got to Oak Creek, but the police with Sitting Bull were not there. Fechet decided to push on, and sent word to Drum of his determination." The cavalry kept on until, twelve miles from the camp of Sitting Bull, they were met by one of the Indian police. He told a story of surprise by the chief's followers, of a fight that followed, of his own escape and the death of his comrades and of a remnant of the police barricaded in Sitting Bull's house, surrounded by the others, carrying on.

Fechet disposed his troops for attack, ordered the men to separate the Indians from their horses and drive them into the brush, then moved to the camp and arriving there at daylight, prepared the charge. Firing was going on. A shell from the Hotchkiss gun the cavalry carried brought a sign in the form of a shirt waved from a window that some of the police were still alive. Fechet ordered a charge.

"We were told to aim low, save our ammunition and make every shot count," said Mr. Connelly. "We separated the Indians from their horses and drove them, about 500 in all, into the brush. We fought on foot, driving them across twenty acres of clearing into the fringe of woodland around the village. Finally they put up a flag of truce and were told to lay down their arms. We formed in two rows and they marched in between, laying down their weapons.

"We found the body of Sitting Bull just outside his house riddled with so many bullets we could not count them. From the police we learned the story of his death. Of the Indian police, Chief Shave Tail, Assistant Chief Bull Head, and First Sergeant Red Tomahawk, in command of the others, entered Sitting Bull's house the night before, finding him in bed. They made him dress and go out with them, saying they would shoot him if he resisted. When he got outside he yelled for help. They shot him down."

It seems that when the police got Sitting Bull outside the house his followers surrounded him. The warrior called for help and Catch-the-Bear and Strike-the-Kettle fired at the police. Both Bull Head and Shave Tail, on either side of him, were mortally wounded, but they killed their prisoner as they fell. Red Tomahawk lived to become a Sioux chief and is such today [1924]. Fechet's men rounded up the prisoners, putting Sitting Bull's body on a wagon, with two of his wives, and escorted all to Fort Yates, where the chief was buried in the post cemetery. . . .

The Flying Squadron [did not take part in the action at Wounded Knee on December 29, 1890, but] spent the remainder of the winter in the field, bringing Indians into the reservation posts and making sure that there were no further outbreaks. Concerning Lieutenant Crowder, his commander then, Mr. Connelly has only words of high praise. "He was the best drill master I ever saw in the army," he said. "He was a splendid officer, and though he might have been nervous, as the rest of us were when we charged Sitting Bull's warriors, he led his men gallantly. He was a fine officer."

Arrest and Death of Sitting Bull (By Matthew F. Steele, lieutenant colonel, U. S. A., retired. From *Winners of the West*, February 28, 1937)

One of the officers who led two troops of Eighth Cavalry through a cold December night in 1890 to arrest Sitting Bull is still alive. He is Lieutenant Colonel Matthew F. Steele, retired, of Fargo, North Dakota. He believes he is the only officer yet living of those who rode from Fort Yates to Sitting Bull's village on Grand River to support the Indian police and help take Sitting Bull to Fort Yates. He described their arrival at the village in a letter to the Smithsonian Institution:

"We found the Indian police besieged in one of Sitting Bull's cabins by his followers, their ammunition exhausted. We drove Sitting Bull's band away and found lying dead in front of the cabin, as I recall, about twelve dead Indians, Sitting Bull's body among the dead. Red Tomahawk handed me Sitting Bull's tobacco pouch, which he had taken off his body. In inspecting his other cabin, where I found his two squaws and his grown son (the latter flat on the floor under a feather bed), I noticed a portrait of the old man in a deep gilt frame on the wall. I forbade the three or four troops that were with me to touch anything in the room. But suddenly I saw one of the extra policemen, whose brother, a regular policeman, lay dead outside, snatch the portrait down and smash the frame with his Winchester and punch a hole through the canvas. He was crying over the death of his brother. I grabbed the portrait from him.

"We took Sitting Bull's body and his squaws back to Fort Yates with us, and I took the portrait and tobacco pouch. A day or so later, I saw Major James McLaughlin, the Indian agent, and told him I had those articles and should like to keep them if his squaws would sell them to me. A couple of days later, I saw McLaughlin again, and he said the women said I might have the things for two dollars. I gave him two dollars for them and I have the picture and the pouch yet. I expect to give them to the state museum at Bismarck or to a museum in Fargo some day."

Two Letters Regarding Fort Yates and Sitting Bull's Death, 1890 (By George B. DuBois, Troop F, Eighth U. S. Cavalry, introduced by George Thomas, formerly of Troop I, Fifth U. S. Cavalry. From *Winners of the West*, March 30, 1935)

I was telegraph messenger at Fort Leavenworth for several months at the time that Captain Edward S. Godfrey was a member of the Tactical Board of the School for Officers of the Infantry and Cavalry at that post, and remember having seen him a number of times while I was a member of I Troop of the Fifth Cavalry under command of Captain John B. Babcock, who was also a member of the Tactical Board. . . . I am taking the liberty of sending to you two letters that were written to me from Fort Yates, North Dakota, on the dates of December 3rd, 1890, and December 18th, 1890, by Sergeant George B. DuBois, F Troop, Eighth Cavalry, then stationed at Fort Yates. The original letters, of which these are true copies, were saved by me until June 14th, 1932, when I placed them and eight others in keeping of the State Historical Society of Colorado, in Denver. They are now on exhibition in that institution.

Sergeant George B. DuBois was my buddy at Jefferson Barracks, Missouri, in 1888, but we became separated when he was sent to F Troop of the Eighth Cavalry and I was sent to M Troop of the Fifth, at Fort Leavenworth, Kansas (M Troop was merged into I Troop in 1890), Captain

John B. Babcock, commanding. DuBois and I corresponded regularly from the time we were separated until we were discharged from the service and I still have his photograph as one of my prized possessions. Captain George D. Wallace of K Troop of the Seventh U. S. Cavalry was on detached service in 1888 and was in command of C Company of Recruits at Jefferson Barracks, Missouri. That is where I knew of him.

Captain John B. Babcock's troop of the Fifth was in the battalion that served under Lieutenant Colonel George B. Sanford at Pine Ridge during the "Messiah" Campaign, and that is why I know something about it. After my discharge from the army (three years act), I went back to my home town, Chicago, and entered the postal service and served Uncle Sam until my retirement. I have forty-one years of government service to look back on. . . .

[DuBois's first letter]

Fort Yates, N. Dakota,
December 3rd, 1890

Dear Friend Thomas:

I still have possession of my black curls, but I have an idea that I came as near losing them as I could, and still have them. Last Sunday night there was great excitement at the post. The two troops were ordered to saddle up our horses and be ready for a dash at any moment. I have since been informed, by a friend who works in the Interior Department, that had the troops gone out there would have been another Custer affair. I don't know why we did not go out. You know the enlisted men are kept as ignorant as possible. We are fortunate in being at a storm center of trouble, but we will only go out when a larger force arrives. If they ever come. If we have any trouble, I think it will come on next Saturday, the ration day of the Indians. If Sitting Bull comes in at that time, he will be arrested, and F Troop will do the job.

It was reported on Monday that Bull was at the agency. We saddled up in no time and rode to the agency at a gallop. But it was a false alarm. Bull was not there. The troop rode around about half a mile and came back to the post.

It was snowing yesterday, and we were ordered to mount our horses but did not leave the post. It is my opinion that we will ride around the post every day to throw the Indians off their guard, then when Sitting Bull does come to the agency we will make a dash and take him prisoner.

I have not seen the famous Ghost Dance, nor do I believe any one here has done so, even if the press does say so. An Associated Press reporter was the closest that any one has been, and he was about five hundred yards from the dancers. He took a snapshot with a Kodak which he gave to our photographer to develop. The picture shows the Indians dancing around a pole in a large circle. There was one lone tepee forty yards away. I suppose it was the medicine man's wigwam. Old Bull [Sitting Bull] and two or three others are shown standing between the tepee and the dancers. The Indians did not know that a picture was being taken of the dance, or it would have gone hard with the poor fellow.

The dance at Sitting Bull's camp is thirty-eight miles from here and the Indians will not allow anyone to come within five hundred yards of it. The Indian scouts of the post have been made to cut their hair so that they will not be mistaken for the Sioux. The Indians at the dance will not allow the scouts to come near them. Buffalo Bill and Doctor [Frank] Powell (White Beaver) were here last week, and Buffalo Bill was going to bring Sitting Bull in to the post. He started for the dance, but when he got to within fifteen miles of it he got bluffed out. He came back without scalp or glory and has gone away now. I suppose that the newspapers will say he had a long talk with the Indians and tell all about the dance. I am personally acquainted with some of the chief dancers, and I would like to see the dance (from behind a big rock).

If the troops do not bother them, I do not look for any trouble, but if they interfere then look for something serious. It will take most of the Army to whip them because they are better off now than they ever have been, and are supplied with more arms than anyone thinks for. Besides, there are plenty of cattle in the country to feed them. I don't think there will be trouble till next spring if the authorities leave them alone. There are a lot of troops at Mandan. It is sixty miles from here, but we may expect them at any time. Our wagons stand packed with ten days' rations, tents, and other equipment, all ready to hook the mules to them. They stood with the harness on all night Sunday, together with the horses for the Gatling and Hotchkiss guns. F Troop takes the Hotchkiss and Corporal McCarthy (you remember him as our gunner), G Troop, handles the Gatling gun.

I will let you know as soon as I take a scalp or eat an Indian's liver for breakfast.

George B. DuBois,
Sergeant, F Troop,
Eighth Cavalry.

[DuBois's second letter]

Fort Yates, North Dakota,
December 18th, 1890

Dear Friend Thomas:

I have enough to tell you to keep me writing for a week, but will condense as much as possible and give you the news. You will know by this time that the fight was fought and Old Sitting Bull has gone to the Happy Hunting Grounds, together with eleven of his braves that I know about. Also five Indian police have gone under.

The plan laid out was for the forty Indian police to go to the camp of Sitting Bull (thirty-eight miles from Yates) at daylight on Monday morning. They were to arrest Sitting Bull, throw him in a wagon, then meet the two troops on the road, and we were to keep off the hostiles. We started from Fort Yates at twelve o'clock on Sunday night and by sun-up we were about three miles from Sitting Bull's camp. It turned out that of the forty Indian police that were to be there with a wagon, only eighteen showed up, and they had no wagon.

But they were brave men and they went into the camp. They brought the old man out of his cabin, then they had a white elephant on their hands. Sitting Bull let out a cry for help. His followers came rallying around him. One Sioux Indian shot Bull Head (the chief of the police) in the leg. As he did this, Bull Head turned and shot Sitting Bull in the head, and as Bull was falling, Red Tomahawk shot Sitting Bull twice, one of these shots going near or through the heart. The fighting became hand-to-hand. It must have been awful. The hostiles soon drove the Indian police into Sitting Bull's cabin. The battle raged until the ammunition began to run short. The police called for a volunteer to go and bring the soldiers. Hawk Man volunteered and made his way to the corral adjoining the cabin, where he found Sitting Bull's best pony with only a piece of rope around its neck. When he got to the bars of the corral, he found that the bars were so tight that he could not lower them.

Red Tomahawk ran out of the cabin and let the bars down for him. Hawk Man began to whip the pony before he mounted, he was so excited, but he managed to crawl on in some way and dashed off to meet us. If those Indians were not brave, I don't know who was. The bullets must have rained around them. Hawk Man met us about two miles from the camp. When he met us, there were exciting times. Captain Fechet, who was in command of the two troops, would have turned back, but the other officers insisted that we must go and rescue the police, and he agreed.

I then got a command to take my squad (No. 1) and move as skirmishers five hundred yards in advance in front of the troops, and ride at a gallop. It was ticklish job and none of the officers dared come up. I moved off till I came to a bluff. It was about a thousand yards from the Indian camp and in full view. Then you should have heard the red devils yell. It was awful. I halted till the troops came up. F Troop was dismounted, thrown out on a skirmish line, and commenced firing. The Hotchkiss on the hill was firing over our heads. The Sioux were soon driven from the brush and they disappeared like magic. The Indian police ran up a white flag, and while they came to us the Sioux Indians made their escape. We went down to the creek on a skirmish line and hunted all around. We found only one buck in the brush and made short work of him.

The Indian police had their blood up. One of them would have killed a kid about six years old. I knocked his pistol up and talked him out of it. The scenes around the camp were awful. I saw one fellow go up to Old Bull and cut him across the face with an ax. One cut him with a knife till his own squaw wouldn't know him. The dead looked horribly cut and shot. The blood and brains lay around in all shapes. There were broken guns covered with blood. The commander ordered the camp to be made so that the men and horses could be fed. I was ordered out with my squad (two corporals and nine privates) for picket duty. We had a hard time of it.

Corporal Ford was playing hide and seek with an Indian on a hill-top. Neither one was hurt. I had a hard time for myself. One buck came riding in toward camp. I thought he was an Indian police[man], as he had a white kerchief the same as the police all wore. When he got to within four hundred yards of our camp, he stopped. It seemed as though the whole of our men started shooting at once, but the Indian spurred his pony and dashed in my direction. He did not see me until he got within five hundred yards of where I was. As he turned away, I let him have it. The first two shots were misses, but at the third shot he threw up his hands and a riderless pony galloped over the plains.

The Indian police went out with a wagon and brought in a dead Indian. While I was on picket duty, the troops cooked dinner and ate it all up. I had nothing to eat or drink, nor did any of my eleven men or horses. They were afraid to stay there any longer so we started out for Oak Creek. We got there just at dark. We had traveled seventy-five miles since midnight the night before, but the funny thing that was of the most interest to me was that I had nothing to eat. We had no wagons nor any bedding. Few of the boys slept at all, as they had one blanket and a saddle blanket each.

At midnight that night two companies of infantry joined us. They had supplies and our buffalo coats. We managed to warm up a little, but not enough to sleep very much. The next morning we pulled into Fort Yates. You bet I was glad to hit the spring bunk a lick once more. I haven't seen any account of it yet, but you will have the true story. I have not written the soldier rumors. Just what I saw myself and what the Indian police told me themselves. So I know what I am talking about.

Bull Head, the man who shot Sitting Bull, is in the hospital. He has a shattered arm and leg. The doctor thinks he will pull through all right [Bull Head subsequently died]. The five Indian police that were killed were buried with military honors yesterday. The whole garrison turned out to the funeral. We are liable to go out at any minute to round up the others. That was what we might have done, but the officers thought it was too big a job to tackle. Most of our boys have some relic of Sitting Bull. I have a knife and a bag of medicine. The troop has the Holy Shirt that Old Bull said was bullet proof. He did not have it on at the time that he was killed.

George B. DuBois,
Sergeant, F Troop, Eighth
Cavalry

Scouting for Sioux in 1890 (By John Rovinsky, formerly Eighth U. S. Cavalry and Seventh U. S. Infantry. From *Winners of the West*, October, 1925)

I served two enlistments, in Troop B, Eighth U. S. Cavalry, stationed at Fort Meade, South Dakota, and in Company B, Seventh U. S. Infantry, stationed at Fort Logan, Colorado. In 1890, we of the Eighth U. S. Cavalry were stationed at Fort Meade, South Dakota, with Colonel Elmer Otis in command. I was all through the Sioux Indian campaign of 1890-91, as Troops A and B, under Captain Almond B. Wells, later raised to major, were sent out against the Indians. We took the field early in the spring, and after several days' march came to the town of Oelrichs, South Dakota, where we made our camp. For a time it was severely cold and we had to sleep on the bare ground, often times amid downpours of rain, hail, and snow. We had no tents or shelter of any kind, and several times we awoke in the morning to find ourselves covered with snow. We stayed at Oelrichs the greater part of the summer guarding that town and patrolling the country for hostile Indians. We next camped at Battle Creek, close to Cheyenne River, and from there we scouted the country along the Cheyenne.

On one of our scouting trips, which were composed of ten soldiers and a noncommissioned officer, we came to an abandoned house known as Dailey's Ranch. We passed this place several times, and on one occasion a rancher came out and warned us that Indians were sneaking around in the thicket beyond the Cheyenne. We continued on but for a few yards, when the

Swedish immigrant Sopphus Borresen joined Troop H, Eighth Cavalry, at Fort Meade, South Dakota. Borresen wore full dress while posing on horseback in ca. 1890-91. *Editor's collection*

Indians began firing on us. Sergeant Ohorn, who was in command, gave orders to dismount and return fire. We dismounted, tethered our horses, and opened fire into the brush where the Indians were concealed. The firing on both sides soon ceased, and a courier was sent to inform the commanding officer of the engagement with the redskins. The whole command soon arrived, but the major did not believe the savages had fired on us and placed Sergeant Ohorn under arrest. He later released him when the ranchers testified to the fact that the Indians had begun the skirmish.

We now received news of the Battle of the Wounded Knee, of the killing of Sitting Bull, with orders to concentrate and close in on the Indians if they failed to obey orders to go back on the reservation. The Indians, however, started for the Pine Ridge Agency, and we followed them, pitching camp near the agency. General Miles reviewed all the troops, after which we returned to our winter headquarters at Fort Meade. We had been here but shortly when the Chinese who ran the laundry near here came running into the fort and said that several Indians had driven them out of their homes. The commanding officer sent three of us, including a sergeant, to arrest them. The Indians were drunk, and we arrested them and brought them to the guard house. Just as the sergeant of the guard proceeded to open the prison door, one of the Indians seized an axe and raised it to hit me over the head. The sergeant grasped the axe and after a short struggle took it away from the Indian and shoved the two Indians into jail.

Some of the officers of Troop B were First Lieutenant John Guest, Captain Edmund Luff, and First Lieutenant John A. Johnston, and Second Lieutenants Farrand Sayre and Ulysses G. Kemp. [Later, during my service with the Seventh Infantry,] Captain Edward E. Hardin was in charge of Company B, Seventh Infantry, a good drill instructor and a fine and efficient officer. He is now retired from the service as lieutenant colonel. I was discharged at Fort Logan, Colorado, on July 29, 1897, for disabilities contracted while in line of service. . . .

Time at Wounded Knee (By William J. Slaughter, formerly of Troop A, Seventh U. S. Cavalry. From *Winners of the West*, April 30, 1937)

About the middle of November, 1890, all was excitement at Fort Riley, Kansas, where the Seventh Cavalry was stationed, on learning that the Sioux Indians of the Pine Ridge Agency [Reservation] had gone on the warpath once more, threatening to kill the agent and burn the agency buildings. The older men of the regiment began regaling we youngsters with stories of the bloody battle of the Little Bighorn, of June, 1876, when Chief Sitting Bull and his Sioux warriors, thousands strong, ambushed and annihilated Lt. Col. George A. Custer and five troops of our regiment. This made us eager to meet the redskins and get revenge for what they had done to our predecessors. The good news from the War Department ordering us to pack up and entrain for Pine Ridge Agency, S. D., reached us a few days before Thanksgiving, so we said good-bye to Fort Riley, Kansas, a band, as usual, playing "The Girl I Left Behind Me," little realizing that many of our comrades would never return.

We made our first stop at Beatrice, Nebraska, at sundown the second day after entraining. We unloaded our stock, consisting of pack mules, cavalry and artillery horses. The idea was to water them and allow them to stretch their legs after being shut up in cattle cars for about thirty-six hours, and believe me those gentlemen mules from Missouri did stretch their legs as the writer well knows, for one of our dear old Irish quartermaster sergeants, knowing him to be a rookie, ordered him to ride one bareback and lead three others to a watering trough about two hundred yards distance, and, after galloping over half of the state of Nebraska in the next hour or so, arrived at said watering trough. That night I saw bootleggers at work for the first time, for our commanding officer, Colonel James W. Forsyth, seeing some of the boys heading for the Stock Yard Hotel, ordered a guard stationed at each door to keep soldiers from entering. The enterprising proprietor, not to be outdone, had three or four men carry a couple of quarts of Tangle-foot apiece and sell it on the quiet to those who had the money, and when the money ran out he had them swap a quart for an army blanket. But a couple of our old timers turned the tables on him. They saw that he was throwing the blankets into a room behind the bar and, climbing through the window, threw them out to other comrades who carried them away.

Once more we loaded our stock and started before daylight over the Elkhorn and Missouri Railroad for Rushville, Nebraska, arriving there early the next forenoon. We unloaded our animals and equipment and started overland for Pine Ridge Agency, about twenty miles distance, when about five miles from our destination we heard firing ahead of us and upon reaching the agency found that some of the supposed friendly Indians had marched out of the agency firing upon some of its defenders, wounding several. Major General John R. Brooke, who was in command at the agency, ordered our colonel to make camp in a hollow on the bank of the creek which ran between two hills, giving us protection from the cold north winds and water for our animals. We then settled down to the regular routine duties of a cavalryman in below zero weather for a week or two. Our rations consisted of salt pork, hardtack biscuit, sinkers, and an occasional can of tomatoes topped off with alkali water coffee. Now, I am not criticizing the government for the quality of our rations, as South Dakota at that time had very few settlers and transportation facilities were not what they are today and potatoes and other fresh vegetables were hard to procure and could not be kept on account of the frigid temperature.

Our Indian and white scouts were continually watching the Sioux and bringing into camp an occasional spy. On December 26, they reported that the Sixth Cavalry had captured a large band of Indians and that Chief Big Foot and his band of . . . Sioux were headed toward the Wounded Knee Creek, about eighteen miles distance, their purpose being to form a junction with another band supposed to be in that vicinity. So our commanding officer ordered Major Samuel M. Whitside, with A, B, K, and L troops of the Seventh Cavalry, to proceed to Wounded Knee Crossing without delay. Just before noon of the 28th, two of our scouts caught an Indian spy taking a survey of our camp and reported Chief Big Foot and his band near Porcupine Buttes, about six miles away. "Boots and Saddles" was sounded instead of "Mess-call," and we mounted and rode after them, accompanied by a platoon of E Battery, First Light Artillery, commanded by Second Lieutenant Harry L. Hawthorne. We came in contact with them near the buttes, and a bloodthirsty looking lot they were, their faces painted green, yellow, and red, with colored feathers in their hair. Each one of them wore a calico "Ghost Shirt" under his blanket, which crafty old Chief Sitting Bull and the medicine men had told them would stop the paleface or white man's bullets from harming them.

While Major Whitside and our interpreter held a powwow with their chief, Lieutenant Hawthorne unloaded and assembled the two three-inch Hotchkiss guns, ready for action. The Indians were very much impressed by them, as they had never seen breech-loading [artillery] guns before. As our orders were to capture and disarm them without bloodshed, if possible, it took our commander and interpreter a long time to talk their chief into ordering his warriors to accompany us back to our camp, as most of the young "Bucks" wanted to try out the bullet resisting qualities of their "Ghost Shirts." We eventually escorted them back to our camp, dividing our rations with them, also furnishing their chief, squaws, and papooses with a tent, as he claimed to be sick. After dark Major Whitside sent a courier to Pine Ridge Agency for reinforcements and formed a chain-guard around the camp. We spent a sleepless night as the Indians wailed and chanted all night long.

At daybreak on the 29th, we found ourselves re-enforced by the Second Battalion of our regiment, consisting of C, I, D, and G Troops commanded by Colonel James W. Forsyth. Also the rest of E Battery, First Light Artillery, commanded by Captain Allyn Capron. After breakfast our officers and Indian interpreters held a consultation and decided that we would give them a chance to lay down their arms and surrender, or [we would] disarm them, as they well knew that other bands of hostile Indians were nearby and there would be probability of another Custer Massacre if we allowed the other bands to come up with us, as we were greatly outnumbered and could look for no more help from the agency. Our commander ordered the interpreter to notify the chief that they must pile their arms in a certain spot, to which he apparently agreed. About a dozen of the Indians laid down some old guns, their medicine man meanwhile exhorting them to fight, and our interpreters told our officers what to expect.

The medicine man threw a handful of dust into the air and blew a whistle which was the prearranged signal to start the ball rolling. They threw their blankets off and poured a volley into our ranks, doing considerable execution as we were at close quarters. In the ensuing hour and a half the red devils got all the fight they wanted. We won, but it cost us dearly, for as well as I can remember, we lost two officers and about forty men killed; and three officers, Lieutenants Mann, Garlington, and Hawthorne and seventy or eighty men wounded, [and] my own Troop A having seven killed and six wounded. There was considerable hand-to-hand fighting. I saw Captain George Wallace down five Indians before he had his skull crushed with an Indian war club. Also saw Sergeant Coffey of B Troop drop four Indians by clubbing them with his gun before he died. And Captain William G. Spencer of the Medical Corps ministered to the wounded under fire as unconcerned as though he were on dress parade. We gathered our dead and wounded, and as we were short of ambulances, some of our wounded had to ride with the dead bodies of their comrades, which must have been a nerve-racking experience for them, on our night trip back to the agency.

Myself and several others were detailed as guards over our wounded Indian prisoners and never heard a groan out of them, although several of them with shattered limbs and other painful gunshot wounds had to ride all night on bare-backed ponies. We arrived at our destination at daybreak on December 30, unloaded our dead and wounded, fed and watered our animals, and had just finished a much-needed breakfast and were anticipating that we would get a well-earned rest, when "Boots and Saddles" sounded once more and the tired bunch had to gallop to the relief of the sisters at the Catholic mission about five miles away, as the Indians had already fired and burned a couple of outbuildings and were about to burn the main buildings in which were several white sisters and three or four hundred Indian children. We drove them off, [but] a few of them acting as rearguard exchanged shots with us to keep us coming after them while the main body of the band prepared a trap for us, into which we would have walked if it had not been for Second Lieutenant John R. M. Taylor, Seventh Infantry, and his half-breed scouts, who located several thousand hostile Indians hidden on each side of the narrow trail through which we would have to ride after those who were acting as a bait for us. We were dismounted, fighting on foot and our horses and pack mules were in our rear, one man being in charge of four horses. In a short while we found ourselves running short of ammunition, as several of the pack mules, being wounded, had bolted with our ammunition. Luckily, several packs came loose, so that we had a chance to pick up a box or two.

Captain Myles Moylan of A Troop ordered the writer and another buddie to pick up a box of ammunition and follow the troop with it as they were returning to a knoll about two hundred yards away. We were making very slow progress as the box was heavy and upon coming up with I Troop, Captain Henry J. Nowlan in command, he asked us where we were going with it and I told him that Captain Moylan had ordered us to carry it to A Troop's new position. He ordered us to deliver it to him and as we hesitated, he pointed his forty-five Colt's revolver at us and the box left our possession immediately, I assure you. I heard afterwards that half of his command had only one round of ammunition left when we arrived on the scene.

Our commander seeing that the Indians were cognizant of the fact that we were running short of ammunition and were cut off from our horses, sent a courier back to the agency for re-enforcements and supplies. The Sioux were crowding us pretty close when Colonel Guy V. Henry arrived with four troops of the Tenth Cavalry and a battery of light artillery. The Indians did not linger any when they saw them and the artillery shells taught them a lesson which they will not soon forget, and we were glad to retire to the agency once more and get some food and rest. Our casualties were very light in this engagement, as the Indians are poor shots at a distance of two hundred yards or more. The next morning we buried forty-eight of our comrades during one of the worst blizzards we had ever experienced. The next few days were taken up with guard duty and hustling to keep warm.

About the middle of January, 1891, Colonel "Buffalo Bill" Cody arrived at the agency with several Indians who had been traveling with his wild west show. After a conference with Major General John R. Brooke, he took a few troops for an escort, rode out a few miles and coaxed the Indians to surrender and return to the agency, telling them that they could never win by fighting us, as the "Great Father" in Washington (meaning the president) had more pale-faced soldiers in numbers than the sands of the hills. It certainly impressed us very much to see what influence "Buffalo Bill" had over several thousand bloodthirsty redskins. There were so many of them that it took a couple of hours for them to file into the camp. That night, when all was quiet in camp, General Brooke had four pieces of light artillery placed on top of a hill to rake their camp if they should break loose again. Each piece had a tent placed over it to hide it from the Indians for the time being. When the coverings were removed the Indians showed a great respect for them, as one chief said to one of our interpreters, "Big guns heap bad. They shoot today and kill tomorrow," meaning that the large shells carried a great distance.

The next word that we received was that the old arch-fiend, Chief Sitting Bull, who was the prime mover in all Indian uprisings for several years past, with several other warriors had been killed trying to escape from their captors [on December 15, 1890]. I think that a detail of the Eighth Infantry, Second Cavalry [sic], and Indian police were in this encounter. Early in February, everything now being quiet, all of the troops who had been called out to help put an end to this uprising were concentrated at Pine Ridge Agency for a review and I understand that it was the largest gathering of regular troops up to that time since 1865. Several days later we packed up, said good-bye to our erstwhile enemies and our comrades in arms who took other routes, and marched back to Rushville, Nebraska, and boarded a train for Fort Riley, Kansas. But it seemed that fate decreed that trouble for some of our outfit was not at an end, as the second and third sections of our train were wrecked before reaching Manhatten, Kansas, killing and injuring several cavalry and artillery men. Captain Edward S. Godfrey lost the use of his right arm. We arrived at old Fort Riley once more without further mishap and it certainly was a joyful homecoming for the officers and men who had the pleasure of meeting the "Girls They Left Behind Them" three months previously. We settled down once more to garrison life, satisfied that we had done our little bit to help win some of the northwestern territory, which at this writing contributes largely toward the nation's bread rations. . . .

An Army Medic at Wounded Knee (By Andrew M. Flynn, formerly of Troop A, Seventh U. S. Cavalry. From *Winners of the West*, November-December, 1939)

I enlisted in New York City in the year 1888. I was sent to Jefferson Barracks, Missouri, was there about four months, then was sent with many others to Fort Riley, Kansas, and joined A Troop of the Seventh United States Cavalry and went through the regular routine of learning my tactics and riding, doing saber drill, etc. There were lots of things besides. I remember very well that there was a heavy rain the day before we arrived at Fort Riley. It was a good thing for us because there was a large detail sent to pull out sunflowers that almost covered the parade ground. Some of the boys in my squad were complaining about this, saying, "I came here to be a soldier." I urged them to pitch in and see if we could not beat the other squads, telling them we came to do what we were told to do, whatever it was. Well, we all stuck to it and our squad was the first one to be done, and it was no small task, for the sunflowers were very tall, some of them almost ten feet.

So much for that. We had very nice new barracks with a wonderful mess hall and good food. Much better than we had at Jefferson Barracks. The "non-coms" there had their own mess hall and, boy, but didn't they live high. But that was changed very soon, as there was a place there where old soldiers from different places came on furlough to reenlist, and they began to complain about the food they were getting, such as "slumgullion" for dinner and a piece of dry bread and about three prunes for supper. There happened to be a quartermaster sergeant among the men and he went to the commanding officer, who was Captain Henry W. Wessels, Jr., of the Third Cavalry, from Fort Sam Houston, Texas. The captain said he did not know what he could do about it, but he said he would try to get it changed. However, this quartermaster sergeant did not wait, but wrote to Washington about it and someone was sent from there to inspect the whole thing. We had a large place where we had cows and lots of pigs and a very fine garden, but we did not get much of it. The man came from Washington incognito. He made out that he was an English lord and wanted to find out how things were done in the United States. He was there for a few days and found out all about it. So he went to Captain Wessels, giving him his card, and said that there must be a change and that every man be well fed, that not only a few were to get all the good things. Every "non-com" there, with the exception of our first sergeant, was sent out to the regiments, which they did not like. So it pays to be honest and kind to others.

Now back to Fort Riley, the geographical center of the United States, they told us. We were treated well there and had a fine set of officers from Colonel James W. Forsyth all along the line. We had fine quarters, a nice chapel, and a good chaplain and a Y. M. C. A. secretary, a very fine man whom I liked very much. In fact, I liked everything there. There were the great open spaces like Pawnee Flats, where we used to drill in the early morning in the "good old summer time," then come in and have a shower and go for breakfast and then had target practice. I never was much of a shot but I thought I was a fairly good horseman.

I had a good horse and was sorry to leave him behind me, but you know, the best of friends must part. I remember we took a long trip to Topeka, Kansas, to a Grand Army encampment, where we were escort to the Honorable Benjamin Harrison . . . . I tell you, we had a wonderful time of it. There were many G. A. R's there, probably between two and three hundred of them. We then returned to Fort Riley to the fall maneuvers in the Indian Territory. That was a great thing for a "rookie" like me. I was not very old, but I tried to do my share in capturing the enemy.

One day, shortly after payday, a farmer came into camp with a load of watermelons, supposedly, and he said the price was from ten cents to a dollar. Well, I bought one for a dime, which was very good, but when the boys who had bought the dollar ones cut into them they found that they were hollowed out and that there was a pint of whiskey inside. I tell you, that load of watermelons soon disappeared and the old man gave the whip to the horse and off they went so fast you couldn't see them for dust. That was the only whiskey that was in camp so far as I know, and it must have been the real squirrel whiskey, for the fellows who drank it climbed the trees yelling, "I'm a squirrel!" When we got back to Fort Riley things were rather quiet, so I started to work to finish learning my tactics. By this time, I was getting very well acquainted with the place and the people there. I used to go to chapel on Sundays and take part in the services and I became acquainted with Major John Van R. Hoff. As they had no children, they invited me to their home and were very nice to me.

About this time, our head sergeant surgeon [hospital steward] asked me if I would like to learn first aid to the injured. I told him I would like to very much and he gave me all the instructions. I learned it very thoroughly, passing two examinations in it. Then I asked for a transfer to the hospital detachment but was refused. I asked my captain, Myles Moylan, who had always been very nice to me, why I had been refused. He told me that he wanted me with him as a "non-com." I told him that I thought that I was too young for that, but he said that I would do all right. About that time there were rumors of the Indians going on the warpath and I said to my captain, "If you were wounded, would you want someone who did not know how to take care of you, or would you rather have me?" He just laughed it off.

Well, we did get into that war. In the latter part of September, 1890, we had word to pack up and to go to Pine Ridge, South Dakota. We traveled over the F. E. and M. V. [Fremont, Elkhorn and Missouri Valley] Railroad and detrained at a junction point named Rushville in Nebraska, which we left as soon as possible for Pine Ridge, where we pitched our tents in a little valley. There were some negro troops there who gave us food.

We were encamped there until the 27th of December, when we were ordered out to Wounded Knee to intercept Chief Big Foot and his tribe of renegade Indians. We had only four troops with us, but we went after the enemy and captured them without a fight and brought them into camp at Wounded Knee. This was on the afternoon of the 28th of December. Half of A and I Troops had charge of guarding the Indians, so we put a chain guard around them and had them pretty well tied up, we thought, though we were not as confident as we might have been because we had a feeling that they had some guns with them. We discovered later that they did, but it turned out that the guns were their undoing because they did not know how to reload them. We were very glad when about eight o'clock we saw the four troops coming on the other side. That evening as I was lying down with a piece of a bale of hay for my pillow and the stars for my canopy, there was a great commotion among the Indians which lasted most of the night. We discovered that it was the old medicine man chanting over a death.

One of our scouts asked me if I knew what he was saying. I replied that I did not. He then said to me, "Have you said your prayers yet?," and I said "yes." [He continued,] "The medicine man is telling the Indians not to give up their guns because they were to be killed anyway."

We were formed in a hollow square which was a bad thing for us because it took our men so long to get out of each other's way when the firing started. That was how so many of our men were killed or wounded before we had a chance to use our guns.

[Once the shooting began,] as I had charge of a squad of first aid men, I handled the bandages and other medical supplies and was quite busy. I may say here that the first man we picked up was our first lieutenant, Ernest A. Garlington, of Troop A. He had a compound fracture of the right elbow. I first stopped the flow of blood, although he had lost quite a lot of it. I took my lance and ripped the sleeve from his blouse. But before I had it all done, he said, "Hell! That's my new blouse!" I cut not only the sleeve of his blouse, but his shirt sleeve, too, and stopped the flow of blood, and then took him to his tent and laid him on his bed.

Then he fainted and I had quite a time with him, but I had a little medicine on my hip and found a silver teaspoon and put some of the "medicine" in it and worked till I got some of it into his mouth and he opened his eyes and said, "The red devils got me!" He wanted to get his pistol, but I told him he did not need it and if he did have it he could not use it. I then went down to the hospital tent and told the surgeon, Major John Van R. Hoff, about Lieutenant Garlington, telling him that I had done the best I could for him and I was hurrying out to look for some more of the wounded, when he told me to sit down and rest. I told him I could not stop and he said that there were a lot more of the men out there who could handle the rest of the wounded. He then went to his medicine chest and brought me something in a little glass. I told him that I did not drink, but he said he knew but that this was medicine and he held up a small mirror to my face. It was as white as a sheet. Then he gave me some more. It did seem to help some.

On my going out on the field again, I met Second Lieutenant John C. Waterman. There were four or five Indians lying on the ground with their blankets on, supposedly dead. But suddenly a shot was fired and we saw a man drop. Lieutenant Waterman and I went around the corner of a tent near the Indians and watched them. We saw one of them raise his head a little and as he saw someone coming toward him, fired on him. Lieutenant Waterman sent for the sharpshooter crew and they came on the double quick and each of them got his man. As I was walking towards the ravine where there was still some shooting going on, I met Second Lieutenant Thomas Q. Donaldson, Jr. He had been shot in the groin. He had his watch in his little pocket of his pants and it was all smashed.

I picked out the broken glass and other stuff and cleaned the wound with medicated gauze and sent him to the hospital. While doing this, we were crouching behind an old wagon. A bullet hit on the rim of the wheel quite close and we hurried to better cover as there were quite a few Indians in that part of the ravine, which overhung, giving a shelter from the outside. The bravest deed that was done to my knowledge was that of a corporal from the artillery. He ran his little Hotchkiss gun right up to the mouth of the ravine and stayed there until he had gotten the last man there. In looking over his gun after the battle, the marks of the Indians' bullets were right over the muzzle of his gun.

There have been various stories told by others and these have been taken from reports. I was there on the job from the beginning to the end—first in the capture of Big Foot and then in the bloody fight. Our men did not have much chance to get at the Indians as we were formed in a hollow square and it took some time to get in position to use our guns and they did good work then, but the Indians were better armed than we were. The old medicine man had about sixteen bullet holes in his body. The first shot was fired by some crazy Indian. The one mistake that I saw was that the Indians should have been made to remove their blankets, for after the first shots were fired, before inspection, there were four or five big bucks who dropped down on their faces as though they were dead and as I was passing near them there was a man a few yards from where I was standing who was shot through the calves of both legs. Some of the first aid men picked him up.

I met Lieutenant Waterman and he asked if I knew where the shots had come from. I told him that I was going to find out. So I went behind one of our tents and hid and by and by there was a man going across from where we stood and one of the supposed-to-be-dead Indians lifted his head and fired at this man. Fortunately, he missed. I told the lieutenant that he should call the firing squad, which he did in a hurry. When they opened fire on those men, they let out a great yell and threw their blankets and guns away. But it was no good. They were all killed. It was shortly after that that I had saved Lieutenant Garlington's life. He was very severely wounded. He had suffered a compound fracture of the right elbow. I know that I saved his life and Surgeon Major John Van R. Hoff will bear me out in my statement, as I reported to him about Lieutenant Garlington. He was our first lieutenant of A Troop. I did not see my captain, Myles Moylan, during the fight, but he was on the job like all the other good soldiers.

As I went up and down the camp to see the wounded and give them a drink of water and speak words of comfort to them, a man called me over to where he was laying in the hospital tent and told me he had some kind of weight on his back. I examined him and found that a bullet had lodged between his flesh and his skin and I just took my little lance and cut a little hole there and took out the bullet and gave it to him as a keepsake. When I fixed him up he felt much more comfortable. I believe this man was Sergeant George Lloyd of Troop I. There were many others whom I helped, also, but the shooting finally ended and I was very glad to get to our troop again. That was a trying time.

As we did not have much room, we had to load up the dead and put the wounded on top of them. Just as I was looking over the field, I came across a dead squaw and a little papoose who was sucking on a piece of hardtack. I picked up the little papoose and carried it in my arms. A little way farther on, I found another dead squaw and another papoose. I picked it up, too, and brought them over near the hospital tent, where there were a number of Indian women.

As I came over to where they were, I met a big, husky sergeant who said, "Why didn't you smash them up against a tree and kill them? Some day they'll be fighting us."

I told him I would rather smash him than those little innocent children. The Indian women were so glad that I saved the papooses that they almost kissed me. But I told them I didn't have time for that.

I also found a white woman who was shot in the wrist. I asked her how she came to be there and she said that she had been stolen from her people. On going a little way farther, we passed an old outhouse and we heard a noise inside, somewhat like a cat, and we looked in and saw a little papoose. She was a beautiful child and clothed in a fine buckskin suit. Second Lieutenant Herbert G. Squires [sic] went in and got it and it began to laugh so he said it's name would be Laughing Swan, and that he was going to take it home to his wife, which he did. After everything was loaded up, we saddled our horses and prepared to march to Pine Ridge and on getting outside of Wounded

Knee we saw that the prairie ahead of us had been set on fire. We had to detour for quite a way before we got on the road to Pine Ridge. Then we met a troop of horsemen. We did not know whether they were friend or foe, so they called out to us to find out who we were and we did the same. We found that they were coming out to help us so we finally got to Pine Ridge, where the wounded were taken care of.

On the following day, December 30, six troops of the Seventh Cavalry were ordered out to White Clay Creek or Mountain. Some claim this was just a mere skirmish, but I say that it was almost another Custer field, as shots were fired at us from all directions as we left our horses in a sheltered place and crawled up the side of the mountain. Major Whitside had to call for a volunteer to go into Pine Ridge and get out the Ninth Cavalry (colored), commanded by Colonel Guy V. Henry.

The volunteer came up to Major Whitside and saluted him and said: "Well, Major, I got to [go?] sometime once, so I will go."

He had a fine horse and then Major Whitside took him by the hand and shook it heartily and said, "God be with you!" and away he went in flying charge and you ought to have seen the bullets fly. He got away safely and reached General Miles at Pine Ridge. His horse dropped dead and he lay down by the dead horse and cried as though his heart would break.

General Miles said to him, "I will get [you] a new horse."

But he said, "Oh, General, there is no more like him. We were great pals."

The reason for sending for reinforcements was that the Indians were coming from all sides. You could take your hat and put it on your gun, and, Bang! The bullets came flying. Major Whitside called for the sharpshooters to get their guns loaded. Then someone put his hat on his gun, so that they could see where the shots would come from. As soon as they found out, they fired two volleys and there were no more shots from the Indians.

In the meantime, Colonel Guy V. Henry's Black Demons came up the side of the mountain yelling and shooting. They came in the shape of a V. Out of this victory we had seven wounded and one killed. First Lieutenant James D. Mann was wounded and died when he reached Fort Riley. We lost two very fine officers—Captain George D. Wallace, who was killed by an Indian war club by a squaw; his skull being partly lifted off his head, but there were six dead Indians at his feet and he still had his gun.

We got down from the side of the mountain and got our field guns across on the other side and fired a volley out of them. It went into the Indian powwow that was being held. We shelled it and broke it all up. There were a large number of Indians seemingly on the warpath and there were strict orders sent to the several chiefs to turn all guns over to the government. There were a few weeks spent in getting the guns and sending the men back to where they belonged, as they had buried a lot of the guns in pits. Then the Indians went into a place which looked like an amphitheater. When they went in they had some cattle and when they had eaten them all up they wanted to get out and get some more.

Some of the chiefs wanted to have a powwow with some of the generals and told them they would not give in [sic—up?] their guns or men. General Miles told them to tell the Indians that they had to give up their guns. In the meantime, the artillerymen during the night had put up the field guns and put a tent over them. They were standing on the side of a hill and the Indians did not know what was in the tent. It was almost directly across from where the Indians were camped and during the powwow General Miles and his staff told the chiefs to come with them and they went right up to the tent and were told that every gun they had in the camp where they were and those guns that they had buried must be given up. They said, "No give up guns! No go back to reservation."

At a given signal, the tent was opened up and the two guns were pointed right at the place where the Indians were camped. They grunted, then they saw the guns. They were told, "Now, you give up the guns and send the Indians back to the reservation or there will be no Indians left." There were two chiefs whose names I remember, . . . Rain in the Face and Young Man Afraid of His Horses, who, by the way, was made chief of all the scouts. So the chiefs were told that there would be wagons placed near them and every man was to give his gun to be put in the wagons. Then Young Man Afraid of His Horse's (which was a misnomer, for he was not afraid of anything) told them to get busy and the first Indian that wanted to go and fight would be shot and I will be the shooter, he said. They gave up their guns and started back to their tepees and it took quite a few days before this was done. There were some scouts sent out around to see if they could dig up any more guns.

I shall never forget that last day when they buried the dead soldiers. They could not fire a volley over the graves for fear of arousing the Indians. All they could do was to blow taps. It was a terribly dreary day—the sky seemed to bend down to earth. Of course, I was just a young chap then and had not seen anything like this before. There were lots of the older soldiers who had never seen it either. We broke up camp from Pine Ridge and camped away towards Nebraska. It seemed the whole United States Army was there. The tents seemed to stretch away about five miles, and you could see the Indians peeking over the tops of the mountains. I had quite a few talks with Old American Indian Horse [sic—American Horse?]. He said that the man that started the ghost dances was a fanatic. Someone was saying that he must have heard the missionaries talking about it. But why blame the missionaries? They had not told this man about the Indians and buffalos coming back at that time. The missionaries did a great deal of good all over the western country.

In closing this narrative of forty-nine years ago, I should like to say that I believe that I have given a true story. [I saw] . . . an article in which appears a list of eighteen men upon whom Congress has seen fit to bestow the nation's highest award, the Congressional Medal for their conduct at Wounded Knee. I should like to know just what those men did at the Battle of Wounded Knee. I myself had charge of a crew of first aid to the injured and was on the field all day taking care of the wounded. I saved Lieutenant Garlington's life, as he had a compound fracture of the right elbow. I administered first aid to Lieutenant Donaldson. I removed a bullet from Sergeant Lloyd's back, and helped many others. To cap the climax, I saved two papooses from someone who would doubtless have killed them and gave them to the squaws, who said "Pale Face heap good."

I believe that I, too, was entitled to a medal for what I did. Of course, I was just a young lad and a rookie, but I did my share of good. . . .

A soldier's leather diary and pencil. *Editor's Collection*

A Memory of the Pine Ridge Campaign (By Henry B. Becker, formerly of Troop E, Seventh U. S. Cavalry. From *Winners of the West*, June 28, 1943)

On the night of December 28, 1890, the second battalion of the Seventh, Troops C, D, E, [and] G, were called to Pine Ridge, South Dakota, to reinforce the troops of the Seventh under Major Samuel M. Whitside, who had captured Chief Big Foot and his hostile Indians [who were] surrounded and guarded at Wounded Knee Creek, about eighteen miles from the agency. I was given charge of a mule carrying two cases of ammunition. When we had covered about half the distance, I fell out of line to adjust the mule's pack, and also took time to tighten the horse's girth. When I remounted, I found myself alone on the trail, the troops having disappeared. I kept on for several miles and then I heard hoof beats from behind. I pulled up short, and when the riders were close enough, I drew my .45 Colt out of the holster and held my carbine ready for emergency use. Then I challenged: "Who goes there?"

"Frank Grouard and Indian scouts."

"Advance, Grouard. Scouts stay where you are."

Believe me, it was a relief to see this well-known scout just then. He asked me how come that I was out here alone, except for the very dangerous company of the ammunition-carrying mule. After we had proceeded a few more miles along the trail, he called my attention to a pony about a hundred yards from the trail. The three scouts fanned out in the direction of the pony, and I saw an Indian mount and disappear in the distance. Then, without further incidents, my escort rode with me in to the camp at Wounded Knee. The troops had made a detour and the captain (Charles S. Ilsley) had sent a few men back to locate me. He told me he would never again entrust me with the care of a mule, especially one carrying such important cargo. I am writing this because I believe Frank Grouard deserves all the credit for my being alive for all these years since December 28, 1890, and I have been informed that his remains rest in sacred ground at or near St. Joseph, Missouri.

A Trooper's Vignette (By Frank Sturr, formerly of Troop K, Seventh U. S. Cavalry. From *Winners of the West*, March 30, 1931)

I was a sergeant of K Troop, Seventh U. S. Cavalry, serving five years in said troop, and mustered out with excellent discharge on May 1, 1892. Took part in the battle in question [Wounded Knee], also the White Clay Creek

Fight later, and it was my business to know what was going on among our men, but at no time did I see or hear of any drinking or carousing throughout the whole campaign. . . .

The renegades . . . were captured by four troops of the Seventh Cavalry and a detachment of E Battery, First Artillery, on December 28, 1890, and we took them into our camp on Wounded Knee Creek and furnished them rations, where they powwowed all that night. A cordon was placed around them with every man in the command on guard. Our officials at once, on the capture, dispatched a messenger into Pine Ridge Agency to notify General Nelson A. Miles, who was in command. General Miles sent out four additional troops of the Seventh Cavalry to join us, with orders to disarm the Sitting Bull renegades [sic—the chief had been killed on December 15], and above all, not to allow them to reach the agency under arms.

About 8:30 on the morning of December 29, 1890, we were ordered to search all tepees and get all the warriors together. When this was accomplished a demand was made for them to turn over their arms. This they hesitated in doing, and all the while the squaws sang and kept up a regular din by beating on tom-toms. Finally the medicine man reached down and took a handful of prairie grass and snow and released same over his head, which apparently was the signal awaited. The Indians at once dropped their blankets, under which their guns had been concealed, and opened fire. . . . That night we loaded all of our killed and wounded into wagons, together with some seventeen wounded Indians, mostly squaws and children, and made a night march to Pine Ridge Agency. Our wagon train was attacked several times en route by bands of hostile Indians. On reaching the agency, a hospital was established under a splendid physician, Dr. John Van R. Hoff, and the Indian wounded received like medical care as our own troopers.

In the agency there were over 3,000 Messiah-crazed Indians, and General Miles well knew to allow Sitting Bull's band to join Chief Red Cloud would be the signal for the whole of the Sioux Nation taking the warpath. Finally, regiments of all branches of service—cavalry, infantry, and artillery, as well as troops of Indian scouts—, began arriving at Pine Ridge from all parts of the country. The First Infantry, from as far distant as California, and our own General [John] Pershing of this period, was there with his Indian scouts. Soon a cordon was thrown around the entire Sioux Nation and gradually closed in the circle until all Indians about the reservation were within. They were then disarmed, with the military rejoicing that their worries were at an end, temporarily at least. . . .

On the Pine Ridge Campaign (By Grant C. Topping, formerly of Troop F, Sixth U. S. Cavalry. From *Winners of the West*, February, 1925)

On November 23, 1890, telegraphic orders were received at Fort Wingate, New Mexico, this post being situated five miles from the station. Colonel Carr was at that time in command of the Sixth U. S. Cavalry. . . . We embarked immediately and on December 9, 1890, arrived at Rapid City, South Dakota, and were given a leading part in the Sioux campaign. General Miles distributed us along the railroad north of Rapid City and along the [Cheyenne] river on the edge of the Badlands . . . .

From December 15, 1890, to February 2, 1891, we were in the field against the Sioux. . . . there were deep snows and intense coldness, and this weather seemed to favor the Indians. The men and horses of the Sixth suffered untold misery but no difficulties were too great for the Sixth to overcome. Second Lieutenant John J. Pershing, with Troop A of the Sixth U. S. Cavalry, met the savages at their own game and none were braver against the savage foe than First Lieutenant Augustine T. Blocksom. The trails were hard to find and the Sixth Cavalry performed a feat during this campaign which is still fresh in the minds of the boys who fought at Wounded Knee.

On December 24 a message was received that Big Foot was moving south on the Deep Fork trail. At this time we were on White Horse Creek. A courier from the Seventh U. S. Cavalry . . . now came into camp being nearly overcome by fatigue and hard riding. "Boots and Saddles" was sounded and Colonel Eugene A. Carr ordered a forced crossing over the [Cheyenne] river . . . , which was covered by floating ice. No obstacles were too great as we were after the redskins. Those who participated in this charge will never forget it as even the alkaline pools were frozen, the weather being so cold. Christmas morning found us on the pinnacle of one of the highest points in the Badlands, from which we could see the country for miles around.

On December 29 the Battle of Wounded Knee started. Little the world knew, especially the people of the United States, that it was the death blow to the Indians. The Indians finally surrendered and the Sioux campaign or war passed into history. Later, the Sixth Cavalry were left here to guard the Badlands and the Pine Ridge Agency against further uprisings and depredations. I will not state nor attempt to state the exact number of cavalrymen and infantrymen killed in this battle as there is a dispute in regard to the actual number of regulars killed.

The picture is too sad to go into details any deeper. We spent many hours digging ditches and into these we pitched the bodies of the dead Indians. I did not count the number of Indians killed. Our boys were buried to the right of the Pine Ridge Agency and later they were taken up and sent to their respected [respective] people. Being the youngest man at the time of this battle, I do not suppose that there are four comrades left of the F Troop of the Sixth Cavalry. All the soldiers of Troop K of the Seventh were killed with the exception of three [sic—this is an exaggeration, although Troops B and K of the Seventh Cavalry together lost more than thirty men in killed and wounded]. I wish to state here that any comrade of the Sixth Cavalry who reads this article can recollect the Ninth Cavalry. The colored boys deserve a great credit for the work they did and I am here to state as a living witness [that] had it not been for them this letter from me would never have been read by the public and especially those who were in Troop F of the Sixth. Sleeping on snow, a saddle for a pillow and a horse blanket for covering was no snap.

Infantry Operations at Pine Ridge (By Richard T. Burns, formerly of Company D, Second U. S. Infantry. From *Winners of the West*, March, 1938)

I was not at Wounded Knee, but close by at Pine Ridge Agency. About the night of November 18 everything was going as usual at Fort Omaha, Nebraska, when orders came for A, B, C, and D Companies of the Second U. S. Infantry, then stationed there, to leave inside an hour, which we did. We left so fast we did not have a sergeant or top sergeant with us and the captain, James Miller, was wild. We boarded the Fremont, Elkhorn and Missouri Special Train and rushed to Rushville, Nebraska, where we unloaded. We had fifteen minutes for coffee and at about 7 p.m. joined up with three troops of the Ninth colored cavalry and made a forced march, taking all night as we halted every few minutes until the cavalry scouts reported all right ahead. Every time we halted, the companies would crowd together. One minute you would be in the center of the company and the next you would be jostled out.

Orders were not to strike a match or speak above a whisper. The boys were all old Civil and Indian war vets but were getting pretty nervous before daybreak and began slipping cartridges into their rifles and the officers warning them not to do so. We could see the campfires and hear the Indians on the bluffs, but got to the agency and took charge. We camped on the hill and the cavalry camped in a hollow. In a day or two the other four companies of the Second Infantry [arrived, along with] the rest of the Ninth Cavalry, the Seventh Cavalry, and E Battery, First Artillery, and F Battery of the Fifth Artillery. Also, one company of the Eighth Infantry with machine guns joined us.

The Seventh and the Ninth cavalry were out every day in squadrons looking for Big Foot's band and scouting all the way to the Black Hills. Young Man Afraid of His Horses was on a hunting trip and came in peaceably, but they could not locate Big Foot's band until a squadron of the Seventh Cavalry surprised them at Wounded Knee. A man of the Seventh Cavalry told me two troops dismounted to search the Indians when they threw off their blankets and a hand-to-hand fight started. With the Seventh Cavalry were a howitzer [Hotchkiss] battery and a wagon train and it was a merry-go-round.

December 29 was the fight and the dead and wounded were brought in that night. The wounded were put in tents back of the woodpile and the dead were laid on the ground with blankets over them. There were over seventy-five killed and wounded soldiers. Also, a lot of squaws and papooses were wounded as it could not be avoided in the mix-up. Captain Wallace was among the soldiers killed, and Lieutenant Garlington severely wounded. They buried the soldiers back of the mission schools in a blinding blizzard on New Year's Day, 1891. While they were burying them, I was on No. 1 Post Main Guard when I heard accoutrements rattling and saw a darker spot on the Chadron, Nebraska, road and turned out the guard. In a few minutes they came into view. They were the First U. S. Infantry. Colonel William R. Shafter and General Nelson Miles were with them. This was the first we saw of General Miles at the agency. The first thing he asked the sergeant of the guard was, "What makes this camp so still?" And the sergeant told him the troops were all to the funeral of the men killed at Wounded Knee. The next question he asked was, "How did they attend?" The sergeant said, "With side arms." Miles went wild and sent an aide to the cemetery ordering all the men except the actual burying party back to camp. Miles said, "The idea, attending the funeral with only side arms in the middle of a hostile country."

That day he ordered the Seventh and Ninth Cavalry and Second Infantry out of the agency right into the blizzard and a mile or two out we got lost and had to make camp. The Seventh were separated altogether. A troop would come along and ask if we had seen anymore of their troops, and they were told several troops went by and said they lost the rest of the regiment. One of them camped alongside of us. The Ninth Cavalry went snowblind and had to go into camp somewhere.

Members of Company A, Second Infantry, at Fort Omaha, in 1893. Left to right, standing, Privates Hoffman, Bartel, Phillips, Mitchell, and Corporal Patrick Prendergast. Sitting, with rabbits, Corporal Regan and Private Jenkins. *Editor's collection*

Speaking of the Ninth Cavalry, I heard of them [earlier?] marching from the Black Hills to Pine Ridge Agency ninety miles, without stopping. They just got into the camp and unsaddled when a corporal rode in and reported the wagon train was attacked. The Ninth Cavalry (Colonel Guy V. Henry) and the Seventh Cavalry (Colonel Forsyth) went to the rescue immediately, some of the Ninth riding bareback.

Then the fun began around the agency. The Oglala Sioux under Red Cloud and some Cheyennes were under guard at the Pine Ridge Agency. The Brulé Sioux . . . from Rosebud came down and started a scrap with the Oglalas, thinking they were holding out on them. Then the Pine Ridge Indian Police . . . made it a three-cornered affair. The cavalry regiments were all out scouting and our companies were laying on the ground, two at each corner of the agency. This was before Wounded Knee. Our colonel, Frank Wheaton, brigadier general from the Civil War, was in command with orders not to fire unless absolutely necessary. It was a rather tough three-cornered scrap, bullets flying all around and the artillery officers begging for permission to fire. In the meantime, Indians were sniping from the bluffs and A and B Companies deployed and ran them off, having a few men wounded and half of our tents were riddled, but no one was in them. There were twelve battles fought in the 1890-1891 campaign, but you never hear anything about it. All newspaper correspondents were ordered to keep out of the war zone, so I guess that is the reason.

Recollections of the Pine Ridge Campaign and Wounded Knee (By August Hettinger, formerly of Company H, Eighth U. S. Infantry. From *Winners of the West*, December 30, 1934, January 30, 1935, and February 28, 1935)

During the fall of 1890 there were rumors of an Indian outbreak on the three Sioux reservations located in [South] Dakota. It seems that all through the summer of 1890 Indian . . . [dissidents] went around among the tribes and spread discontent; some of these complaints were based on facts, but ninety per cent of them were pure fiction. They promised the Indians, among other things, the assistance of the Great Spirit in the extermination of the white man, and as soon as this small feat was accomplished the buffalo were to return automatically in countless numbers. All this meant an easy life to the Indian and, as he is human, he took considerable stock in it. . . . While none of us soldiers were bloodthirsty, all the reports from the scene of trouble was good news to us, for the reason that we had been stationed at Fort Niobrara, [Nebraska,] since 1886, when the Eighth Infantry came fresh from the Geronimo Campaign in Arizona.

Only a soldier can realize what we suffered—or thought we did—during the four years in the sand hills of Nebraska, for with the exception of a short summer maneuver there was absolutely no excitement whatever. But the storm finally burst on November 25, 1890, and the Sioux Indian "Messiah Craze" campaign, as it is officially known, was on. As the order came at 9 a.m. to march at 2 p.m., there was sure some excitement in the fort, and to make matters worse—or better—most of the soldiers started a jollification at the canteen. The officers also laid in a supply for strictly private use, but I regret to say a good deal of this private stock disappeared in a mysterious way before the wagon train left the fort. To my own knowledge the quartermaster came to me and stated that two of his gallon jugs had been found empty and he asked me to take care of one. I managed to get the one he turned over to me to the Rosebud Agency by putting it in a nosebag and filling it to the top with oats.

Promptly at 2 p.m. the "General" call sounded and we were off; A, B, F, and H companies of the Eighth Infantry, and two troops, my own Captain Daniel T. Wells in command, and Luther Richardson . . . of the Ninth Cavalry. We crossed the Niobrara River and then left the main road to Valentine, turned sharply to the right, crossed the Minicatosa and climbed the steep bluffs along the north side of the river and followed a dim trail leading straight north across the prairie to the Rosebud Agency, forty miles away. Unluckily, on crossing the Minicatosa, the H Company wagon upset and the boys had the pleasure of seeing their bedding, extra supply of tobacco, stationery, etc., going down the river. Everything was fished out again, but the supplies were ruined; writing paper and postage stamps were at a premium during the coming winter. But the funny part of it was that the teamster of this wagon, a noted character of our company known by the nickname of "Limber," always bragged that all he needed was a piece of buckskin to drive a six-mule team around a ten-cent piece, and then he upset our bed wagon with all our precious possessions in the river before we were two miles from the fort.

Before we got away from the fort, a little incident happened that nearly landed me in the guardhouse. It seems that at the last moment the department commander decided to organize a battery of one-pounder Hotchkiss [guns] as a part of each expedition, the members of which were to be drawn from the different companies. I was detailed to drive the four-mule ammunition wagon. That sure got my goat; here was a likely campaign in sight, for which we had waited for years, and . . . I was told to drive mules in a different organization. Only a soldier can realize my predicament. The company means everything to a soldier, but as the first sergeant threatened to put me in the guardhouse unless I reported to the quartermaster immediately, I had to go or miss the expedition altogether. The whole incident proved to be a piece of luck afterwards, for the reason that my own company was left at the Rosebud Agency during the campaign, while the two troops of cavalry, the battery of light artillery and Company A of the Eighth Infantry were detailed to go to the assistance of the Seventh Cavalry just before the Battle of Wounded Knee, and by being a member of the battery I got to see the whole show.

The forced march of forty miles from Fort Niobrara to the agency was a heartbreaker to most of the infantrymen, but nevertheless we arrived there at daylight in the morning. It was just bright enough to see Short Bull pull out with about 1,500 warriors in the direction of Eagle Pass. A forty-mile march is no particular feat for an infantry command to make after they are two or three days on the road, but to make forty miles under heavy packs the first day out can only be accomplished by the American doughboy. In this connection, it may be mentioned that at that time, in 1890, K Company, Eighth Infantry, held the world record—they marched fifty-eight miles in twenty-four hours during the Geronimo Campaign in old Mexico. But this feat was tied by A Company, Eighth Infantry, during the march from the Rosebud [Agency] to the assistance of the Seventh Cavalry when they made fifty-eight miles in twenty-four hours in from twelve to fifteen inches of snow, and in three days and three nights they marched 128 miles.

But I am digressing from the story. After breakfast, we pitched camp in the agency and for nearly a month the command was busy getting in shape for a winter campaign. The weather was unusually cold, but everybody was busy drilling, [conducting] target practice for the recruits, breaking in a string of sixty pack mules, drilling a detachment of Indian scouts, organizing the remaining 500 or 600 Indians, and issuing rations. The Hotchkiss field guns amused the Indians a great deal; we used a big lime rock and for a while an old cabin a mile away as a target, but as the cabin lasted only one hour for a target we had to fall back again on a large limestone cliff across the valley. They could understand the workings of the gun, but the explosion of the shell remained a mystery to the old Indians, and they actually were afraid of the shell. You could not get one to as much as touch a cartridge.

About a week after the outbreak, General Miles took command of all the forces in the field, and as he had no superior as an Indian fighter and organizer everything went off according to schedule. The weather was fierce at times, but right at the start General Miles equipped all the troops with suitable clothing. His strategy consisted in making a big drive from all directions to one common center; this center was the Pine Ridge Agency. And he succeeded in this admirably. When the roundup was complete there was something like 18,000 hostile Indians in one camp in White Clay Creek guarded by something like 3,500 soldiers in four different camps. But I am getting ahead of the story. Nothing very exciting occurred at the Rosebud except that we received a big batch of recruits which nearly doubled the strength of the companies. It was of course quite a change for these boys from some quiet farm in Indiana where most of them came from, to an Indian agency in the middle of winter, where to go beyond the protection of the camp meant certain death. The issuing of beef on the hoof to the Indians was

Non-commissioned staff at Fort Niobrara, Nebraska, 1886. Standing, left to right: Hans Schroeder, Assistant Hospital Steward; Hans Petersen, Principal Musician, Eighth Infantry; Raymond Wiegand, Post Quartermaster Sergeant; Simon Askins, Commissary Sergeant. Sitting, left to right: Albert Fensch, Hospital Steward; Charles Cramer, Drum Major, Eighth Infantry; Professor Carlsen, Band Leader, Eighth Infantry; George Castle, Sergeant Major, Eighth Infantry; "Billy" Edwards, Regimental Quartermaster Sergeant, Eighth Infantry. Hospital Steward Fensch attended the dying Lieutenant Colonel William H. Lewis at the Battle of Punished Woman's Fork in 1878, and prepared the account of that engagement presented in this book. *Editor's collection*

a revelation to most of them, for it was nothing to see an Indian riding through the camp at top speed with 100 feet of gut tied to the horn of his saddle, rope fashion. The gut represented his share of the beef. Or to see a number of otherwise attractive young squaws sitting around the agency building chawing raw beef gut, the same as a white girl would gum, while the blood was running down both sides of their jaws. However, they [the recruits] soon got bravely over being surprised at anything and by the time they got into Fort McKinney the following spring they were veterans in every sense of the word. The American soldier in every case proves his adaptability. They had also no more illusions about the Indian.

Christmas day came and went a little more dreary than it would have been at a fort, but not much more so. (This holiday is always a heart-wringer to young soldiers no matter where stationed. A soldier in the Regular Army in those days had to depend on his own resources for recreation; companionship outside of the fort we had none.) . . . . Like a flash out of the sky came the order to march at 9:30 p.m. on December 27, 1890. This made a stir, as it was thirty minutes after taps had sounded. The camp was full of wild rumors, but nobody outside of the commanding officer knew even where we were going. All we knew . . . was that we had to march at midnight. The command consisted of two troops of the Ninth Cavalry, the mountain guns, and Company A, Eighth Infantry, to guard the wagon train. Captain Folliot A. Whitney was in command and Charles Taggett was chief of scouts, of which we had six. Young Spotted Tail was a member of the scouts. This Charles Taggett was a half-breed, his father having been a missionary for forty years among the Brulé Sioux. He was highly educated and all the tribes had the greatest confidence in him. He became chief interpreter during the big powwows the Indians and General Miles had in February, 1891, as the Indians refused pointblank to have Frank Grouard act in that capacity. I nearly forgot to mention Foolish Elk, the best Indian scout at that time in Dakota—outside of Charles Taggett. I was sorry that my own company was not selected as an escort because A Company had the worst reputation in the Regular Army as a feeder, and I was assigned to this outfit for rations. No matter what the ration consisted of, in this company you received only hardtack, bacon, and coffee. Even beans were considered a luxury. On the other hand, my own company furnished the most substantial meals I ever saw anywhere. Here, as nowhere else, one can see the value of management and honesty [wherein] the members of one company perpetually went hungry while the next company lived on the fat of the land on the identical same rations.

Promptly at midnight we pulled out. The new moon went down before we were a mile on the road. The cavalry disappeared in the darkness, so we just plodded along the best we could. Sometimes we noticed that we were on a trail, sometimes for miles we followed old buffalo trails. If we were going into action, we knew it could not be a surprise, for we could see the Indian signal fires sixty miles to the northwest as soon as we left the agency, and so the chances were the Indians in the badlands knew more about our movement than we knew ourselves. But we never worried over the future. We were happy to be on the road again, no matter where it would lead us. It was bitterly cold, but we were equipped for a winter campaign, were young and optimistic. It sounds funny, but the only thing we ever worried about was to keep our stomachs full of chow, and to tell the truth we had good reason to worry about that if we had to live with A Company. We did suffer terribly at times for the want of water. This was on account of the sowbelly diet, improperly cooked, and sometimes, in these badlands, where there was no wood, not cooked at all.

But on the whole we could eat snow, but we could not help but be sorry for the mules. We fed [them] corn, all they could eat, but no hay sometimes for weeks at a time. All the springs were frozen tight unless we came to a good-sized spring, and this happened but twice in 128 miles. The work and pack animals received no water. We could, of course, not turn them loose for a minute, for the Indians would stampede them in spite of all we could do. But you must remember that the field army is always made up of young men who can stand anything; the same rule applies to the mules. We received most of the pack and team mules fresh and unbroken from Kentucky and they were a congregation of devils. There were only a few that would not bite, strike, and kick at the same time, and what that means with sharp shod animals after being tied all night in a blizzard to a wagon wheel, without hay, must be lived through. You cannot imagine it. The wagon boss nearly had his ear bitten off one day by what was supposed to be a mule, but really was a bull dog.

Well, just at break of day we came to White River, quite a large stream at this place, something like 150 feet wide and from three to four feet deep. The ice was thick enough to hold up the cavalry horses, but not the heavy-loaded six-mule wagons. So a passage had to be cleared out, and after much difficulty getting the wagons down the steep banks without upsetting them, we got the wagon train across and camped on the other side to cook coffee. One six-mule team would not tighten a tug for some reason after they got in the stream, and so another six-mule teamster had to get in that ice water up to his hips and hitch on another team. While this was going on, the atmosphere turned blue, and it was not from the cold, either. After we filled up on sowbelly and alkali water we pulled out again about 8 a.m. The cavalry left us here again and we did not catch up with them until next day about noon, when we found them standing by their horses near a dry lake during a blizzard. We ourselves camped at 9 p.m. on a bare hillside without wood or water that night and raw bacon and snow was our supper. We had marched twenty-one hours and were fifty-eight miles from the Rosebud Agency.

At 4 o'clock sharp [December 28] reveille sounded and as there was nothing to cook and the mules would not eat their corn unless they were watered, and there was no water, it did not take us long to get ready, and at 5 a.m. we pulled out in a blizzard. We pounded along in the cavalry and then pulled about four miles further to where the scouts thought we could get some water. We camped here about one hour and watered the poor mules and filled them up on corn, for we were told that there was nearly a twenty-mile hike ahead of us before camp would be made for the night. We made camp this night something like three hours after dark at an old deserted ranch. In spite of hunger and cold, we slept like dead men and it seemed only an hour when reveille called us again to put icy harness on the mules and frozen shoes and overcoats on ourselves. At 5 a.m. we were on our way. By daylight, when we were something like six or more miles out, Foolish Elk, who was always the furthest out, came loping back to the command with another scout, a white man. After they had a short talk with the major, we left our line of march and struck out northwest through those desolate hills of Dakota. We knew that this scout had brought important news. The command was kept in close order, only the Indian scouts were from one to three miles out. We were told that no stop would be made for coffee that day and not to spare the buckskin. As we had been running a race with the devil for the last three days and nights, we were as anxious as the commanding officer to get some place, no matter where, and we all pushed to the limit. We naturally thought that the race since five in the morning was made for the purpose of heading off a band of Indians and the day's march would wind up with a fight. We knew that Short Bull had left the badlands with nearly 1,000 warriors, and several other subchiefs had done likewise. But we were disappointed in our hopes before the sun went down on this day.

Between 2 and 3 o'clock in the afternoon we saw several of the Indian scouts galloping back to the command, and a few minutes later we were halted and the command given to corral the train. In the meantime, Captain Whitney advanced over the hill with the cavalry, but before we got the train in shape for defense an orderly came back and ordered us to advance again. About a half mile further on, we crossed the brow of a small hill and beheld a small valley about one-half mile wide spread out in front of us. A small creek fringed with brush and cottonwoods meandered down through the center and finally disappeared to the northwest in some pine-covered rough hills. This was our first sight of Wounded Knee Creek. Between us and the creek there was a small egg-shaped hill, approximately fifty feet higher than the surrounding bottom land. This hill was occupied by the cavalry, whom we soon joined. We were told that a battle had taken place the day before, on December 29th, just across the creek from us, but with whom we had no way of knowing. We could see on the other side of the creek the ground strewn with the bodies of horses and even wagons and the remnants of a burned camp, and what looked like the bodies of human beings could be seen over an area of 200 or 300 acres. The first thing the troops did was to start a trench large enough to hold all of the 120 men in the command. The job actually took several days, for the ground was frozen as hard as flint. Before we got something to eat, Captain Whitney took the scouts, the doctor, and the stretcher bearers and my ammunition wagon with hospital supplies and went over to the battlefield to take care of the wounded if there were any. I just got as far as the first dead pony and Indian when the mules gave the place just one whiff and look and stampeded, as luck would have it, toward the creek, where they finally tangled themselves up in the woods and here I tied them, took my gun, and went back to the battlefield.

The dead Indians were laying around single and in bunches over about 200 acres, and the first sight of the mutilated bodies and the expressions of the faces had the effect of turning one sick. But, of course, you get used to it. Our first effort was to look for wounded in order to find out what regiment had been in the fight. We found, after a careful search, five wounded Indians. We packed them to an old cabin and made them as comfortable as possible. They didn't, however, answer a single question of the scouts. The only word they ever uttered was "water." We never found out until the next evening that the fight had been between the Seventh Cavalry and Big Foot's tribe. These wounded had been lying on the battlefield a little over twenty-four hours and we knew they could not live. One squaw was shot five times through the body. But to the last they were defiant and our reward for making them comfortable were looks of the blackest hate. You could not help but admire such courage in the face of the dead. As I stated, we made them as comfortable as possible for the night, but we found them all dead next morning. The battlefield was divided by a deep washout thirty to forty feet wide and all of fifteen feet deep; several cow trails crossed this dry gulch and near the lower end, toward the creek, a wagon road crossed also. In searching for the wounded, I ran down this road and on coming out on the other bank I was confronted by a pile of dead Indians. On top of all, and in a sitting position, with his arm extended full length and the forefinger pointing straight up in the sky, was an Indian, painted green as grass from head to toe, and looking with wide open, clear eyes, straight at me. It startled me and the next second I had a bead on his forehead, but second thought made me hesitate about pulling the trigger, for while a soldier will kill in the line of duty, unnecessary shooting is murder nevertheless, and so, after looking at him for a minute over the sights of the gun, I noticed that he never batted his eyes and so I came to the conclusion that he was dead and so he was. Lucky for me I did not shoot—the boys would have guyed me to death.

The next day we were busy getting the camp in shape for defense; we even dug a round trench deep enough at each end of the hill to hold the Hotchkiss, for after all we were only a small command of ninety-six men and officers and there were from 30,000 to 40,000 Indians roaming around, and about the poorest policy a commander of troops could follow was to get careless or underestimate the fighting qualifications and determination of the Sioux Indians. Along in the afternoon a scouting party with dispatches from General Miles came into camp, and as the escort of the dispatch rider consisted of troopers of the Seventh Cavalry who had been in the fight, we got the first account of the battle. We tried to get one of these troopers to go over the battlefield with us to show us on the ground just how it happened, but he stated that his bunky got killed and he never wanted to see the place again.

[The following account of the fighting, while hearsay, represents an apparently commonly held view of the action among the troops.] It seems that the Seventh Cavalry had been on the road for several days from the badlands to the Pine Ridge Agency, with the tribe of Indians as prisoners, but they were not disarmed. The government throughout this campaign insisted on the Indians giving up their arms, but the Indians refused to the last to comply with this condition. They told General Miles again and again they would [not?] surrender their arms, and the Battle of Wounded Knee was proof of their contention. The night before the battle they camped on what turned out to be the last camping grounds for all of the Indians but one tiny papoose and a great many of the soldiers. The guy ropes of the soldiers tents and the tepees joined. Forsyth had orders, it seems, to disarm this tribe before bringing them to the agency, and as this was the last day's march he called the chiefs for a powwow early in the morning of December 29th to his tent. While this powwow was going on a row started among the soldiers and Indians and at the first shot the chiefs pulled their war clubs, which they had concealed under their blankets, and fell on the officers, knocking the brains out of Captain George D. Wallace and wounding several others. In two minutes it was a free-for-all fight, and the mix-up was so great that the soldiers were killing one another, so the general sounded "Boots and Saddles," the soldiers extricated themselves as best they could, made for their horses, mounted and rode over a low hill, halted here, formed into their proper organization again, and prepared to charge the Indians and their own camp. At this stage of the game, the Indians made a fatal mistake. When they saw the soldiers ride over the nearest hill 400 yards away, they thought they were running away, so they crossed the dry gulch on foot and horseback, and some even in wagons, and started across the short flat and up the hill. The leaders, who were on fast horses, nearly got to the top of the hill when the soldiers came back as fast as their horses could charge. The Indian furthest up the hill was a young squaw on a pinto pony and it looked as if she received the first fire from all the troopers in the regiment, for she was literally riddled with bullets. I counted over forty bullet holes in the upper part of her body. The troopers shot and ran the Indians across the flat and into the dry gulch; they got no chance to make a stand here, for the soldiers were right on top of them. The gulch was literally piled full in places with horses, wagons, and dead Indians. Some tried to climb up the cow trails on the other side, but few managed to do it and get to the tepees, which were just beyond. At the bottom of every trail there was a pile of dead, and you could see by their positions that they tumbled back down in the gulch after being shot on the trail above. The whole thing happened so quickly that all of the Indians did not get a chance to pursue the soldiers. About seventy-five bucks, most of the squaws, and all of the papooses were in and around the tepees yet, and these now cut slits in the tepees and opened a murderous fire on the soldiers on the other side of the gulch only 75 to 100 yards away with telling effect. But the Hotchkiss opened up on these with case shot and soon silenced them. During this last phase of the fight, all the papooses but one were killed. Of course, this was very sad, but it could not be avoided. (This one papoose was found alive and uninjured by an officer, who raised and educated it as his own daughter.)

As soon as the firing ceased the soldiers gathered around their tents. One lifted up the flap of the tent to step inside, when he was shot down by a wounded Indian who was concealed behind the stove inside. All the soldiers were of course very much excited from the battle, and when they saw their comrade shot down three others pulled their revolvers and started for the tent only to be shot down dead one after the other. At this stage of the game, a corporal in charge of the Hotchkiss told them all to stand away. He trained his gun at the center of the tent and let it fly; the shell made a clean hole through the stove and caught the Indian, who was lying on his stomach behind the stove, on the chin and ripped him wide open. The fire from the stove was scattered over the bedding and everything went up in flame, roasting the Indian like a barbecue beef. This battle was not a massacre, but a fight to a finish. The evidence on the ground showed that the squaws fought as desperately as the bucks. I counted as many as twenty-three empty shells by the side of dead squaws. This tribe [group] of Indians consisted of about 354 members, was Sitting Bull's own tribe, and was the most desperate in the Sioux Nation. About ten days after the battle, General Miles sent out under a heavy escort a bunch of Indians to bury the dead. They [the dead] were all laid in a long trench on top of a small hill back of the camp. If my memory serves me right, they buried a few over 300 only because every night the friends of these dead Indians would steal the bodies of prominent bucks and bury them according to their own rites. Strange to say, they never took Big Foot until he was buried, when they stole him out of the grave and packed him off somewhere.

The Seventh Cavalry lost something like eighty men. These were immediately transported to the Pine Ridge Agency while the rest of the regiment rode across the country to relieve the mission from the attacks of Short Bull. During this fight at the mission, the Seventh was extricated from what may easily have terminated in another Little [Big]horn catastrophe by the timely arrival of the Ninth Cavalry. Sitting Bull was killed by the Indian police some time before the Wounded Knee battle, and as the Seventh Cavalry had been the heaviest sufferer at the hands of the Sioux during nearly thirty years of warfare, it was fitting they should administer a severe and last lesson with a heavy hand. During the final windup of the campaign in January and February, 1891, it was a privilege to be a member of the Regular Army at the Pine Ridge Agency. Such an exhibition of Indian life will never be seen again.

The Indian camp extended for four miles down White Clay Creek, with all their dogs and countless horses. . . . For fifteen miles around their camp the hills were literally dotted with their [dead] cayuses. You could see hundreds of braves walking around the agency in all their finery, and what is more, see all the scouts from Buffalo Bill down. It was their last meeting. The Indians, too, . . . for the last time could look at the old army commanders when [who] they met on many hard-fought battlefields, such as Forsyth, Carr, G. V. Henry, and Miles, the peer of them all. If my memory serves me right, we were in camp near the battlefield about three weeks. During this time, the work, pack, and saddle animals suffered greatly for the want of hay. There was abundance of forage on the range, but we could not of course make use of it for the reason that nearly every day scouting parties of Indians would make their appearance on the surrounding hills, watching for an opportunity to commit some depredation.

But the Regular Army officers had learned Indian warfare during nearly thirty years of continued conflict, and during this whole campaign not a serious mistake was made. All this accounts for the small loss of lives and the shortness of the campaign. In plain English, the Indian found out in less than four weeks that he had no more show than a rabbit; no matter which way he turned, he found himself opposed by a detachment of regulars ready to smoke the pipe of peace or fight him to a finish. But I am digressing again. The commanding officer learned from the scouts that there were about five tons of hay scattered in small bunches of from 500 to 1,000 pounds each at Indian homesteads up and down Wounded Knee Creek, some being as far as ten miles from camp. So when the coast was clear I would empty my wagon of ammunition and hospital supplies, get an escort of six or seven mounted men, and go after a wagon box of hay. It meant only a mouthful of hay to the horses and mules, but it was better than nothing. But we liked it for the excitement there was in it, for it was a gamble every time we went out. However, I knew that my four mules were faster than any Indian pony, so we used to beg the quartermaster to let us go. On one of these trips up the creek, we came to a store building. We put out guards and searched the place cellar and all, but the Indians had stripped the place clean. The only thing that was left was a tobacco cutter which was screwed to the counter. One of the boys took that for a souvenir, I believe. In the hillside at the back of the store we noticed a dugout. Upon investigating it, we found it full of chickens, nearly dead from starvation. At first sight my mouth began to water at the thought of fried chicken, but all we could do was to liberate them and forget about that chicken diet.

A few days after this, while out foraging, we ran across a small mission. A short distance from the mission was the preacher's house. Everything here was smashed into kindling wood. The preacher's wife had a fine collection of fancy dishes, for in one room there was a pile of dishes two or more feet high smashed into small bits. But strange to say, in another room there was a whole trunk full of the finest kind of ladies' dresses, some of silk, uninjured. They did not do this out of gratitude to the lady, for most of them do not know the meaning of gratitude. For example, there was a colored cook at the agency for nearly fifteen years. He gave a handout to every hungry Indian during all these years, but in December he ventured too far from the agency and they skinned him alive. On this occasion, we had one of the preachers along from Arizona, an old timer wise to the game, and he evidently knew what he was looking for and the proper place to search for it. He finally got a box from the yard to stand on and searched under the roof in what appeared to be the preacher's study, and here to our surprise he found three quart bottles of whiskey, one half empty. As no whiskey is allowed on Indian reservations, we immediately confiscated this supply. We did not report the preacher to the commanding officer as we should have done, for the culprit being a preacher and probably a stout member of the A. S. L. [American Sobriety League?], we felt sure that he kept this small supply for medical purposes only. But that night about a dozen of us had a meeting in an empty wagon by a shaded lantern and along about 2 a.m. we defied Short Bull, Two Strikes, Young-Man-Afraid-of-His-Mother-in-Law, and all the rest of the Sioux tribe to come and take us. After this, we made the roofs the main point of attack in searching abandoned dwellings, but you know the saying "lightning never strikes twice in the same place." At any rate, we never made another lucky find, but then we never had another opportunity to search a missionary's private dwelling.

A few days later, at about 2 p.m., two Indians came to the camp and stated that about seven miles up the creek there were two helpless wounded Indians at an old cabin. They stated that apparently before they became helpless they had killed a beef a short distance from the cabin, took the liver and tongue and made themselves at home in this old cabin, but that they were in bad condition now and without food. Charles Taggett and myself, with six infantrymen as escorts, were told to go out and bring them in the same evening. The proposition looked fishy to Taggett from the start, for the reason that the Indian scouts had searched every nook and corner within fifteen miles looking for wounded or dead Indians, and it was queer they never discovered these two wounded right in the valley of Wounded Knee. He acted, therefore, accordingly.

It took us a little over an hour to get to the place described by these Indians. We saw a dead critter in the center of a 160-acre flat and, on the opposite end of the flat near the creek bank, a cabin. We stopped in the center of the flat; Taggett instructed us not to leave the wagon for a minute and be ready to move on up the creek—not back to camp the way we came—as fast as the mules could travel if we heard any shooting at the cabin. He told us not to look for him, for if there was an ambush at the cabin he would either be dead or would catch up with us further up the creek. He then went back the way we came to the creek crossing and followed the creek bed on the ice until he came opposite the cabin. Here he tied his horse and sneaked up to the cabin. All this time he was out of sight from us, but we finally saw him coming out of the brush only ten feet from the cabin. We saw him jump for the cabin with Winchester in hand, kick in the door and disappear inside. Our hearts were in our mouths at this moment, but nothing happened. A few seconds later, he came on his horse across the flat and told us that no wounded Indians had ever been in the cabin, and in all probability they meant to trap us on the way back to camp. We therefore proceeded that night about six miles further up the creek to the Sixth Cavalry camp and fooled them.

Along towards January, after the Indians had killed the last estray beef and were getting hungry and consequently docile, the big drive started according to schedule from the badlands east of the Black Hills, the Standing Rock Agency in the north, and the Missouri River in the east. The day we entered the Pine Ridge Agency we had the pleasure of marching for about ten miles with that crack cavalry regiment, the Sixth, Colonel Carr in command. I see him sitting on his horse, a powerful man with flowing black whiskers, the very picture of the Civil War cavalry officer. The powwows over the treaty were dragging along day after day; the Indian refused constantly to give up his arms until finally General Miles sprung a great bluff on them, as follows: All the regiments were camping from eight to ten miles around this Indian camp in four main camps. Every outlet was closed. One night we got orders to march at daybreak and attack the Indians. We put in most of the night getting ready, for we knew it would be a fight to a finish, but there was no doubt of the outcome in our minds, in spite of the great odds. The next morning at break of day we pulled out from Wolf Creek and as soon as we got on a high mesa we could see the Indian camp some eight miles away in a cloud of dust as the ponies were driven in by the countless thousands. We could also see a cloud of dust some fifteen miles south which we knew was Colonel Stafford's command [sic—possible reference to a command under First Lieutenant John Stafford, Company G, Eighth Infantry] . I am glad to say that when we got within shooting distance of the camp the Indians hung out the white flag everywhere. That afternoon they agreed to deliver their arms but they never did it. I saw wagon loads of guns brought [in], but they were nothing but obsolete junk and everybody knew they were better armed than the soldiers. We admired the Indian for his grit just the same.

After Miles concluded a peace treaty [an accommodation] with the Indians, we had a grand review of 3,500 fighting men. First in line were about 500 Cheyenne scouts. They made a sight never to be forgotten. Then the famous Seventh Cavalry. This was not the usual garrison affair [with] brass buttons; as a matter of fact, no two soldiers were dressed alike. They had not shaved since they left their home garrisons, they were gaunt as greyhounds, they looked and were a fine body of fighting men of which the country had reason to be proud. We were all very sorry for General Forsyth, colonel of the

Seventh Cavalry, he of Beecher Island fame [sic—Hettinger mistakenly identifies George A. Forsyth here], who was under arrest at the time for some unknown reason. He stood behind the wagon train and watched his regiment march in review. He must have felt neglected and bitter in his heart that morning. The following season, Congress decorated him with his Medal of Honor [sic—Forsyth did not receive a Medal of Honor]. I remember the first troop of his regiment was only a skeleton. The rest of the troop was either dead or seriously wounded in the hospital. A lieutenant was in command of this troop when they passed in review and he could not salute General Miles for the reason that one arm was in a sling and his head was bandaged so you could only see his eyes, but it is a safe bet he would not have traded places with Creosus. The glory of this review and the spirit which was behind it more than repaid us for the hardships we had endured. The commands soon broke camp and departed for their home garrisons and there was no more excitement until the railroad strike started in 1894. But this is another story.

On the march from Pine Ridge Agency to Chadron, Nebraska, by the Sixth and Ninth cavalry and my own outfit, all speed records were broken on account of the boys having four months' pay which was burning a hole in their pockets. The peaceable population that night took to the hills or barricaded their homes, and the boys proceeded to decorate the town a bright red. They were so interested with the job on hand that they never noticed the eighteen inches of snow that fell during the night until they looked for their equipment the next morning, which was carelessly thrown down anywhere the night before. There was enough equipment left under the snow to equip a company of militia. I myself lost a cartridge belt and trench knife. From Fort Robinson we proceeded to Merino by rail (the end of the railroad—the present name of the station is Upton). While at Merino the thermometer registered never less than thirty degrees below. This weather was hard on everybody because our shoes and clothing were worn out. Some had socks on their feet in place of overshoes, and besides the wood was so scarce we could not dry our clothing at night.

From a high point at Donbary Town (near Gillette [Wyoming]) we got the first glimpse of the Big Horn range. We knew the end of our journey was somewhere at the foot of the range. From what was known as the "Corral" to Kinney crossing, a distance of only fifteen miles, it took us all day on account of the blizzard that was raging. But the main cause of delay was the road, which was so sidling that we could not keep the heavy loaded wagons right side up. I can yet see the band wagon tumble down a steep side hill with the band instruments flying in all directions. We were royally received in

Buffalo, where we arrived early in the afternoon from the "Cheese Brown" Ranch, and after a few ceremonies we proceeded to Fort McKinney. The only thing that marred our happiness here was the great number of deaths we had from an epidemic of pneumonia that broke out the second day after our arrival and which was only checked by the timely arrival of Dr. George E. Bushnell in the spring. Headquarters and four companies of my own regiment were ordered to Fort McKinney. I never got back to Fort Niobrara again, but joined my company at Fort Robinson and came overland by way of the Black Hills to what was known at that time in the army as the best fort in the United States, Fort McKinney. . . .

Incidents of Wounded Knee (By Joseph Monnett, formerly of Company H, First U. S. Infantry. From *Winners of the West*, May 31, 1936)

So far as I know, that [Pine Ridge] campaign may have hit other men pretty hard, but I can hardly believe any of them could have been in a worse predicament than we boys of the First U. S. Infantry. We were stationed in the warm climate of California, and in the month of October, 1890, were ordered to South Dakota with no heavy underwear or extra covering for head, hands, or feet. Notwithstanding the suffering experienced, the boys stood it well, and we were not issued heavier clothing until the last week in January, 1891.

We arrived at Fort Niobrara, Nebraska, one beautiful, cold day with the thermometer registering twenty degrees below zero and no quarters for us. We had to clear away the snow before we could set up our tents, and then we were moved into quarters after the Ninth Cavalry were ordered out into the field, but only for a stay of a short week when we were ordered to Valentine, Nebraska, to take a train to Hermosa, South Dakota. General Nelson A. Miles ordered the First U. S. Infantry to what I believe was called Fox Creek, through snow to our waists and bitter cold. Well, we finally reached Fox Creek at about 5 p.m., and the men were preparing to make some hot coffee and enjoy a grand meal of hardtack, when a man on horseback rode into camp and the next thing we heard was the drum beat call to break camp and again we were on another hard march back to Hermosa, where a train was waiting for us, which we boarded and was dumped off at Chadron.

We camped at Chadron for ten days, and one cold morning, with sleet and snow to face, we were ordered out once more and marched to White River and camped, as the men were exhausted with marching against a head wind. We had just about settled down for the night when a rancher and family drove into camp and reported to Colonel William R. Shafter that a band of Indians was headed toward his home. One captain and five men from each company were ordered to go to the rancher's home and remain there until the officers were satisfied that all was safe and then back to camp again. The following morning we started for Pine Ridge Agency, and there we remained until after the Battle of Wounded Knee. I had the pleasure of being in the detail to bury the dead Indians and it was a terrible sight. The dead lay around everywhere, and we took both young and old and buried them in a trench which was dug by half-breeds, sixty feet long, six feet wide, and six feet deep. Big Foot and his daughter were placed side by side at one end of the trench.

After all was straightened out, we returned to Pine Ridge and there to experience other thrills. First of all, Colonel Shafter wanted the regiment mounted and the infantry turned into cavalry. So the government ordered cow ponies for us, and as a result our men had broken arms and jaws and numerous other injuries. Those cow ponies sure could kick. A sergeant was instructing on mounting, and dismounting was left to the ponies and they sure knew how. After several attempts, I succeeded in getting on a pony's back and quite firmly seated in the saddle. The pony started ahead for dear life and ran about 300 yards and stopped suddenly, but I did not. I went over his head into a deep snowdrift and was lucky to be able to walk back. Many other such bright stunts happened, too numerous to mention. A movie picture man would have reaped a harvest if he had been there.

Maneuvers in Montana during the Ghost Dance Crisis (By James E. Wilson, formerly sergeant, Company H, Twentieth U. S. Infantry. From *Winners of the West*, February 28, 1933)

It was December, 1890. There was great commotion among the soldiers in camp on the Yellowstone just above old Fort Keogh. What was it all about? Sibley tents were being hastily taken down and rolled up and with stakes [and] poles loaded into great army wagons with six mules hitched to each, with a "mule skinner" in the saddle, a jerk line in his left hand and a blacksnake whip in his right, ready for the command to go. . . . This was the beginning of my experience in that well-known campaign of 1890-91, known as the "Messiah Campaign," against old medicine man Sitting Bull and Big Foot of the Sioux.

Early in the winter of 1890 it was known that the Sioux were becoming restless and showing signs of going on the warpath. About the first week in December, troops began to assemble at the nearest point to the seat of the trouble. The Twentieth U. S. Infantry and three troops of the First U. S. Cavalry were stationed at old Fort Assinniboine, away up north on the Milk River, about forty miles south of the Canadian border and over 100 miles from the nearest settlement. Orders had come to send two companies of infantry and three troops of cavalry to old Fort Keogh, near Miles City at the mouth of Tongue River where it empties into the Yellowstone. The two infantry companies were G, commanded by Captain Abram A. Harbach, and H, commanded by Captain John N. Coe, the two senior captains of the Twentieth U. S. Infantry at that time. A troop train had been assembled on the railroad about one mile from the fort, where we entrained, and after about three days of rambling down through the Shasta Mountain [sic] and river valleys we arrived at Fort Keogh and went into camp in our Sibley tents on the Yellowstone River, where there were many other troops and one company of Crow [sic—Northern Cheyenne] Indian scouts under command of First Lieutenant Edward W. Casey, [Twenty-second Infantry].

The snow was very deep and the river frozen over. We were compelled to melt snow in our tin cups in order to get water for the company cooks. Now here was a new experience for men. I had never been out on a campaign in Montana in the winter with weather 15 to 30 degrees below zero, and I was destined to learn something. Now to any of you old-timers who have never had to melt snow in a quart cup, it might appear easy, but I'll say you will have to know your snow before you can do it. We were now in camp in a big forest and fire wood was plenty. We hauled it in with six mule teams, loads at a time. The first sergeant gave the order, "everybody outside." "Now men, every man melt snow in your cup until you have a quart of water for the cook. Every man who fails to melt a quart of water and turn it over to the cook gets no supper tonight." Well, some of us sure had a time, and we nearly burned our cups to pieces before our good old First Sergeant Patrick Farrell, who had been on many a campaign in Montana in the winter, showed us how, and after that it was easy.

For three weeks we just had routine duty gathering wood, company inspection, and guard duty. On December 29th there was great commotion in the camp. Word came that the Indians had broken out and there was trouble. Our entire camp on the Yellowstone was ordered out. Everybody was happy and eager to be on the move. Now there was a scene never to be forgotten. Three troops of the First U. S. Cavalry, one troop of Indian scouts, all mounted and in marching formation [rode] ahead, and two companies of the Twentieth U. S. Infantry brought up the rear. Flanking the line of march were newspaper reporters and photographers in action. Then, flanking both sides of the line at a distance of 200 to 300 yards, were Indian squaws with their papooses strapped on their backs, all of them singing a war song, the most weird noise I had ever heard. We crossed the Tongue River and struck out in a southeasterly direction and soon out-distanced the squaws and heard their songs no more, and I am sure any surviving veterans who were on this march will remember this incident.

We marched all day through the deep snow and as the cavalry and mounted scouts had broken the trail it made marching much easier for the foot soldiers. We made only twelve miles the first day, and on account of the excitement no one seemed very tired, although our equipment was heavy, including knapsack, haversack, canteen, and web belt with 100 rounds of ammunition. We made camp in a low valley, set up our Sibley tents, and helped the cooks to build up fires from wood we had brought with us. The next morning, December 30th, was clear and cold with the sun shining bright and we were up early and after a hurried breakfast the old army wagons were loaded up and we were on the march once more. The cavalry and Crow [Cheyenne] Indian mounted scouts soon left the infantry behind, and we did not catch up with them again for nine days.

The two companies of infantry made twenty miles the second day, and eighteen miles December 31, 1890, and made camp upon a wooded ridge of pine trees, and here is where a good many of us made a mistake that we did not soon forget. After setting up our tents and banking up the snow to keep the wind out and from flapping the tents, as it was blowing a gale through the pine trees, we were told to melt snow in our tin cups for water for our coffee. Our squad had built a fire beside a fallen pine tree, and it being very cold we had taken off our overshoes and sat around the fire with our feet probably too close to the coals, and before we knew it the intense heat was cupping the soles of our shoes. The next morning, many of the boys could not get their shoes on and were obliged to march in their overshoes. That was a weird night on "Tin Cup Ridge." The wind howled, and the timber wolves also. There seemed to us to be thousands of them and they would come very close to our camp as if to attack us. They howled the whole night through and then slunk away at the break of day, and the wind died down as we broke camp at sunrise New Year's morning, 1891.

Our seventeen miles march and camp that day was uneventful, and on January 2nd we marched nineteen miles, which brought us to camp on the west bank of the Powder River. On the 3rd, we crossed the river on the ice and had to help pull and push our six-mule wagons up the opposite bluffs. Marching was very hard all day, as it was much colder and the snow deeper and much harder to walk on. It rolled up under our feet and we were slipping and falling against each other all day. We were only able to make fourteen miles that day and all were tired and glad to make camp on Timber Creek, although why it was so named we did not know as there was no timber in sight and our only fuel was sage brush. January 4th was the most eventful day we experienced since breaking camp near Fort Keogh on December 29th. We were tired and foot sore, so much so that we could hardly get going at all. We were climbing to a higher level of a rough country where one could look for miles and see nothing but the snow and where the sky and earth seemed to meet. Suddenly, we came in view of a lower ridge running parallel to our line of march [and] which was covered with thousands of antelope, running as they caught sight of us and disappearing in the distance. It was one of the most beautiful sights we had ever witnessed.

We also saw scores of jackrabbits, as white as the snow, and great flocks of sage hens would fly up so suddenly and so close to us they would startle us by their noise. We were now so far from civilization that the wildlife was showing up in all of its splendor. One would wonder how the wild animals could find anything to feed [upon] with the whole plains covered with a blanket of deep snow. By four o'clock in the afternoon the sun had disappeared and it was almost dark when we came to camp in the Blue Mud Hills of the badlands of Montana. We had marched twenty miles that day against a strong wind and flurries of snow that would bite one's face. It was the most dismal evening we had as yet experienced. We were tired and nearly frozen and supposed to be somewhat in the neighborhood of hostile Indians, although we did not know where we really were. The officers knew, but told us nothing. As we sat in our tents that bitter cold night, with our furs to keep from freezing, one soldier spoke up in a very weak voice and said, "I wonder when we will find them Indians." Another replied, "I hope we find them soon and don't care if they kill us all and put us out of pain." We had experienced much difficulty during the day in keeping some of the men on their feet. We had no ambulance and only one six-mule team to each company. During that long, long night more snow fell and that made our next day's march more difficult than ever. January 5th we made twenty-two miles toward the dreary Black Hills and made camp on Dry Creek.

On the 6th, after a march of only five miles, we came to camp on the Little Missouri River in company with the three troops of the First U. S.

Cavalry and one troop of mounted Crow [Cheyenne] Indian scouts which had preceded us. We had at last reached the end of our trek. On the morning of the 7th, the cavalry and scouts were out early while the infantry lounged in camp and built fires to get themselves thoroughly thawed out. There we remained for two weeks and had a chance to cook some good warm food for the first time on the trip. Also, to have a change of clothing and do some laundry work for the first time since leaving Fort Keogh. We cut holes in the ice on the river but did not know it was alkali water, so that the more soap we put in it the greater the accumulation of alkali on the surface. The Indian scouts were camped about 100 yards from the infantry and would remain quiet during the day, but when night came they would sing their weird songs and beat their tom-toms. This was the routine until January 21st. Each day, and in fact, each hour, we were expecting something to happen.

Along about noon on the 21st an object appeared in the distance. The officers discovered it with their field glasses. Soon it came near enough for us to determine that it was a man mounted on a mule. He came riding up to the tent of Captain Harbach, the commanding officer, and delivered him a large envelope. It developed that the man was an orderly from headquarters sixty miles away. We all gathered around him and learned that there had been a battle and that Captain Wallace and his famous K Troop of the Seventh U. S. Cavalry had been almost wiped out. Well, we all know the story of that Battle of Wounded Knee Creek. We learned but little of what had really happened in that battle, but found the object of the long march of the three troops of the First U. S. Cavalry, one mounted troop of Crow [Cheyenne] Indian scouts, and two companies of the Twentieth U. S. Infantry was intended to head off the Indians from escaping to the badlands, where they would have been difficult to dislodge.

The next morning we were ordered to break camp and march back again to old Fort Keogh. We had marched 150 miles through deep snow and weather 25 to 35 degrees below zero, and now we were ordered to march back again with all the weather conditions equally as bad. As before, the cavalry and mounted scouts soon were out of sight of the infantry. We were lonesome, miserable, and a sorry lot of unshaven men. Our overshoes gave out when we still had 100 miles of marching ahead. Then there came a break about the fourth day of our backyard march. The wind changed to our backs and the sun was warmer. It was what the Indians called a Chinook wind. We could now raise the ear flaps on our [muskrat] caps. We were allowed much more freedom going back. Now and then, we could step out of ranks and shoot at game. Company H had some crack marksmen and they brought in quantities of sage hens and rabbits. Well, we finally arrived at our old camp on the Yellowstone and settled down. At Fort Keogh, where the Twenty-second U. S. Infantry headquarters was located, we were able to get shaved and cleaned up and a change of clothing. We felt like new recruits just arrived from Columbus Barracks. . . .

The Leech Lake Uprising of 1898 (By Harry V. Wurdemann, who investigated the incident. From *Winners of the West*, August 30, 1933)

In 1898 there was an insurrection of the Chippewa Indians, the young bucks of the tribe becoming disgruntled and going on the warpath. This started at Bear Island, Leech Lake, Minnesota, during the month of October—an Indian uprising, which may well be called the last of the long series of bloody encounters in which the red man and the white man have clashed in the struggle for a continent! The War with Spain was then occupying the attention of everyone and a skirmish in the woods in an obscure corner of Minnesota passed with little notice. The incident is really of considerable historical interest, however, not only because of its local significance, but also because the cause was typical of those of many similar Indian uprisings and because it was the last time that a band of Indians actually engaged United States troops in battle and inflicted considerable loss upon them.

The fighting which took place between a disaffected band of Chippewas and a detachment of the Third Regiment U. S. Infantry was of so hot a character that it recalls some of the encounters of Custer's day against the warlike Sioux. The shores of Leech Lake were the scene of the affair. This lake is a good-sized body of water in the north-central part of the state, the very heart of the lake region. About sixty miles west is Lake Itasca, celebrated as one of the sources of the Mississippi River, and north about forty miles are Cass Lake and Lake Winnibigoshish. The Chippewa reservation practically surrounds Leech Lake on the southwestern shore of which is the town of Walker, at the time of the uprising a place of about five hundred inhabitants. The country was covered with pine woods with occasional patches of hardwood timber, and was very sparsely settled. The lumberjack, the squaw man, and the backwoods farmer were the builders of most of the log cabins and little frame dwellings on the edge of clearings studded with stumps and girdled trees. It was one of our last frontiers, and the men of those backwoods clearings were, for the most part, of that rough but picturesque type of pioneer which has filled so large a place in the American conquest of a continent.

In the case of the Leech Lake uprising, one of the inciting causes was, apparently, certain irregularities in regard to the disposal of the dead and fallen timber on the Leech Lake Reservation. The Indians complained bitterly that they were being defrauded by white speculators, and it seems that on account of these complaints the cutting of dead and fallen timber was stopped shortly after the outbreak, pending an investigation by the Department of the Interior. If the petition of October 22, signed by fifteen Pillager chiefs and 112 of their tribesmen, is an index to the sentiment of the band, this action, also, incensed them, for in this petition they stated that they depended on the continuance of logging operations during the winter to supply their families with groceries and clothing.

Much resentment and bitter feeling had also been occasioned by the rather indiscriminate arrests of Indians by United States marshals and the trouble at Leech Lake was really precipitated by the attempt of a deputy marshal to arrest certain Indians concerned in whiskey-selling practices on the reservation. On September 15, 1898, two Indians were arrested by deputy marshals and were rescued by their comrades. This was an open violation of the authority of the United States and warrants were issued for the arrest of more than twenty Indians who had taken part in the rescue. As the Indians assumed a rather threatening attitude, the marshals asked for troops to arrest them. It was believed that a show of force in the form of a detachment of regular troops would induce submission. Twenty men of the Third Regiment United States Infantry were dispatched to Walker, but as the Indians showed no signs of yielding a request by telegraph was made for more troops and on October 4 eighty additional men of the Third Infantry left Fort Snelling for the scene of the trouble.

Two days later the War and Interior departments in Washington received a bombshell in the shape of the following telegram from the assistant adjutant general at St. Paul:

> In answer to a telegram to your marshal at Walker, Minn., have received reply giving location of [Brigadier] Gen. [John R.] Bacon on mainland, southwest corner of Leech Lake and saying:
>
> ["]Commenced fighting at 11:30 yesterday. Indians seem to have best position. Not moving. Maj. [Captain Melville C.] Wilkinson, five soldiers and two Indian Police killed. Awaiting reinforcements.["]
>
> Press dispatches and private Western Union dispatches seem to support these statements. Reinforcements will doubtless reach the

Soldiers of Company E, Third Infantry, deployed near the railroad station at the time of the Chippewa uprising at Leech Lake, Minnesota, in October, 1898. *Editor's collection.*

command this evening. Reliable information indicates Indians quiet in vicinity of engineer dams to the northeast. No report yet from Gen. Bacon. No need for further reinforcements unless to send to vicinity of Leech Lake dam to cut off escape of Indians. Would suggest authority be given to utilize one battalion of Minnesota volunteers in case of need. Reports just received of arrival of [Lieutenant] Col. [Abram A.] Harbach's [Third Infantry] command at Walker about 4 o'clock.

It was fully decided that in any event a force should go to a point on the northwest side of the lake where Bugonaygeship, one of the two Indians rescued from the marshals on September 15, and a number of his rescuers were known to be living. The force consisted of seventy-seven men from the Third Infantry under Captain Wilkinson and Second Lieutenant Tenny Ross, etc. One of the Indians near the hut, Mahqua, was identified by Deputy Marshal Timothy J. Sheehan as a dangerous member of the Pillager band who had taken a leading part in the rescue of the two Indians from the officers. Mahqua resisted arrest most vigorously, twisting the handcuffs from the hands of the marshal and attempting to hit him on the head with them. The marshal parried the blow, the irons bruising his right hand. Sheehan and the Indian grappled, several of the soldiers and deputy marshals joined the fray, and the Indian was overpowered, handcuffed, and sent on board the *Flora* under guard. While the arrest was being made, five Indians armed with Winchesters left the house and made their way to the nearby woods. But, as none of them were recognized as persons wanted by the authorities, they were allowed to leave unmolested.

After a brief consultation it was decided to scout the adjacent woods for Indians and a skirmish line of twenty-five men was sent out across the clearing and a short distance into the woods with orders to bring in any Indians seen. This searching party returned in about fifteen or twenty minutes, having seen two armed Indians, and those running along the shore at such a distance as to make their capture impossible. There were three small Indian villages on the point and the next step was to visit these and see if any of the men wanted by the marshals might not be apprehended there or in the nearby woods. Lieutenant Ross with about sixty men was left to guard the landing while the detachment of twenty-five soldiers, General Bacon, Captain Wilkinson, Marshal Richard T. O'Connor, three of the deputy marshals, and the four newspaper correspondents set off on a hike across the point. They followed a path which, leading out from the west side of the clearing and along the shore of the lake, came to an inlet about fifty feet wide and two or three feet deep. This had to be forded. They all waded through with the exception of Deputy Marshal Sheehan, who was strongly opposed to a wet-feet campaign and who turned back to the clearing. The others followed the path, which meandered through the woods for about two miles. Three Indian villages were passed, and although numbers of old men, women, and children clustered about the log and birch bark huts looking at the soldiers, no young men and no arms were seen. After a short halt at the last village, the party returned to the clearing.

Here nothing of any importance had taken place except that a brave who had taken part in the rescue of Bugonaygeship had given himself up. He was sent on board the *Flora* under guard together with two sick men, a hospital steward, [and] the marshal O'Connor. Morton, the correspondent of the *Globe*, also returned to the *Flora*. It was now about 11:30 and the men were drawn up near the house and ordered to stack arms preparatory to dismissal for dinner. As nearly as can be made out, one of the recruits' rifles was fired accidentally as the men were stacking arms. This, according to most of the witnesses, was followed by two shots from the woods, evidently fired as a signal and then by a volley from the three sides of the clearing. The men without waiting for orders snatched their guns from the stacks and jumped for the cover afforded by the house, the stumps, and the irregularities of the ground. A soldier who was present told the writer that in half a minute after the first fire from the Indians there was not a man in sight. There were only nineteen veterans in the detachment, the remainder being raw recruits who had never been under fire before and some of whom scarcely knew how to load and fire their own rifles. That there was a sort of panic for a few minutes, as stated by some of the eyewitnesses, is not strange. The suddenness of the attack from the concealed foe would have shaken the courage of veterans. Encouraged, however, by the shouts and example of their officers and by the old soldiers in the force, the men quickly recovered themselves and formed a rough skirmish line in the shape of an irregular crescent facing toward the wooded sides of the clearing and with their backs to the lake.

Here from the best cover they could obtain, they vigorously returned the Indians' fire. General Bacon with Captain Wilkinson took charge of the center of the line, Second Lieutenant Tenney Ross the left, and Deputy Marshal Sheehan, who was an old soldier, the right. General Bacon, rifle in hand, fought like a common soldier, while he continued with the other officers to encourage the men by word and example. All the officers exposed themselves freely to the Indians' fire, walking up and down the line to see to the disposition of the troops. Captain Wilkinson proved himself true to the traditions of the brave though profane old army as he walked along the line shouting: "Give it to them, boys; give 'em hell! We've got 'em licked! Give 'em hell!" He was in full uniform of his rank and evidently drew the fire of the Indians for he soon received a slight flesh wound in the right arm and a few minutes later a bullet struck his left thigh just above the knee. He fell to the ground saying to Lieutenant Ross: "I'm hit, Ross, but not badly. Keep 'em at it." He was carried behind the log house where the hospital steward dressed his wound as the captain sat propped up against the wall. But nothing could keep him out of the fight and as soon as his wound was dressed he was back on the firing line. He had scarcely returned when a bullet struck him in the right side, passing completely through the abdomen and he fell mortally wounded. "Give 'em hell!" he shouted to General Bacon as he breathed his last a few minutes after being hit.

For a time both Indians and soldiers kept up a hot fire although neither side had much to aim at save the puffs of smoke. By the volume of fire from the woods it appeared that the braves were about equal in number to the soldiers. It was very easy to distinguish the rifle fire of the Indians for most of them were armed with Winchesters whose duller reports were punctuated by the sharp staccato crack of the soldiers' Krag-Jorgensens. At the end of about half an hour, the fusillade from the woods slackened and there was a short respite after which it broke out again more fiercely than before. Altogether, there were six separate attacks, or rather bursts of fire, from the woods with short intervals between until about three o'clock in the afternoon, when apparently the main body of the Indians withdrew. Occasionally a few shots would come from the woods but the main attack was over. It had lasted for three hours and a half and had resulted for the troops in the loss of one officer and five men killed and ten men wounded. There were plenty of narrow escapes among the remainder. A number had bullet holes in their clothing, one man had a bullet graze his chin, and another had a bullet take a piece of skin from the bridge of his nose. A bullet went through General Bacon's hat, passing within an inch of his head. All from the general to the last recruit fought well and instances of individual gallantry were common. General Bacon, Lieutenant Ross, and Marshal Sheehan, as well as Captain Wilkinson, all showed great coolness and resolution, as did the noncommissioned officers, particularly First Sergeant Kelly, who took charge of the center of the line after the fall of Captain Wilkinson. Sergeant Butler was killed by a bullet through the head while exposing himself in the carrying of a message. The hospital steward, Burkhard, distinguished himself by his disregard of danger while bringing in the wounded under fire. The surgeon, Dr. Henry S. T. Harris, was equally devoted to his duty. He was on board one of the steamers when action began, having accompanied one of the sick sent to the steamer. He returned to the command again by rowing ashore under fire in a small skiff. Together with his hospital steward, he upheld the highest tradition of his department for matter-of-fact courage and efficient performance of duty in the face of danger and difficulties.

At the commencement of the firing the steamers lying off the point were exposed to a sharp rifle fire from the Indians and in a short time they stood out from the shore and returned to Walker, where no little excitement and consternation was caused by the report which they brought. Indian Inspector Arthur M. Tinker, Marshal O'Connor, and several of the deputy marshals were aboard, and their rather hurried return to Walker, leaving the soldiers to fight it out or be driven into the lake, caused a great deal of unfavorable comment and a good many broad hints that the courage of those aboard was rather questionable. It seems, however, that both Inspector Tinker and the marshal were desirous of getting to town to hurry up reinforcements as well as to send food and blankets to General Bacon's detachment. The boats themselves were quite unable to render any material assistance as their sides and pilot houses were readily pierced by rifle bullets.

The night was an anxious one for General Bacon's men. The wounded were made as comfortable as possible, and a trench and some rifle pits were dug and pickets posted. Several alarms took place and an Indian policeman was killed by a sentry who mistook him for one of the hostiles. The provisions were scanty and the men did not have their blankets. When morning came the little force was well intrenched and felt confident that it could easily repulse the Indians if again attacked. Most of the enemy had apparently left the peninsula but occasional shots from the woods proved that some of the Indians were still lurking there. A chance shot killed a soldier digging potatoes in the neighboring field, and the situation was hardly a pleasant one, particularly for the wounded. The arrival of a steamer from Walker with blankets and a quantity of food greatly cheered the men. The steamer was fired upon and consequently was able to take off only one of the wounded.

About 3:30 p.m., October 6th, Lieutenant Colonel Abram A. Harbach, with a force of two hundred and fourteen men and a Gatling gun, arrived at Walker to reinforce the detachment at Sugar Point. About two hours later, the steamer *Flora*, returning with the dead and wounded of General Bacon's party, brought the report that fighting had practically ceased and that the steamer had established satisfactory communication with the shore. Indeed, from about noon on the sixth no Indians were seen and only one or two shots were fired. The wounded were sent to the Walker hospital and the bodies of the dead were taken to Bailey's warehouse near the dock. About noon on Friday, October 7, General Bacon's force embarked on the steamer *Leila D.*, arriving about 5:30 in the afternoon at the Walker dock where they were warmly greeted by the citizens and by the men of Colonel Harbach's command. The next morning the latter force went to the Indian agency five miles north of Walker where they pitched tents and went into camp. Runners were sent out inviting the Indians to come to the agency for council to discuss the surrender of the braves for whom warrants had been issued and to investigate and settle the complaints in regard to the disposal of the dead and fallen timber. The United States Commissioner of Indian Affairs, William A. Jones, arrived from Washington October 10, and the next morning he and Father Aloysius Hermanutz, a priest who had great influence over the Indians, went to Bear Island, where they had a long and friendly conference with those chiefs of the Pillager band who were principally concerned in the outbreak.

The news of the clash between the troops and the Indians spread like wildfire and resulted in a general alarm throughout the northern villages. The settlers and timber cruisers poured into the towns for protection and telegrams were sent to the adjutant general of the department requesting that troops be sent to Walker, Bemidji, Farris, Cass Lake, Deer River, and Aitken, while, at the same time the citizens of these towns armed and organized for the defense of their homes. At Bemidji, something like a panic took place. The women were collected in the court house and two hundred armed citizens kept watch and ward. The arrival of detachments of troops in the villages soon quieted the alarm and caused the excitement to subside.

Troops were poured into the Indian country, not only for the sake of actual protection in case of an extensive uprising, but also to impress the Indians with the fact that recourse to arms was hopeless and that the government was determined to suppress any armed resistance to its authority. At the same time, a thorough investigation of the Indians' complaints in regard to the disposal of the dead timber on their land was promised. Influenced by the tact of the Indian commissioner, persuaded by the chiefs and the leading men of the tribe, which has always been conspicuously friendly to the whites, and also, probably, impressed by the military force brought to the scene, the Bear Islanders gradually acceded to the demands of the marshals and by the middle of October practically all the men for whom warrants had been issued were in the hands of the authorities. They were transferred to Duluth for trial. When their cases came up before Judge William Lochren on October 21, all were found guilty and were given sentences varying from sixty days imprisonment and a fine of twenty-five dollars to ten months and one hundred dollars. On December 13, the Indian office recommended that the term of imprisonment be commuted to two months and that the fines be remitted, and finally on June 3, 1899, the pardons were granted.

B. Central and Southern Plains

The area of modern Kansas, Oklahoma, Texas, and eastern Colorado held proximity to many of the principal emigrant arteries west, as well as collateral overland trails, roads, and railroads between the 1850s and 1890s. During that period thousands of whites entered the region seeking land and fortune, some passing through to the goldfields of California and elsewhere and others remaining to gain their livelihoods from the land. The inroads disrupted Indian societies and brought warfare as the tribes attempted to dissuade the invasion. Ultimately, the army, as instrument of the federal government committed to the protection of American citizens, waged brutal campaigns against them, and in the end the native people met defeat and were placed on reservations. Military expeditions on the Central and Southern Plains in many ways mirrored those in the north, particularly in the grueling extremes of climate posed by torrid summers and freezing winters, and in the mobility and fighting prowess of the native people targeted by the army. Among the reminiscences presented here are several dealing with the Cheyenne and Arapaho War of 1867-69 (which included the notable engagements of Beecher's Island, Colorado Territory, Beaver Creek, Kansas, and Washita, Indian Territory [Oklahoma]), which is represented here by accounts from veterans of state forces as well as federal commands, and the Red River War of 1874-75, which included the noted Battle of Palo Duro Canyon in west Texas.

Supplies for Colorado in 1864 (By Elias J. Quick, formerly of Tyler's Rangers. From *Winners of the West*, January 15, 1926)

During the summer of 1864 the Indians were on the warpath and stopped supplies going to Denver, Colorado Territory, and there was no mail for several weeks. Denver sent out scouts every day and night to see if the Indians were mobilizing to attack the city. Every commodity in the market that was scarce was bought up and prices raised. Common salt was 75 cents a pound wholesale. Pork products were all 50 cents a pound. Certain kinds of nails even brought $1.00 per pound. All provisions were getting scarce, prices higher, and it looked like starvation as well as the probability of being massacred.

Governor John Evans called for volunteers to open up communication with the states. Clinton M. Tyler of Black Hawk, Colorado, raised a company of ninety-five men, calling themselves Tyler's Rangers. These men were sworn into the service . . . on August 15, 1864. The government had no arms or ammunition, so we furnished our own horses, guns, ammunition, clothing, bedding, and cooking utensils. Officers and men had no tents, sleeping in the open, rain or shine, hot or cold. Government furnished us four mule teams and wagons loaded with bacon, hardtack, and grain for the horses. The hardtack must have been made two years, and before we could eat it we had to boil it, skim the worms off, and then fry in bacon grease.

We left the city [Denver] three days after being sworn into the service, going down the Platte River, scouting both sides of the river, and did not see a white man until we came to Fort Cottonwood, Nebraska, a distance of 300 miles. We had trailed Indians from Colorado to here, and as Nebraska had issued a law that they would protect all peaceful Indians at Fort Cottonwood on a certain date, that stopped us. We followed another bunch of Indians over on the Republican River, but ran out of provisions and had to return to Fort Cottonwood, where was stationed a regiment of soldiers under Brigadier General Robert B. Mitchell[, commander of the District of Nebraska]. We drew rations here for our return trip home.

At Fort Cottonwood there was over a hundred teams loaded with provisions that the soldiers were holding for Colorado. We escorted them to Denver. We established a mail and express line to Denver, and living again became normal. The territory had no money to pay us, and so we were conditionally discharged. On our return to Denver the government addressed us, saying we had accomplished much that would do credit and add luster to the fame of the most valiant veterans of any war. "A more noble and patriotic service than yours has not been rendered by anybody at any period in the history of our country." This is recorded in Denver.

Campaigning in Colorado and New Mexico, 1860s (By Luke Cahill, formerly of the Third U. S. Infantry and Fifth U. S. Infantry, and former National Commander, National Indian War Veterans, Denver, Colorado. From *Winners of the West*, August, 1924)

During the winter of 1867 and 1868 I was stationed at Fort Lyon, Colorado, along with Companies G and I of the old Third U. S. Infantry. Captain Lee P. Gillette was then with Company G but was succeeded by Captain J. Ford Kent. Its first lieutenant was John W. Hannay. Company I was commanded by Captain William H. Penrose, First Lieutenant John W. Thomas, Second Lieutenant Thomas B. Briggs, and First Sergeant Conway. I served nine months in camp with Buffalo Bill and also Wild Bill Hancock [Hickok] in that terrible expedition in the winter of 1868-69, commanded by Major Eugene A. Carr of the Fifth U. S. Cavalry, and Captain Penrose of the Third Infantry. The campaign was against the Cheyennes and Arapahos. . . .

On the 4th day of May, 1866, I enlisted in the regular army at Chicago, Illinois. [I] was sent to Governors Island, New York [Harbor], then to Fort Leavenworth, where 1,500 of us soldiers with 100 wagons started on our long march across the Great American Desert to Fort Union, New Mexico Territory. We were under the command of Lieutenant Colonel George Sykes. Colonel Sykes, then brevet major general, commanded the Fifth Army Corps and captured Little Round Top at the Battle of Gettysburg. Our quartermaster on that expedition was Major George A. Forsyth of Beecher Island fame. From Fort Union I was assigned to Company A, Fifth U. S. Infantry, then at Fort Sumner. Here three companies of infantry and one troop of cavalry were trying to keep 20,000 Navajo Indians on a reservation. We had daily trouble, and many of our men were killed.

In August, 1867, a courier arrived at Fort Sumner with a message that the little town of Trinidad, Colorado, was surrounded with Ute Indians and all the whites [were] about to be killed. A company was sent out and at once marched day and night until we arrived at Trinidad, beat off the Indians and saved the lives of the people. In the meantime, the Navajos broke out, surrounded the three remaining companies, and we were ordered back from Trinidad on another day-and-night march to help relieve our surrounded troops. Troops came from Fort Stanton, [Fort] Bascom, Santa Fe, and our Company A from Trinidad in time to save the garrison.

Thirty-six soldiers were killed. The Indians began leaving by thousands and the troops were unable to stop them. General William T. Sherman was sent out by the War Department to try to make peace with them. He gave them twenty-four hours in which to surrender and return the guns they had taken from the dead soldiers. The little headstones at Fort Sumner tell the history of those poor boys who gave up their lives there in defense of their country.

The Navajos were without control. Their head chief, Manuelito, was a good Indian but he could not control the young braves of the tribe and they went back to their own country. The great General [Colonel] Kit Carson [had earlier] defeated those Indians and put them on the Fort Sumner reservation in the winter of 1863. He killed all their horses. The Fifth Infantry was relieved from duty in Arizona in November, 1867, and ordered to report to General Hancock for duty on the great plains of Colorado and Kansas. My company arrived at Fort Lyon [on] November 7, 1867. The fort [second Fort Lyon] was just being built, and we were compelled to lie out in tents all winter. It was terribly cold and much snow.

The Indians were troublesome. They stopped all ox trains and the mail coaches had to be constantly escorted by soldiers and the traveling all done at night. This was hard duty for us, as there was no wood to cook with and we were compelled to hunt buffalo chips from under the snow to provide fuel to cook with. In February, 1867, Colonel Kit Carson arrived in Bent County with his family consisting of his wife and six children, whose names were Terresina, William, Charley, Josefeta, Stefineta, and Kit. He settled on a claim on the Purgatory (Picket Wire) River about four miles up from its mouth where it empties into the Arkansas River, which is about two miles east of Las Animas. He had come from his home at Rayada, New Mexico.

Soon after his arrival in Colorado the Indians stampeded and ran off all of his mules and horses and a portion of my company and of Troop C, Seventh Cavalry, were sent to capture them. Four of our men were killed and some of the Indians also, and they outnumbered the troops forty to one. The Indians became worse and worse, tying up all wagon trains and stopping travel east from Fort Lyon to Fort Dodge, Kansas. President Andrew Johnson and General [Ulysses S.] Grant sent for Colonel Kit Carson to appear before them in Washington to consult as to the best means of subduing the Cheyennes, Comanches, and Arapahos. After Colonel Carson's return, he reported to Captain William H. Penrose at Fort Lyon that he advised the president and General Grant that the only way to subdue the Indians was by the same means he had used to defeat the Navajos in 1863, which was to make a winter campaign against them and kill their horses. Soon after the return of Colonel Carson from Washington, his wife was taken ill and died on April 15, 1868, in childbirth. Soon afterwards, Colonel Carson was taken ill and Dr. [Henry R.] Tilton, the post doctor, had him removed from the ranch of Thomas C. Boggs to Fort Lyon. He became worse, and died May 23, 1868. At his deathbed were Dr. Tilton, the hospital steward of Fort Lyon, and this writer. I was holding his hand when he breathed his last. Colonel Carson was the most wonderful man in all the West. Faithful, true, and honest. He was buried with military honors at Boggsville, Colorado. On January 1, 1888, Hon. Thomas O. Boggs and John S. Hough, county judge, had the remains of Colonel Carson and his beloved wife removed to Taos, New Mexico.

The Indians became so bad that the government was obliged to declare war against the Comanches, Cheyennes, and Arapahos, and General Philip H. Sheridan and Lieut. Col. George A. Custer took command to form an army. Troops assembled at Fort Leavenworth, Fort Hays, Fort Sam Houston, and Fort Lyon, Colorado, and in the month of November, 1868, the troops commenced to march on the Indians. Captain Penrose left Fort Lyon with the Tenth U. S. Cavalry. His chief of scouts was Wild Bill. Major Carr with the

Fifth U. S. Cavalry and a detachment of the Third and Fifth U. S. Infantry became a part of his command. During the very first night on Butte Creek there arose one of those terrible Colorado blizzards. Nothing but the tops of the tents could be seen of the camp. The wagons were buried in snow, and the ground became so soft [that] the wagons would sink to the hubs in mud during the day. At night the cold would register more than 25 below zero. Thirty-six mules and horses were found dead, and four men froze to death. Scores had to be returned to Fort Lyon for treatment, too badly frozen to be able for duty. We had 300 to 400 head of cattle, many of which perished and all the rest drifted off into the deep gulches and never were found. This left us entirely without meat. William F. Cody ("Buffalo Bill") was chief of scouts for the Carr command. Finally with forced night marches all the commands met, surrounded the Indians, killed all of their ponies, and thus the great idea of Colonel Kit Carson as outlined to the president and General Grant at Washington as to how to subdue and conquer the Indians was carried out to the letter.

[William F. Cody's letter to Luke Cahill, March 8, 1913:]

My Dear Comrade:

Your letter of February 28th was a happy surprise, and your memory is perfect. You have mentioned many things in your letter that brought back to me the hardships and the endurance that we had to pass through that terrible winter of 1868 and 1869. From what I have read of Napoleon's retreat from Moscow in the winter, that expedition of ours was nearly as bad. I remember you very well as a plucky young sergeant of the United States army, butchering the buffalo with your men after I had killed them, and although it was freezing cold to butcher buffalo out in the snowdrifts and not a complaint from you or your men, and had it not been for what we were doing to supply meat for our command, when we were nearly out of rations, there would have been much more suffering among the troops than there was. I would like to meet you and talk over the experiences we had during that terrible winter. . . .

Service with the Eighteenth Kansas Volunteer Cavalry in

1867 (By Henderson Lafayette Burgess, formerly of Company D, Eighteenth Kansas Volunteer Cavalry. From *Winners of the West*, August 30, 1929)

At the close of the Civil War a large amount of territory embracing what is now central western Kansas, eastern Colorado, and the Indian Territory was inhabited by numerous tribes of hostile Indians. The general government at Washington had turned its attention to the development of the West, the opening up of a public thoroughfare across the continent to the Pacific Coast. To this end, aid was being granted by the government in the construction of a line of railroad across the plains, and the eastern division of the Union [Kansas] Pacific Railroad, in the spring of 1867, had been completed to Fort Harker, Kansas, and was in course of construction from that point west. The hostile Indians, and especially the Cheyenne, Kiowa, Arapaho, and Comanche tribes, were upon the warpath and determined to prevent the building of the railroad and travel and transportation across the plains by the method then in use, to wit, ox and mule teams with long wagon trains. The United States mails were interrupted. Men, women, and children were being massacred, stock stampeded, wagon trains captured and contents burned and destroyed by these hostile tribes to such an extent that the United States Government troops then on the frontier were inadequate to afford protection. Therefore, by order of the War Department at Washington, the first battalion of the Eighteenth Kansas Volunteer Cavalry was organized and enlisted between the 5th and 15th days of July in 1867, and on the 15th day of July was mustered into the United States service at Fort Harker, Kansas. It was armed, uniformed, and equipped by the United States Government, and within three days after it was mustered into service under command of the late Horace L. Moore, of Lawrence, Kansas, entered upon an active campaign of four months' duration against these hostile Indians.

On the day the regiment was mustered in, the command was attacked by Asiatic cholera and a number of deaths occurred at Fort Harker on the 15th, 16th, and 18th days of July, 1867. Major Moore, who had recently been mustered out of the United States service as colonel of the Fourth Arkansas Cavalry, being a man of excellent judgment and having at heart the interests of the troops under his command, took the best method of preventing a greater loss by disease by putting the command immediately into active service and moving it from Fort Harker across the country by way of Pawnee Rock to Fort Larned. While en route to Fort Larned under the command of Second Lieutenant Henry J. Hegwer of Company D, a detachment of twenty-two men was sent in pursuit of a band of hostile Indians that had stampeded a train and run off some stock belonging to freighters. Three fine horses were recaptured and later returned to the owners by the government. At Fort Larned, we lost the regimental surgeon and one commissioned officer, First Lieutenant Samuel L. Hybarger of Company B, and a number of enlisted men from cholera. However, the troops fit for duty were immediately sent forward from Fort Larned to Fort Hays to cooperate with the Seventh and Tenth United States cavalry regiments in an expedition against the Indians in the north and northwest part of the state.

At our camp on Walnut Creek, while en route to Fort Hays, more deaths occurred from cholera. I remember at this point a boy belonging to Company C was sick with the cholera. When the four companies broke camp early in the morning, this young soldier was breathing his last, and as Company D passed by where he lay on a stretcher, he expired. A detail was made to dig a grave. He was taken from the stretcher, wrapped in his blanket and buried on the banks of Walnut Creek, and the four companies continued the march to Fort Hays, where we sustained no further loss from cholera.

About the middle of August, Companies B and C, under the command of Captain Edgar A. Barker and Captain George B. Jenness, with Company F of the Tenth United States Cavalry, the entire command being under Major George A. Armes of the regular army, were ordered on a scouting expedition to the northeast in pursuit of Indians who were making raids from the northwest, killing and scalping those engaged in surveying and building the Union [Kansas] Pacific Railroad. A number of men had been killed near what is now Bunker Hill Station, west of Ellsworth, and along the line of the road, and a large force was necessary to drive these Indians out of the country.

Major Moore, with Companies A and D under command of Henry C. Lindsey and Captain David L. Payne, was sent upon this expedition, his command to move to the northwest from Fort Hays. The troops carried three days' rations and the two commands under Major Armes and Major Moore were to cooperate in the campaign against the hostiles. The rations proved to be entirely insufficient for the raid, which lasted for eight days. The buffalo had been driven out of the country by the Indians and a large part of the prairie burned over to prevent our obtaining forage for our horses and mules. The herds of buffalo that usually ranged through this district would have afforded an abundance of fresh meat. Both men and animals suffered greatly for want of food and water, it being exceedingly hot and dry during the entire summer.

After reaching the Saline River, Major Armes with his three companies of cavalry proceeded to follow the river until he formed a junction with Major Moore with Companies A and D of the Eighteenth. Major Moore with his command proceeded to the northwest, while Major Armes with his three companies took a northeasterly course, each of the two commands intending to cut off the possible escape of the Indians, and to form a junction on the Solomon River. By this movement the Indians were driven farther to the northeast, where a part of Major Armes's command engaged them, and the Battle of Beaver Creek ensued. This battle was a most bloody fight. The small detachment of troops separated from the command were placed at every disadvantage and exposed to the greatest danger from their relentless and savage foes. Captain Jenness was severely wounded in the thigh. The chief scout, Captain Allison J. Pliley, was twice wounded by the Indians, and a number of the troops were wounded, some dying from their wounds, while several were killed. The soldiers fought bravely, and when finally joined by Major Armes and the rest of the command, succeeded in forcing the Indians to retire with a severe loss in killed and wounded. The exact number, of course, could never be ascertained, as Indians carry their dead and wounded with them when it is by any means possible to do so. On the other hand, they rarely fail to torture and kill their enemies when they fall into their hands.

This account of incidents of the service of the Eighteenth Kansas Cavalry is prepared from memory. It is impossible now to recollect the names of all those killed and wounded. In fact, I never knew the names of all the brave men who fell during the campaign, but I remember, in addition to Captain Jenness and Chief Scout Pliley, the names of Thomas G. Masterson of Company C, who was killed in the fight on Beaver or Prairie Dog Creek, and of James H. Towell of the same company, who was wounded several times and afterwards died of his wounds in the latter part of August at Fort Hays; also the name of Thomas Anderson of Company B. Of those who died of cholera at Fort Harker, I remember the names of Bailey McVeigh and William P. Maxwell, of Company D. Maxwell was a fine young man and had been promised promotion; he was in perfect health, a man of splendid physical development. He was taken sick in the evening and was dead and buried the next morning. I helped to care for Comrade Maxwell during his very short illness. His body is buried at Fort Harker on the Smoky Hill River, as is also the body of Bailey McVeigh and many others belonging to the battalion who died of the cholera. Others are buried at Fort Larned on Pawnee Creek, on Walnut Creek, at Fort Hays, and on the Beaver. Some were killed in action; others died of wounds received in action in various places between the Republican River on the north and the Arkansas River on the south. The Eighteenth was constantly engaged in drilling, marching by day and by night, fighting Indians, guarding government trains, making its basic operations at Fort Hays, Fort Larned, and Fort Dodge, from which government posts it received its rations, ammunition, and supplies. It marched over two thousand miles in four months and engaged the Indians on several occasions, affording protection to government property and the United States mails, as well as to private citizens. It greatly aided in making safe the then unoccupied plains for settlement by the sturdy and industrious farmers who have for the last sixty years planted and reaped golden grain over the graves of these brave men who gave their lives in the protection of the frontier. They suffered all the hardships endured by the soldiers of any war. The last service rendered, in October and early part of November, 1867, was in guarding a train of provisions, arms, and ammunition, together with four hundred head of native cattle, sent by the government to the peace council at Medicine Lodge for the use of the Indians. Here most of the Indians agreed to the unmolested occupation by white men of this great agricultural territory. But this agreement was wholly disregarded and violated the very next year by these same hostile tribes.

The Eighteenth Kansas Cavalry served with the Seventh and Tenth United States regiments during the summer of 1867. These were brave soldiers and entitled to a large decree of credit. At one time the entire command was with the Seventh Cavalry in the northwest part of the state, and under the command of Lieutenant Colonel Custer pursued the Indians and drove them out of the country. . . .

On the Kansas Plains during Hancock's Campaign, 1867 (By James P. Russell, formerly of Troop H, Seventh U. S. Cavalry. From *Winners of the West*, March, 1925)

I was a member of H Troop, Seventh U. S. Cavalry. [I] joined H Troop at its organization in the fall of 1866, stayed at Fort Riley, Kansas, until the 26th of March in 1867, when we were sent to Fort Larned Kansas, with a peace commission to make a treaty with the Cheyenne Indians. However, the Indians did not like the terms and vamoosed in the nighttime leaving their tepees standing. So we took their trail the next morning, going north across the Smoky [Hill] River until we came to Lookout Station on the overland stage route, where we found they had killed and burned five men by tying them to the wheels and boot of a stage coach. We turned them, and kept the trail to the next station. It was Stormy Hollow, and was burned, but the men got away to the next station, which was Downer Station.

When there we met part of a company of colored troops. The Indians went north, crossed the Saline and Solomon rivers, and we came up with them on the Republican River. We got a few of them before they took to the hills, and as it was late in the afternoon we lost them near the Nebraska line. As our rations were run out, we had to go back to Camp Fletcher or old Fort Hays, where we were in camp a couple of weeks.

We again took the trail for the Republican River, and again we had a running fight with them and followed them to Fort McPherson, Nebraska. Here they signed a treaty. We left Fort McPherson on Monday morning and on Wednesday eve we were again on the Republican River. On Thursday morning we were attacked by the same Indians who had just signed the treaty. Their object was to stampede our horses, but they failed and we again chased them a couple of days up the Frenchmen Fork of the Republican. We returned to our camp on the Republican and Colonel Custer, who was in command, sent our wagons south to Fort Wallace for supplies.

The guard of two troops with the train had to fight both to the fort and back. We then took up the march up the Frenchmen Fork of the Republican and went to the Platte River west of Fort Sedgwick, Colorado. Then back to our old camp. We learned here that dispatches had been sent to General Custer by Second Lieutenant Lyman S. Kidder of the Second Cavalry. We found him and his escort of ten men and guides had been killed, and their bodies shot full of arrows. As it was now pretty late in the fall of 1867, we went to Fort Wallace, and in a short time the regiment was sent to winter quarters. Our troop was sent to Fort Harker, where we made our headquarters, and patrolled the Saline and Solomon rivers, where settlers were beginning to come in, and it was H Troop . . . that had the scrap on the Saline in '68.

A Skirmish with Kiowas in Colorado Territory, 1868 (By Edward Mayers, formerly of Troop L, Seventh U. S. Cavalry. From *Winners of the West*, September, 1924)

I was so glad to hear from one of our old-timers, especially one who served in the same column at the same place, Fort Lyon, Colorado, but find we [he?] had forgotten about Company L, Seventh U. S. Cavalry.

We camped at the fort the evening of August 31, [1868,] and the next day we started down the river to join the regiment. When about ten miles out we were overtaken by a courier with orders to return to the fort and remain there. Captain William H. Penrose was in command of the post, our troop was commanded by First Lieutenant Henry H. Abell and Second Lieutenant Jacob H. Shellabarger. We camped near the post bakery and spent the first few days getting the stables in condition to shelter our horses and fixing up our company street.

On the morning of the 8th the guard was in line on the parade ground when all at once the cry of "Indians" rang out and we four of the cavalry guard ran to the stables to find that the boys were galloping down to the crossing of the river. We did not take time to change our parade uniform, but were soon racing down the river also to the crossing. The troop formed as we rode, Captain Penrose taking the lead. We never thought of the Boggs family until we ascended the bluff and saw about 200 Indians riding out of the timber directly from the Boggs ranch and making straight across our trail to the tableland, about 500 yards distant. Then began a long chase of some forty miles, the distance between the two little armies remaining about 500 yards. All at once the Indians split, the larger bunch with the horses going off to the right, but we continued after the smaller bunch, and forming to prevent another split. Then something began to happen. Our company baker's horse took a sudden notion to plunge ahead at full speed and Little Phil in trying to check him broke one rein of the bridle at the bit, and "Barney" then began to fly around almost in a circle, as Phil pulled for dear life, but Barney came very near running into the Indians. But Phil finally got Barney turned the other way. A few shots were fired by the Indians but without effect. Then Sam Rickie cried out, "I am going to get that fellow with a flag." It was the medicine pole of Chief One Eye Bull, and Kicking Bird, the medicine man, making themselves conspicuous in the bunch. From that time on the Indians began to lose some of their horses, lancing them as they gave out. Ahead of us was a broken country with that peculiar formation of rocks, and the Indians made a break for them, disappearing suddenly in their natural shelter. We quickly dismounted to prevent them from splitting again. But the Indians were now well fortified in a cave-like formation which time had hollowed out in funnel shape. The first man killed was Little Phil, and . . . next Sam Rickie went down. While in the act of firing my carbine a bullet shattered the wood under the barrel, breaking the ring and wounding my left hand. But the fight was soon over and when we went to look for our horses we found them where we had left them standing, but five of them had dropped dead. So we wrapped our dead comrades in blankets, strapped them to their horses and started back. We called the place Bloody Spring because the blood of the Indians had run into the water so we could not use it, neither could we water our horses because the sides of the hole were sandy and would give way when trod upon.

Captain Penrose was one of the bravest men, and was always in the lead. He, as well as some of the others of us, was satisfied there was a large force of Indians in that section. But we started back, arriving at Fort Lyon [on] September 9, just at guard mount, having made the 120 miles in twenty-four hours. . . .

Combat near Fort Hays, Kansas, 1867 (By George W. Ford, formerly first sergeant, Troop L, Tenth U. S. Cavalry. From *Winners of the West*, November, 1925)

In October, 1867, Private John Randall, G Troop, Tenth Cavalry, in company with two civilians, was attacked by a band of Cheyennes numbering sixty or seventy near a spring about forty-five miles west of Fort Hays, or the present Hays City, on the line of the Union [Kansas] Pacific Railroad. In the fight that ensued the two citizens were killed and one of them scalped. Randall was shot in the hip and received eleven lance wounds in his shoulder and back. These wounds were received after he and one of the citizens named John Parks had taken refuge in a hole under a railroad cut. The Indians had caved in large portions of the bank upon Parks and dispatched him with their spears. The savages, worn out with trying to get Randall out of his hole and doubtless also weary of losing so many of their number, disappeared, leaving thirteen warriors dead, so effective had been the fire of Randall and his friend up to the time of the latter's death.

The Indians then attacked the main camp on the railroad, which was protected by Sergeant Charles H. Davis and eight men, and were repulsed. The sergeant ordered the horses saddled, but thought it best to force the fighting and attack the enemy on foot. As soon as the warriors saw the soldiers advancing, they mounted their ponies and rode leisurely away along the line of the railroad until they met an ox team and wagon with two men. They at once fell upon the men. One escaped to the camp; the other remained and fought until his last cartridge was fired. Three of the warriors dismounted to take his scalp. Just at this critical moment, Sergeant Davis and his detachment arrived and opened fire upon the war party with such success that the Indians abandoned their victim and galloped away for the river bottoms. Returning to camp with the rescued teamster, Davis ordered his men to mount, and, at the head of the detachment, rode with greatest speed toward the river to ascertain, if possible, the whereabouts of Private Randall, who was then lying under the bank, bleeding and exhausted, by the side of his dead companion, Parks. On nearing the river and ascending a little rise of ground, he discovered an Indian picket on the lookout. Dismounting his eight men as quietly and quickly as possible, leaving the horses to be held by two of the men, he, with the remaining six, crept up to the top of a hill and a single shot from a carbine put an end to the savage sentry.

As soon as the man fell, the Indians who had been secreted in two ravines on his right and left rear to the number of seventy-five or eighty, advanced to give battle. The sergeant, finding his squad partially surrounded, divided his little band so as to engage those in rear and front, with, as he feared, little chance of success. The men who held the Indians off on the sergeant's left rear fired so rapidly that the warriors broke and concentrated on his right. At this juncture, the ponies belonging to the Indians which had been left in the ravines, became frightened at the firing and stampeded. The hostiles finding themselves afoot concluded to give up the fight and fled from the scene in disorder. The sergeant followed in hot pursuit until close to the stream, when he concluded to return for his horses and to the two men who stood at their post holding the fretful animals in check. One of the horses had been killed. The men had not only been able to keep the horses together, but defended themselves against overwhelming numbers. The sergeant and his eight men were alive and without a scratch. The path of flight of the hostiles was strewn with war bonnets, quivers, arrows, skins, robes, belts and other paraphernalia.

Davis, in returning toward camp, found a fresh scalp of a white man lying on the ground. Concluding that this must tell the tale of the death of one of the citizens with Randall, he began at once to make search for the soldier and companion, dead or alive. The detachment passed close to the bank under which Randall was lying, and seeing evidence of a struggle, the closest investigation was made. The Indians killed by Randall and Parks had been removed, but the marks of warfare were more than visible. Randall, hearing the voices of the soldiers, cried out until he made himself heard. He was dragged from his hiding place more dead than alive. The dead men were buried near where they fell, and Randall was carried to camp where he rapidly recovered. Considering the number of soldiers and the number of foe, the amount of punishment inflicted upon the savages, the amount of war material captured, and the success in bringing out of the fight all of the men Sergeant Davis took into it, this engagement must be regarded as among the most notable of the period to which it belongs. . . .

A Memory of Beecher Island, 1868 (By Reuben Waller, formerly of Troop H, Tenth U. S. Cavalry. From *Winners of the West*, August, 1925)

I want to add one . . . boast, and it is that Captain Louis H. Carpenter and myself were the first of the rescuers to reach Major Forsyth on the morning of September 26, 1868. I was Colonel Carpenter's hostler and when . . . Carpenter dismounted to lift Forsyth out of the rifle pit, I held his horse. If any of those Beecher Island fighters are living and remember the circumstances, I hope they will come forward and testify to what I have said. They ought to remember Colonel Carpenter and his colored orderly, as we charged up to where they were lying in their rifle pits, and how we all cried together as we helped them out of their starving condition. . . .

Sully's Campaign in the Autumn of 1868 (By A. Clinton Rallya, formerly of Troop I, Seventh U. S. Cavalry. From *Winners of the West*, May 30, 1927)

I will now relate a few things that I remember in the Sully campaign of 1868. Troop I, Seventh U. S. Cavalry, left Fort Wallace in the spring of 1868, being ordered to join the regiment at Fort Hays. Arriving there in good shape, we were surprised to find that the Seventh U. S. Cavalry had a new commander, Lieutenant Colonel Alfred Sully, as Lieutenant Colonel George A. Custer had been suspended from the army for one year, and let me say right here that I think it should have been for all time, and I think it would had it not been for Major General Philip H. Sheridan. No doubt you know why. We stayed at Fort Hays only long enough to be fitted out for the warpath. Before leaving we were told that I Troop would have a new commander, as Captain Myles W. Keogh would be on Colonel Sully's staff. This was sorrowful news as every man in the troop idolized Captain Keogh. However, we were not going to lose him entirely and would see him every day and did as he kept close touch with us to see that we were properly treated. Second Lieutenant Charles G. Cox was our new troop commander; don't know where he came from, but did not amount to much.

We did not know where we were going, but were on our way, bringing up at Fort Dodge. After a short stay there, we crossed the Arkansas River and started south. On our way, we were told that this was to be known as the Sully Campaign after Indians, and right here let me say that it will never be forgotten by those who took part in it, and will be remembered as at least the worst the Seventh U. S. Cavalry took part in. We did not have much fighting to do until we got into the sand hills, and there and then we were up against it proper. In trying to cross forks of Canadian and Cimarron river, we lost several wagons and mules swamped in the quicksand. The only one of the scouts and guides, in my estimation, that amounted to anything was California Joe Milner, and he knew but little of that part of the country.

California Joe was a tall, rawboned, red-headed old scout whose appearance and makeup would indicate that soap, water, comb, and brush had been forgotten for a long time. What he lacked in makeup he more than made up in bravery, as he was like a tiger in that respect. His only aim during life was to kill Indians, in revenge for the massacre of his wife and children. He joined our expedition at Fort Dodge, and wanted nothing for anything that he might do to help us along, which he did on many occasions. His only wish was to be given a free hand in killing Indians. He said, "Give me a horse and mule, something to eat, also plenty ammunition, and when you see the smoke from my old Long Tom you can reckon there is one Indian less to fight." We did see the smoke from that Long Tom many a time. He usually wore an old blue army overcoat and government boots, with cartridge box, saddle pockets and nose bag full of ammunition. He had a quart bottle of forty rod in the overcoat pocket, and you can imagine perhaps his appearance riding a small mule and his No. 14 boots almost touching the ground. I never saw him take a drink of water, and one day I asked him why it was. His reply was that water would rot your boots, and he would not take any chances with his stomach.

When Colonel Jack Romeo [Scout Raphael Romero] could not find a passage way through the sand hills, we were obliged to turn back and re-cross the river. From that time on we were kept busy fighting Indians, and every day brought more. We were told not to waste our ammunition, but wait until the Indians came close in and were about to pull us out of our saddles, then fire. [Our] wagon train was doubled up in order to be able to corral our wagons rapidly should occasion require it. However, we did make out to fight our way back without doing that. The Indians circled our train several times, drove our advance and rear guard in, also flankers. The Indians, however, were darn poor shots, and once in a while they would hit a wagon or mule. The only man lost on the trip that I can recall was Captain Louis M. Hamilton's orderly. He was allowed to lag behind the rear guard one morning as we were starting on our day's march. A bunch of Indians swooped down on the poor man and took him off. That morning our troop was at the head of the column and close to headquarters. Sergeant Andrews of our troop hastened to Keogh and requested permission to take a detail and try to rescue the man. Keogh requested permission of Colonel Sully, and he reluctantly gave consent. Andrews grabbed a dozen or so of us kids that had the best horses, and we were off, not giving a thought of our own lives, as the hills and ravines were lined with Indians.

They had perhaps two miles the best of us, but we gained on them rapidly. My horse was not fast, but could run all day, so I was at the head of the party. After a few miles run, we got so close to them that they drew their bows and arrows, and thinking that we would rescue our man, they shot several arrows into his body. He did not fall from his horse, as I think he was tied on, but loped down in the saddle badly hurt. At that time, the Indians did not have many firearms, and this bunch did not seem to have any. However, I would prefer a bullet to an arrow any time.

Colonel Sully had gotten out of his ambulance and was keeping tab on us. He perhaps thought we were getting too far from the command, so he had his bugler sound the recall. Andrews called our attention to it, and said the only thing to do was turn back or get into trouble, so you can imagine the status of our minds when turning back and leaving our comrade to his fate. Maybe you think I did not say some hard words for a long time after that, and yet, we cannot tell what might have happened to us if we had kept going. There might have been another Kidder or Major Elliott slaughter. However, on occasions like that, we never thought of danger, but would ride through hell to rescue a comrade.

The Indians seemed to think they had us licked, and every day they would receive reinforcements. They became more daring, and when they became too numerous and daring Colonel Sully would crawl out of his ambulance, have his orderly help him on his horse, then look things over and perhaps order a charge made. This state of affairs continued from day to day for some time, and finally the Indians commenced disappearing. Don't know why, unless they thought we were not worth wasting any more ammunition on. We went into camp not far from where Camp Supply was established a little later. We stayed here until Custer was restored to command, and poor old Colonel Sully went back in his ambulance to his former command at Harker, and so ended the Sully Campaign.

The Fight at Beaver Creek, 1868 (By Edward M. Hayes, formerly first lieutenant, Fifth U. S. Cavalry. From *Winners of the West*, February, 1940)

Early in October, '68, seven troops of the Fifth Cavalry under command of Major William B. Royall left Fort Hays, Kansas, on a campaign against Roman Nose's band of Cheyenne Indians who were supposed to be on Beaver Creek, a tributary of the Republican River, northwest of Fort Hays. This campaign was bare of results, but later the same command under Major Eugene A. Carr, who relieved Major Royall in command, was very successful. I was at that time quartermaster of the expedition, and had a wagon train of about seventy-six mule teams and a half dozen ambulances under my charge. The trail covered was partly over the same ground as the first expedition, but more directly toward the headwaters of Beaver Creek, as Major Carr had information that the Indians were located in that vicinity.

Orders were given for forced marches, and on the third or fourth day out, late in the afternoon my wagon train, which was about three miles in the rear of the column of cavalry, owing to its inability to keep up on account of inexperienced teamsters and the poor condition of the mules, was suddenly attacked by a band of 300-400 warriors, who had apparently risen as by magic from the prairie and formed line on a slight ridge bordering on a small stream, and in a perfectly open country about three-quarters of a mile from the train. The wagon train was in two columns, about a hundred yards apart, and somewhat lengthened out on account of the rapid gait and poor condition of the mules, but the sight of the Indians had a startling effect, and the straggling wagons closed up almost at a run.

The Indians presented a gorgeous spectacle with their war bonnets, arms, and so forth glistening in the blinding rays of the setting sun. This impressive sight was only momentary, when the larger part of the Indians composed of young warriors, I suppose, dashed forward to the charge, the others remaining apparently as a support to their charging brothers. The time given, however, was sufficient to get the train and guard in position to meet the attack. Two scouts were sent forward on the run to notify Major Carr of the condition of affairs, and succeeded in reaching him. The escort to the train, including convalescents, numbered about forty men and was divided into advance, rear guard, and flankers, covering the open space between the columns of wagons, front and rear of the teams, and forming a line of flankers on the side next to the enemy. The whole was kept moving all the time during the maneuvers and attack, and never once halted. The flankers were in charge of an old sergeant, whose name, unfortunately, I cannot recall, but whose coolness, bravery, and judgment was far above the average. The men were dismounted, their horses being sent to the shelter of the wagon train, the line marching in open order so as to cover the flank of the train, on which the attack was expected to fall. This line was reinforced by a part of the teamsters, who, after having tied their lead mules to the rear of the preceding wagons, were ordered to join the flankers. These men were armed with old-fashioned muzzle-loading Springfield rifles, and did good service.

Orders were given to reserve fire until the Indians were within fifty yards, and then "fire at will." The charge was repulsed with considerable loss to the Indians in both warriors and ponies. In the meantime, Major Carr had detached three troops to the assistance of the train. The Indians discovering the reinforcements before we did, drew away to confront the cavalry. Then took place one of the most interesting and exciting engagements of Indian warfare ever witnessed. The Indians receiving the charge of the cavalry and vigorously returning it, for a time it was charge and countercharge, and doubtful as to which would give way, until finally a determined charge of the troops drove them back across the stream—both Indians and cavalry disappearing over the ridge. The train continued to move on, and joined the remaining troops with Major Carr who had gone into camp about four miles beyond. This was at sundown. The firing of the three troops and the Indians could be heard until dark, when Major Carr sent orders for the troops to withdraw and return to camp. The Indians followed, opening fire on the camp, which continued about two hours, but with little effect on account of the darkness and poor marksmanship. This was the first and only time in my experience that I witnessed a night attack by Indians.

Before starting early next morning, Major Carr decided to burn up a number of wagons, all the forage and camp equipage, in order to lighten the train and increase the number of mules to the teams of the remaining wagons. The pursuit was then taken up and continued from early morning till late at night, the Indians being in plain view on all sides of the command and fighting desperately with the advance guard to retard our progress and give their village [with its] women and children, which was only a few miles ahead and our objective, an opportunity for escape. Dark had overtaken us when we went into camp, the Indians skirmishing with us all the way. That night their small camp fires were discernible a short distance from us, but no attack was made.

Before daybreak next morning, Major Carr started out with the cavalry, directing me to follow with the wagon train, the troops pressing the village so closely that the Indians were forced to throw away all of their belongings, including bundles of buffalo robes, dried meat, tepees and tepee poles, and abandon many of their ponies. The pursuit was kept up by the cavalry for two days and nights, until the Indians scattered in every direction, leaving no trail to follow. On the third day the train rejoined Major Carr, and all marched back to Fort Wallace, Kansas, where the campaign ended. This campaign cleared the country of nearly all hostile Indians between the Platte and Arkansas Rivers, their favorite hunting ground, and practically ended the Indian troubles in that section. William F. Cody was our guide on this campaign, and had his first experience as a government scout, displaying all the well known qualities of bravery and skill which later made him the most famous scout of the United States Army.

A Buffalo Soldier Recalls Beaver Creek (By Reuben Waller, formerly of Troop H, Tenth U. S. Cavalry. From *Winners of the West*, October, 1924)

While stationed at Fort Wallace, Kansas, in October, 1868, the Indians were bad, and there were only two troops of cavalry at the fort. A scout brought in word that there was a large camp of Indians about one mile northeast of Fort Wallace, on Beaver Creek, at a place called Short Knolls. Troops H and I of the Tenth Cavalry were all that could be had at that time. Major Eugene A. Carr came to Fort Wallace on an inspection tour. The demand was so great for cavalrymen that Major Carr got the two companies of black soldiers together and looked them over and tried them out as to horsemanship and marksmanship. He found us expert horseback riders and dead shots with the Spencer seven-shot carbines. . . . I at that time was Lieutenant Colonel Henry C. Bankhead's orderly, and the conversation which ensued between Colonel Bankhead and Major Carr is still very fresh on my mind. I can hear Major Carr as he said: "Why, Bankhead, I can take those two troops of negroes and whip hell out of all the Indians in Colorado." Colonel Bankhead[, who commanded Fort Wallace,] replied in words like these: "Very well, General Carr [referring to his brevet rank], they are at your service."

Major Carr sent for a scout named Grover Sharp [Sharp Grover], who was chief scout and had several scouts under him. Immediately upon being informed that the Indians were thus situated nearby, Major Carr ordered boots and saddles sounded, and further ordered eleven wagons loaded with forage for the horses. Early the next morning we hiked out for Beaver Creek where the Indians were reported to be. It required three days for us to make the trip to Beaver Creek. Here we found about twelve hundred Indian warriors, besides women and children. We struck them about dark on the third day. The Indians gave us quite a round that evening, and we went into camp about three miles distant from them.

Bright and early the next morning, the Indians were upon us and they made things look serious for us. I recall Major Carr having told Captain Carpenter of my Troop H that we had better retreat. Major Carr ordered a retreat and the Indians left us to dispose of their women and children, and let us go until about three o'clock that day. Twelve hundred strong, they overtook us upon the bare plains. We, being well disciplined, corralled eleven wagons, while one troop kept the Indians at bay. We placed the horses and mules inside the corral and took the forage out of the wagons and made breastworks. By the time we had finished this work, the Indians had completely encircled us and it looked bad for Major Carr's scalp. We fell back behind the sacks of forage, and being dead shots the Indians melted away like snow beneath the burning rays of a summer's sun. The Indians came up eight-to-ten deep within fifty yards of our breastworks. We slaughtered them unmercifully. Major Carr said to us that he had never seen such superior marksmanship among soldiers in all of his military experience. He said, "Men, you have surely gained the day." We said among ourselves, "Yes, General Carr, and we have also saved your scalp." Our soldiers also scalped some of the Indians, but we soon put a stop to that kind of barbarity among the Tenth cavalrymen.

Kansas Troops and the 1868 Campaign (By W. R. Smith, formerly of Company F, Nineteenth Kansas Volunteer Cavalry. From *Winners of the West*, March 30, 1926)

The western plains sure had no welcome greeting for the Nineteenth Kansas Cavalry in the latter part of November, 1868. Scarcely had we reached this then unknown pathless wilderness before old King Winter sent down his storms upon us. There was a succession of rain, sleet, hailstorms, snows, raging blizzards, and intense freezing cold.

In the blinding storms, all trains and landmarks were lost sight of, and the regiment floundered about in the deep snows for two days before we reached Sand Creek, a tributary of the Cimarron River, where we went into camp. Some weeks later, *Harpers Weekly* published an illustration of our going into this camp. It was a wild and dreary scene. "Camp Starvation" we called it, and that name gave a most correct idea of its fitness. Those sand hills along the north side of the Cimarron, among which our camp was located, were formed by the action of the wind in past ages by blowing the sand out of the river bed. They were at that time covered by a growth of young timber, their only redeeming feature as they thus supplied us with wood for fires.

Supplies for our regiment had been sent to Camp Beecher, now Wichita, but had been partly consumed by the troops stationed there. As it was urgent for us to reach Major General Philip H. Sheridan at Camp Supply on the Canadian River, we had marched on with what rations and forage were left, scarcely half enough for the trip. There we were, 1,200 men and twice that many horses and mules, without food, forage, or tents, snowbound by winter storms among the sand dunes of the Cimarron, a bleak, desolate, and forsaken place. The continued storms had driven the buffalo far away, and only an occasional old stray stag could be found in some sheltered cove. They were killed and brought into camp and the meat was ravenously devoured without leaving a scrap. Even the bones were roasted and broken open for the marrow they contained. The boys roamed over the brush-covered hills in search of anything that would sustain life, but game of all kinds was hard to find outside of their burrows under the deep snow. Large quantities of hackberries were gathered and eaten and made into tea by some of the half-starved boys, which afterward caused them much pain and trouble.

We had not received our full supply of clothing to protect us from the terrors of a winter on the plains, and some suffered greatly from lack of it, wrapping their feet in pieces of blankets or buffalo hides. Sheridan said afterward that he greatly feared the whole outfit had perished. Our horses suffered terribly, some of them freezing to death, and in their starved condition acted like wild animals in their frenzy. We cut cottonwood poles and brush and carried it to them to gnaw the bark and twigs from. That was all there was for them to eat. Having gone nearly a week without much food, many died from starvation and cold. In after years, our line of march from this camp to Fort Sill [sic—Camp Supply] could be followed by the bleaching bones of our noble horses. A detail of fifty men with the best horses, under the command of Captain Allison J. Pliley, was sent out in the storm over the snow-covered plains, without rations or forage, to find

Sheridan's camp on the Canadian and send relief back to the regiment, which later we received and then went on to Camp Supply. While at this cold, blizzard-swept, and starving camp, Thanksgiving Day was passed, but I fear few of the boys felt that they had anything to be thankful for. When we went to the plains we expected to fight Indians and maybe lose our scalps, but we never thought of those other worse enemies—cold and starvation. That ill fate followed us almost from the first to last, without much glory, if any, for services rendered.

Trials of the Southern Plains Campaign, 1868-1869 (By Henry Pearson, formerly of Troop I, Nineteenth Kansas Volunteer Cavalry. From *Winners of the West*, December 30, 1926)

In the latter part of October, 1868, the governor of Kansas issued a call for one volunteer regiment to fight Indians in Kansas and New Mexico, [and] Indian Territory. The regiment was soon formed and the shipment of supplies to Topeka, Kansas, had arrived. After being mustered into service, the uniforms, ammunition, and equipment were drawn and our horses had begun to arrive. After drawing the horses, bridles, and saddles, we were sent out to drill, and a greener, rawer bunch was never brought together. After drilling for two days, the emergency and haste being so great, we were prepared for the march into the Indian Territory.

On the fifth day of November we marched up Kansas Avenue, four abreast, with bright shining equipment and being well mounted on fine horses. A gayer-hearted bunch of boys certainly never marched up Kansas Avenue. Little did we realize what we were going out into—we supposed to fight Indians, but instead to a great extent we fought starvation and one of the worst blizzards ever known in Kansas. Governor Samuel J. Crawford resigned his office as governor and was appointed colonel. He was loyal to his officers and kind to his men, and if they had hunted the territory of Kansas over a better man for that position could not have been found.

After marching several days we finally struck Fort Beecher, which is now known as Wichita. There we received orders to replenish our supplies enough to carry us on through to Camp Supply. As the wagon train from Fort Hays hadn't arrived, we decided it best to go on with half rations. After staying in Fort Beecher a day and two nights, we marched out across the Arkansas River and bid good-bye to civilization. We marched on for two days and on the third day a rainstorm set in and we camped on a small stream. Every fourth man was ordered to hold out four horses to graze until nine o'clock at night. Our scouts had been on ahead finding the trail for us to follow the next day. About dark one of them came into camp and, jumping off his horse, hastily pulled off the bridle and saddle and started to head his horse to where the others were feeding. The saddle had not been entirely unfastened and was dragging along the ground. The horse became scared at this and broke away from the scout and ran as fast as he could toward the other horses, who became scared at the noise and they started to run. This caused a stampede among all of them and away they went over the prairie, four fastened together. The bugle sounded to fall in, armed and equipped, and we supposed the Indians were upon us and we would have to fight. But when we marched up the line to the colonel's tent, we were informed that our horses had stampeded. For two days we searched the prairie for them and succeeded in finding all but one hundred and thirty head. The next morning we marched on, a hundred and thirty of the boys walking, but our provisions were becoming too short to wait longer.

For several days we marched and then it began to snow. All the trails were covered and the scouts had to go by their knowledge of the lay of the land. They disagreed about the direction of Camp Supply from where we were located, but we tramped on while all the time the snow was coming down faster and the thermometer registering lower and lower. We finally came to a small stream and, brushing away the snow, we camped until morning. When morning came it was still snowing and steadily getting colder, so we pushed on, our supplies being nearly exhausted. At noon we were stopped and two hardtacks was issued to each man, and that was all we had all that day. Just as night was coming on we came to a small tributary of the Cimarron River and here we went into camp. The officers and scouts had a meeting as something had to be done soon. They agreed there was no use in going further as we didn't know where we were, so it was decided we stay here until the scouts could locate Camp Supply and bring back provisions.

One of the scouts believed Camp Supply lay due south of where we were camped and the other one believed it lay southwest. They were told to pick out twenty-five men each and push on to where they believed Camp Supply lay and bring back provisions for man and beast. At nine o'clock that night Pancy Bill took twenty-five men and started south. Johnny Stillwell took two hundred rounds of cartridges, two carbines, and two revolvers, an extra horse and started southwest alone. About noon the next day, Pancy Bill returned to camp with his twenty-five men, but two of his horses died on the trip. He then decided that Camp Supply lay to the southwest. There we were, nothing to cover us but the sky and snow, nothing to eat but hackberries, and wondering how long it would take us to starve or freeze to death. We found a little wood with which we built a fire and we cut down some trees so our horses could gnaw the bark.

The second day, some of the boys began to talk about deserting and taking the back trail. The trail was completely obliterated and was almost impossible to be found, but about midnight about twenty-five of them gathered plenty of ammunition, picked out some of the best mules and horses, and started back. The rest of us decided we might as well stay there and starve or freeze, whichever it was to be, as to get lost and freeze out on the prairie. We were taking chances on Johnny Stillwell finding Camp Supply. We had a lot of confidence in Johnny Stillwell even though he was but a boy of twenty years. The morning of the third day, one of the boys from Company A and myself went out to see if we might find some animal or bird that we could use for food. After wandering around for quite a while we found a sage hen and the boy from Company A shot and killed it. Being reasonably close and with an ounce ball in his gun, and the sage hen being small, it was torn into pieces. But he gathered up all the parts he could find and took it to camp and cooked it and God only knows how many hungry boys feasted on that little sage hen. On my return back to camp, a squirrel was unfortunate enough to let me see him run up a tree and I shot him. When I took him into camp we skinned him and put him in the camp kettle, but about all the boys got from that squirrel was about a pint of soup.

When the fourth day had dawned and we were still held prisoners, the boys began to talk about a suitable name for our camp. One of the boys, sitting with his head bowed ready to meet death, said, "Let's call it 'Camp Starvation,'" and so it was named; a more suitable name could not have been procured had we had all the names in the book to select from. Four days and nights and we had been wondering if Johnny Stillwell had succeeded in finding Camp Supply, or whether he had gotten lost and frozen to death, leaving us out on the prairie away from all civilization and with no way to communicate with the camp which was so near and yet so far away. But, as if our thoughts [were] answered, we heard the squeaking of the wagon wheels on snow and then we knew Johnny Stillwell had been successful and we would soon have food and provisions enough to carry us on to Camp Supply. We were so filled with joy and thanksgiving that some began to shoot off their guns, but the officers soon stopped that for we would probably need all the ammunition we had before we were through with our campaign.

The wagons drove in, one wagon for each company, and two guards were placed over each wagon. We were formed into camp messes, about twelve in each mess, and each man was issued one hardtack and some coffee. We were told we could have more hardtack and coffee at midnight. Some of the boys refused to sleep for fear they would oversleep and not get their meager lunch at midnight. We stayed one more day, feeding our horses and letting them gain a little more strength so they could carry us on. We had only a few left, as the others had starved or frozen to death. During the time that Stillwell had been gone, Captain Allison J. Pliley and his company, with the best horses in the command, had started south. The rest of us, after resting and eating for a day and two nights, started for Camp Supply with two hundred of our horses dead and two hundred boys wading the snow, which was from sixteen to eighteen inches deep.

Lieutenant Colonel George A. Custer had been waiting at Camp Supply for the Nineteenth regiment to reinforce him in his march to the Wichita [Washita] River, but fearing that we had all perished, he started on with his few mounted men, and at Antelope Hill he met Black Kettle and his little band of Indians. He had quite a little battle with them, and lost a few of his men but killed a good many Indians. As Custer looked down the valley he saw it was red with Indians so he decided he had better go back to Camp Supply as we had probably arrived there by that time. When he returned to Camp Supply we were there and partly recuperated. He said there was no time to be lost as the Indians would be getting further away. All of the Nineteenth who had horses joined with Custer and he also took the Third Infantry. We marched out of Camp Supply for the Washita River and after several days marching we came to a small stream where the Indians were camping, supposing Custer had given up and that they could live there in peace. [This was in March, 1869.] But when they saw Custer returning with reinforcements they knew they had reckoned with the wrong man. They decided to fight, but when Custer was forming his lines for battle they soon changed their minds and thought it best to surrender without losing any more of their warriors.

We were very much disappointed to think that we had suffered starvation and laid out half frozen, many with their feet and hands frozen and our uniforms in rags, and then we wouldn't get to fight those Indians after all. From one camp to the other ran the messengers and interpreters with messages of truce. Custer finally went into the Indian camp and brought back four Indian chiefs. They were asked many questions in regard to the white women who had been captured eight miles west of Concordia [Kansas] in the fall of '67. They claimed the Sioux had them and that they didn't know just where their camp was located. It was decided that . . . [three] chiefs should be held in our camp until the white women were found and given to us. The Indian messenger was sent back to the Indian camp with the message that if the white women were not brought to us by sundown, the chiefs would be hung. The Indian came back and asked for one more day in which to bring the women. Custer granted one more day to them, but told them no more time would be given them, that if they didn't bring the white women we would hang their chiefs. About four o'clock the next day we could see an Indian ride up over the hill and look down into our camp and then ride back and after a while another would ride up and look down to see if we still held the chiefs. Finally an Indian came into camp and asked for just one more day, but Custer said "No—if those white women are not here by the time the sun is sending its last rays over that hill in the west, we will hang those . . . chiefs." Just as the sun was setting, a big chief riding a beautiful black horse came up over the hill, and following him came the two white women on a gray pony. The chief brought them up to our lines and surrendered them to us. Custer turned to Colonel Horace Moore and said, "You are from Kansas. You receive and welcome those two women." We had prepared a tent for them, and two guards had been placed over it, one at each end, and the women were escorted to the tent and everything was done for their comfort that was possible to be done out here in the wilderness. The old chief who had brought back the women then demanded we give up to him the . . . chiefs, but Custer said, "No, we'll keep them a while." He went back to camp and the Indians began to prepare for battle and we were very much delighted to think we would get to fight them after all. But at the last moment we were disappointed for they gave it up. We stayed in the camp for a couple of days as Custer thought maybe they would decide to start on the warpath, but they decided to let us keep the chiefs without a fight. The time for the Nineteenth to be discharged was drawing near, and so we were ordered to take the back trail for Fort Hays, where we duly received our honorable discharge. . . .

With Custer at the Washita, 1868 (By Henry Langley, formerly of Troop C, Seventh U. S. Cavalry. From *Winners of the West*, December 15, 1925)

In reference to the Black Kettle fight we had in Wichita [sic—at the Washita River], we had a pretty hard time getting there on account of snow and sleet and things of that kind. We were in sight of the Indians but out of reach. They had their women and children with them and were going to camp. They would throw out fighting men every once in a while to detain us from catching up with them. We followed them for several days in the snow, eighteen or twenty inches on the level. We had Ute [Osage] Indian trailers and guides. We followed the Indians for several days and finally lost sight of them. After a few hours one of the Ute trailers was on ahead and signaled for us to stop. Colonel Custer rode up with his aide and the Indian reported the tribe on the Wichita [Washita] River, which was only about a mile from where we were. The sun was going down at the time and Custer thought it wouldn't be right to go for them that night.

We were ordered to dismount and stand by our horses to keep them from making any noise, as the Indians were right under the bluff. You could hear the dogs barking in the camp. We laid all night with our horses, cold, wet, and mad! But finally, just before day, the order was given to get ready to march. We had our band with us, which Custer ordered to play the grand charge. As soon as it was light enough to see, the command was given to mount and charge. The band was stationed at the crossing of the creek, and Custer ordered it to strike up some lively tune. As soon as the command was given to charge, the band struck up "Garry Owen," a lively Irish quickstep. Our horses were tired and we were mad before that, but as soon as the band struck up that tune the horses seemed to take new heart and the men, too, and when we went into the village the Indians didn't know what it was, thinking it was some serenade, and they came running out of the tents without their arms. As soon as they saw Custer and his command, they rushed back into their tents and got their guns, commencing firing. We did nothing but return the fire, and left a great many of them on the ground, between eighty and ninety, I believe. Captain Louis M. Hamilton, of our regiment, was killed early in the fight. Major Joel Elliott, with nineteen [seventeen] men, was ordered on a scout to look out for outlying Indians[sic—Elliott went after escaping Indians on his own volition]. He went off and they kept us fighting all day, off and on, but Major Elliott never turned up. Sometime afterwards we found him and his men in a canyon in the mountains, all dead. We buried them and got ready to go back [sic—Elliott's party was not found until two weeks later when Custer's command returned to the scene; the dead were buried at that time].

After the fight at Wichita was over, we had orders to destroy the camp. We burned their tents and their camp equipment and had to shoot the ponies, after which we started back to Camp Supply, I. T., with the Indian women and children. [In March, 1869, Custer's command pursued the Indians into the Texas panhandle.] There we met a lot of Indians, but they had no fight in them. Colonel Custer sent for some of the chiefs and main men to come in for a talk. There were three chiefs and some other Indians came in. . . . After the talk, Colonel Custer placed the three chiefs under guard and sent the balance of them back to their camp to bring two white girls which they had captured before, and bring them back at a certain time. If they didn't bring them back by that time, Custer would hang the three chiefs to a cottonwood tree. They started off and in a very short time came back with the two girls. . . .

I was wounded slightly twice during the fight at Wichita, in the left wrist and in the left leg above the knee. This all occurred in the latter part of September, 1868. [sic—the Washita encounter took place on November 27, 1868.]

The Battle at Palo Duro Canyon, 1874 (By John B. Charlton, formerly sergeant, Troop F, Fourth U. S. Cavalry. From *Winners of the West*, April 28, 1942)

During the summer of 1874, while Colonel Ranald S. Mackenzie's command was in quarters at Fort Clark, Texas, rumors became rife of unrest among certain tribes of Indians on the government reservations. These rumors were soon verified by a threatened outbreak. Shortly after this news reached the post, I was sent by Colonel Mackenzie with dispatches to Fort Sill, and my orders were to travel by night only, as the country at that time was infested by numerous small bands of Indians; so by traveling at night much delay was avoided and many dangers evaded. By changing horses at each army post on the route, I was able to make the ride, a distance of about 580 miles, in six nights. Upon my return, I found the general's command at Fort Concho, Texas, and there learned that the threatened outbreak had occurred—that Lone Wolf's band, strengthened by warriors from other tribes, had left the reservations, and with their families had established themselves in winter quarters somewhere well within the border of northwest Texas, and that Colonel Mackenzie had been ordered out with his command, consisting of seven troops of cavalry, to intercept them and break up their camp.

I reported to the colonel and was placed with the scouting party then being formed. This party consisted of six white men, thirteen Seminoles, and twelve Tonkawa Indians. First Lieutenant William Thompson was made chief of the scouts. The command left Fort Concho immediately, moving in the direction of what was then called Blanco Canyon, but is now known as Yellow House Canyon. The supply trains, accompanied by four companies of infantry from Fort Concho, followed. After several days' marching, we reached this canyon where a supply camp was established. Rain fell in torrents that night, and a "norther" blew up, which added greatly to the discomfort of the troops. The next morning, September 26th 1874, with fifteen days' rations for each man, the troops were on the march again, this time the objective point being Tule Canyon, about a day's march ahead of us. After reaching the level of the plains, the scouts were ordered out on duty, as we were nearing that part of the country where it was hoped reliable information might be gathered as to the location of the main body of Indians. Lieutenant Thompson had orders to travel in a direction deviating somewhat from that taken by the command. We rode all morning without any sign of Indians, but about noon came to a slight break in the plains where we drew rein to make a survey of the landscape. Some distance away I noticed what appeared to be a herd of about a hundred buffalo. I called Lieutenant Thompson's attention to them. Looking through his field glasses for a moment, he exclaimed: "They are Indians, sergeant, and they are going to attack us. Get your men ready for action."

I dismounted the men, placed six of them in charge of the horses, and the remainder was formed in line of battle around the horses. Lieutenant Thompson watched the approaching savages intently until they were near enough to make sure of their approximate number, then he rode over to us and gave orders to fall back toward the command, as we were outnumbered four to one. "Hold steady, men, and reserve your fire until they are within easy reach," said the lieutenant. They were approaching rapidly, about 120 of them, and yelling like demons. The scouts numbered thirty-one men, all told. When the Indians reached a point about sixty yards from our defense line, they suddenly turned to the right and began circling us. Then we opened fire. Step by step our scouts fell back, fighting every inch of the way, and hoping meanwhile that we were traveling in the direction of the command. An Indian buck, mounted on a white horse, kept riding toward us, firing and yelling, then riding back into line. Each trip he grew bolder and approached nearer to our men. Just how many of the scouts decided to stop his bluff, I cannot say, but this Comanche soon went down with several bullet holes in his carcass. The Indians continued to harass us until about sundown, when luckily we reached the trail of the command. Our foes, realizing from the size of the trail the presence of a large body of troops in that vicinity, disappeared as if by magic. We then mounted our horses, took up the trail, and reached camp about 10 o'clock that night. Several Indians were killed by our men, but by good luck we had no casualties to report.

When Colonel Mackenzie heard of the skirmish with the Indians, he ordered about one-third of the company, including the scouts, placed on guard that night, as he, with the rest of us, strongly suspected that we would be attacked before daylight. His suspicion proved correct, for at "moon up" they were upon us, this time several hundred strong. That portion of the men not on guard rested on their guns, so at the first alarm from vidette we were up and ready for them. At the first fire from our men, the Indians withdrew, no doubt somewhat surprised at the number of troops. At no time during the night did they approach so closely again, but kept circling the camp skirmishing, presumably for an opening to stampede our horses. Ten wagons in charge of Wagonmaster James O'Neal arrived at camp during the night. These wagons were loaded with forage and ammunition and were accompanied by one company of infantry, the other three companies having been left to guard the supplies at Yellow House Canyon. It is a mystery why this train of ten wagons was not attacked, for, owing no doubt to some atmospheric condition peculiar to the plains, the drivers heard none of the firing and came noisily into camp cracking their whips and yelling at their mules, which were floundering in the mud.

At dawn the following day, the Indians left us. A laughable incident occurred about this time. As the Indians disappeared, the attention of the troops was attracted by the sight of a solitary Comanche riding a brown pony. He was on a little rise out of range of our rifles, and appeared nonplussed as to the direction taken by his companions, from whom he had evidently been cut off. He scanned the horizon for a moment, then attempted a short cut in the direction taken by the other Indians. This brought him in range of our rifles, when Henry, a Tonkawa, shot his horse dead and the horse in falling threw the rider. Henry then rode forth against his fallen foe. Now, in those days an Indian wore his blanket in this fashion: taking the blanket lengthwise, he wrapped it around his body. His cartridge belt, with pistol in holster, was buckled around his waist, and the top part of the blanket then turned down over the belt. The Comanche had risen to his feet, but was somewhat dazed from the fall when Henry arrived upon the scene. Henry's rifle was strapped to his saddle, and he was so sure of victory that he had neglected to draw it until it was too late. He fumbled desperately for his pistol which still remained entangled in the folds of his blanket. In the meantime, the Comanche, fully recovered, had made a spring for the Tonkawa, dragged him from his horse, and, drawing his bow, began to give him the trouncing of his life. At every cut of the bow, Henry leaped about three feet in the air, making frantic gestures toward the troops and yelling, "Why you no shoot? Why you no shoot?" The whole command was laughing, but we had enjoyed the fun long enough, so somebody shot the

Comanche and Henry took his scalp with great satisfaction, but he nursed a grouch against the whole bunch of us for several days.

After the troops had breakfasted, Colonel Mackenzie sent for me and told me to take two Indians and follow the trail of those who had attacked the command the night before. So, accompanied by two Tonkawas, Johnson and Job, I took up the trail at once, and we rode rapidly for several miles before I began to notice numerous other trails, all converging and fresh. The country over which we rode appeared level as they eye could see, and was covered with undulating waves of rich grass. Suddenly and unexpectedly, we came in view of Palo Duro Canyon, a colossal crevice which breaks the plains of northwest Texas for a distance of sixty miles. I dismounted at once, left Job in charge of the horses and, with Johnson, crept on hands and knees to the edge of the canyon precipice. I felt overawed at the depth of the walls of the canyon, which at this point had a sheer drop of about 1,500 feet, the distance from wall to wall being about [one-]half mile. A small stream of water was running through the canyon. Flecks of valley land was visible, intermingled with dark cedar tops which cast darker shadows on the ground. In the open, hundreds of horses were grazing. Viewed from our immense height, the horses appeared as tiny moving objects. Tepees thickly dotted the banks of the stream as far down the canyon as I could see. I afterwards learned that this Indian camp was three miles long. At any rate, from my vantage point I had gotten a pretty comprehensive view of the whole situation. Time was pressing and there was a ride of twenty-five miles back to the main command. "Heap Injun!" grunted Johnson, close to my ear. "You bet your life, old scout, and some canyon, too," whispered I, as we backed off cautiously and made a run for our horses.

I lost no time in reporting to Colonel Mackenzie what I had seen. In a short time the troops were again in the saddle, marching against Lone Wolf's stronghold, in the depths of Palo Duro Canyon, and its defense of 1,500 warriors. The colonel left one troop of cavalry with the remaining company of infantry to guard the wagons at Tule Canyon. This reduced the strength of the main command to less than 600 men. After an all-night march, the command reached the Palo Duro Canyon at sunup on the morning of September 28th, 1874. The scouts, as was their duty, were slightly in advance of the main column. As the rear of the column swung into line, Colonel Mackenzie rode over to us and said: "Mr. Thompson, take your men down and open the fight." "Very well, sir," said the lieutenant. Now the only means of ingress to the canyon available was a rocky and precipitous buffalo trail, down which the men were forced to go in single file. Lieutenant Thompson led us down here, and as we went over the brink, McCabe, an Irishman and one of the scouts, murmured dolefully: "And not even a cup o' coffee to stay me stummick."

When we had reached a point about two-thirds of the way down, an Indian sentinel to our left leaped to his feet from behind a rock and uttered a war-whoop that awoke the echoes far and near. That yell, with the shot that finished his earthly career, aroused the multitude of Indians below. The din became terrific. And then we went down into that inferno of howling redskins. Kiowas, Comanches, Arapahos, and Cheyennes attacked us from every quarter, first by dozens, later by hundreds, as the warriors gathered from the lower part of the camp. Many were concealed behind rocks, while others were ambushed in the foliage of the cedars. We were being reinforced as rapidly as the troops could make the descent of the tortuous and precipitous trail. The smoke from our rifles settled down, adding further obscurity to the darkness of the canyon. But I could hear Colonel Mackenzie's voice giving orders somewhere in the thickest of the fray. The Indian warriors held their ground for a time, fighting desperately to cover the exit of their squaws and pack animals, but under the persistent fire of the troops they soon began falling back, slowly at first, toward the head of the canyon.

The herd of Indian ponies, frightened by the uproar, fled first to one pass and then to another, only to have their leader shot down by a trooper, thereby blocking the trail. The main body of Indians retreated in the open along the banks of the stream. Here the troops suffered their greatest casualties, being subjected to a crossfire from numerous snipers hidden in the timber on both sides. It was about five miles to the pass where the squaws left the canyon, and it was well toward sunset when the warriors, now in full retreat, reached that point. The command followed closely the going out of the Indians, but long ere the rear troops had reached the level of the plains, Lone Wolf's magnificent band of warriors had fled. We followed them for a short distance, but as the men had been twenty-four hours without food, and as our dead and wounded were in need of attention, Colonel Mackenzie thought it best to turn back. Upon re-entering the canyon, we passed over dead Indians everywhere. Their wounded they took with them. After a careful search, we found our casualties to be two dead and quite a number wounded. One man was shot through the bowels, but he got well. His recovery, the doctor said, was due to the fact that he had been without food so long.

The Indians, although no doubt apprised of the approach of the troops after the attack at Tule Canyon, were evidently not looking for a pitched battle so soon, otherwise they would have gathered their ponies and packed their tepees, all of which were left behind. Colonel Mackenzie ordered the

This Southern Plains warrior posed for a photographer after the conflicts between his tribe and the Army in the 1870s. The cavalryman, from the same period, typified those who routed the Kiowas, Comanches, and Southern Cheyennes at Palo Duro Canyon in 1874. *Editor's Collection.*

tepees and everything of value to the Indians burned. This was done, after which the horses, numbering about 2,200 in all, were rounded up and driven out of the canyon, when the main command started on the return trip to Tule Canyon. Everybody was tired and hungry, but the scouts, who had done extra hard duty the preceding forty-eight hours, were utterly worn out. So try as I would, I could not keep awake. Several times during the night as I slept in the saddle, I felt Colonel Mackenzie's hand on my shoulder shaking me. "Wake up, sergeant," he would say. "Wake up your men and look after your horses." This I did, rousing the other weary scouts and rounding up the straggling ponies, only to fall asleep again immediately myself. The command reached Tule Canyon in the early morning, when the colonel ordered the captured horses shot. Some questioned the wisdom of this act, but it was the only thing to be done, as there were too many horses in this herd to be taken care of by the limited number of men in the command.

The Battle of Punished Woman's Fork, 1878 (By Albert Fensch, former hospital steward, Nineteenth U. S. Infantry. Fensch became National Adjutant General of the National Indian War Veterans and helped found the United Indian War Veterans. From an unidentified newspaper dated November 25, 1923)

Early in the month of September 1878, a body of Northern Cheyennes numbering about 300 men, women, and children under the leadership of Chief Dull Knife left their reservation in the then Indian Territory in an effort to return to their old hunting grounds in the Black Hills. They passed a few miles to the west of Dodge City, [Kansas,] killing and scalping settlers of Ford County, destroying ranches and running off stock. Troops composed of a squadron of the Fourth United States Cavalry, from Camp Supply, ninety miles south of Dodge, commanded by Major Clarence Mauck, took up the pursuit. These troops were joined at Fort Dodge, a military post four miles from Dodge City, by Companies G and F, Nineteenth United States Infantry, commanded respectively by Captain James H. Bradford and Second Lieutenant Cornelius Gardener, all with Lieutenant Colonel William H. Lewis, Nineteenth Infantry, who had been designated to command the expeditionary forces, and pursuit of the Indians was taken up.

On September 27th, 1878, the command overtook the savages and a battle took place, which has been officially designated by the War Department as "The engagement at Punished Woman's Fork." Here Lieutenant Colonel Lewis, the commander, received a bullet wound in the thigh which severed the femoral artery—this while reconnoitering near the line of the enemy. The writer with two comrades ran to his assistance when he fell from his horse and at the same time the Indians made a rush to capture him. He was brought, under heavy fire from the enemy, to the shelter of a large boulder and a messenger sent to the rear for reinforcements and medical assistance. A young contract surgeon with two privates responded to the call under fire, a tourniquet was applied to the wounded leg and the commander sent to the rear. A few hours later, he was placed in an ambulance and started across the unbroken prairie to Fort Wallace, some forty miles away. On the road over the rough country the tourniquet became displaced and this brave and gallant officer bled to death, and was so found on the arrival of the ambulance at Wallace. . . . [Major Mauck renewed the pursuit of the elusive Cheyennes.] At the Wyoming [sic—Nebraska] border the pursuit was taken up by troops of the Third United States Cavalry under command of Captain (afterwards General) Henry W. Wessells, and the

Private Thomas A. Lewis, Company K, Twentieth Infantry, possibly at Fort Gibson, Indian Territory, ca. 1881-85. Lewis wears a canvas cartridge belt first issued to soldiers in the mid-1870s. *Editor's collection*

troops from Dodge and Supply took train at Cheyenne and returned to their stations.

C. Mountain West

The Mountain West included the inter-mountain country embracing Idaho Territory and western Montana Territory, stretching south through the Rocky Mountains of Colorado. These lands attracted an influx of white Americans interested in settlement and in extracting mineral wealth from the land. Despite treaties with the tribes, their exploitive presence and ill treatment of the Indian people around them eventually culminated in prolonged culture conflict, invariably causing death and destruction and resulting in the Indians' loss of most of their lands. Notable army campaigns waged in the Mountain West included those against the non-treaty Nez Perces in 1877 (including battles at White Bird Canyon, Idaho, and Big Hole River, Montana), the Bannocks in 1878, and the Utes of Colorado in 1879. By the 1870s, many of the native tribes in this region had adapted their life ways to incorporate physical traits and some material characteristics of those people of the neighboring Great Plains, and to a great extent the modes of warfare were largely the same. In the following accounts, veteran soldiers describe incidents of fighting Nez Perce, Bannock, and Ute warriors in the above-mentioned campaigns.

The Fight at White Bird Canyon, 1877 (By Frank Fenn, Mount Idaho Volunteers. From *Winners of the West*, January 30, 1926)

In 1877 we were among the volunteers who accompanied the troops under Captain David Perry on that disastrous expedition that ended in the White Bird defeat. Then, in the early '80s, we lived on White Bird Creek for several years. In those days what by courtesy was called a road followed from the top of the hill straight down a gulch for nearly a half mile, the descent for considerable distance being at the rate of three feet to the rod. Later a grade was constructed to the eastward of the original road so as to cut out the worst part of the earlier way . . . .

As the writer bowled along over the smooth highway surface many events of the earlier times were recalled to mind as familiar points were passed. For the first time he saw the beautiful shaft beside the highway

A rare photograph of troops afield near Kamiah, Idaho Territory, during the Nez Perce War of 1877. *Courtesy of Douglas D. Scott*

erected to the memory of a soldier who fell on that spot the fatal day of the White Bird Fight. The soldier was an old gray-headed sergeant, one who had, no doubt, passed through many campaigns against hostile Indians. He was killed in as fair a duel as ever was fought. So far as the writer knows, there are but two living witnesses of that fatal affair, himself and Herman A. Faxon, who now lives at Tillamook, Oregon.

These two were among the volunteers that joined Perry's command and were with their companion volunteers on the extreme left of the firing line when the White Bird Fight started. Faxon was wounded, shot through the thigh, while on the firing line. When, after Perry's bugler was killed at the very beginning of the engagement, the troops began to fall back, the retrograde movement soon became a rout. The volunteers, because of their position in the line, were in the rear of the soldiers when the rout started. As was customary when the troops, cavalry, dismounted to take position in the line of battle, one soldier was left behind to hold the mounts of [himself and] three of his comrades. When the line broke and soldiers started back pell mell, the holders of the horses seemed to be animated chiefly with a desire to get to the front of the retreating men and, largely, they did so, thereby leaving their comrades afoot to shift for themselves. Thus it happened that a great many of the soldiers were left on foot to be overtaken easily by the Indians who were well mounted. The old sergeant referred to was one of the unfortunates thus abandoned.

It so fell out that the writer and Faxon were the last two of the volunteers in the line of the retreat and, because of this fact, were closest to the body of soldiers who were without mounts and nearest to the advancing Indians. Faxon and the writer were perhaps fifty yards, certainly not more than that, from the old sergeant when he and his antagonist, who had left his horse and was also on foot, began their duel. They were probably fifteen paces apart. The sergeant would fire and fall back a few steps, the Indian would fire and advance. Each combatant must have fired four or five shots before the sergeant was hit and fell. Thus ended the tragedy. It was not until Sunday that the writer knew where the memorial shaft had been erected, and he was not aware that it marked the spot where he can testify that a brave old soldier, fighting heroically, fell with his face to his foe. Possibly the fact that the dead soldier was a sergeant may aid somewhat in his identification by the War Department, so that his name may be given the place it deserves on the honor roll of those men who gave their lives fighting worthily that day in June, 1877. . . .

Reminiscences of White Bird Canyon (By John P. Schorr, formerly sergeant, Troop F, First U. S. Cavalry. From *Winners of the West*, March 15, 1926)

I was very much impressed with the article of Comrade Frank A. Fenn, a volunteer in the Nez Perce [War]. . . . I was one of the survivors of that battle

[White Bird Canyon], on June 17, 1877, our first engagement with Chief Joseph's band of redskins, who outnumbered us six to one.

We left the fort [Fort Lapwai] on June 15th and made forced marches, being in the saddle for forty-eight hours with only about two hours' rest. On the 17th, about 3 a.m., we located the Indians, but before we could get in battle formation they fired on us from all directions and practically had us all hemmed in. It is still a mystery that any of us escaped, for out of ninety men from Troops F and H, First U. S. Cavalry, thirty-three comrades fell in less time than it takes to tell it. Among the first to fall was Trumpeter John Jones, Troop F. The brave old sergeant who fell with his face to his foe, fighting heroically, gray-headed and on his fourth enlistment, was Sergeant Patrick Gunn of Troop F. He was as fine a "non com" as anyone could wish for as a comrade. I know, for I was under his instructions as a young recruit, which served me later to further my own advancement. As far as I know, Sergeant Gunn was buried at Fort Lapwai, taken there by a fraternal organization, while the rest of the comrades were buried where they fell. First Lieutenant Edward R. Theller of the Twenty-first Infantry also fell, selling his life dearly. The Indians had the advantage over us for most of them carried magazine guns. Brave Sergeant Gunn, heroic Lieutenant Theller, and other comrades gave their lives fighting worthily that day, and they answered their last call by never flinching in the line of duty.

The Nez Perce War and the Battle of the Big Hole, 1877 (By Charles N. Loynes, formerly sergeant, Company I, Seventh U. S. Infantry. From *Winners of the West*, April, 1924; May, 1924; March, 1925)

Those were eventful days from '75 to '80 in the then Territory of Montana. Colonel John Gibbon at that time commanding the regiment, with headquarters and six companies stationed at Fort Shaw; other companies were at Fort Benton, Fort Ellis, and Camp Baker. On the 17th of March, 1876, with drums and bugles playing "St. Patrick's Day in the Morning," we left Fort Shaw, the snow knee deep, and did not return until October. The Seventh was to be part of the force ordered to meet Brigadier General Alfred H. Terry for the Yellowstone expedition and attack the Sioux under Sitting Bull. In the month of June, two days after the Custer massacre, we were in the vicinity of the Little Bighorn country, when First Lieutenant James H. Bradley, who had charge of the mounted detachment [of the] Seventh Infantry, and was in advance, sent back word to the main column that

Lieutenant Colonel George A. Custer and his command had been massacred. Of course, officers and men could not credit such a report, but soon found it to be true. The regiment immediately advanced and rescued Major Marcus A. Reno, who, with the remaining companies of the Seventh Cavalry, had made such a gallant stand against the savages, by using their dead horses and hardtack boxes for breastworks. During that summer the Seventh Infantry marched over twenty-one hundred miles.

After the expedition to the Yellowstone, the companies returned to their respective forts for the winter, and not until the following year, 1877, did they move again. At that period, the government intended to establish a post west of the Rocky Mountains in the Bitterroot Valley, near a small settlement called Missoula. For that purpose, two companies of the Seventh, Companies I and A, commanded respectively by Captains Charles C. Rawn and William Logan, were ordered there. On a beautiful June day we entered the then-struggling village of Missoula, composed at that time of a grist mill, about twenty log houses, and a camp of two or three hundred friendly Indians of the Pend d'Oreille tribe, under an old chief about eighty years of age by the name of Big Canoe. We soon crossed the Blackfoot and Hellgate rivers, which meet at that point, and after passing over a level stretch of prairie four miles across, we found ourselves under the shadow of the Bitterroot Mountains and near the river of the same name.

Many will remember that at that time Brigadier General Oliver O. Howard, with cavalry, infantry, and a section of the Fourth Artillery, started on his long trip from Oregon to the Missouri River in pursuit of the Nez Perce Indians under the great Chief Joseph. Being advised of the approach of the Indians in our direction, we at once commenced to fortify our camp as best we could, by throwing up rifle pits, cutting away the brush that would shelter the Indians, and piling up the sacks of grain in such a position as to give protection to the wives and children of officers and the laundresses of the companies. About seven miles to the south of our camp was what is known as the Lo-Lo Pass, through which we expected the Nez Perces to come. A detachment from both companies was accompanied by a few friendly Indians and thirty or forty citizens, all under command of Captain Charles C. Rawn, and a better officer never lived. His entire force numbered about one hundred, while that of the Indians was about five hundred, and mostly armed with Winchester repeating rifles, while we had the Springfield single loader, caliber .45.

We soon arrived at the entrance to the pass, or canyon, and with our skirmish lines thrown out in front and on flank, we advanced to meet the

Indians. Going forward about three miles, we were suddenly accosted by a number of shots coming in our direction from brush in front, evidently fired by the outposts of the hostiles. Our answer was a yell, and the friendly Indians with us giving their war-whoops, we pushed forward, the few Indians in front retreating back to their main body.

The canyon at this point was becoming less broad. On our sides were high stone precipices, some underbrush, and scattering Norway pines, and a small stream of water called the Lo-Lo [Creek] . . . . Men with axes were soon felling trees across the canyon in our rear; a tree would be dropped, then another, called a headlog, would be placed upon it, with a small limb in between, giving the required space to get the rifles through.

In the meantime, the shades of evening were coming on, a drizzling rain had set in, and the citizens who accompanied us, principally for the ponies they might capture, perceiving the large body of Indians we had to contend with, had already deserted, with the exception of about a dozen. Among those who remained was a man by the name of Andrews, as we remembered him, who ran the grist mill at Missoula, and a daring brave man he was, too. During the early evening his attention was attracted to a slight noise in front where he and some soldiers were posted, so getting over the works they advanced cautiously forward and soon covered four Indians with their rifles, and brought them in prisoners. They were conducted to the rear, their feet and hands tied, and a guard placed over them. Among the prisoners was one by name of John Hill, who had a good English education. Another was what is termed a squaw Indian, who had during the trip from Oregon killed a ranchman's wife, and was consequently, when captured, enjoying the privileges of a brave. He afterwards escaped from the guard tent one dark rainy night, while guarded by a drummer boy.

Chief Joseph must get by us, for he knew General Howard's command was coming up in his rear; in this, he might be successful, but only at a great loss to himself, so during the night we made preparations to receive him, believing he would try to force his way through on the following morning. Before the first streak of daylight every man was on the alert, with rifles ready, to meet the expected attack. At last daylight came, and with it an occasional shot, just enough to keep our attention. We were beginning to get somewhat impatient, and were preparing to throw out a skirmish line to feel them, when, on a high rocky point to our right, were seen six or eight Indians working their Winchesters right into us. Volunteers were called for, and fourteen sprang forward—led by First Lieutenant Charles A. Coolidge . . .

and started up the steep mountainside to drive them off. We had gotten quite well up when they vanished out of sight.

We soon discovered that during the night Joseph had moved his whole camp up the steep mountainside, had passed around us, and was then making rapid time to get to the Bitterroot Valley, and at the same time had left a number of his warriors to keep our attention and delay us as long as possible. When he arrived at the mouth of the Lo-Lo Pass, he turned to the right and went up the Bitterroot Valley, going in the direction of Corvallis and Phillipsburg toward the Big Hole Basin, where a week later, or on the 9th of August, we attacked him. Not having at the time force large enough to follow, we at once returned to camp near Missoula.

On August 3, Colonel Gibbon arrived at Missoula from Fort Shaw with Companies D, F, G, and K, and men from other companies attached. The day following, the above named companies, including A and I, left Missoula in pursuit of the Nez Perces. In addition to our command were a number of citizen volunteers, making the entire force about 182 men, including a four-pound howitzer. We followed over the roughest country imaginable. In places the trail was so steep that the mules were detached from the army wagons and with ropes were drawn up the steep sides. The scattered settlers were congregated in a square-built adobe fort for protection, and the men informed us that if necessary the women could use firearms as well as they. One night we encamped on a high point of the mountains, with no water or food. The next morning we descended to the valley below, where we got water for men and animals who by this time were nearly famished. Here the Indians had camped four or five days previous, many "wicky-ups" being in evidence. They are made by bending over the young willows, forming a circular arch, upon which are thrown buffalo hides or blankets for protection of the occupants.

About the third night, Lieutenant Bradley with the mounted detachment, and accompanied by First Lieutenant Joshua W. Jacobs, started ahead to locate the Indians. Two days following their departure, we had entered what is called the Big Hole Basin, when Lieutenant Bradley sent word back that the Indians were encamped about seven miles in our front. We then marched to within three miles of their camp, halted, and made preparations to attack. Here we left our wagon train in charge of Hugh Kirkendall and Sergeant John W. H. Frederick, also our Howitzer in charge of Sergeant William W. Watson and Corporal Robert E. Sale, both former artillerymen, both of whom lost their lives the next morning, although Watson's wound caused his death some few days later in Deer Lodge. They had orders not to advance

A Nez Perce village along the Yellowstone River in 1871, as photographed by William Henry Jackson. This camp typified many of those attacked by troops on the plains and in intermountain areas during the 1870s and 1880s. *Courtesy of the National Archives*

until they heard us attack the camp. After eating hardtack with water, and being issued 100 rounds of ammunition per man, we waited until about 11 o'clock at night, when we received orders to "fall in" in single file, all orders being given in whispers. At this time we were in a deep valley quite thickly covered with underbrush and scattered Norway pines. Taking the side of the hills on our left, we advanced quietly toward the Indian camp. It was quite dark, where there was brush; now and then a soldier would stumble or fall in some manner, but absolute quiet was demanded.

About one o'clock, we found ourselves on the side of a hill, facing the Indian village, their herd of ponies on the crest of the hill, in our rear. It was part of the plan to capture that herd. With the exception of the restlessness of the Indian ponies, it was very quiet just at that time, but it was the quiet that precedes the tornado before death and destruction follow. How unsuspicious they were of approaching danger. Now and then a tepee would flash up with light, as perhaps someone in it would throw a stick on the fire, for the nights were chilly there. Private Patrick Fallon of I Company could not resist an inclination to smoke, so he lighted a match for that purpose, but soon discovered that he had made a mistake. Thirty or forty yards below us flowed the Big Hole or Wisdom River, into which we must soon plunge, for the camp was on the other side. The river was fringed on either side by alder bush.

Chief Joseph intended to move his camp that day, so, at the first signs of the coming morn three Indian herders were seen coming in our direction on their way to their herd. Concealment now was no longer possible. We had previously received orders to give three volleys through the camp and then charge, so that as the Indians stepped up the bank on our side of the stream, they instantly fell, and as we gave three volleys into the camp we rushed to the water's edge, everyone seeming to want to get to the opposite side first. So into the water we leaped, not knowing its depth in the dim light of the moon, [waded] through it and into the camp of the Indians. We followed with a yell that would do credit to the Indians themselves.

We will never forget that day, how we fought with those savages, kill or be killed, no time to load our rifles. With the butts and muzzles of our guns we struck right and left. The shouts of soldiers, the war whoops of the Indians, the screeching of the squaws, who with Winchesters in their hands were as much to be feared as the bucks. Our attack was a complete surprise, and we gradually forced them back to the opposite side of their camp, where the river makes a complete bend. Into the water they jumped, some of them who had a blanket first throwing it in and getting underneath, trying thus to escape. But they had to have air, so as soon as we discovered this trick we only had to notice where the blanket or buffalo hide was slightly raised, and a bullet at that spot would be sufficient for the body to float down the stream. Although at this time the sun had not yet risen, it was quite light.

Most of the Indians had taken to the brush on the east side of the camp, where they soon discovered how few in number we were compared with them. Soldiers were constantly falling, and we soon discovered they were being hit by shots coming from the tepees occupied by Indians who had not time to get away or had retreated into them at the first attack. It was necessary to get them out at once. To do so, three or four soldiers would throw a lariat over the top of the tepee, and with others on the opposite side lying on the ground with rifles ready, the tepee would be pulled over, exposing an Indian who, of course, with his last shot, at so close a distance, would kill or wound a soldier. Those detailed to run off the Indian ponies had failed in their mission; many of the Indians at the first firing had gone to save their ponies and succeeded. When we rushed them in early morning, many Indians had gone in the direction of our field piece, which was hurrying to our relief, and we met it quite near to the camp. Above the din of firing we heard one or two shots. We killed or wounded those in charge. Corporal Sale's body was afterward found stripped, and one of the horse collars about his neck. Privates Charles B. Gould and Scott were never heard of again. Private John Bennet, a veteran of the Civil and Mexican wars, who rode the horses attached to the field piece, merely escaped with his life.

We supposed at this time we were masters of the camp. It was not so, however. It was the old story of the government in those days sending a handful of soldiers against a host of Indians better armed than ourselves. They rallied from all directions and soon every bush and tree covered an Indian. Something must be done quickly. At this point, Colonel Gibbon, while washing a wound he had received in the foot or ankle, directed Captain Rawn of Company I, then the senior captain in the regiment, to form and deploy his company toward the brush, some eighty yards distant, now full of Indians. Then the discipline of the regular soldier showed itself, for the company formed under fire and advanced toward the Indians. On they went, over dead and wounded soldiers and Indians. The move was simply to cover the retreat of the main body who were to fall back, cross the creek, and fortify as best they could on the side of the hill, where today [1924] stands a monument erected by Congress to commemorate one of the most stubborn conflicts in frontier history. The main body had now left the camp. Captain Rawn must now retreat with the remnant of his company. With faces toward the exultant savages, we gradually fell back. As we did so, those of our wounded would clutch at our legs and beg not to be left behind.

Poor Private Herman Broetz, whose knee had been shattered by a ball, reached up and grasped Sergeant [Corporal?] John D. Murphy's rifle and would not let go; the sergeant quickly found another. Fighting thus every step of our way, we slowly retreated. But what a sight met our view in that short time. There was Henry Bostwick, our scout and guide, sitting with his back against a clump of alders, a bullet having pierced his chest, the blood streaming from his mouth and his hands tearing at his shirt. In agony, he realized his situation when the Indians would find him. There lay dead the gallant Captain Logan, for he was a soldier who won his shoulder straps through bravery in the Civil War, his iron gray hair mingled with the green grass.

Here lay Lieutenant Bradley, and no regiment ever had a more fearless or better officer; First Sergeant Frederick Stortz with the glaze of death coming in his light blue eyes; First Sergeant Robert L. Edgeworth, who left two sisters in England whom he was never more to see; Sergeant Michael Hogan, with a mother in Dayton, Ohio; Sergeants William H. Martin and Howard Clark; Corporals Daniel McCafferey, Dominick O'Connor, William H. Payne, and Jacob Eisenhut; and the many privates making a total of over sixty killed and wounded.

First Lieutenant William L. English, with other wounded, was carried to Deer Lodge, where he afterwards died. Sergeant Edward Page of L Troop, Second Cavalry, also Private Charles B. Gould of the same regiment, who accompanied us, were also killed. One incident made an impression upon our minds which is not easily forgotten. A squaw was found lying on her back, dead, with wide open eyes staring heavenward, an infant upon her bare breasts, alive and crying as it painfully waved its little arm, which had been shattered by a bullet. It was probably hit when we sent three volleys into the camp before charging, and perhaps the shot that killed the mother wounded the little one.

Among the last to leave the camp was Captain Rawn and the few members of his company. Recrossing the creek [and] going in a westerly direction for about two hundred and fifty yards, they met the main body trying to entrench by throwing up the dirt using the Rice trowel bayonet for the purpose. One man would scrape up the dirt, while every second man would continue to fire. We were now completely surrounded by the savages, some of whom would climb the trees on the upper side of us. But our best marksmen soon dislodged them. We now lay in a square, probably forty feet each way, the Indians on every side, and not a man expecting to leave alive.

That was a long day to us. The sun seemed to stand still. We wanted the night to come that we might get water, for the cries of our wounded for water were most distressing. On the lower side of us flowed the Big Hole, or Wisdom River, only distant about thirty yards. Oh, for the darkness of night, for by this time we had no water or food, nothing since the day before. But as there must be an end to all things, so there was to that day. As the shades of night came on, so the Indians kept closing in, particularly upon that side where the water was. When it was dark, a few volunteered to get water, and loaded with canteens they crawled out into the darkness. But soon we saw the flash and heard the reports of rifle shots, and Lockwood, a citizen, and one soldier had lost their lives in the attempt.

Among the head war chiefs of Joseph were Looking Glass and White Bird, the latter a brave warrior and great chief whose strong voice could be heard all through the night, first on one side of us and then on the other, urging his braves to get ready to charge us in the morning, for he told them we had killed their braves and squaws. Every word he uttered was interpreted to us in a low voice by a half-breed by the name of Pete Matt, whom we had met on our way up the Bitterroot. The officers were a little suspicious of Pete, so a sergeant and two privates rode beside him with orders to shoot him on sight if he proved treacherous. He was a horse thief with $500 on his head offered by ranchmen in Idaho. He was afterward captured and hung.

During the time we lay there, digging and fighting for our lives, we could hear the last cries of our helpful wounded in the camp below, as the Indians closed in and finished them. Pitiful and awful as they were, they rang in our ears for days afterwards. The first night there was not much we could do to strengthen our position, for what few limbs of trees were scattered about we had already used. To the north, or upper side, were a few saplings, so Corporals Charles W. Loynes and Levi Heider were ordered to leave their guns behind, crawl out, and with the Rice trowel bayonet, which is sharp on one side, try to cut down a few. The former, followed by Heider, was soon chopping them down, but the noise quickly attracted the Indians, and their dark forms were seen creeping in that direction by the men who were stationed on that side to watch. The cry, "come back quick," soon brought them back amidst a volley from both sides.

Colonel Gibbon's horse, a large dark sorrel, had been with us up to the time when we were first surrounded, but he was soon hit, and with pain he commenced to rave and pitch, greatly to the danger of Second Lieutenant Charles A. Woodruff (now [1924] General Woodruff, retired), who was wounded through the hips and with a revolver in each hand was doing his best to repel the Indians while sitting with his back to the tree to which the horse was tied. "Better finish him, Woodruff," an officer cried out, "for we may need him." During the following night some crawled to where the bloated dead horse lay. They cut off some of the flank, but, being without salt or a fire, preferred to remain hungry.

The night passed with a shot now and then, mingled with groans of the wounded and their cries for water, some of whom at times became delirious, when the name of mother or some loved one could be heard. When the first signs of day were seen, most of us were posted on the west side, for at that point we expected they would charge us, because twenty yards away was a narrow ravine, the opposite side being covered with a dense underbrush. We had not long to wait, for soon a heavy column of smoke began to arise. We saw their intention was to either smoke us out or more probably to charge under its cover. We crouched down behind our slight earthwork with rifles loaded and cocked, prepared for what we believed to be our last struggle. But the smoke did not take the direction the Indians hoped for. It rose steadily, going in a direction to the right of us, and our hearts beat more hopefully for that.

As it became lighter, the firing increased. We were cautioned now to use our ammunition sparingly, for it was getting low. The sun was getting higher, and as its hot rays beat down upon us, our throats became parched, and the deep sunken eyes and powder-stained faces of our comrades told of the strain which was upon them. We realized our situation was a desperate one, but there was a fight left in that band of the Seventh infantrymen, as there always is in the American soldier. Generals Howard and Miles, and a few remaining officers and men who at that time met the Nez Perces, will testify to the fighting qualities of the Indians while under the leadership of the great Chief Joseph, many of the Indians at Big Hole showing courage to a marked degree. One great warrior was particularly noticeable. He crept through the light brush to within thirty yards of us in daylight wearing a blue shirt, upon the front of which was a red star, and as the red glistened a second it made a shining mark, and he fell dead.

Thus the fight went on, but we had one hope. We knew that grand soldier, General O. O. Howard, was some three days back on the trail of Chief Joseph, and if we could hold them off a while longer we would be saved. It was during the third day that the shots from the enemy became less and less and finally ceased entirely. Evidently their outposts had discovered the approach of General Howard. Suddenly there appeared in our midst one of the advance scouts of General Howard, who soon informed us that the general was only a few miles back and would soon be here. Needless to say, it was a happy moment to us when we saw him approach with the First Cavalry and detachments of the Eighth and Twenty-first infantries, also a band of friendly Bannock Indians as scouts uniformed in blue blouses, bucktails hanging from their black campaign hats. Very soon his surgeons were at work on our wounded. Generals Howard and Gibbon had a conference, and soon the cavalry bugles [sic] sounded , and they [Howard's command] dashed away to the south of us after the fleeing Indians. The Bannocks soon found the dead Indians who were too near us to be taken away, and commenced to scalp them. They took the entire scalp from the head, and after carefully washing it had what they most highly prized. But to us it was not a pleasant sight, considering the state of our empty stomachs, and the air laden with the stench of dead bodies and ponies from the camp below mingled with burning sagebrush and the ether the surgeons were using.

A detail under Captain George L. Browning was soon deployed down into the abandoned Indian camp, where we found our dead comrades stripped of all their clothing, their bodies swollen to twice their normal size from the heat of the sun, very few being mutilated. They were buried as best we could at that time, but some few weeks after, a detail was sent to more properly perform that duty. (Some of the bodies were found torn up by bears and wolves that inhabited that wild region.) In the meantime we went back and were surprised to find our wagon train safe. We at once made preparations to move our wounded to Deer Lodge, probably sixty miles distant. They could not be carried in the army wagons, for the jolting would be too rough, so we took tepee poles, and then skinning the dead ponies lying around, we cut the hides into strips and braiding them over the poles improvised what is termed a travois, upon which we laid our wounded, the other ends dragging upon the ground, where a soldier walked for the purpose of lifting it while crossing streams or when the ground was too rough.

We finally arrived at Deer Lodge, where we left our most dangerously wounded, some of whom died there. First Lieutenant English, who had been married only a few months previously in the States, and whose wife was among those who came to greet us as we entered the town, was one of the number. Deer Lodge at that time was only a small place of log houses, but the people did everything for our wounded they could, and they felt only too grateful that the Indians turned in another direction, for Deer Lodge was in the path of the hostiles. . . .

The Bear's Paw Campaign and the Surrender of Chief Joseph

(By Luther Barker, formerly of Company D, Fifth U. S. Infantry. From *The Oregon Veteran*, December, 1922, January, 1923, and February, 1923)

As the Nez Perces had long been a peaceable tribe and had lived neighbors to the white settlers in Idaho, they had imbibed many of the white man's ways. The cause of their going on the warpath was that the government had decided to remove them to another reservation. This was not pleasing to the Indians, and to hasten the climax some white trappers and hunters had trespassed on their hunting grounds. In the quarrel that followed, the Indians killed some of the white men and after a hurried council they decided to go on the warpath. They traveled east across the mountains intending to join Sitting Bull and fight it out in eastern Montana. The troops under Colonel Nelson A. Miles on the Yellowstone River had been kept pretty busy after Sitting Bull, Crazy Horse, Lame Deer, Iron Star, and the many bands of Sioux and Cheyennes. We little thought that it would fall to our lot to capture Chief Joseph and his band.

Early in August, 1877, Joseph encountered a small command of regular infantry and a few volunteer citizens under command of Colonel John Gibbon, where the Battle of the Big Hole was fought. The courier that brought the news of this battle down to Fort Keogh claimed that Colonel Gibbon had been worsted in the engagement with the Indians. The dispatch stated that there had been seventeen men killed and thirty-five wounded. It further stated that Joseph had captured some supplies and a cannon. Of course, they had no use for this piece of ordnance, so they upset it over a bank down in a deep ravine. Joseph was now in eastern Montana. He skirted the settlements along the Gallatin Valley, killing some citizens and capturing others. . . . As Colonel Miles commanded the District of the Yellowstone, and Joseph was in the Yellowstone country, the colonel took steps to capture the band. He at once dispatched Colonel Samuel D. Sturgis with eight troops of his regiment, the famous Seventh U. S. Cavalry, and 300 Crow Indians, in pursuit of Joseph. . . . Sturgis came up with Joseph and forced him to battle. The Crow allies proved to be rather a weak support to the troops, and once more Joseph stood his enemies off while his women and children, with their supplies, made a successful escape.

After waiting a considerable time . . . Colonel Miles decided that he would have to go after Joseph himself. On September 17, just after midnight, about the time the colonel usually started on a hunt for Indians, there was a tremendous rapping at the orderly room of Company D, Fifth Infantry. We heard the headquarters orderly tell the first sergeant to turn out the company for a thirty-day scout in light marching order. Fort Keogh was soon in a buzz with preparation for an Indian campaign. By daylight the next morning the command, consisting of six troops of cavalry, two of the Second and four of the Seventh, and five companies of the Fifth Infantry mounted, two companies, D and K, Fifth Infantry, under Captain David H. Brotherton of K Company, as train guard, had crossed to the north bank of the Yellowstone River. Considering that there were thirty wagons drawn by six mules, two ambulances, and two pieces of artillery drawn by four horses each, all the cavalry horses and 150 pack mules, it was no small task to cross all this stuff from 1:00 a.m. till daylight on a small and rickety ferryboat. The entire command consisted of about 400 men with the usual complement of scouts, teamsters, and packers.

While eating breakfast, there were many conjectures as to our destination. Not a word had been dropped by the officers for our enlightenment. We had heard nothing from Colonel Sturgis's command, but hoped they had captured Joseph's band. The wagon train was the first made ready to start, led by the infantry company of seventy men. After passing through the canyon to the high land, we headed for the northwest in the direction of Fort Peck. We had been over that trail before when after Sitting Bull during the winter of 1876. The mounted troops passed us two hours later with jokes, saying that they were sorry for the doughboys. Let me say that before this campaign ended I saw some of these cavalrymen carrying their saddles to the first wagon after dispatching their mount when he could no longer go. The weather was ideal, and the twenty-five-mile march this first day was only exercise for the train guard. The next day we marched thirty miles. No one seemed to notice the extra five miles except a few recruits that had never been on a real campaign. We were camping each night with the mounted men, and when on the third day we made thirty-five miles, the recruits and some of the heavyweights were beating Uncle Sam by riding on the hind feed box.

We were adding a few miles each day to the march. Sometimes we would make the cavalry camp as late as 9, 10, and 11 o'clock at night. We thought that this was pretty strenuous campaigning. The colonel was breaking us in by degrees. The day before we made the Missouri River, we broke camp before daylight. Captain Brotherton, being mounted, increased the pace to a higher rate than we had ever experienced. By three in the afternoon the train guard company was getting somewhat jaded. By nine that evening our ranks were thinning, and when we finally made the cavalry camp at 12 o'clock, there was just six of us stacked arms out of the seventy-five men that composed the train guard. When the ambulance carrying the odometer pulled in and the instrument examined, it read forty-five miles. . . . My bunky and I never knew when the wagon train all finally pulled in that night, for as soon as we found our blankets, we arranged our bed under a tree and were soon dreaming of better days gone by. Colonel Miles instructed Captain Brotherton that he should let his men sleep until sunrise the next morning. There were many expressions of gratitude for this, and some hoped the colonel would soon be wearing a star.

A short march the next morning brought us to the Big Muddy. Soon after arriving at the Missouri River, there could be heard a steamer whistle down the river. It was decided that the steamer was moving downstream, and Colonel Miles knew that it would be his one chance to cross the river without much delay. There was a good trail and a level country on the north side of the river, while the south side was very rough. A scout by the name of [George] Sandy Johnson, a brother of the famous scout Liver-Eating Johnson [sic], volunteered to swim his horse across the river and catch the steamer. His noble horse carried him across the river all right, but the bank was too steep, and after many efforts, the man and horse were drowned. His brother, being present, saw Sandy drown, but could not help him. A raft was soon constructed and two men rowed the raft with saddle and equipment [piled on?], swimming the horse. After making the opposite shore with the aid of the two soldiers, the horse made the bank in good shape. After resting his mount for a brief time, the trooper chased down the steamer and turned it back to cross the command to the north side of the river. The battle was not always the test of man or beast in winning the great west. After the ice broke up the next spring, Sandy Johnson's body was found seventy-five miles below, near Fort Peck.

While waiting for the steamer to return, a negro in a skiff suddenly hove in sight. He seemed greatly excited. The fact was, he was scared within an inch of his life. His story was that he was watching some stores on Cow Island, fifty miles up the river, that belonged to the post trader. There was also a sergeant and six men guarding the government supplies on the island, and that Joseph's band had captured the island . . . but he had made his escape in the only boat. . . . The detachment of soldiers on the island had built a strong dugout for winter quarters as well as for defense. When they saw several hundred Indians crossing onto the island they decided that discretion would be the better part of valor, so they barricaded their dugout and let the Indians help themselves. After Joseph had taken what he wanted from the island, he crossed to the north bank of the river and captured a wagon train of supplies on the way to Fort Benton. He gave the teamsters each a mule to ride to Fort Benton, helped himself to the supplies, and burned the wagons. By the time the steamer had returned to cross the command, Colonel Miles had decided to take the mounted troops and the pack train and go after Joseph in light marching order. Captain Brotherton, with train guard, would remain on the south side of the river and have a good time fishing and hunting, while the mounted fellows captured Joseph's band.

When Colonel Miles with the mounted troops and pack train had crossed the Missouri River, the steamer once more headed downstream, and as the cavalry with their belongings moved out of view to the north, the train guard congratulated themselves on being rid of a troublesome crowd. In less than an hour after their departure, we heard the little breech-loading cannon boom, then again and again. Finally, the steamer answered by several long blasts. This made the train guard wonder what was coming. We didn't have to wait long to learn our fate, as a cavalryman soon hailed Captain Brotherton from the north bank of the river to make ready to cross the river at once. A soldier in active service never knows what is before him until it happens. The writer and his Irish bunky with others had just been posted on a high mound as picket guards for the night when we learned that the wagons must be unloaded and the supplies all carried onto the steamer and the wagons had to be taken apart and carried a piece at a time on board the steamer. The men on guard felt that they were in luck for once. It was ten o'clock that night when the last of the wagon train was crossed to the north side of the river. After moving out a mile before a suitable camping place could be found, the train guard rolled in their blankets about the usual hour, eleven o'clock at night.

For the next three days we made long weary marches over a barren country, with scarcely no timber and little water to be found, and that was bitter with alkali. The course of march led to the northwest, toward the Little Rocky and the Bear Paw mountains. Colonel Miles had pushed on with the mounted troops and we were following their trail at a full forced march. We entered a narrow valley that divided the Little Rockies, through which flowed a small stream called Beaver Creek. The Little Rockies presented some very beautiful scenery, and the sparkling waters of Beaver Creek abounded in mountain trout, of which we managed to catch a number whenever there would be a brief halt of the wagon train. We encountered a snowstorm the afternoon of the day we passed through this mountain range which spoiled our fishing and sight-seeing. The next morning, the 30th day of September, when we had passed the Little Rockies we could see the tops of the Bear Paw Mountains glittering in the sunshine twenty-five miles to the north. We crossed a valley of some twenty miles in width that separated the two ranges of mountains and we camped that night at the base of the Bear Paws. For the first time we here could plainly see the trail made by Chief Joseph's band of Indians. Colonel Miles had struck their trail at this point the day before, as we were about twenty-four hours behind the mounted command.

The next morning, October 1st, there was a heavy fog, and Captain Brotherton feared to move the train under such conditions. Although everything was packed and teams hitched, we still waited for the fog to raise. While roasting buffalo veal on our steel ramrods and tucking away a supply in our haversacks for future emergencies, a scout rode in among us unobserved. We had been discussing the probable fate of the mounted command, and wondering how much farther we would have to go when the man in buckskin handed a message to Captain Brotherton. Our loitering abruptly came to an end. At the command, "Fall in!" every man was eager to hit the trail. The fog was so dense we could not see fifty yards in advance. But we soon learned from the scout that Colonel Miles had Joseph surrounded about eighteen or twenty miles away at the east base of the Bear Paws, on Eagle Creek. As we were moving on quick time, the scout rode by the side of the column and gave us many details of the attack, [and told us] that quite a number of our boys had been killed and many more wounded. [He said] that the fog made it difficult to see and hold the Indians, and we were needed very bad. Although we had marched 300 miles and brought the wagon train over some very rough country, when we learned that the object of our search was so near we felt like new and were anxious for the fight.

When the fog finally lifted there was a most wonderful landscape revealed. The Bear Paws loomed up on our left with piles of snow, while the country to our right was brown and free from snow, with hundreds of buffalo roaming everywhere. But we were after other game now and cared but little for the surrounding country or the herds of buffalo. When we finally arrived at the base of a ridge extending from the mountains across the trail, the scout told us that the mounted command was deployed in line of battle just west of the ridge while Colonel Miles with his aides crawled to the top of this eminence and planned the attack. A scout well in advance of the cavalry had spied out the Indian camp from this point and Colonel Miles was taking advantage of the situation. The plan of attack was the four troops of the Seventh Cavalry would oblique to the right and attack the camp from the

Company K, Seventh Cavalry, in dress uniforms, ca. 1877-78. *Editor's collection*

south, while the five companies of mounted Fifth Infantry would charge direct to the front and attack in the center, while the two troops of the Second Cavalry would oblique to the left and cut off the Indian herd that was grazing well to the north of the Indian camp. The Second Cavalry troops succeeded fine in capturing nearly all their ponies, about 1100 head.

But not so with the Seventh Cavalry battalion. They executed the movement as directed in fine shape and dashed in on the south side of the Indian stronghold. But not until they were within close range of the Indian rifles did they discover a steep bank some twenty-five feet high that they could not force their horses down. At this critical moment, the Indians opened fire on their unprotected line. Men and horses went down pretty fast before the battalion could fall back over the ridge out of sight. The Fifth mounted infantry found a high bank in their front, and only one company, I, of the Fifth, found a passage through a ravine down into the Indian camp. They lost a number of men before they could find a way to get out and take position behind a friendly ridge nearby. By the trumpet call to halt and deploy skirmishers, [the troops] encircled their camp and the boys began to dig in and so were able to hold their ground.

And when the train guard marched over the divide we were cheered by the men who were watching for us to aid them. The wagon train carried picks and shovels for road repairing, and these were distributed around the skirmish line that night, which was an improvement over their entrenching tools. Toward evening, the white flag was raised over in the Indian camp, and acknowledged by one being displayed from headquarters. Chief Joseph accompanied by a few braves met Colonel Miles for a parley. While this conference was going on, Second Lieutenant Lovell H. Jerome of the

Second Cavalry bolted the skirmish line and went down into the Indian stronghold. He was made a prisoner and securely bound. So Chief Joseph was held as hostage until the lieutenant was released. Joseph was brought over to the train guard for safe keeping. A tent was pitched for him and a comfortable bed arranged. The colonel ordered an extra strong guard should be placed over him. A darkened lantern was placed in the tent and an infantryman sat on a camp stool with fixed bayonet with orders to use it if he made an effort to escape. On the outside of the tent there were two cavalrymen walking post. The writer had the honor of the first and last relief on guard over Chief Joseph inside the tent. When he awoke in the morning he greeted the writer with, "How John." I returned his greetings by saying, "How Chief." He kicked his foot from under the blankets and showed the writer that his moccasins were wore out. He said that he was heap tired of war, so we had a pleasant little visit. Joseph was a fine looking Indian and could speak the English language quite well. About sunrise, Lieutenant Jerome was turned loose, and when he was safe the chief was escorted beyond the line and given his liberty. So the siege went on for five [three] days longer.

The following day a detail of the train guard was sent with wagons up in the mountains to get wood, as sagebrush and wet buffalo chips made poor fuel. The afternoon was spent in a fruitless search for wood. Timber was always in sight, but always out of reach. We returned that night at about ten o'clock wet and bedraggled, as the snow was knee deep up in the mountains. On coming to camp, a part of that detail was ordered out to occupy a high hill to the north of our lines to keep a sharp lookout for Sitting Bull, who was just over in Canada. The nights would not have seemed so long or the duty so strenuous could we have had hot coffee or warm food, but dry hardtack and salt pork constituted our daily menu. After dark the evening of the 3rd of October the train guard company relieved the two troops of the Second Cavalry and occupied the line of rifle pits to the north of the Indian camp. As we passed the first rifle pit on the bank of Eagle Creek, just opposite headquarters, three men on the left of the company were given this pit, the writer being among them. From this rifle pit, we had a good view of the Indian stronghold, only 200 yards to their first dugouts. Just under the bank from our rifle pit some of the I Company, Fifth Infantry boys were shot from their mounts. Instead of being tomahawked and scalped, the Indians helped them to a safe place where they would not be run over by charging horses or ponies. They filled their canteens with water, then rushed into the fight to shoot other soldiers out of their saddles. This was the equal of any civilized warfare on record, and all who pursued and fought Chief Joseph have nothing but praise for him and his gallant band. In the best regulated armies there are always radicals and outlaws, so Chief Joseph's band was not an exception to this rule. There were some bad Indians in Joseph's band, and it was reported that there were twenty-five renegade white men with Joseph [sic]. But they made their escape during the dark, stormy nights as it either rained or snowed most every night. The Indians claimed that these white men were responsible for most of the outrages committed on the trail while near the settlements. There was always in-fighting of this kind, some strange and even pathetic experiences.

Yellowstone Kelly [Luther S. Kelly], chief of scouts for Colonel Miles, accompanied by Corporal John Haddo, Company B, Fifth Infantry, who scouted with Kelly a great deal, came to the battlefield one night with important information for Colonel Miles and was to leave in the morning with dispatches for some other command. While their horses were eating, Corporal Haddo says to Kelly, "I am going out on the firing line and take a few shots at the Indians." He selected a good position and in raising his shoulder a little higher to get a better view of the Indian stronghold, he received a rifle ball through the center of his chest and sank down dead, without getting a single shot at the Indians. The Indians had fortified a deep ravine that extended back to the south from Eagle Creek. This ravine was in the form of an L with high rugged banks interspersed with smaller ravines and breaks that made it a natural stronghold. It was on the south side of this ravine where two troops of the Seventh Cavalry were so badly shot up in the charge. The Indians had plenty of picks and shovels, and no doubt the white renegades helped and showed the Indians how to strengthen the position by making indentations in these high banks that gave them a good view of our rifle pits while they were perfectly sheltered. A bullet from one of these notches got Haddo and a lot more of our boys. We had one advantage over Joseph; he was cut off from the creek and could get no water in daylight, only during darkness.

Our company cooks would traverse the line of rifle pits after dark with a day's rations, and we saw them no more until the next night. A troop of cavalry with a lot of wagons made a trip to the north base of the mountains and found plenty of wood. So we had coffee, cooked pork, and beans afterwards. The white flag would be displayed over in the Indian camp, usually in the afternoon and the headquarters bugler would sound cease firing. The children in the Indian camp knew what that call meant. They would come scampering out of their dugouts and caves, fixed for their safety, and enjoy a romp and play like schoolchildren. Even the soldiers enjoyed these brief opportunities to walk about and get some exercise. But when the white flag returned in their camp, every man and Indian hunted his hiding place. When the fight would grow dull the Indians would sometimes put up an old hat on a stick or ramrod. The soldiers would also trick them. It would always bring a rattle of rifle shots. But this fun, as we called it, was soon brought to an end at our rifle pit. Captain Brotherton's tent was pitched just under the creek bank behind our rifle pit. The captain's dog robber reported us when the captain inquired why there was so much firing at the Indian camp, so he informed us that we should stop at once. You see, the captain was a very tall man and he did not enjoy the whiz of those bullets. We could not blame him much either, as he had just brought a new wife from the East only a few days before starting on this campaign.

There was a division in the Indian camp. Chief Joseph wanted to surrender the evening of the first of October when we held him a prisoner overnight, but Chief White Bird and his party refused, believing that Sitting Bull would come down from Canada and help them out. We were a little concerned about this matter ourselves. We were in no condition to fight any outside enemy with seventy-five men killed and wounded [sic] and some sick and all about worn out. Still the fight went on, but we could see the resistance was growing less. The evening of the 4th of October, the writer's birthday, just about sunset, a large party of warriors came out of their stronghold and formed a camp on the creek only about fifty yards from our rifle pit. An officer came over and talked with the writer to inform us that these Indians would give up their arms in the morning, and that we must not fire on them in the night. We thought that it would be safer for us if they would give up their arms that evening, but he said they were all right as they had surrendered. We were wide awake that night at our rifle pit, as it did not seem good to us to have so many Indians as our neighbors unless they were disarmed. There was but little firing that night as the word had been passed around the lines to only fire when we were fired on. There was a bad bunch that would not surrender over in their stronghold that we paid our respects to, as we decided the fight was about over.

The Nez Perces laid so low in the daytime that it was hard to get a shot at them, so there was usually more firing at night than during the day. At night they would be moving about, and we could hear them talking, so the man on watch at each rifle pit would fire at every sound. There were two reasons for this: we might get our Indian, and another reason was to let them know the man on post was wide awake. During the night of October 5th [4th], Brigadier General Oliver O. Howard and son, Second Lieutenant Guy

Howard, came to the battlefield with a bodyguard of the Seventh Cavalry. General Howard had been on Joseph's trail since February [sic—June] and he wanted to be in at the surrender. When it was light enough to see on the morning of the 6th [5th], it revealed the fact that the Indian camp across the creek had been greatly augmented during the night. Most of their fighting men had joined the friendly camp, although there was a number who still showed fight. At about nine o'clock, Chief Joseph, followed by a number of his chiefs, moved out to meet General Howard and Colonel Miles. General Howard was somewhat in advance of Colonel Miles when they halted to receive Joseph and his party. Joseph walked stiffly by General Howard and handed his gun to Colonel Miles. The warriors turned in their guns; they were almost all of an obsolete pattern. Colonel Miles knew that they had been using better guns than these, so he ordered two troops of cavalry to take charge of the Indian stronghold.

The first thing to be done was to capture the outlaw Indians. They had fired several shots after Joseph had surrendered. They were soon disarmed and bound and the Battle of the Bear's Paw Mountains was over. A large number of breech-loading rifles were found. In one place there were twenty-five magazine Henry rifles. They had carefully cached these improved rifles for some future use. The order was that no one would be allowed over in the Indian stronghold, only these two troops of cavalry. We were all anxious to see this place, and at our rifle pit we hadn't had a chew of tobacco for so long that we could not smile anymore. So we planned that we would go in turns and would carry our guns and if any objection were raised we could say that we were one of the guard. The only trouble we experienced in this was the difference in the length of our gun barrels. There were so many dugouts and pits that one had to be careful where they stepped or they would go headlong into some hole. We secured the object of our search; while we could not eat anything they had in the way of food, we sure could relish the tobacco.

As there had to be litters made to carry our wounded, so many being so badly shot that they could not ride in the wagons, we did not get away from the sinister place until the afternoon of the seventh of October. Had it been two months earlier, or under more favorable and peaceful conditions, it would have been a lovely place to have spent a summer vacation. But we were in rain, snow, and mud until our uniforms of blue were the color of a Montana clay bank. We were five days in making the Missouri River, where a steamer was in waiting to take the wounded to hospitals at Fort Buford and Fort Lincoln. Some that were shot through the body died that first night on the steamer, after relaxing their energy. These men's wounds had not been dressed since the beginning of the battle, September 30th, until October 12th. We were winning the Great West in those days and giving Uncle Sam the best of our manhood. What class of veterans have done more? There was a temporary hospital established here at the river and a number of amputations performed. Colonel Sturgis was here with eight troops of his regiment, and we lost the four troops of the Seventh that were with us at the Bear's Paw battle.

After being relieved of the wounded, and the train guard being all mounted, we made better time. When about two days march from Fort Keogh we were met by two troops of the Second Cavalry, completing the battalion, as we had had two troops of the Second at the battlefield. Joseph and his band were held at Fort Keogh for a time, but were finally sent to the Indian Territory. It was claimed that 480 all told surrendered to General Miles at the Bear's Paw Mountains. They became sickly after staying in the Territory a few months and were later [1885] sent back to their reservation in Idaho. Joseph was the guest of [later] General Miles at several expositions. He had lots of respect for General Miles, as he was the only one that had whipped him in an equal fight. And thus ends the campaign and capture of a great chief and his fighting band, the Nez Perces.

Bannock War Service, 1878 (By Ernest F. Albrecht, formerly of Troop A, First U. S. Cavalry. From *Winners of the West*, November, 1924)

About the 18th or 20th of June, '78, we were ordered to leave Camp Harney[, Oregon,] to hunt and fight Indians. At that time there were stationed at Camp Harney A and G, First Cavalry, and Company K, Twenty-first Infantry.

Troop A, under Captain Thomas McGregor, and Troop G, under Captain Reuben F. Bernard, at once left, leaving Captain George M. Downey with Company K, Twenty-first Infantry, to guard the post. We shortly struck an Indian trail as wide as a city street. After following it for a few days, the scouts reported the Indians a short distance ahead. We were halted and ordered to tighten our cinches and get ready, then mounted again and we struck the Indians about five miles further on, as far as I can recollect, the 23rd of June. When we first sighted them, they were in a small round valley about twelve to fifteen hundred yards in diameter. From about the center of this valley to a gap in the surrounding hills there were the headwaters of a stream covered with thick willow brush about ten to twelve feet high. Near the end of this brush, the chiefs of the different tribes were riding in a ring, waiting for us. As soon as we sighted the redskins, it was a trot, gallop, charge while they fired at us. As soon as their revolvers were empty, they fled along the bushes towards the outlet of the stream.

Here they had a narrow trail leading out of the level valley to a palisade-like cliff that ran almost parallel with the bushes about five hundred yards from them. We were ordered to dismount, firing at them and following them as fast as we could. Now that was just what the Indians had expected, as the whole thing was a trap. The bushes to our left were full of Indians, planted there to massacre us from ambush, and the cliffs to our right were lined with Indians lying down firing at us, without giving us a chance at them. Not a man would have come out alive had it not been for two things. The first was that the Indians on the bluff, fearing to hit the bushes, fired a little too low, their bullets raising a cloud of dust about four or five yards to our right. The other was the fact that McGregor, being an old Indian fighter, saw the trap we were in and had the trumpeter sound cease firing and recall, besides sending Second Lieutenant Frank A. Edwards to bring us back. We then went back to where the officers were and remained here with our mortally wounded corporal, Peter F. Graentsinger. We remained here in the hail of Indian bullets to keep him from the torture until he died, without disobeying orders [and] not firing at the Indians. We were then ordered to a small hill on the edge of the valley and "dug in," that is, built a small breastwork, expecting the redskins to attack at daybreak next morning. We were, however, disappointed. It was either the loss of . . . [one of their chiefs, Little Bearskin Dick, killed] or the nearness of General Howard's big command. We were left alone until night came.

I was detailed for guard on the picket line that night and received the second relief from eleven [p.m.] to one [a.m.]. Punctually at twelve, three shots were fired at us from the bushes, one striking the ground under the horses' feet, another making a couple of holes through Captain McGregor's tent, and the third went wild. The next morning a burial and firing party was detailed for poor Graentsinger. As we rightly surmised, the redskins had gone. I asked some of the burial party afterwards how Graentsinger had looked, but even the most callous of them told me it was too revolting to relate.

During all this time, one of our scouts was missing and we believed he had taken French leave [deserted]. Little did we dream what a terrible fate was his. He had been badly wounded in the first part of the battle, had fallen off his horse, and crawled into a nearby hole in the ground, thinking that he had not been seen. But the squaws had seen him and as soon as we were out of the way they pulled up sagebrush, piled it on top of the hole, and set fire to it. Any one that ever burnt sagebrush knows what that means. It will flare up, but the thick stems will scale off and burn through anything they fall on, so they slowly tortured him to death. We never found this out until afterwards when everything was over and the Indian prisoners boasted of it. Strange to say, the very Indians boasting were graduates of the government schools, and one of them a talented sculptor. After the burial we broke camp and took up pursuit, and kept so hot after them that they had no time to go murdering through the country. The rest of the war is too well known to take your time, except that all prisoners after the war agree with Sally [Sarah] Winnemucca that the Indians we struck was the whole of the Indian force, numbering between 1,200 and 1,500, all well armed with Winchesters, Sharps, Centennials, and other such then modern rifles. It was really the fact that they had taken us to be the advance of General Howard's force that saved us from being massacred.

After the war was over, and we had to chain-guard the prisoners at Camp Harney, it fell to our lot to learn a brand new method of making good Indians. The inventor of this new method was First Lieutenant Thomas Drury, a wise Irishman. He evidently knew Indians, because in a private conversation he was heard to say that he would kill more Indians than the war, and he came near doing so. He was commissary officer, and he saw to it that the redskins got all they could eat, and the redskins promptly gorged themselves until they died like flies. Out of between 600 and 700, the number first in the prison camp, scarcely 200 were finally delivered to Father James H. Wilbur [Indian agent] at Fort Simcoe. . . .

It was Captain Thomas McGregor with Troop A that transported the prisoners that winter over the mountains in frost and snow to Fort Simcoe, for on that trip I contracted my rheumatism that gives me h-ll now. After delivering the redskins, we stayed for a little while at the agency and had an opportunity of observing Wilber's method. It was simply justice and severity. During our stay there, one of the Indian farmers came to Wilber complaining that one of his cows was stolen. Wilber took out his whistle, blew one blast, and the chief of his police came running across the parade ground. In two hours both cow and Indian were on the parade ground, and in three the prisoner was chopping wood with a ball and chain on him and a policeman with a blacksnake whip and a revolver over him. Later we went to Ellensburg and camped within easy reach of Fort Simcoe all summer. That was the last Indian trouble in the Northwest.

Fighting the Bannocks in 1878 (By George Buzan, formerly of the Oregon Militia. From *Winners of the West*, May, 1924)

I am acquainted with a few of the boys that served in the Bannock Indian War of 1878. . . . [Here is] a few lines in behalf of the . . . [soldiers who] stood before the reds on that hot afternoon in July, 1878, at Willow Springs, where three were killed and a number wounded. . . . We will start with the first warning on the 3rd day of July, 1878, [when] about 3 a.m., a friendly voice came to our mountain home—"roll out, roll out, the Bannocks and Snake Indians are on the warpath." And 20 miles from Pendleton, Oregon, we made a run for a near town, and on July 4th, 1878, organized a company of volunteers, and on Dec. 10, 1878, we were mustered in by Adjutant General J. H. Turner, as Company B, 2nd Regiment, Oregon State Militia, Captain Robert E. Eastland, with headquarters at Elk Horn School House, Umatilla County, Oregon, near the line of the Umatilla Indian Reservation. We had our own horses and met once a week for drill. We also built a stockade. There were three Indians captured for the killing of two white men. This made the Indians very sulky. (This was in the fall of 1878.)

They (the Indians) were tried and executed, two in January, 1879, and one later in 1879; and at the January execution, 1879, the fears of the people and sheriff were great that the Indians would cause trouble. The sheriff called the volunteers, or a part of them, to Pendleton, Oregon, as guards and the balance as scouts. He also had a company of U. S. troops from Fort Walla Walla, Washington [Territory], and before the last Indian was executed it looked like another outbreak was inevitable. However, a number of the whites and Indians held a council and we had no more trouble. With all candor, I hope that the [pension] law may change so that the few that are left of Company B may receive their just reward.

There were fifty-eight in the company. There has been a good many dropped out in that time. Our time in the service was one year, eleven months and six days, without pay. Horses don't count.

Action in the Ute War of 1879 (By Eugene Patterson, formerly of Troop F, Fifth U. S. Cavalry. From *Winners of the West*, November, 1925)

The field of battle was well chosen by the Indians, and had it not been for Major Thomas T. Thornburg's advance guard, commanded by Second Lieutenant Samuel A. Cherry, discovering the Indians, the entire command would have been annihilated. Cherry saw a small party of Indians disappear over the hills and rode back and notified Major Thornburg, who had already begun the descent into a deep ravine which was intended to engulf the entire command. The Indians were concealed upon the hillsides and the troops were dismounted and deployed in line of battle. Cherry moved out and approached to within a couple of hundred yards of the Indians, took off his hat and waved it. The response was a shot which killed Private Michael Firestone. This was the first shot and Cherry deployed along the hill to prevent the Indians flanking his position.

The wagon train was then parked, Company F, Fifth Cavalry, on the left, and Company E, Third Cavalry, on the right. Captain J. Scott Payne with Company F was ordered to charge the hill, having his horse shot under him [in the process] and several of his men wounded. The Indians were driven from this point, and the company rallied on the wagon train. Lieutenant Cherry called for twenty volunteers who responded promptly. Sixteen were wounded and two were killed before he reached the wagons, and he brought every wounded man in with him. Major Thornburg started to the wagon train and was killed when hardly halfway to the train. Captain Payne, then in command, began shooting horses for breastworks. The red devils then set fire to the dry grass and some of the wagons caught fire, which required all the force possible to smother it with no water, and the smoke was suffocating.

The Indians kept up a constant fire and Captain Payne was wounded for the second time. At an early hour in the morning of October 2nd, Captain Francis S. Dodge with D Company, Ninth Cavalry, dashed up and entered the beleaguered camp without losing any men. Early in the morning of October 5th, the command under Colonel Wesley Merritt reached us, which sure looked good. His command had marched 170 miles in less than forty-eight hours. Those killed [in all the fighting] were: Major Thornburg, First Sergeant John Dolan, Privates Michael Firestone, John Burns, Samuel McKee, and Amos D. Miller, all of Troop F, Fifth Cavalry; Privates Thomas Mooney, Michael Lynch, and Charles Wright, all of Troop D, Fifth Cavalry; Private Dominick Cuff of Troop E, Third Cavalry; William McKinstry, wagon master; Thomas McGuire, teamster, and C. Grafton Lowery, guide. Those wounded were: Captain Payne, Second Lieutenant James V. S. Paddock, Sergeant John Merrill, Trumpeters Frederick Sutcliffe and John McDonald, Privates James T. Gibbs, John Hoaxey, Emil Kussman, Eugene Patterson, Frank E. Simmons, Eugene Schickedonze, William Esser, Gotlieb Steiger, all of Troop F, Fifth Cavalry; Sergeants James Montgomery and

Allen Lupton, Corporal Charles F. Eichwurzel, Privates Frank Hunter, James Conway, William H. Clark, Orlando H. Duran, John Donovan, Joseph Budka, Thomas Ferguson, Thomas Lewis, Edward Lavelle, Willard W. Mitchell, John Mahoney, Joseph Patterson, William M. Schubert, Marcus Hansen, John Crowley, Nicholas W. Heeney, Thomas Lynch, Frederick Bernhardt, E. Miller, Dr. Robert Grimes, and Teamsters Thomas Kane and Fred Nelson.

Merritt's Relief Column to Milk River (By Jacob Blaut, formerly of Troop B, Fifth U. S. Cavalry. From *Winners of the West*, April, 1924)

As I recall, three companies left Fort D. A. Russell, Wyoming [Territory], going into the hills of Colorado to pacify the Ute Indians who had a dispute with Nathan C. Meeker, the Indian agent. Before the soldiers' arrival there, the Utes killed Meeker and his clerk, Shadrack A. Price, taking with them Mrs. Meeker, her daughter [Josephine], and Mrs. Price.

About a week later a message came to Colonel Wesley Merritt, commander of the garrison at Fort Russell, saying the Indians had killed all the horses of the three companies and had surrounded the soldiers in a sort of canyon. A relief expedition of Companies A and B was immediately sent out. It was nearly a week later at daybreak when we reached the scene of the Meeker massacre and saw the dead horses of the companies lying where they had been killed by the Indians. We soon found the companies, finding many soldiers and citizens dead or wounded, among the dead being Major Thomas T. Thornburgh and the scout. We found the Indians had withdrawn and a little later we came across several Indian commissioners with some peaceful Utes who told us they had gotten the three women from the Indians and sent them on to the lower agency with some peaceful Utes.

The commissioners and friendly Indians now left and we buried the dead men, removing the wounded to a safe place. We then proceeded to White River, pitched camp, sending out scouting parties to look for the hostile Utes. First Lieutenant William B. Weir of the Ordnance Department, First Lieutenant William P. Hall of the Quartermaster's [Hall was regimental quartermaster] and ex-Sergeant Major Paul F. A. Humme went with one of the parties and about 10 o'clock that evening Lieutenant Hall came back to camp and told Colonel Merritt the party had been attacked and he had lost sight of his two comrades. Every man in camp under Major Edwin V. Sumner was sent out to look for the two men. Lieutenant Hall secured permission of Captain Robert H. Montgomery to take ten men and myself and go to the place where they had been attacked. We arrived there and waited for the rest of the command. Major Sumner refused to go in the canyon, and so Lieutenant Hall and my small command went into the canyon, shouting for the missing men, but this brought no results. I then reported back to Major Sumner, who ordered me to dismount with my men and go on foot up the hills. I found several hats which I thought belonged to the missing men, but they turned out to be old Indian hats. After picketing for several hours, we were recalled and found out Lieutenant Weir's body had been found and was later shipped east while we buried ex-Sergeant Major Humme's body where we found it in the mountains of Colorado.

Reminiscences of the Ute Uprising (By Jacob Blaut, formerly of Troop B, Fifth U. S. Cavalry. From *Winners of the West*, March 15, 1926)

[On the] Ute Reservation in southern Colorado, [the] agent . . . had given orders to the Indians to work, which they refused and rebelled by killing Agent Nathan C. Meeker and three assistants, captured Mrs. Meeker and daughter, and Mrs. [Shadrack] Price. An expedition in pursuit of the Indians [was] commanded by Major Thomas T. Thornburg from Fort D. A. Russell, Wyoming [Territory], and five companies cavalry and infantry. I was in the relief expedition in the command of Colonel Wesley Merritt, two troops of Fifth U. S. Cavalry, and two companies of infantry. We found that Major Thornburg, First Sergeant John Dolan, and two privates of F Troop, one private of A Troop, one scout and several teamsters, and all the horses were killed and six privates wounded, the dead lying unburied in a ravine for a week. We buried the dead.

We came up to the Indians in a canyon and charged them, when they raised a white flag and advanced with two Indian commissioners who had arrived from the southern agency and spoke to the officers. Then we moved the troops up on the hill out of the canyon, where the stench was unbearable from the decay of the dead horses, and proceeded to the White River. After leaving White River about thirty-five miles, two companies took the wrong trail, leaving two companies in command of Major Edwin V. Sumner. First Lieutenant William P. Hall asked for a sergeant and ten men to go in advance, and I was detailed with ten men of Troop B, Fifth U. S. Cavalry. We rode up near the canyon where First Lieutenant William B. Weir and [former] Sergeant Major Paul F. A. Humme were attacked. [While] dismounted waiting for the two companies to come up with Major Sumner, the lieutenant asked if he, Major Sumner, was going in the canyon. He replied, "No, I will not." Then the lieutenant asked me if I would go in with my ten men. I replied, "Yes, certainly. "

Then we started up the canyon, calling for Lieutenant Weir, but received no answer. At the end of the canyon we turned back. As I came back to the company, the major ordered me to leave the horses and proceed up the mountain with my ten men on picket duty. Advancing about 200 yards, I found two hats, sending them back to the major asking if he recognized them as the hats of the lieutenant and sergeant major. He returned word that they were Indian hats. About daybreak, two scouts came up and ordered me down. On arrival at the company the major asked me why I did not come down when he called me. I answered him that I did not hear him and did not think that his voice could be heard about a mile and a half up the mountain. Then Captain Robert H. Montgomery said, "Never mind him, sergeant, get your horses." I found out later that the major intended to leave me and my ten men, and that was the cause of the captain telling me not to mind the major. The next day we returned to the camp and found the body of the sergeant major and buried him there. The lieutenant's body had been brought in by some of the men before.

The Fifth Cavalry Comes Through (By Arthur S. Wallace, formerly of Troop A, Fifth U. S. Cavalry. From *Winners of the West*, September 30, 1933)

[Here are some] memories of the Fifth [U. S. Cavalry] at White River, Colorado, in '79 [when] I again sat along side my bunkie, huddled under a dog tent as we watched a wood fire in a small round of stones in front of our tent, and he remarked, "This beats our last winter's 'four left' into a sand bank in the Sand Hills." He had no sooner said this than we heard a picket cry out a challenge and a horse was heard coming down the hill and a few moments later splashed across the shallow ford of White River and coming up the bank, we heard the rider call out, "Orderly Bugler." The cry brought Colonel Wesley Merritt to his tent door immediately and the rider proved to be First Lieutenant William P. Hall, regimental quartermaster, who, jumping off his horse, stated his errand. In a few minutes, "Boots and Saddles" rang out and we raced to our herd, brought in our horses, saddled up, and fell into line, and with Lieutenant Hall leading began a night ride Indian file, time about 10 p.m. in late October.

Some time after midnight, we came to a halt on finding we had lost contact with the company ahead of us. It seems the last rider in the company in front of us discovered he was riding blind with no one in front of him, and on halting so advised our captain Augur. It was therefore decided to stand to horse and wait for daybreak. At dawn, we backtracked and found that the rider who reported himself as lost had crossed a ravine, while the preceding riders had turned at right angles and ridden up the ravine, and this we now did also. Coming out on to a hillside, we soon saw a long distance away in the valley a cavalry troop and on their near approach it proved to be Troop B of the Fifth, and on the back of a horse was bound the body of First Lieutenant William B. Weir, naked but not scalped.

A few days before this ride of ours, Colonel Merritt ordered Troop B to advance toward Grand River, or Green River, to find a plausible way should it be found necessary for a quick movement of his command in that direction. Accompanying Troop B under his orders were Quartermaster (First Lieutenant) William P. Hall, First Lieutenant William B. Weir, and ex-Sergeant Major Paul F. A. Humme. Lieutenant Weir was an unassigned second lieutenant fresh from West Point [sic] who with the consent of Colonel Merritt came with us when we left Fort D. A. Russell, [Wyoming Territory], under orders to effect the rescue of three of our Fifth Cavalry troops corralled by Ute Indians at Milk River, Colorado. This rescue was accomplished on October 5th. Humme had been discharged in the field and on account of his experience and expert marksmanship was employed by Colonel Merritt as a scout.

The talk about the camp was that Lieutenant Weir was placed in Lieutenant Hall's care and that under no circumstances were they to leave the troop to hunt. Evidently, if this was the instructions [sic], the death of Lieutenant Weir occurred as a result of the disobedience of orders. Hall, Weir, and Humme, while hunting deer, ran into a Ute Indian picket of seven Indians and Weir was killed by the first shot from them. Humme let his horse go and took to the brush fighting on foot. Hall kept to his horse and succeeded in getting away and rode into our camp for help.

Resuming our march now with Troop B and Weir's body, we returned to headquarters camp and the officer in command reported to Colonel Merritt. Colonel Merritt, always a very soft spoken man and soldier, we heard give his reprimand for not bringing in Humme in no gentle tones, and in consequence, after a night's rest we started out again, this time to find

Humme. On our second morning out, we saw some Indians at a distance on a hillside, and we got ready for trouble. The Indians dismounted and signaled for a parley. Two of them advanced on foot and a lieutenant and bugler of ours walked out to meet them. One of them turned out to be a white man, a commissioner ordered out from Washington to negotiate the surrender of Mrs. Meeker and daughter, who had been captured by the Utes when they sacked the Ute Indians' agency on White River, killing the agent, Nathan C. Meeker, and all other whites except Mrs. Meeker and daughter, whom they forced into captivity. The commissioner brought the parley to an abrupt end when he tried to place the blame of the deaths of Weir and Humme on the soldiers. Shortly after this, they showed us the body of Humme, which as I remember was buried where it fell. It was reported that Humme killed three of the Utes before they got him.

We returned again to headquarters and now began to settle for the winter. Snow had not come as yet. The ground was dry. Weather clear and cold. We cut logs on the hills and made shacks for four men to each, about eight feet square with stone chimneys, all of our own architectural design. Our entire furnishings consisted of bunks on each side of the rooms supported by forked willow, covered with small willow branches and snake wood from the hills for a mattress. The Indians had left plenty of cattle behind them when they fled, with which we supplied ourselves with meat, very generously killed by Chris Madsen on whom we especially relied for game when in the field. For stables for our horses, we cut and planted long willows in trenches, bringing the tops together for a roof, which served very well until the roof gave way under the weight of heavy snows. Our horses, like ourselves, were hardened to cold and exposure and lived through that winter minus flesh and plus bones and hair.

We lost one man from our troop that winter by fever, and had to ride horses over the trail of snow very deep to a neighboring hillside for burial. Second Lieutenant Frederick W. Foster spoke the Episcopal burial service, a distinct compliment to his early religious training as there was not a Bible in the camp. The ground was frozen too hard to dig a grave, so we laid his body on top of the frozen ground and the infantry which remained after we left for Fort D. A. Russell said they would bury his bones. The coyotes would do the rest. We left on March 31st [1880] for Russell, and as so many became snow blind the first few days, we rode for a time at night until we got away from the snow fields. Our wagon wheels were chained to runners under them, and with riders on the side of the trail steadying the heave loads by holding to ropes against their slipping and swaying, we got along fairly well.

Occasionally one would tip over and then the mess of lifting and reloading it was done with the use of much polite language common to old-time cavalry men in time of trouble.

Winding up the memory trail, I feel that if this comes to print that Sergeants Madsen and Hauser can recall this picture of '79 more vividly and accurately than I have portrayed it. And perhaps Sergeant Madsen will hear again the night howling of the big timber wolves easily seen from our camp on moonlit nights as they dark-lined the white snow on the foothills. And perhaps [he will] remember when he went at midnight in his underclothes to the log crossing at the river to try for an engagement with a mountain lion whose appealing cry brought him out from under his blankets.

A Sidelight of the Ute Campaign (By Earl Hall, formerly Troop D, Third U. S. Cavalry. From *Winners of the West*, October, 1924)

It was during the memorable campaign of 1879 against the Utes, in northwestern Colorado. The disturbance which prompted the campaign was known as the Meeker Massacre. Nathan C. Meeker, the Indian agent, was killed, and his wife and daughter carried into captivity. Major Thomas T. Thornburg and quite a number of his men, including a large per cent of Troop E, Third Cavalry, were killed. All the horses of this troop were slaughtered on the battlefield.

I did not see the scene of the conflict until after the battle. I was a recruit of Troop D, Third Cavalry, which comprised part of the force under Captain Guy V. Henry, ordered to the front from Fort Sanders, Wyoming, after the news of the slaughter. We proceeded rapidly to the scene of hostilities until we reached White River, where we went into camp. Our camp was located about seventy-five miles from Bear River, where Major Andrew W. Evans of the Third Cavalry was camped with another force. Both forces were awaiting orders from Colonel Wesley Merritt of the Fifth Cavalry, chief commander of this expedition, who was already in the field, in advance of us. It became important that immediate communication should be opened between our camp and Major Evans. It was decided to send two men, one an experienced soldier, and the other a recruit. They selected Francis "Pug" Malone of F Troop and myself of D Troop, both of the Third Cavalry. Fully armed and equipped, possessing the two best horses in the command for speed and endurance, we started toward dusk. We aimed to make a night ride of it in order to minimize danger of being discovered, as we had to travel through a hostile territory. After we had traveled a distance from camp and darkness approached, we halted and muffled our horses' feet by binding remnants of an old saddle blanket around their fetlocks, and repeating as often as needed.

After sufficient time had elapsed at our rate of speed to cover nearly the distance we expected to go, we slowed up as we approached the ledge of a mountain, which brought us out in the clear from the timber and gave us a view of the surrounding territory. We at once observed campfires in the plain below, very many of them. This latter fact puzzled us and made us hesitate, as it was well known that it was the custom of the Indians to make many fires when in camp, while on the other hand, it was the custom of white men to build but a few large fires. We were not sure whether the camp contained friend or foe, but after looking to our weapons in order to be prepared for trouble, we determined to advance cautiously and ready for instant action. All at once, breaking the stillness of the night, came to our ears the hee haw, haw haw, hee haw of the camp mule. Can you blame me, a recruit, not yet twenty-one, dog tired, for calling this mule bray sweet music?

We quickly descended into the camp, were duly challenged, and conducted, after all preliminaries, to the commander. Our object accomplished so far, we were in the saddle and on our return trip after one hour of rest. Just as day broke, as we were on our way back, we discovered the dead body of a man. We found his body inside the entrance of a shallow cave, where we had tracked him after he had made a desperate fight for life, indicated by the empty cartridge shells, which made a trail for his last resting place. He was over six feet tall from appearance, fine looking, but roughly dressed in the style common to the western man of that day. He had wedged himself closely in the cave, his feet nearest to the entrance, and had not been scalped. His boots had evidently been taken by the murderers, as no doubt had been his other property, for carved over his head in the solid rock, which was low enough for him to reach in his reclining position, was this inscription: "In my pocket you will find $20 in gold and my watch. Please send to my mother, Dayton Ohio." No further inscription, no name or address, so it appeared that he had expired before he had completed his message. We found nothing on him, and so we assumed his watch and money had gone with his boots. After the hasty inspection of this sad affair, we turned to mount, reminded of our own danger and the importance or our errand, but I could not help casting a last glance at the reclining martyr of the frontier days. . . .

I may add the fellow had no martial cloak left [on] him, not even his boots. The cave as far as I ever learned became his grave. We were compelled to leave him as we had found him. Without further adventure we arrived at our camp. I would have liked to have taken a few snapshots of the scenery, as the Utes had left their mark all the way. We had covered a distance of 150 miles in less than thirty-six hours, without change of horses, and now we and our horses were excused from duty until we had recuperated. The effects of the trip showed more on the horses than it did on us, but I can say I felt it.

I have heard some fine music in my life, before and since this event, which has appealed to my soul. But none has appealed to me with the force, carrying a message of safety and friendship to two poor and poorly paid cavalry boys daring the dangers of death or torture, that the dignity of the United States might be sustained and its citizens might be protected, as the bray of that army mule.

Occupation Duty in Utah, 1879-1880 (By George K. Lisk, formerly sergeant, Troop H, Fifth U. S. Cavalry. From *Winners of the West*, February, 1925)

In the fall of 1879, H Troop of the Fifth Cavalry left Fort McPherson, Nebraska, proceeded by rail to Rawlins, Wyoming [Territory], and there took wagon train to White River, Colorado. At this place, Agent Nathan C. Meeker, with the blacksmith and two or three citizen employees, were massacred by the Indians. Mrs. Meeker, her daughter Josephine, the blacksmith's wife and her two little girls were captured and taken away by the Indians. We buried those that were killed. Meeker, himself, had a barrel stave run down his throat and a log chain around his neck. We then pursued the Indians and rescued the women and children after a short fight in which Major Thomas T. Thornburg, First Lieutenant William B. Weir, [former] Sergeant Major Paul F. A. Humme, and several others whose names I do not remember, were killed. We remained there in snow and suffered severely with the cold.

[When we left] . . . in March of the following spring [1880], the snow was so deep that as we were coming through the mountains we had to cut our way, taking six days to make eighteen miles. We had to put snowshoes on the wheels of the wagon. Striking the high divide, we removed the snowshoes, allowing the wheels to roll over the ground until we again struck snow. In the canyon we replaced the snowshoes and slid along like a sled. Going into camp at night we could not pitch our tents owing to the depth of the snow. Some of the men would dig into the snowdrift, cut the tops of brush and carry them inside for a bed and then covered themselves with blankets and buffalo robes. Others would cut brush and lay it on top of the snow, place their blankets on top of this and cover themselves with their buffalo robes. Over this they would place their shelter tents. This is the way we suffered to open the country for civilization. Coming back to Rawlins—there we took [the] train for Fort D. A. Russell. From there we took wagon train again and marched north to Fort Laramie, Wyoming, and thence to Fort Robinson, Nebraska, where we went into permanent quarters. During this expedition many of the boys went snow blind. This condition would last for three or four days and was very painful.

D. West Coast

By the time white Americans began settling in the area of the Pacific Coast (Washington, Oregon, and California) in the 1840s and 1850s, the Indian population had dramatically declined from the effects of Spanish rule and colonization there. That trend continued between 1850 and 1880, as state and local militias wiped out hundreds of small, loosely organized tribes. The U. S. Army was not involved in this extermination, but in the 1850s and 1860s took action against several Rogue River, Paiute, and other tribes in Washington and Oregon when they resisted the whites' spoliation of their country. Most of these people were ultimately placed on reservations. Rebelliousness over treaty agreements, however, persisted among one group, the Modocs, leading to full-scale army operations against them in 1873-74. Most of the campaign, which included a high-profile assassination of an army commander during a peace council, took place in the rugged lava country of northern California, during which troops were forced to maneuver over some of the roughest terrain imaginable. The following veterans' accounts include a perspective of an incident in the Paiute country of southern Oregon, as well as personal reflections of the Modoc War.

A Close Call in Oregon, 1868 (By John M. Smith, formerly of Company C, Twenty-third U. S. Infantry. From *Winners of the West*, May 30, 1927)

I served three years from June 12, 1867, to June 11, 1870, in Company C, Twenty-third mounted U. S. Infantry. . . . On October 15, 1868, I was ordered by my commanding officer, First Lieutenant John W. Lewis, to take eight mules and deliver a load of provisions to a detachment of our command on station at a place called O'wyhee Ferry where they were doing duty as stage guards. The distance was 100 miles from Camp Smith, [Oregon,] headquarters of the command. My intentions were to make the distance without camping, for the country was infested with [Paiute] Indians who would not hesitate to murder me and take my supplies. Water was scarce in that part of the country, but there was two springs about half way distance between points, and one of these springs was reported to be good water, the other poison.

I arrived at the springs about 1:30 o'clock in the evening and watered the teams and drank some myself. I then started on my way, but had gone but about eight miles when one mule took sick and died. I then decided to go into camp and spend the night there, which I did, and in the morning I left the dead mule's mate to rustle for itself and proceeded on to the ferry. I arrived there in the evening and remained in camp until the following morning. During the night snow fell to the amount of about fourteen inches, but I made a start. However, I went but a little ways when I decided it best to go back to camp for several days, until the snow was partly gone, and give the team a rest. I started out again on the second day, and when I arrived at the springs on my return trip it was getting late, near sundown, and the wind was getting terribly cold. To my surprise, I was joined here by the mule I had turned loose, and who had stayed here with its dead partner.

My route laid to the north, up over a high land country and all covered with ice and snow. I had no way to tell where the trail was, and the full force of the blizzard struck me squarely in the face and I could see nothing. After a time I was compelled to give up trying to direct the team and got down in the wagon and covered up my head and ears to keep from freezing. I called on the good Lord to direct the course of the team and take me safe and alive into Camp Smith, a distance of about forty-five miles. I don't know how long I remained down there in the wagon, but after a time I aroused myself to find that the team had turned and was following the back trail toward the springs.

I got up and managed to turn them around and head them in what I believed to be the direction of Camp Smith and then I laid down again.

Until this day I have visions of that wagon and team rumbling along over cliffs and rough country. At one time I was sure the wagon was turning over, but in time it righted itself and rumbled on. After a long time, seemingly many hours, I heard a cock crow and knew that I was in the vicinity of Camp Smith, Oregon. I was unable to move, but shortly I heard the familiar challenge of "Who Comes There[?]," and although unable to answer the challenge or move, I knew the good Lord had answered my prayer and I had arrived in camp. The guards stopped the wagon and took me out and carried me into quarters where there was a good big fire going, and I soon recovered from my chill. Until this day I have never reported to my commanding officer, First Lieutenant Lewis, and if by chance these few remarks should come under his notice I ask that he receive my belated report of the trip to O'whyee Ferry, Oregon, in October, 1868. . . .

Scouting during the Modoc War, 1873 (By Oliver C. Applegate, formerly captain, Oregon Militia. From *Winners of the West*, February 28, 1930)

The 12th day of this month was the fifty-seventh anniversary of a scouting episode which occurred early in the Modoc War, a little over a month after the first fight with Captain Jack's band of Modocs on Lost River and the massacre of the settlers at the head of Tule Lake which occurred the same day. . . . The forces in the field were divided at that time. Captain Reuben F. Bernard with his command, consisting of his own troop of the First Cavalry, Captain James Jackson's troop, Sub-Chief Dave Hill's Klamath scouts and some other forces, which I cannot now recall, were stationed at or near the southwest corner of Tule Lake, on or near the Land cattle ranch and near the point where Captain John C. Fremont camped in May, 1846. Tule Lake is here about twelve miles wide, the historic lava beds resting on its southern border, and the Modoc stronghold, where the hostiles were encamped, was within four miles, or a little less, of the high volcanic ridge bounding the lake and lava beds on the west, usually known as the High Bluff.

Major John Green, a veteran soldier who had come up from the ranks, was field commander. He with his forces was encamped at the springs at the head of Willow Creek, a tributary of lower Klamath Lake, a place then known as Van Bremmer's ranch, eleven miles west by a trail winding among the rocks to the top of the High Bluff, already mentioned, three or four miles west of Captain Jack's stronghold known later as one of the most remarkable natural fortresses encountered in all the experiences of our army. Frank Wheaton, then lieutenant colonel of the Twenty-first Infantry, a major general in the Civil War, and one of the finest men in the U. S. Army, commanding all the forces in the field, was also at the Van Bremmer ranch with his staff. He was contemplating a plan to surround the Modoc stronghold, Captain Bernard to advance his command from the east and Major Green from the west, moving up on either side on January 16th, so that on the 17th his troops would be near enough, all conditions being favorable, to advance in skirmish order and surround the stronghold, Captain Bernard's right flank resting on the lake and Major Green's left flank also touching the lake. The colonel hoped that should the Modocs find themselves surrounded we could open communications with them through our Modoc scouts and perhaps close the war without serious casualties, possibly without any loss of life.

As I have mentioned before, to reach the High Bluff, the distance from Van Bremmer's by the horse trail was eleven miles through a very rocky terrain, but to reach that point overlooking the Lava Beds with the artillery, etc., on wheels would necessitate a trip of at least twenty-five miles, first north ten or twelve miles to the old emigrant road at the south end of lower Klamath Lake; thence along the old road to a point nearly north of the High Bluff; and thence about fifteen miles through a rugged undulating region, climbing gradually up among the crags without a road. To ascertain whether it was possible to take wagons through this little-known fifteen miles of lava upheavals, a reconnaissance was made over the horse trail to the High Bluff on January 12, 1873. Major John Green with Captain David Perry (in later army life a general [sic]) of the First Cavalry with thirteen men and the famous scout Donald McKay, with five Klamath scouts, left the encampment at about 9 a.m.

I was then a captain of Oregon state troops, having with me at the encampment fifty men of my company, half of them enlisted Klamath and Modoc scouts from my home station at Camp Yainax on the Klamath Indian Reservation. My orders were to remain an hour in camp after Major Green's departure, and then follow up with a reserve force of thirty men. This I did, taking with me fifteen white men and fifteen Indians of my company, and the regimental surgeon of the state troops. When we reached the second escarpment about three miles west of the High Bluff we heard firing, and, forcing our way down the declivity among the great boulders as rapidly as possible, we rode with the utmost speed up the rugged ascending

Oliver C. Applegate, who served in the Oregon militia at the time of the Modoc War. His recollections provide insightful testimony by an eyewitness of the events. In this picture, taken in 1926, Applegate sports his old officer straps on a buckskin jacket, along with his National Indian War Veteran membership badge and two badges commemorating the fiftieth anniversary of the Battle of the Little Bighorn in that year.

Editor's collection

plain to within a hundred yards of where I could see troops dismounted at the top of the bluff. Dismounting my men and leaving them with the horses, I ran on foot to where Major Green, seated on the ground, was eating his lunch (it was not an exciting day's work to the old soldier), at the point where the trail begins its descent of the cliff. Captain Perry, Donald McKay, and a few Klamath scouts and soldiers were about him, and a skirmish line of Perry's men was crawling up to a rocky elevation five hundred yards to the left where the Modocs had a picket station, from which point the Indians had evidently fired on Perry's men.

The Modocs, from their stronghold below, appeared shouting, talking, and sounding the war whoop. They were advancing in diverging lines toward the foot of the bluff. Evidently, they had been informed from their picket station that the opposing force was only about twenty persons, not knowing of the arrival of reinforcements, and they were running to climb the escarpment and attack Perry's men. At that moment I heard firing at the picket station, saw men dodging among the rocks, and Perry's men, having driven the Indians from their station, were starting on their return. Running back to my men, I sent Sergeant Pierce, a Confederate veteran, with about two-thirds of the men, to occupy the rim rock on the right of Major Green and Perry, to carefully conceal themselves among the rocks overlooking the cliff. Leaving a few men with the horses, with First Sergeant Neil and the remainder of the men we ran along the rim to the left and reoccupied the rocky elevation from which Perry's men had driven the Indians; from that point, at intervals of a hundred yards or so, where there were large boulders, were stationed Indians, the line extending down the cliff and well into the lava field at its base. A wounded Modoc whose rifle we picked up passed down the cliff, assisted by the Indians who occasionally appeared from behind the boulders and fired at us, though without effect. The situation was that we held the rim rock for six or seven hundred yards, our men well concealed, and Captain Jack's main party, diverging, were approaching our approximately fifty rifles. There doubtless would soon have been a serious crisis for the enemy had not a sudden change occurred in the program.

Major Green, having finished his lunch, rode up to my position and said, as nearly as I can recall his words, "Captain, draw out your men and escort us back to headquarters." We were not out to fight that day it appeared, but to cover Captain Perry's small detachment sent to examine the rough volcanic region between the High Bluff and the old trail at the south end of lower Klamath Lake, to determine the possibility of getting over it with the artillery, etc., on wheels, preparatory to the plans maturing for surrounding the Modoc stronghold. We had made it safe for Captain Perry's reconnaissance and he started on his way down toward Klamath Lake, while my command returned with Major Green to camp on the Indian trail by which we came in.

Colonel Wheaton's plans for the investment of the stronghold I did not yet know, but the next day after this episode I proposed to go into the Lava Beds at night with my company and one other, guided by my Modoc scouts who knew the ground, secure good positions in the lava fields, and the next morning invite attack. The colonel then explained his plans fully to me, saying that if my plan should be successful it would probably be at heavy sacrifice, but that he hoped by his plan of surrounding the Modocs in their stronghold to secure their surrender with little or no loss of life. My plan, if approved by the colonel, would perhaps not have been a success. Colonel Wheaton's might have succeeded had it not been for a dense fog which prevented the use of the artillery on January 17th, when the effort was made in full force from the east and west. We had forty-one men killed and wounded, and did not dislodge the enemy. We did not know beforehand the awful ruggedness of their position.

Murder of the Peace Commissioners (By Oliver C. Applegate, formerly captain, Oregon Militia. From *Winners of the West*, January 30, 1926)

During the Modoc War of 1872 and 1873, a truce was declared by the authorities at Washington, and a commission was sent to the headquarters of the army in the lava country south of Tule Lake in northern California. After a month or so had been consumed in communications with the hostile Modocs, mainly through Indian messengers, it was arranged for the commissioners to meet the hostile chief and four of his principal men in the Lava Beds, between the military camp and the Indian stronghold among the rocks, distant from the army camp three-fourths of a mile.

The commission then consisted of Colonel Alfred B. Meacham, formerly superintendent of Indian affairs in Oregon, chairman of the commission; Major General E. R. S. Canby, U. S. Army, department commander; Reverend Ezekiel Thomas, a Methodist minister of California; and Hon. Leroy S. Dyer, U. S. Indian Agent of Klamath Agency, Oregon. The interpreters of the commission were Toby Riddle (since known as Winema), a Modoc Indian woman, a second cousin to Captain Jack, the hostile chief, and her husband Frank Riddle, a Kentuckian. On the part of the

Modocs, Captain Jack, chief of the hostile Modocs, a signer of the great treaty of 1864 as Kientpoos; Sconchin John, sub-chief of that band, brother of Old Sconchin, chief of the friendly Modocs then at Camp Yainax on the Klamath Reservation; Black Jim, half-brother of Captain Jack; Boston Charley and Hooker Jim, headmen of the band. It is true that there were other warriors at hand when the attack was made on the commission whose presence was not authorized.

Captain O. C. Applegate, officer in charge of the Modocs, Paiutes, and Klamaths at Camp Yainax on the Indian reservation, was under detail to assist the commission, and at the request of General Canby brought to the headquarters of the commission at Colonel Alvan C. Gillem's camp in the Lava Beds the loyal old Chief Sconchin from Yainax, to assist the commission in negotiations, or more particularly to observe while with them the conduct and appearance of the hostiles, and to determine whether or not they were acting in good faith. Meetings were held on successive days at the agreed place in the Lava Beds, Sconchin being present with the commission on two occasions. Before the third meeting, word was received from Camp Yainax that some of Captain Jack's emissaries were there, probably for the purpose of influencing the old chief's Modocs to join the hostiles.

The old chief, being greatly disturbed by the news, asked General Canby to return him at once under conduct of Captain Applegate to Yainax, to prevent dissatisfaction among his people. This the general agreed to. The evening before departure, with the few Modocs who had accompanied him from Yainax, Captain Applegate conferred with Colonel Meacham and Mr. Dyer of the commission and they both, being experienced men with Indians, assured Captain Applegate that Captain Jack's party was coming every day to the council armed and in a morose temper, and they felt that they were risking their lives at every meeting at a place so remote from the camp of the army, and in a rugged terrain where hostile warriors could be easily concealed. Neither General Canby nor Reverend Dr. Thomas seemed fearful of danger, and were bent on continued efforts for peace, and Mr. Meacham and Mr. Dyer were determined to take chances with them at any risk. Captain Applegate took from his pocket a little two-barreled Derringer and gave it to Mr. Dyer, saying: "Put this in your pocket with these cartridges. In some possible emergency it may help you." Mr. Meacham already had a little pocket pistol, but neither General Canby nor Dr. Thomas would consent to carry arms, even such innocent weapons as these little pocket pistols.

The next morning, before Captain Applegate started to Camp Yainax with his party, he, with the old chief and Littlejohn, his Klamath interpreter, went into the peace commission tent at military headquarters to say good-bye to the commissioners, who were all seated around a table. Mr. Meacham, evidently wishing confirmation of his own views, said to Captain Applegate: "Oliver, can you give us any hope?" The answer was not encouraging. It was that the commissioners were in great danger, dependant as they were upon the caprice of Indians already proven treacherous and having an evident advantage. The meeting with Captain Jack and his cabinet passed that day without unusual incident, but Winema, who was sent with a message to Captain Jack after he had returned to his stronghold, was secretly intercepted on her return by Faithful Williams, one of Jack's Men, an old-time friend of hers, with the statement that the Modocs had already decided to kill the commissioners, and if they should go to the place of meeting that day it would surely be their death. This dread news she immediately communicated to the commissioners, and she and her husband plead[ed] with them vehemently not to go.

The morning of the fatal day, April 11, 1873, General Canby and Reverend Dr. Thomas, being still unconvinced, the entire party went as before, and with them Bogus Charley, one of Jack's men who had remained overnight in the military camp with the soldiers, professing warm friendship. The council opened peacefully as usual, General Canby distributing cigars among the party and expressing his hopes for peace. As the council proceeded, however, signs of an approaching crisis appeared and finally Kientpoos, springing up and drawing his pistol shouted, "Otwe Katuck"—"Now it ends"—and shot General Canby in the face at a distance of probably not over eight feet. The attack on all the commissioners began at once, each Modoc knowing beforehand who his victim was to be. Other warriors appeared armed from the surrounding rocks. General Canby and Dr. Thomas were soon killed and their clothing stripped from them. Colonel Meacham, bleeding from several wounds, was prostrate and unconscious among the rocks.

Mr. Riddle succeeded in escaping to a rugged lava field near the lake shore, and Mr. Dyer ran toward the military camp through the rocks, pursued by Hooker Jim, who fired at his intended victim as he ran. Mr. Dyer expected momentarily to be killed, but marvelously escaped being shot by one of the best marksmen in the hostile band. At a distance of probably a hundred yards from the place of attack, he turned toward his pursuer, menacing his foe with the Derringer, but not firing, as the books have it, for it would have been impossible with such a weapon to have harmed his foe at a distance of fifty yards. The menace was effectual and Jim threw himself on the ground to escape a possible shot, while Mr. Dyer gained distance enough to meet the relief party of soldiers from Colonel Gillem's camp, who had been notified from the signal station on the cliffs above the camp of the attack on the commissioners. Winema remained on the ground where the murderous attack occurred, was once knocked down by an Indian gun, and prevented one Indian from shooting Mr. Meacham through the head and another from scalping him while he was yet unconscious. At last she cried out in the Modoc tongue, "Sojers capcopila" ("soldiers are coming") and the Modocs stopped the bloody work and soon disappeared in the rugged fastnesses of the Lava Beds.

The noble Canby, famous as a major general in the War of the Rebellion, and Reverend Dr. Thomas, peace-loving divine as he was, lay prone and naked among the rocks, and Alfred B. Meacham, enthusiastic and almost fanatical friend to the redman, lay bleeding where he had risked his life rather than desert his companions, who could not realize the danger with him. He slowly recovered from the awful ordeal and lived for several years, and until his death remained a friend to the Indian.

Mr. Dyer's escape was marvelous, for both Black Jim and Hooker Jim had been selected to kill him, but their bullets went wild and, as he claimed, the menace with the little pistol had saved his life. Captain Applegate made him a present of it. After more than fifty years, when Mr. Dyer finally passed away, his daughter, Miss Helen Dyer, of Ontario, California, sent the little pistol by mail to Captain Applegate at Klamath Falls, Oregon. It is only a month ago that he received it, and you may be sure that he prizes it as one of his most interesting souvenirs of the tragic drama of the Modoc War.

Incident in the Charge on the Modocs, January 17, 1873 (By Jasper N. Terwilliger, formerly of Troop F, First U. S. Cavalry. From *Winners of the West*, April 30, 1926)

We all remember the cold dismal foggy day, the fog being so thick we could almost cut it with a knife. Captain Oliver C. Applegate with his [militia] command on our extreme right could hardly be discerned for the fog. Several of F Troop, First Cavalry, were wounded as the line advanced. [Privates] Guttermuth and Hollis, close to myself, were victims. We took Hollis under cover, took off his belts, gave him a drink of water, and as he was badly wounded we signaled the hospital corps, and two men were shot in attempting to reach him. The bugle sounded to the left and we were to cover the position occupied by Captain John O. Fairchild of the California volunteers, whom the Indians were picking off. As we were advancing along, Paddy Doyle, who was just ahead of myself, raised his hand and said, "See the white flag the Indians have raised?," which was a false move on the part of the Indians. Just then two shots were fired so close together that they sounded like one. Paddy was shot in the arm and, dropping his carbine, jumped down and said, "I'm shot all to paces." Captain David Perry said, "Terwilliger, get that carbine and smash it," and I did.

We then crossed over to the lines of G and B troops, where the wounded were attended to by the surgeons. In crossing this open space, Captain Perry and Corporal Iseman were wounded. After the wounded were taken care of, we then moved back a few miles to the temporary camp of B and G troops, where we had coffee and what there was to satisfy hunger. We rested and had a few hours sleep and then, with the wounded upon horses, we started back on a twenty-mile hike to the permanent camp of B and G, everybody good and tired. Being acquainted with the cook of G Troop, I sauntered down to the cook's tent and, I tell you, I surely did enjoy the meal. In the meantime, the cook took an axe and broke open a cracker box. It sounded just like a shot, and every trooper was out of his tent with his carbine, but it was a false alarm. The next morning we were separated from the rest of the troop under Sergeant Coppell and had a sixty-mile hike to get back to F Troop headquarters. . . .

E. Southwest

Southwestern campaigns took place in West Texas, New Mexico, Arizona, and southern Utah, where pressures by settlers and miners aroused the native peoples to offer resistance to the intruders. Campaigns against the Indians began soon after conclusion of the War with Mexico and carried intermittently through the Civil War, and especially involved the large tribe of Navajos and smaller and more diverse groups of Apaches. Again, many of these peoples were physically forced onto reservations, and their resistance to this control, both initially and sporadically thereafter, proved the root of much of the conflict that proceeded well into the 1880s and beyond. In many ways, the Apache wars were the most difficult of all the Indian wars, for the troops labored over grueling deserts and tortuous mountain terrain in pursuit of incredibly smart and elusive people as the warriors and their families

Men of Company H, Tenth Infantry, stand with their officers at parade rest before their barracks. They wear dress uniforms and hold their Springfields in this image taken at Fort Union, New Mexico Territory, ca.1890.

successfully evaded the army time and again. The following veterans' statements offer insights into this difficult warfare, describing actions and personal tragedies and experiences regarding Utah's Black Hawk Indian War and the various Apache conflicts that permeated Arizona and New Mexico throughout the 1870s and early 1880s. Most of the accounts relate aspects of the famed Geronimo Campaign of 1885-86, providing highly personal views of the pursuit and surrender of the famed Chiricahua leader, while a single remembrance describes the exhausting effort to subdue the Apache Kid in the 1890s.

Pursuing Indians during Utah's Black Hawk War, 1865 (By Joseph S. McFate. From *Winners of the West*, February 15, 1926)

About the middle of December, 1865, the Indians made a raid on Kanab, Kane County, Utah [Territory], and drove off a bunch of horses. About the same time they drove off horses and cattle from the St. George country. I was living at Virgin City. As soon as we got word, several of us left home to join the boys from St. George who were ahead under James Andrews, while we went with Sextus Johnson. It had been raining several days when it turned to snow, which was eighteen inches deep when we got to Pipe Springs ranch. Dr. James M. Whitmore and Robert McIntyre had been killed before the snowfall on an alkali flat of over one hundred acres, with not a bush or spear of grass on it.

After we had been there several days, some of the boys went out and captured a young Indian, brought him to camp, but he would not talk. After trying several days, I—who spoke the language well—was told by Captain James Andrus [Utah Militia Cavalry] to tell him that if he would tell where the men were that were killed [Whitmore and McIntyre] we would not hurt him but set him free, otherwise he would be killed. He then said if we take him and seven or eight men on horses to the flat about four miles from the ranch we would find them. He took us to the northeast corner and pointed west, had us ride about twenty-five rods west, four or five feet apart, all abreast. Then he had us turn to the south, back to the place of starting. Then he had us go on the north side. When we went about half the distance, about ten feet to the right I discovered the feather end of an arrow above the snow. It was shot into one of the men's bodies (do not remember which) after he was killed and stripped of his clothing. As soon as that was seen, the Indian turned his pony's head, would not look that way. I told him to turn, but he would not. When I asked him where the other man was, he asked me if that was the man with whiskers. After telling him, he pointed to the other about ten or twelve feet from the one just found. Sextus Johnson then asked Hyram Morris and myself to go to camp and get a wagon to take [the] bodies home. It was about four miles, all up grade. About a mile off, we looked back, saw James Andrus coming from the southeast with his men that went out that morning. They had seven Indians, took them to where the dead men were, showed them what they had done, and [they] were shot right there. When we returned, we put the bodies of Whitmore and McIntyre in the wagon, covered them with snow, and took them to St. George, getting home about 10th or 12th of February.

The little village of Kanab was in peril as the Indians from the extreme north to south were all on the warpath. The Utes under Black Hawk, all the different tribes with their leaders, . . . and Paiutes, with the Navajos hissing [cheering?] them on. When the settlement in Long Valley was not considered strong enough to protect themselves, I with about fifteen others went as guard about the middle of May and were there until about the middle of July, when James Andrus came with another bunch of about twenty-five men and guarded them into larger settlements. At the same time, the settlements on the upper Sevier had to leave their homes and take their families to better protection. Their good crops was their only show for bread. I went again as guard and to help gather the crops. . . .

An Apache Fight near Camp Bowie, Arizona Territory, 1871

(By John F. Farley, formerly of Troop K, Third U. S. Cavalry. From *Winners of the West*, September 30, 1935)

My army service dates from March 1, 1867, to March 1, 1872, when I was honorably discharged at expiration of service. The first two months after my enlistment were served at a military school at Carlisle, Pennsylvania, after which I was attached to a group of 300 recruits who went from Carlisle to Fort Leavenworth, Kansas, for assignment to the Third United States Cavalry, located in various forts in New Mexico. After a few weeks delay at Fort Leavenworth, we were equipped with arms and mounted. We started on the march over the plains over the Santa Fe Trail, some 800 miles of a march. On reaching Fort Union in New Mexico, we were assigned to our various troops in our regiment. With some twenty other recruits, I was assigned to Troop K, located at Fort Seldon, some 400 miles from Fort Union, where we arrived one month later.

I served with my troop at Fort Seldon for two and one-half years, during which time I was in several Indian engagements in New Mexico and western Texas. After two and one-half years in New Mexico, our regiment was transferred to Arizona, my Troop K being located at Camp Bowie. On July 19, 1871, my Troop K was stationed with one infantry company of the Twenty-first regiment at Camp Bowie. On July 16th there occurred near Camp Bowie an Indian depredation which caused Major Andrew W. Evans, the commander of Fort Bowie, to issue orders to Captain Gerald Russell, the captain of Troop K, to take all the men who could be spared from the post from Troop K and go in pursuit of these Indians. Captain Russell acted accordingly, taking about seventy men from the troop, leaving some twenty men to do escort duty for daily mail carrying in and out of the post. These men were subject to my orders as first sergeant of the troop under order of Post Commander Major Andrew W. Evans. About 3:00 p.m., July 19, 1871, a report reached the post that the post cattle herd of about 150 head located near the post had been stampeded by hostile Indians, and that one of the herders had been killed and the other desperately wounded. On receipt of this report, the commanding officer of the post sent his orderly to me with orders to take all the cavalrymen of Troop K I had in the post and take after the Indians, and that in event that we caught up with the Indians to try and hold them engaged until the infantry company which he would order out to our assistance would reach us. I acted upon this order of the commanding officer at once, but found that I could muster only six men, including myself, to take after the Indians on horseback.

The daily escorting of the mail in and out of the post every afternoon was a longstanding order by the commanding officer of the post and could not be dispensed with. This was a detail of twenty men, leaving only six men, including myself, to take after the Indians on horseback. It will be noted that the Indians stampeded the cattle herd of the post at the time of day when our force at the post was the weakest. On leaving the post with my small squad as per commanding officer's orders, I confined myself to following the trail of the Indians and the cattle herd which was very broad. This we followed, very rapidly for about five miles from the post, when we came to a small hill over which the trail led us. Our horses having been ridden so rapidly to this point, each of our squad dismounted including myself and started leading our horses up this hill in single file. I was in advance when we had reached about half way up this hill and one single gun shot from the top of this hill took effect in my left hip. Immediately after this shot was fired it was followed by a volley of several shots aimed at us which for the most part went over us doing no damage. I immediately tried to mount my horse, but found that the gunshot had disabled me so that I was unable to do so. Following the volley fired at us, the Indians who were mounted on ponies rushed down on both sides of us, intending to cut us off from the post. Fortunately for me, three of my men abandoned their horses and the four of us without horses aimed to reach a deep arroyo some few hundred yards distance with a heavy growth of brush which would enable us to make a dying fight by getting together. We succeeded in reaching this arroyo after many narrow escapes from being shot down by armed Indians all around us.

Our fight was with a bunch of dismounted Indians as all those mounted Indians for the time were drawn from us in trying to head off two of our party from making their escape to the post. When they failed to head our two men off from the post, the mounted Indians returned and joined the bunch of dismounted Indians who were trying to dislodge us, but they finally gave up their efforts to get us out of the arroyo. This was about 6:00 p.m. The July sun was generally intensely hot; this increased the pain of the wound received in my hip which was bleeding very profusely. At about seven o'clock a heavy thunderstorm passed over with heavy rain which was a great relief to my wound, which was becoming much inflamed and intensely painful. I of course thought that my wound was a fatal one.

We remained in the arroyo until ten o'clock expecting relief from the post and wondering why it had not reached us sooner. At that, I noted in the darkness approaching us on horseback, a man. When near enough, I challenged, "Who comes there" and received in reply, "A friend." This man was in charge of a squad from the post which had come to our rescue. The rescue party had an ambulance and was looking the ground over for our dead bodies, not expecting to find any of us alive.

We arrived in the post about midnight where I was taken to the hospital. My wound was examined by the doctor, who gave it as his opinion that it would not be fatal if I would keep up my courage. For the first two weeks while I was in the hospital, I suffered intense pain from my wound before it commence to heal. The only medical attention that could be applied to the wound was a wet cloth laid over it to keep down the inflammation. I came out of the hospital at the end of five months.

While I was confined in the hospital, my regiment had been transferred to Fort Robinson [sic—Fort McPherson], Nebraska, and it then being within a few months time of the expiration of my service, I remained at Camp Bowie. I received my discharge from the service on March 1, 1872, and did not return to my regiment again. On the return of Captain Russell from his pursuit of the Indians who had been committing depredations mentioned above, he came at once to the hospital to see me. He was very much interested in my report and escape from death. When I reached the part where I mentioned about the two men who had made their escape to the post and who were followed by all the mounted Indians until they safely reached the post, the captain disapproved their action in leaving the party in that way and especially so when they knew I was wounded. He advised that they should be prosecuted on charges of cowardice, but after hearing my further report and my reasons for disapproval of charges against them, he finally agreed with my views that no charges should be preferred against them. I explained to him that those escaping to the post from our party drew all the mounted Indians away from myself and the others with me for about one hour's time so that we had only a few dismounted Indians, about six or eight, keeping us under fire until the mounted Indians returned to where we were located. On their return, the four of us were together in a good position in the arroyo to defend ourselves. There were about twelve or fifteen mounted Indians who followed the two men into the post and I gave it as my opinion that if they had not been drawn away from us as they were in pursuit of those two we would have all been killed, as the Indians were all well-armed with up-to-date guns and they outnumbered us by at least three to one. The captain agreed with me then that no charges should be preferred against the two men who had made good their escape to the post.

Combat at Salt River Canyon, 1872 (By an "Old Non-Com" of the Fifth U. S. Cavalry. From *Winners of the West*, November, 1924)

During the years 1872-73, General George Crook, commander of the Department of Arizona, organized a special campaign against the bands of hostile Apaches who were certainly raiding the little settlements scattered at wide intervals in a few of the watered valleys of Arizona. The force consisted of several detachments each generally consisting of two troops of cavalry, with some friendly Indian scouts. Each detachment had its own field of operations and I will merely give an account of one engagement with the hostiles by one detachment, of which my troop formed a part. It was commanded by Captain William H. Brown of the Fifth Cavalry, his force consisting of Troops L and M of the Fifth U. S. Cavalry and some friendly Indian scouts, being afterwards joined by Captain James Burns with his Troop G, Fifth Cavalry, and a number of Pima scouts under First Lieutenant Earl D. Thomas, Fifth Cavalry.

The objective of Captain Brown was an Apache stronghold known to be somewhere in the frowning canyons of Salt River. A friendly Apache scout who had once lived there agreed to act as guide, provided that the march was made at night, for in daylight, he said, the command would surely be seen, ambushed, and wiped out. He further stated that the Apaches could in that part of the country easily defend themselves against any available force, if forewarned. It must be remembered that in those days the entire army of the United States numbered about 23,000, and was expected to control all the Indians from the Mexican line to the British line, besides garrisoning ocean forts.

The horses together with the pack train were left under guard. Each man had a blanket roll and in it plenty of cartridges to supplement those in his thimble belt, also a very little food, and of course a canteen of water. It was bitterly cold, and all night we marched in Indian file along the narrow, rocky trail. Shortly before daybreak [on December 28, 1872,] a light was seen in front and two scouts were sent forward. They soon returned with the information that the light was made by a party of Apaches returning to their stronghold from a raid on the Pima Indians and the few white families living in the Gila Valley, and that they had left a number of weary mules and horses, stolen from thence, in a little canyon and [had] gone on. Captain Brown ordered Captain Burns with his troop to stay where the stolen horses were, so that if any more Apaches came up he could hold them and prevent the command being caught between two fires. The main body was halted and Second Lieutenant William J. Ross with the Indian guide and fifteen men followed the trail of the returning Apaches toward the stronghold, and in less than one-half a mile the guide signaled halt, and whispered "Apache." Then he, together with Lieutenant Ross and two scouts, crept along to a turn in the trail, and looking around saw the Apache stronghold about thirty-five yards in front.

It was a long, wide, open cave, and a few yards in front of it was a rampart of huge blocks of stone, a natural fortification, but probably added to by the Apaches. Just at the outside of the cavern a fire was burning, and a band of Indians were dancing and singing around it, evidently celebrating their bloody raid through the Gila settlements. A few of the women were cooking a meal, and a number of Indians could be seen sitting in the cave and watching the dance.

The men were whispered forward by Lieutenant Ross and sent a volley into the dancers, several falling dead. The others at once rushed to the cave or manned the rampart, and in less than three minutes opened fire upon the soldiers, whom they could just get a glimpse of in the early dawn. At this moment, Second Lieutenant John G. Bourke with between forty or fifty men came at the double down the rocky trail just in time to save Ross and his handful of men from a counterattack, Captain Brown having rushed them forward the moment the first volley was fired. Lieutenants Bourke and Ross hastily posted their men so as to cut off retreat of the Apaches by either flank, and when Captain Brown came up with the rest of the men, they surrounded the Indians, the cave being under an unclimbable cliff. For about two hours an interminable fight was maintained, until broad daylight showed that the roof of the cave was all rock and would deflect bullets all over the cave.

The men therefore fired volley after volley at the roof, and the effects were soon seen. A number of Indians then made a determined charge, one party at the front, the other at the right flank, while still another party mounted the rampart and fired rapidly, evidently trying to help out the charges, which, however, were repulsed, with much loss to the Indians, and several of those on the rampart were also killed. The troops then commenced firing volleys into the cave, and at this time Captain Burns with his troop came up on the cliff, above the cave. It was impossible to get down to attack the Apaches below, so they started rolling rocks down upon them. The Indians, however, still continued defiant, singing and yelling. After some little time, it was plainly seen that the end was near. The death song had died away, and Captain Brown, after signaling Captain Burns to hold up rolling rocks, ordered a charge, and after it was over not a warrior was left alive except some mortally wounded. In this charge, however, one Apache did get away. He must have thrown himself flat upon the ground in the midst of the charge and wormed his way through, but when he considered himself safe, he could not resist leaping upon a high rock and giving a yell of defiance, which brought a shot from Blacksmith Cahill of the pack train, which killed the Indian. [It was] an 800-yard shot.

Between eighty and ninety Indians were killed in this fight. The boots of most of the men were well ventilated by this night march over this trail of sharp rocks. Many had bleeding feet and some could not wear their boots, but rode barefooted for several days. This is a fair sample of work done by this Fifth Cavalry during their three and one-half years in Arizona in the early seventies. I may add that our Pima allies all quit temporarily and departed to fast and mourn for their comrades killed in this fight.

Memories of Lieutenants Hudson and Tyler (By Peter Lacher, formerly sergeant, Troop D, Fourth U. S. Cavalry. From *Winners of the West*, January 15, 1926)

I, a sergeant, Corporal Henry R. Davis, Privates Peter Carrigan, W. K. Davis, E. Edwards, and Private Maple of Company D, Fourth Cavalry, on detached service at Fort Clark[, Texas,] were assigned to Company I and rode with Captain Napoleon B. McLaughlen in that memorable charge through the camp of the Kickapoo Indians at Santa Rosa, Mexico, May 19th [, 1873]. I regret to say that the only man to lose his life in the fight was one of my four men, Private Peter Carrigan. He was mortally wounded on May 19, and passed away at Fort Clark, May 23rd.

When I read the name of First Lieutenant Charles L. Hudson, Company I, [in a recent issue of *Winners of the West*,] it reminded me of a very sad affair that happened December 31, 1873. On September 29, 1872, I saw Lieutenant Hudson lead Company I through a camp of Comanche and Kiowa Indians on the north fork of the Red River. Although his horse plunged into a mire, his charge was a success. First Sergeant Billy Wilson kept the company in line until Lieutenant Hudson got out of the mud, unhurt. There were over 200 Indians killed in two hours, 163 prisoners taken, and over 1,000 horses captured. Our casualties were one man killed, two mortally wounded, and one slightly wounded.

On the 19th of May, 1873, I rode with Lieutenant Hudson at the left of Company I in that memorable charge upon the camp of Kickapoo and Lipan Indians at Santa Rosa, Mexico. Later in the year, Lieutenant Hudson, with thirty-five men, was ordered to take up a position made vacant by the promotion of Second Lieutenant Frederick D. Grant of Company F, who went on the staff of General Sheridan at Chicago. His duty was to guard surveyors on the Grand Trunk Railroad to Mexico. While on that duty, Lieutenant Hudson intercepted a band of thieving Indians who were making a raid in that vicinity. In the skirmish that followed, fifteen Indians were killed and thirty-five horses captured, which he brought into Fort Clark at about Christmas time, 1873, where he also found that he had a roommate. This roommate was a new second lieutenant right from West Point. His name was Augustus C. Tyler, a grandson of President John Tyler.

On December 31st, Lieutenant Hudson was still congratulating himself on the fact of having gone through three sharp Indian fights in thirteen months without being hurt. Hudson was dressed in his bright uniform, all ready for muster and monthly inspection. As he was putting on his belt, Lieutenant Tyler, who had picked up a Winchester carbine which Hudson

A trio of infantry non-commissioned officers wearing fatigue uniforms and campaign hats, probably in the early 1890s. *Editor's collection*

had carried with him while in the field, asked, "How does this thing work?" It worked. The charge went off. The ball struck Hudson under one arm pit and came out under the other.

Lieutenant Hudson fought his last battle with death and surrendered five days later [on January 5, 1874]. After receiving due military honors at Fort Clark, his body was sent to San Antonio for burial. At his request, the thirty-five men that were with him in his last Indian fight escorted his body to the grave. Poor Lieutenant Tyler was heartbroken over the mishap, and his bright hopes for the future were dimmed, and perhaps his whole career was wrecked. I cannot say, as I left the service two months later. Such is life. [Tyler resigned from the Regular Army on July 1, 1878.]

A Personal Bout with Apaches (By George O. Eaton, formerly second lieutenant, Fifth U. S. Cavalry. From *Winners of the West*, September, 1938)

The following manuscript was written by George Oscar Eaton some months before his death on September 12, 1930, at Fort Myers, Florida, at the age of eighty-two. Eaton served in the Fifteenth Maine Infantry in the closing year of the Civil War, was appointed to West Point by [U. S. Senator] James G. Blaine, and was graduated in the class of 1873. He was assigned to the Fifth Cavalry, and shortly after his arrival in Arizona took part in an engagement at Sunset Pass (November 1, 1874) wherein his able handling of a detachment, and the heroic conduct of a sergeant, resulted in the rescue of the seriously wounded commander of the expedition, First Lieutenant Charles King, later a widely known novelist. An expedition in the same region, November 17 to December 5, led by the young officer, is known as "Eaton's Scout." It was shortly after this that the incident described in the manuscript took place. In March, 1875, Second Lieutenant Eaton was given the difficult assignment of moving the Mojaves, Yumas, and Tontos from Camp Verde to the San Carlos Reservation—with a fight between the tribes as a complication on the way. At the beginning of the 1876 [Sioux] campaign, Eaton was accidently shot during a stampede of the regiment's herds, and shortly afterward [sic—in 1883] retired from the army, achieving considerable note as a civil engineer. He was the original [model] of "Jack Truscott" in *The Colonel's Daughter* and other stories by [later Brigadier] General Charles King.

In the first paragraph, "you" refers to General King, to whom the original manuscript was addressed.

Not very long after you left Camp Verde to take your Indian bullet-broken arm to northern climes, I sought recreation by a few days trip to department headquarters at Fort Whipple, Arizona, three miles from

Prescott. Attended by my orderly and mounted on a good horse, I speedily passed over the forty miles. It being late in the afternoon upon my reaching there, I decided not to dismount until I had formally reported my presence to General Crook. As I rode across the parade ground, I noticed that everything was very quiet and the only soldier to be seen was a sentry on a distant post. I dismounted and knocked at the general's door.

"I am indeed glad to see you," he said grasping my hand, "for I am greatly in need of getting a message through to the commanding officer at Camp Beale Springs. A bad Indian outbreak between here and the San Francisco mountains has called out all the infantry and cavalry from this post, and with the Wallapais (Hualapais, perhaps) at Camp Beale Springs reported restless, it is vital that I get orders to the commanding officer there."

He said he disliked to order me to go as "it would be impossible to get enough men together to furnish me with even a half-way decent escort."

I said, "I'll go, and perhaps I will not need any escort."

He said, "Do you mean to chance it all alone? There is much chance for Indians to pick up a single man."

I said, "Yes, true, but a single man not traveling over usual trails and quietly going through a more or less wooded country, might slip through without encountering any Indians."

"Just what have you in mind?" he asked.

I explained, "The locations of the traveled train between Camp Beale Springs and this point, over which the paymaster comes with heavy escort of soldiers, has long been a source of unspoken query to me. I have been over it, and also stood at both ends and gazed across and wondered.

"As you know, general, the trip from here to Camp Beale Springs is a long wearisome journey of a full day over a comparatively level country. But the trail followed as a whole, is in the shape of a gigantic oxbow, with the two ends represented by Camp Beale Springs and Whipple Barracks. From your front window we can look across the open end of the oxbow and see the general location of Camp Beale Springs and it is surely not more than one-third of the distance across to it than it is around the traveled trail. Now there likely is a reason why the long distance trail was first used, but I have often wondered if the fates would not permit me the opportunity of attempting to get straight across from one point of the oxbow to the other—and it seems this is my opportunity, with your permission."

"I am of course glad to give it," he said, "and all good luck go with you. As to the country you will pass over, I have no idea, but if it is a rough and almost impassible country you are not likely to encounter Indians there. I am glad indeed that you do not propose to go the regular trail because Indians surely would be lying in wait to pick up any unfortunate settlers who unsuspectingly came along."

At daylight next morning before any movement in camp, I started with Winchester rifle and a belt full of cartridges, a canteen of water, and a far from fresh horse to brave the uncertainties. To aid me in pursuing a straight line was the landmark of Cross Mountain, far away to the north, so named because of snow lying in deep ravines on its side taking the form of a cross of white against a dark background.

In ten minutes time I was traversing a wild but level open glade with scattered trees and no underbrush to impede the horse's fast walk. Things were going well for perhaps a half hour, when in front of and to right angles of my course appeared a very black streak of ground seemingly hardly three or a few more inches high. That I knew by Arizona experience was the very top line of a dreaded box canyon. This section of Arizona is covered by a sheet of lava perhaps 300 feet deep. In the ages that have passed since this lava cooled, earthquakes had split this sheet like glass from top to bottom here and there (mostly here), leaving the vertically torn apart sides fifty to a hundred feet across at the top. These cracks might extend for miles. Strange to say, these box canyons, as they were called, were mostly parallel with each other, so that if one was laboriously crossed, a few yards further progress might bring the traveler to a place where he could gaze at the distant bottom of a duplicate to that just painfully negotiated.

There was no way to get across the first box canon I met save to lead my horse either up or down the ridge in search of some place, perhaps a mile or so out of my way, where the side wall had for some reason partly broken down, at least sufficiently so to enable me to lead my horse down to the bottom without damage to him or myself. Once in the bottom, I must follow along in similar fashion to find a place where I could scramble out. This I did, and only lost about two miles, but I had hardly resumed my general direction when I met another box canyon. This part of my journey is covered by saying I had to cross a regular series of such canyons, all of which used up hours of time and lots of physical and mental energy. But after a while I felt I was safely through that formation, and I tried to think that with distant Cross Mountain still showing white in the midday sun, that while I had surely found the answer to my problem of why the trail went around instead of across the oxbow, yet at least I had not been molested in my investigation.

But just then a serious discovery was made. The forenoon's hot sun poured down through the scattered trees upon us, and there was not a breath of air stirring. My horse and then myself were a reek of perspiration and we both suffered for lack of water. My canteen had become very hot but the water was wet—while it lasted. From time to time I took a small mouthful from the canteen, moistened the inside of my mouth, and then spirited it directly into the nostrils of my horse. He shied from it at first, but soon got so he did not flinch in the least and it kept the dust out of his nostrils, which had begun to dry when perspiration ceased. We were in a bad way from thirst, but had reached a more level country, although the trees were very few now, and here and there small isolated and ragged buttes stuck up. There would be several of these buttes in sight at one time, perhaps a quarter mile or more away in front of me. Of course it was a part of my business to scan them very closely to see if any Indians might be lurking about them.

All at once I saw, or thought I saw, one of these sizable buttes distant a half mile or more, actually moving toward me. I said to myself, "You are a sane man and you know perfectly well that it is your thirst that plays this illusion upon you, and if you will summon all your will power and command that butte to be fixed in the ground where it belongs, it will obey you." Thus my intellect spoke, but when I summoned all my resolution and commanded that butte to "stand still," I did not have the luck that Joshua had with the sun, for the butte continued to come on, although fortunately it never reached me. All the buttes in sight by this time were moving toward me in like manner. I did not yield my mind to the illusion for a moment, and believe that the buttes did move, but I could not make my vision see them otherwise than as moving.

By this time, I was leading my horse, but I did not stop and continued to keep Cross Mountain in view, determined to keep on as long as could be. And so, without hardly knowing it, we passed out of the region of those buttes and into an area where the trees grew more thickly. Then, right on the edge of the new ground, we found water! A little spring welled up and a small rivulet led its water away, and around it were plenty of signs that animals of many sorts resorted here for water. It was difficult to control either my horse or myself, but I did have resolution enough to take the water very slowly, and if possible get perspiration started over our bodies before becoming gluttons. I did not like to take chances, but I did loosen the saddle girth, which several times I had tightened, to give the horse the best breathing possible, for it was necessary after a moderate rest and safely filling up with water. But it was astonishing how the water rejuvenated us. We actually moved away in mid-afternoon with some evidence of strength and spirit.

I estimated that if we could go in a straight line from this point to our destination I would not have more than twelve to eighteen miles to go and I hoped to get over that distance without trouble, although I was now nearing the old reservation of the Hualapais and almost anything might happen, for even General Crook did not know anything save that they had become restless because of other sub-tribes of Apaches being off their reservations. There could be no secrecy about my movements. It was a clear case of assuming that the Indians hunting trouble just were not there. And if they were off the reservation, obviously they were not on it, and there was little prospect of accomplishing killing or torture in its vicinity to tempt them to linger about. The only thing I had to fear was a chance encounter with a straying band of independent Indians, and that is just what I did run into.

I was pushing along at quite a fast walk, mounted this time, when as I was passing through a bit of low ground with a rising slope on my right, suddenly there appeared on its crest and leisurely coming toward me five Indians. Seeing me clearly was a great surprise to them. They had no squaws with them, which looked bad for me, as it might be a war party. They also had lots of paint on, but they seemed uncertain and somehow gave the idea they were footsore. They were about 300 yards away when I first saw them, and I motioned them with my hand to stop, and they did for the moment, but I did not stop and kept quietly urging my horse along to try to get beyond the point where they would cut me off if they continued in their present direction. I would have been glad to get away without any closer knowledge of them, and if they really were footsore I felt that my horse could outrun them into Camp Beale Springs.

But suddenly as I was quietly moving my horse along and thinking over these things, one of the Indians without any previous indication stepped out from his companions and took a quick shot at me, the bullet striking the ground near my horse. I already had my Winchester lying in the hollow of my left arm, and almost as quick has he fired, I pumped two shots, not at any single Indian but at the group of them as they stood in consultation, and they being on my right, I had to twist in my saddle to get in the shots I did. Evidently one of my shots at least struck something, for instantly they were dragging one at least apart, and in a moment each Indian was covered by a tree [sic]. It is a most remarkable thing why they did not, like any other Indians I ever saw, . . . at once seek cover and begin shooting at me. My horse was perfectly gun-shy and stood like a rock while I fired my two shots, but immediately after firing I was not interested in anything more there, and before the Indians could think or do very much shooting or anything else, I had started up my good horse for a race from there to Camp Beale Springs if they wanted it.

But I never saw any of them again and just about sundown I rode into Camp Beale Springs, inquired for the commanding officer, saluted, and said I had a packet that was directed to him for which at his leisure I would be glad to get his receipt. His response was: "Where on earth did you come from; how did you get through, and where is your escort?"

The Fight at Cibicu, 1881 (By Anton Mazzanovich, formerly of Troop F, Sixth U. S. Cavalry, relating the account of Sergeant John A. Smith, Troop D, Sixth U. S. Cavalry. From *Winners of the West*, April, 1925)

In 1871, General Grant, then president of the United States, called a council and powwow of some Indian chiefs and medicine men of the Southwest at Washington, D. C. Each Indian in attendance at that powwow was presented with a medal commemorating the occasion after smoking the pipe of peace. Among the medicine men who received one of these medals was Noch-ay-del-klinne, of the White Mountain Apaches. This same medal . . . was loaned to me by Sergeant John A. Smith, late of Troop D, Sixth U. S. Cavalry, who in 1881 was stationed at Fort Apache, Arizona. The medal was secured by Sergeant Smith under thrilling circumstances.

In the spring of 1881, affairs at the White Mountain Apache Reservation were becoming very serious. Medicine Man Noch-ay-del-klinne was going from camp to camp on the reservation telling the Indians that in August of that year all the Indians who had gone to the happy hunting grounds in the past would return to earth again and then the entire tribe were to meet in the Tonto Basin and start from there to wipe the hated paleface from the land. At every camp where the medicine man stopped the Indians held war dances, and nearly all of the bucks joined in as he went about endeavoring to foment trouble. At that time of year the agent would issue passes to the White Mountain and Chiricahua Apache tribes located at the White Mountain and San Carlos reservations, granting them permission to hunt in the Tonto Basin.

The Indians were holding nightly dances, which started at Apache then circulated to Cedar and Careisco creeks, eventually winding up at Cibicu Creek, which was located some fifty miles from Fort Apache. The regimental headquarters of the Sixth Cavalry were at Fort Apache, [and] Colonel Eugene A. Carr received orders from the department commander to start out and locate the troublesome medicine man of the White Mountain Apaches and bring him in as a prisoner. Colonel Carr was an officer with a most gallant record of long and distinguished service in the United States Army, having been conspicuous in the Civil War. . . . After the Civil War he participated in many campaigns against the Indians in Kansas, Nebraska, . . . Colorado[,] Wyoming, Montana, Dakota, and Arizona. He was conspicuously presented to the attention of the country by a gallant and successful defense against the attempted massacre of his command by the White Mountain Apaches at Cibicu Creek in August, 1881, because of the arrest and subsequent killing of the medicine man and prophet, Noch-ay-del-klinne.

Colonel Carr started to attempt the capture of this troublesome Apache with Troops D and E, Sixth Cavalry, and one company of Indian scouts. Troop D was commanded by Captain Edmund C. Hentig, noncommissioned sergeants John E. Blackburn and John A. Smith, and Corporals Burton and Bowman. Troop E was in command of First Lieutenant William Stanton and Second Lieutenant Thomas Cruse. Company A, Indian scouts, was commanded by Lieutenant Cruse, noncommissioned officers Dandy Jim, Dead Shot, and Skitashe and Mose. First Lieutenant William H. Carter was acting adjutant. The balance of the command consisted of Post Surgeon George McCreery; sixty-five enlisted men; twenty-five Indian scouts; Nat Nobles, boss packer; George Hurle, interpreter; Colonel Carr's son, Clark Carr, who was on his summer vacation, also was with the command.

After a vigorous march, this small column overtook the medicine man and his followers, who were camped on Cibicu Creek. They were just on the point of starting to hold a council when Colonel Carr's command arrived. Without wasting any time or mincing words, the medicine man was placed under arrest and three noncommissioned officers from the company of Indians scouts—Dandy Jim, Dead Shot, and Skitashe—were detailed to guard him.

Some days prior to this, it had been deemed advisable to withdraw the ammunition carried by the Indian scouts. Colonel Carr, however, thought it more judicious to have a plain talk with them and assume an air of confidence. No overt act had been committed by any of them, and in past years they had accompanied the troops on innumerable scouting expeditions, showing at all times courage, untiring energy, and vigilance. The object of the present expedition being explained to the scouts, their ammunition was returned to them. Chiefs Juh, Nana, and Sanchez asked Colonel Carr why the medicine man, Noch-ay-del-klinne, was placed under arrest. The colonel replied that his orders came from the War Department. He also advised the chiefs to go to their different camps on the reservation [and] settle down and behave themselves.

After making the arrest, Colonel Carr moved down the creek with Troop D to locate a good camping place for the night, leaving Troop E as rearguard to keep the Indians from crowding in. After crossing the creek a few miles below, the colonel located a good spot to bivouac. The horses of Troop D and the pack mules were sent out on herd. Meantime, many Indians had gotten past Troop E on the right and left flank and crowded in close. Captain Hentig thereupon ordered the interpreter to tell the Indians to keep away. They were in an ugly mood, however, and paid no attention to the order but continued crowding in closer than ever. It looked as if trouble was imminent and a fight likely to start at any moment. The Indians were coming to camp on horseback and on foot, all armed with the best of weapons.

Captain Hentig again ordered them away from his camp. He gave his orders in a loud and businessman-like tone of voice. He was standing near an Indian scout sergeant by the name of Mose. The latter exclaimed, "I am a soldier." The captain ordered him to move once. Mose slipped around behind the captain and shot him through the heart, killing him instantly. That single shot was the signal for the first volley, which was fired by most of the Indians, including the scout company, directly into the ranks of the small command. Troop E came dashing to the scene of actions, after which the troopers started hunting for cover. During the excitement, Dandy Jim and Skitashe tried to smuggle the medicine man away, but a bugler [trumpeter] from Troop D named William Ahrens pumped three bullets into his head from an army Colt.

Other troopers dashed in and disarmed the three scouts and placed them under arrest. The firing lasted about an hour. Sergeant Smith told me that Colonel Carr's son was in the thick of the fight and seemed in his element—a "chip off the old block"—and that he fought like a seasoned trooper. Those killed at the first volley included Captain Hentig and Privates Henry C. Bird [sic—Bird was wounded but died later], John Sullivan, William Miller, Edward D. Livingstone and Sonderegger. Those wounded were Sergeant John F. MacDonald and Privates Ludwig Baege and Thomas J. F. Foran [both of whom died later]. One man was reported missing. The horses of Troop D and also the pack train mules were stampeded and captured by the Indians. Colonel Carr assembled the officers under him and held a council of war. They decided to start for Fort Apache under cover of night. It was not learned if any Indians were killed during the fight or even wounded.

Sergeant Smith said that at the first volley the firing was at close range, and that undoubtedly some of the Apaches were killed. The first shot was fired at about 5 p.m. Scouting parties were sent out, composed of volunteers from each troop, in an effort to locate the Indians. Meantime, guard was mounted. Sergeant Smith was sergeant of the guard. A detail was burying the dead. The scouting detail returned with the information that the Indians were camped five miles south of the command. They were engaged in rounding up their stock from the creek bottoms.

Just as the men were placing the last body in the grave, Sergeant Smith observed the medicine man crawling about on the ground. He had not been killed, despite the fact that he had three bullets through his head. Not daring to shoot for fear of alarming the command, Smith grabbed an ax which had been carried along by the pack train and dispatched the wounded Apache. The sergeant said that it was a rather unpleasant method of sending the medicine man to the happy hunting grounds, but that it was the only way under the circumstances. As the sergeant knelt beside the body to make sure that life was extinct, he observed a beaded necklace and a large medal around the medicine man's neck. This medal and necklace he appropriated. The medicine man was then buried in the same shallow grave with the dead troopers.

At 11 o'clock that night, after everything had been put in good order and the wounded troopers placed in as comfortable positions as was possible, the march to Fort Apache was begun. It was a terrible journey, as the hostiles followed the small command all the way in, harassing them at every opportunity. It must be remembered that half the command were on foot, taking turns about at riding with those of the command which were mounted. The command reached the post without any further casualties. Private Foran of Troop D, who had been seriously wounded, died a few hours after reaching the post. Sergeant John A. Smith is now [1925] living in Burnett, Washington. He is sixty-nine years of age and the only white man in possession of a medal . . . [as described.] The dies for the medal were engraved by Paquet, who at that time (1871) was assistant engraver at the United States Mint in Philadelphia. . . .

Notes on the Cibicu Creek Fight and the Fight at Fort Apache (By William Baird, formerly captain, Sixth U. S. Cavalry. From *Winners of the West*, April, 1925)

I am seventy-three years old, and the hardships and exposures of the service in Arizona and all over the West in the "early days" have left me not very robust. . . . I brought into old Fort Apache the bones of Captain Edmund C. Hentig and the men who were killed in the Cibicu Creek fight with him. That was about a year after the battle. The bodies had been dug up by the Indians, as they had been buried hurriedly when the command under Colonel Eugene A. Carr had to retreat to Fort Apache to look after the women and children, as very few troops had been left there. The bodies had been buried under the picket line, hoping the tramping of the horses would hide their graves and prevent the Indians from mutilating them. But you know you can't fool an Apache. Afterwards they were buried again. I think the Indians dug them up twice. I took out a small detachment of B Troop, Sixth U. S. Cavalry, and we brought the bones in on pack mules, using gunny sacks to carry the remains in to the post, where they were again interred with full military honors in the post cemetery. . . .

[Regarding the fight at Fort Apache on January 9, 1876,] William Gurnett belonged to Captain William S. Worth's Company K, Eighth U. S. Infantry, in 1875, when I first joined from West Point. He could write you a story about that fight on January 9, 1876, in which both he and myself were "among those present." Indeed, I helped to get him recognition after many years for his part in it. He shot Diablo when the Indians fired into the post. My duty consisted in rallying and leading a part of the command up the hills against the renegades, as I was the only officer in the post when the sudden outbreak occurred down at the Indian scouts' camp, all the other officers having gone down there. D Troop, Sixth Cavalry, was hurried down in their stable clothes with their carbines from the afternoon stables when the first shot was fired. All officers were cut off from the post for quite a while. The commanding officer's horse came galloping back covered with blood, so things were pretty lively for a while.

Major General William H. Carter of Bluemont, Virginia, who was [then a second lieutenant] in the Sixth Cavalry, was acting adjutant at the Cibicu fight. He received a Medal of Honor for rescuing men in that fight. His wife was with Mrs. Mary Carr at Fort Apache when the general outbreak occurred. There were very few troops left at the post and Colonel Carr had to retreat back there in a hurry to protect women, children, and settlers.

Campaigning in Arizona in the 1880s (By John E. Murphy, formerly of Company C, Twelfth U. S. Infantry. From *Winners of the West*, June, 1924)

I have a horrible recollection of Indian disturbances, having served three years in Arizona after going through the Sioux Campaign in 1876, where we lost more men in one battle in less than one hour's fighting than the New Hampshire troops lost killed outright in battle during the World War. I refer to what is known as the Custer Massacre.

Speaking now of the years I spent in Arizona, one might say it was three years of continuous war. The first thing I got was a 500-mile walk from Fort Yuma in the southwest to Fort Apache in the northeast. How is that for a hike in the Arizona sun in the summer month of July? At that time the Apache chief Victorio was overrunning New Mexico and the eastern part of Arizona. Troops were brought in from surrounding sections and he and his followers took flight down into Old Mexico, where the American troops were [mostly] barred from entering.

Then the White Mountain Apaches took the warpath [in 1881]. They put up a good fight, and if the fight had commenced early in the day it might have been what the papers, when they got the news, said it was. The papers in the East came out in great headlines saying: "Another Custer Massacre. Gen. Carr and His Whole Command Wiped Out." But Carr pulled out in the night and got back to Fort Apache where the Indians surrounded the fort the next morning. [At Cibicu,] the Indian scouts with the command deserted and fought with their tribe. The whole Indian outfit was taken in time. Some of the Indian scouts were shot to death and more of them sent to prison. The War Department had all the say about the scouts. But the main body of Indians always were turned over to the Interior Department, where they got new blankets, and when they arrived back on the reservation found that their women and children had been well taken care of.

Here, in order to give the public an idea of Indian cruelty, I'll state a nerve-stirring scene. At the top of what was called Seven Mile Hill we came onto a Mormon outfit that was on its way from Utah to settle in Arizona. They were all butchered by the noble red men. All except one old man who put up a gallant fight for his life. But at last he was overpowered by the redskins, who bound him to a wagon wheel and burnt him to death. That was their way of honoring a brave enemy, so we were told by Mr. Indian after their capture. Anyhow, all that was left of the old man were his iron pant buttons. I bear witness to that, as I was the one who picked the buttons out of the ashes.

In the spring of ' 82 I was stationed at Camp Thomas on the Gila River, near the San Carlos Indian Reservation. [It was] a two-company post, one troop of cavalry and one company of infantry. Everybody has heard of Geronimo, the old Apache chief, and his war party of Chiricahua Indians that left San Carlos Reservation and took the war trail. Something the Indians never did before was to cut the telegraph wire, as they considered them bad medicine. Well, old Jerry Mo, as we called him, cut the wire running between Camp Thomas and Fort Apache. This wire was cut right in the center of the reservation. Two troops of cavalry had passed by where the wire was cut, but being on what was called a hot trail, gave it the go-by. To make a long story short, I was sent out to connect that wire. The chances were against a man getting back alive. I was to strike the outskirts of the reservation at nightfall, connect the wire and get off the reservation before daybreak, as it was considered sure death to be seen by any of the Indians. I did it all right, but what the poor regular army enlisted man does is never told in song or story. My friend, Charles Willey, now of Belmont, this state [New Hampshire], who stood in the bunch and saw me go out, well remembers what I said to him as I started: "Well, Willey, if the Indians get me, when you get back to Concord just tell them that you saw me."

The Fight at Black Mesa, 1882 (By Earl S. Hall, formerly of Troop D, Third U. S. Cavalry. From *Winners of the West*, March, 1924)

Speaking of hardships experienced by "regulars" in Indian war times in the covered wagon days, I wish to relate just one campaign in Arizona by Major Andrew W. Evans, commanding our troops. I was with Troop D, Third Cav., Albert D. King (now deceased), captain; George A. Dodd, First Lieut.; Franklin O. Johnson, Second Lieut. Dodd had command of thirty Indian scouts. Keog, an old westerner, who could talk Apache and was able to handle the Indians, was chief of scouts.

The campaign lasted but two weeks, but was a forced march from first to last owing to the serious necessity of overtaking a band of renegades who had deserted the U. S. service, taking the guns and ammunition and other supplies with them, and had gone on the warpath, stealing stock, murdering ranchmen and their families. Many a burned ranch was evidence of their depredations. [I have] no language to fitly describe the torture of this short campaign. The Indians chose the most impassable trail known to them in order to impede, if possible, or delay our pursuit, to enable them to make a "getaway." They failed to fully realize the relentless determination and courage of their pursuers and the added incentive caused by their atrocities.

On our march, we were undergoing intense heat, often 130 above, following dangerous and narrow trails up and down mountains, sometimes on the march sixteen hours a day, our tongues swollen in our mouths for lack of water, with every stitch of our clothing saturated with perspiration, as if drenched by a "cloudburst." Hardtack for diet. Well, on 17th July 1882 (Sunday) our advance scouts struck them. A volley first apprised us of this fact, although we already were prepared to meet them any moment because of the live coals in the last burned ranch, and other signs. Command was quickly given to dismount and link horses. Each set of fours allowed No. 4 horse to hold horses 1, 2, 3 of each set, [and] went into action at the front. The Sixth or Gray Horse Cavalry, deployed to the right. The third or Bay Horse Cavalry, of which I was a member, deployed to the left in skirmish line. The Indians at sight of us retreated to top of mountains about 400 yards distant as the "bullet flies." Command was given to charge down through the intervening valley and up against them where they had hastily entrenched themselves. The mountain range [sic] was called Black Mesa . . . one of the Mogollon range.

Not a man faltered, although all were staggering with exhaustion and intense heat. Not a shot was fired by us as we ascended the mountain, although [we remained] a target for the Indians. When we reached the top the Indians retreated after a short time to the heavy timber and rocky ravines which furnished a good hiding place and natural fortress. We closed in on them slowly but steadily, keeping up a well-directed fire on them or where we reckoned they were. After about five hours fighting against an almost invisible enemy, [with] darkness approaching, we rested on our arms—that is five of us—Lieutenant Johnson, Paddy Maher, Mike Devlin, Frank Lenke and myself. We held a strategic point of the battlefield all night while the balance of the troops retired further away (we were accidentally forgotten) and pretty near froze to death that night, although the temperature was over 100 above in the daytime.

Left alone on the battlefield, we did not feel very optimistic when we heard a great hubbub among the Indians, the noise increasing indicating that they were coming head-on toward our position. We opened fire on them in the darkness—this changed their course slightly, and perhaps saved our lives, as if they had run into us pellmell and discovered our number we would have been five more dead heroes—Winners of the West. At daybreak, Major Evans trumpeted over to us from the retired position of the main command, expressing surprise that any of the troops were on the battlefield and still alive. Lieutenant Johnson explained the cause of our position. Orders were given to explore the surroundings and the Indian scouts and we five "Casibiancas" moved forward, reinforced soon by the main command.

We were pretty sure that the Indians had vamoosed during the night (what was left of them). It is only fair and just to state here that owing to the natural features of the ground that it was most impossible to intercept the Indians' getaway, especially at night. The battlefield did not present much a different spectacle from the usual ones of this kind, excepting the wounded Indians died fighting. Not that we wantonly killed them, but they knew no other mode of warfare and expected no quarter, especially as they were "renegades." Therefore, as they spied us coming they opened fire, which we returned. One squaw and a little papoose is all we captured alive. The squaw had been wounded and our surgeon amputated her limb. The band was completely broken up and scattered and 250 head of stolen stock returned to their owners by our command.

After we returned to Fort Apache we weighed ourselves and approximately the average weight of the men had been decimated fifteen pounds or an average of one pound per day per man. Excepting the casualties of killed and wounded, no serious results followed our exposure. But I've often thought it was a kill or cure dose physical culture.

Certificate of Merit for Combat in New Mexico, 1885 (By Sylvester Grover, formerly of Troop C, Fourth U. S. Cavalry. From *Winners of the West*, December 30, 1925)

In October, 1885, I was stationed at Lang's Ranch, New Mexico [Territory], directly on the line of the panhandle of New Mexico and the Mexican State of Chihuahua. On the 9th of that month, I was ordered, with Private Hickman, Troop F, Fourth Cavalry, to carry dispatches which had arrived from Captain Emmet Crawford, in Mexico, to Brigadier General George Crook, at Fort Bowie, Arizona Territory. We left about 11 o'clock a.m. and put up for the night at a ranch about forty miles from our starting point. Next morning before daybreak we started off and traveled at good speed towards Cowboy Pass. The country through which we passed is perfectly level, except [for] piles of rocks called Mal Pais, with which the plain is covered and through which the road winds. None of these piles are more than the height of a man and horse, and we had a good view of the country around us and had no idea that any hostile Indians were in the vicinity, as the last we heard of them located them below the national boundary.

About 9 o'clock a.m., while passing near one of these rock piles, we were suddenly fired upon by about fourteen Indians, who upon delivering the fire suddenly rose up around us. Hickman fell at once from his horse, dead, as I found out afterwards. My horse dashed away with me and got about five hundred yards when he fell dead. I dragged myself from the saddle, got the dispatches out of the saddlebags, and with my carbine crawled to a pile of rocks about twenty yards off. I could see part of the Indians chasing Hickman's horse, and the rest followed me up on foot. I opened fire on them at once and held them at bay. They did not know that I was wounded, and to that fact I undoubtedly owe my life.

After the Indians caught Hickman's horse, they all made a break at me. I fired as fast as my wounds would let me, and at last had the satisfaction of seeing them leave toward the mountains, which gave me a chance to look at my wounds. I found that I was shot through the fleshy part of the thigh below the hip, and through the left wrist and hand. For over two hours and a half I was lying under a burning sun, without water, and I felt that my last moments were coming when I saw a wagon approaching. With it were seven citizens, some of whom were discharged government scouts and packers. I called out as well as I could, and managed to make them hear me at last. They stopped, brought me water, washed my wounds, and made me as comfortable as possible, and brought me to the post hospital at Fort Bowie.

Hickman was shot in seven places. The Indians did not mutilate his body, only took off his belts. I have since recovered entirely from my wounds, and through the recommendation of my captain have been awarded a Certificate of Merit by the President of the United States.

The Campaign against Geronimo (By Henry W. Daly, formerly Chief Packer, U. S. Army. From *Winners of the West*, December 30, 1933)

In March of 1885 I was ordered from Fort Apache to Whipple Barracks, at Prescott, to take charge of the pack train at the headquarters of the Department of Arizona. I found the mules run down. The clerks at headquarters had been riding them into Prescott to take in the sights of the town. Not that the sights of Prescott were any great shakes in the view of a young fellow looking for a little excitement. There were saloons aplenty and wide open gambling, but Prescott had the name of a quiet place by the standards of the West of that day and date.

By April the pack train was in condition to take into the field. Brigadier General George Crook and a small party went to the Grand Cataract, a tributary to the Grand Canon of the Colorado, to settle a little Indian trouble between the Havasupai and the Moqui [Hopi] tribes. This business was so soon over that the excursion turned into an outing more than anything else, much appreciated by me after a winter of sleeping under a roof for the first time regularly in a good many years. In May we were at Whipple, with nothing but garrison duty to pass the time. For nearly eighteen months now, the Apaches, the terrors of the Southwest, had trod the white path—that is, had been at peace. A long and bloody road indeed had been traveled to this end, and it had been my fortune to have traveled most of it in person, serving through the Tonto Basin War of 1872-74, the Mescalero Outbreak of '79 and '80, the Warm Spring campaigns against Victorio and Nana in '80, '81, and '82, and the Sierra Madre Campaign that wound up with the surrender of Naiche in the fall of '83. . . .

My professional acquaintance with Geronimo was made during the Sierra Madre Campaign against Naiche, head chief of the Chiricahuas, the most blood-thirsty of the Apache clans. This campaign took place in northern Mexico, where by special arrangement we were permitted to pursue the Chiricahuas. This campaign brought Go-yath-lay, or Geronimo as he was known by the whites, to the fore as a war leader. Geronimo was then no longer a young man, being forty, I should say, and about medium tall. His frame was well-muscled and, like those of most of the Apaches, capable of fabulous endurance. The countenance of Geronimo was the most arresting I have ever seen on a human being. There was in it a look of unspeakable savagery, or fierceness, and yet the signs of an acute intelligence were also present. Geronimo was of a nervous type, which is, or was, rather rare among Indians. His countenance was mobile rather than mask-like. When he was mad he simply looked like the devil and an intelligent devil at that. This type of leader was well calculated to advance himself under Naiche, an able Indian but a loafer when he could find a subordinate capable of assuming his responsibilities.

Three weeks after our return to Whipple, the humdrum of past life was interrupted by the startling news that a band of Chiricahuas under Naiche with Geronimo as war chieftain had left the reservation near Fort Apache and were making a trail of blood across Arizona headed for their hangout in the Sierra Madres of Old Mexico. There is, I think, still some mystery as to the cause of this outbreak. My diary, kept during the sixteen months of the campaign that followed, gives a simple and I think the correct explanation of it. The lieutenant in charge of the Chiricahua reservation was an excellent young man, but untrained in dealing with Apaches. He won the friendship of Chatto, a rival of Geronimo, which in itself was a good thing, except that the matters were so tactlessly handled that Geronimo became jealous and took the warpath to avenge himself.

An Indian chief was as proud as Lucifer and that always has to be borne in mind. It is an error to assume that because of their ignorance of the ways of civilization they were of a childlike order of intelligence and that their feats in war were due mainly to superior physical endurance. Most Indian leaders I have known or observed were equals mentally of the white leaders with whom they dealt, and as often as otherwise they were superior. This statement applies to the old-time Indian in his semi-primitive state. One of life's mysteries to me is the way civilization has blunted the native intelligence of the Indian.

Two expeditions entered Mexico after the hostiles, one on the Chihuahua, or eastern, slope of the Sierra Madre range, and one on the western, or Sonora side. I served with the latter, under command of Captain Emmet Crawford, the best Indian fighter I have ever known. His force consisted of Troop A of the Sixth Cavalry, numbering forty-five men, ninety-two Indian scouts, with the celebrated Al Sieber as chief of scouts, and three pack trains with two months' supplies. I had charge of one of these trains. Crossing the border at Black Springs, south of Tombstone, on June 12, a nine days' march (during which the temperature reached 120 degrees in the shade, and no shade, as the saying was) brought us into camp in the foothills of a spur of the Sierra Madres, a hundred miles below the line. To the east toward the Sierra Madres proper, their summits high above the fleecy clouds that hugged the slopes of the foothills—a truly inspiring scene, and I find in my diary a glowing description of it [sic]. But after our throat-parching march, what we appreciated most was a rivulet that cascaded down the timber-clad crags; its water seemed literally as cold and clear as ice.

Little time was left to admire the beauties of nature, however. The scouts spread out to feel for signs of the hostiles and on June 23rd they had a small fight, capturing twelve squaws and children, two full-grown boys, and the aged chief Nana. They were sent back to Arizona under guard, and we broke camp and pulled out in the wake of the scouts on a trail that led straight up into the Sierras. A few days later there was another small fight, and we pressed on with all possible speed in the hope of a decisive engagement. With each day's travel the going became more rugged. The dense growth of pine shut out the daylight. Steep descents and steeper ascents were made more difficult by fallen timbers. It will suffice here to summarize briefly the remainder of the history of this particular expedition, which is only remarkable for its marches, as we did not get Geronimo. The Indians lured us more deeply into the mountains. Our maps were worthless. The cavalry horses and the men were worn out, and the clothing of us all was in tatters. Captain Crawford sent me back to the border for more supplies. By trail this was a journey of four hundred miles. On my return in August, I found that he had also sent the cavalry troop back, deeming it useless in such country. The hostiles were in the Sierra Madres proper, where no military expedition had ever attempted pursuit. Nevertheless, Crawford pursued them with his scout company and two pack trains.

I would not attempt to say how many times I have crossed the mountains by trail from Canada to Mexico, but this was the most notable feat in that line of my experience. We crossed the Sierra Madres from the Sonora to the Chihuahua side, being, I understand, the first white persons to do so in that region. We made it in fifteen days without losing a man or a mule, though there were some narrow squeaks. We got fairly close to Geronimo a few times, but that was all. A party of scouts under Second Lieutenant Charles P. Elliott preceded us down the eastern slope. Arriving at the town of Casa Grande, they told the authorities that they had come over the Sierra Madres. They were told that no one had ever crossed those mountains and were locked up until the arrival of the main body under Captain Crawford confirmed their story. Geronimo's trail had been lost and the expedition turned north, arriving at Fort Bowie, Arizona, in mid-September.

In my article, "Scouts Good and Bad," published in the *American Legion Monthly* for August, 1928, I described the expedition, headed by Captain Crawford, which conducted the [1885-86] winter campaign that almost resulted in the capture of Geronimo. . . . [During this expedition,] Captain Crawford was shot—perhaps by Dutchy, one of his own scouts—during an engagement with Mexican troops who attacked his Indians under the impression they were Geronimo's own band. Geronimo's braves, warned through treachery, had scattered before the Mexican attack took place. I rejoined Crawford's command just after this episode. The unconscious captain was sheltered in the one "A" tent. I was alone at his side at two in the morning, the only white man awake. Presently I heard a low hum of voices and a padding of moccasined feet outside. The ashes of a fire were stirred into a small blaze. I peered out, and imagine my astonishment when the flickering light revealed the unmistakable countenance of Geronimo, talking and signing to some of our scouts. He was not alone. I recognized Naiche, Chihuahua, Josanna, and one or two others. It was a weird scene. A few yards away, rolled in their blankets, slumbered the few white men of our command. The Indians talked for a long time, one speaking at a time, Indian fashion. Now and then one would stand up, pull his calico blanket closer about him, and sit again. From signs and glances in the direction of the "A" tent, I learned that, among other things, Geronimo was inquiring as to the condition of Captain Crawford.

Just before dawn, the hostiles departed and when the camp was awake I informed First Lieutenant Marion P. Maus of what had happened. About noon, Geronimo and his chiefs reappeared and asked for a conference with the lieutenant. The result was an arrangement for a meeting between Geronimo and General Crook at the Canon de los Embudos, about twenty-five miles south of the border. Geronimo had become convinced that his position between the Mexican and American forces was untenable, and he chose to make terms with us. Five days later, Crawford breathed his last on the march, and three days after that we laid him to rest in the sun-baked little village graveyard at Nacori, Sonora, while a parcel of goats browsed among the wooden crosses. There was no service, and for the want of a bugle, no "Taps," but we moistened the earth with our tears and, kneeling in the dust, repeated in unison "The Lord's Prayer." We moved on up toward the Canon de los Embudos and camped not far from the camp of Geronimo to await the coming of General Crook.

Matters were almost at the breaking point when on March 2, 1886, the scouts shouted news of the arrival of General Crook and party. On his saddle mule, Apache, the general rode at the head of the procession with his busy beard in two braids. The Gray Fox was the name the Apaches had given to General Crook, and when they saw him with his beard in braids they knew he meant business. A council ground was selected by representatives of both sides and the parties of General Crook and Geronimo took their places in a semi-circle. Squatting on the ground, Geronimo began his address. He spoke with fire and eloquence. I have never heard a trained orator make a more moving presentation of a case that rested on such flimsy foundations.

General Crook listened with impassive countenance and eyes fixed upon the ground. Amid perfect silence, General Crook spoke. He ridiculed the pretensions of Geronimo, which is the surest way to discountenance an Indian. He wound up by saying unconditional surrender was all that he would consider, and if Geronimo did not accept those terms, "I will keep after you until the last one of you is killed, if it takes fifty years." Geronimo was bitter. An Indian dearly loves to parley for terms. For two days the

Indians debated the situation among themselves, roaring drunk on mescal. Finally, Geronimo, with bad grace, and with a mind inflamed by cactus whiskey, decided to surrender. The terms were stiff and included two years of exile on the Atlantic seaboard before being allowed to return to Arizona.

When this was accomplished, General Crook returned to Fort Bowie, leaving Lieutenant Maus to bring in the prisoners. That night Geronimo got drunk. He was in no shape for the trail the next day. We covered little ground that day, but next morning got an early start with the prospect of reaching the border by nightfall. This hope, however, was promptly disappointed. Geronimo and his people were marching in front of us. In the mid-forenoon, they halted and prepared to camp, explaining that they were "tired." Then and there, I made up my mind that Geronimo was playing a game and so informed Lieutenant Maus. The Chiricahuas were encamped in two parties—Geronimo on the top of a small mesa, and Chihuahua, his subordinate, at the foot of it. We packers made a camp about fifty yards from Chihuahua's camp in such a way as to prevent a surprise or meet an attack. From my experience with Apache tactics, I did not like the look of things. That night I outlined a plan of resistance to the packers in case of attack.

With our entire camp asleep, I got the lead or bell horse of the pack train and quietly led him around in the rear of Geronimo's camp and put him to graze. Pack loads are borne by mules, but the file is always led by a horse. A mule will follow a horse, but will not follow another mule. Any stir in Geronimo's camp would send the bell horse trotting back to where I was and I would know that something was up. Having posted my bell horse, I lay down with rifle and ammunition handy, but purposely kept awake. At about three o'clock I thought I heard a faint tinkle of the horse bell. Placing the palm of one hand to the ground and pressing an ear to it, I could hear distinctly the bell and the trample of horses' feet. The bell was drawing nearer. With rifle in hand, I aroused Lieutenant Maus. The bell horse was now coming our way as fast as he could travel. The packers were awake and one of my men, Willis Brown, came running in from a brief reconnaissance. "Geronimo's gone!" he shouted. Geronimo and Naiche with seventeen braves, fourteen squaws, and four children had skipped toward the Sierra Madres. Chihuahua with something like eighty people of all ages remained.

Second Lieutenant Samson L. Faison, with a large part of our force, took Chihuahua into Fort Bowie while Lieutenant Maus led the pursuit of Geronimo. The chase was of short duration, as it was evident that he had made good his escape into the mountains. It would take another expedition to get him, and so we retraced our steps toward the line, arriving at Fort

Bowie on April third [1886]. I shall pass over several painful incidents that happened after our return. Suffice to say that Brigadier General Nelson A. Miles succeeded Crook in command of the Arizona Department, and with great energy began assembling troops for the capture of Geronimo and his handful of followers. The intrepid Apache gave the new commander a warm reception. Leaving his squaw camp in charge of one or two bucks, with seventeen fighting men he made two remarkable forays into Arizona. Slipping from mountain range to plain and from plain to range, making unbelievable marches, passing in front of, behind, and between pursuing forces, he fought two skirmishes with regular troops, one with the Tucson Rangers, and after keeping our entire army in that part of the world and a large part of the citizenry on the run for forty days, retired back into Mexico with the loss of but one man, and he a deserter.

On June sixth, Geronimo re-crossed into Mexico for the last time. The principal force of pursuit consisted of infantry, and what was more helpless than infantry, dismounted cavalry, under command of Captain Henry W. Lawton, Fourth Cavalry. They had with them a few Indian scouts, ably directed by Tom Horn. The wisdom of sending a force of this character into a difficult and unfamiliar country to pursue the Bedouins of Geronimo is obscure to me to this day. In company with First Lieutenant Abiel L. Smith and Billing Long, a dispatch rider, I was ordered to join this command. On July 29th, we met up with it in camp about a hundred miles, as a bird flies, below the border and fifteen miles south of the lonely hamlet of Nacori, where we had buried Captain Crawford. The force was in a sorry condition. Captain Lawton immediately summoned me to his tent where he spread his maps on a blanket. Explaining what had taken place in my absence, he asked the opinion of Tom Horn and myself as to where the hostiles might be. As it developed, we were both wrong—not that that made any great difference. With the command at his disposal, pursuit of Geronimo in force would have been futile no matter where he was.

On my arrival at Lawton's camp, I was suffering greatly from sciatica, due to sleeping in wet clothing and blankets. The pain was so intense that Dr. Leonard Wood gave me a dose of morphine and said I would have to return to Arizona, as campaigning would aggravate the trouble. I started back that day, Captain Lawton jokingly telling me to inform General Miles not to send him any more soldiers, as one might as well try to hunt Geronimo with a brass band. On my return march I met a troop of the Fourth Cavalry under, if I am not mistaken in the name of the officer, First Lieutenant James Parker. I directed him to Captain Lawton's camp. I was feeling so badly that I did not recognize First Lieutenant Charles B. Gatewood, Sixth Cavalry, who was with the party. Had I done so I would have entertained higher expectations for the success of the expedition than then filled my mind. The death of Captain Crawford left Gatewood the best versed officer of our army in the subtleties of Apache diplomacy. His selection to join Lawton meant a radical change in the Miles policy of all force and no parley with the hostiles.

Shortly after Gatewood reached Lawton, a report was received at the camp of Geronimo's presence in the vicinity of Fronteras, seventy miles to the northward. With his chief of scouts contending that Geronimo could be found south of the camp, with me contending for the east and now with this report from the north, Captain Lawton was in a quandary such as had been responsible for the indecision of more than one pursuer of the slippery Apache. Taking Tom Horn and six Indian scouts, Gatewood set out for Fronteras. After long marches and a series of skillful maneuvers which included the outwitting of Mexican officials, Lieutenant Gatewood finally achieved a meeting with Naiche and Geronimo. He said that General Miles's terms were unconditional surrender and exile in Florida. Geronimo said he would fight to the last rather than accept, but Naiche was not so belligerent. Gatewood had made effective use of the fact that the mother and daughter of Naiche were already in Florida. This fact resulted in a second parley at which Geronimo capitulated, one of the stipulations being that Gatewood should march, eat, and sleep with the hostiles until they reached Arizona. He did this, and twice forestalled attempts by men of Troop B, Sixth Cavalry, to kill Geronimo in revenge for a defeat the year before. These circumstances and others caused strained relations between Gatewood and Captain Lawton.

On August 31, 1886, Lawton's command and the hostiles reached Skeleton Cañon, in Arizona. On the evening of September 3rd, General Miles and escort arrived and went into camp. Geronimo mounted his horse and presented himself at the tent of the American commander. A lengthy conference took place, and on the following day Naiche, as the titular head of the Chiricahua Apaches, formally surrendered his band, which, if I remember rightly, numbered twenty-seven persons of both sexes, including three papooses. Thus ended the last of the Apache campaigns, sixteen months in duration, and requiring the entire military forces of Arizona, New Mexico, and western Texas to overcome a foe which never numbered as many as eighty fighting men. In a plentiful distribution of honors among the victors, it is a matter of regret to record that Lieutenant Charles B. Gatewood received no recognition, though it must be that there are men now living who will agree with me that no one did more than he to bring Geronimo in.

The Fight in Guadaloupe Canyon, 1885 (By Emil Pauly, formerly sergeant, Troop I, Fourth U. S. Cavalry. From *Winners of the West*, September, 1938)

According to a memorandum in my possession, the fight at Guadaloupe Canyon[, Arizona Territory,] occurred on June 8, 1885. On that day our squadron, consisting of Troop B—Captain Henry W. Lawton; Troop D, Captain Charles A. P. Hatfield; and Troop I, Captain Abram E. Wood, were camped at Cloverdale Ranch. By direction of Captain Lawton, who was the senior officer commanding the squadron, Troop I, of which I was a member, was ordered to scout the San Simon Valley, as there were reports of an Indian raid in that region. We picked up the trail that afternoon and as it seemed to point towards our supply camp, we rode at a trot and gallop until dark. Resuming our march the following morning, we entered Guadaloupe Canyon at about 8 o'clock a.m., and as we came around a bend of the canyon a gruesome sight met our eyes. Not a vestige was left of the wagon train, excepting the tires, bolts, and nuts. The grass had caught fire and burned over a great part of the canyon. Blue dots near the canyon walls indicated the location of our slain comrades, whom we buried with military honors.

After the surrender of Geronimo at Skeleton Canyon, September, 1886, we escorted him and his band to Fort Bowie, Arizona. It was there I met Private John Schnitzer. I asked him to give me the details of this affair, and after a lapse of over half a century I will try and be as accurate as my memory will permit. Quote: "It was about noontime when Cook Oscar Niehouse, Troop D, Fourth Cavalry, called out, 'Come and get it!' Everyone got their mess kits and started for the cook tent to get their dinner, including the man on picket duty on the north wall of the canyon, leaving no one on guard. I was about halfway to the cook tent when the firing started and of course we all rushed back to our tents to get our guns. The only protection we had were the covered army wagons, from behind which we fired, and they soon caught fire when someone evidently fired two close to the wagon cover of one of the wagons.

"About this time I thought of Sergeant Peter Munich, Troop G, Fourth Cavalry, who was very sick with pneumonia. I called Private William B. Jett to help me get the sick sergeant up the north side of the canyon, as he had already been wounded and was unable to walk. We got him nearly to the top when a bullet struck him in the back and he expired in my arms. Private Jett, George J. Schillinger, and I then got behind some rocks and started firing at the Indians, when the ammunition wagons exploded with terrific force. We held our position till late in the evening and then decided to take a chance and get into Cloverdale, which we reached late that night, pretty well exhausted."

When I came back to Arizona last year [1937], I intended to locate the graves of those slain in that fight. However, I was informed by [NIWV] Comrade William H. Kane, who served in Troop D, Fourth Cavalry, that the bodies were disinterred and shipped to Sawtelle, California, and buried in the national cemetery. . . .

After the Apaches, 1885-1886 (By Clarence B. Chrisman, formerly of Company F, Thirteenth U. S. Infantry. From *Winners of the West*, March 30, April 30, May 30, June 30, and July 30, 1927)

On September 22, 1885, three companies of the Thirteenth U. S. Infantry—F, D, and H,—and the regimental band, assembled in front of their quarters at Fort Wingate, New Mexico. The band was at the farther end of the row of quarters, and as it struck up an air and came marching by, the three companies fell in behind in their turn and were off to the time of a lively quickstep amid the cheers of the women and children and the remaining soldiers of the garrison. Little did we dream at that time that we were entering upon what would prove to be the longest, most exciting, and most arduous campaign that the white man ever carried on against his perpetual foe—the red man. Yet this turned out to be the case, for this campaign, from start to finish, lasted well over a year—almost two. And before it was over, two great Indian war generals were in command of it, and under these generals were thousands of the best soldiers of Uncle Sam's army, which is to say, the best soldiers the world ever saw.

That such soldiers were needed goes without saying, for they had to march hundreds of miles over hot and desolate sandy plains, almost utterly devoid of vegetation and water, and across ranges of mountains that seemed to pierce the very sky itself, often in midwinter through almost impenetrable drifts of snow and sheets of ice. And always with death hovering over, for no one knew at what moment he would fall the victim of an ambuscade, perhaps sent to his eternal rest by the noiseless arrow of his foe. Soon after the band had turned to one side and made its way back to its quarters, our real work began. For just back of Fort Wingate rises the range of the Zuni Mountains, and we found ourselves marching on the upgrade almost from the moment of leaving the fort. And I must say we were all rather soft at that time.

For a while there was some joking and talking, but soon it ceased, and the only sounds to be heard were the creaking of the wagon wheels of the supply train, the cracking of an occasional whip and the shuffle of our feet as we toiled wearily up this steep incline. The day was hot and the sun caught us fairly on that side of the mountain, and by the time we had reached a level place on the top of that immense plateau it seemed as though we had traveled a thousand miles. After a short rest the march was resumed, every one being cheered by the thought that we would soon be on the downgrade on the other side of the mountain and that would be easier. So it was, in a way, for we could have easily rolled down. But that would not have been very dignified. So we marched like the true soldiers we were, but every step on that steep declivity, weighted as we were with rifles and ammunition, seemed to drive our knee joints right up into our hips. But everything comes to an end, and finally we reached our first camp. . . .

I wish to call particular attention to the group of noncoms of Company F, ... for all of these men are to play an important part in the events which follow. All of this group were comparatively young men, the only one along in years being First Sergeant Downs, and next to him in point of age and service being Sergeant Maguire. This Maguire was a wonderful soldier, hardy as an oak, one of the best shots in the army and a man withal who held in contempt any sort of weakness. When he spoke, which was none too often, he drew down one corner of his mouth, and the words emanating from that particular corner sounded as though coming through exceedingly thick flannel. More about him later. . . .

On the particular campaign about which I am writing, I carried with me a little leather-backed notebook about four-by-six, and in this precious little volume I have a record of every march and every camp we made on that memorable campaign. And besides, as I was handy with a pencil, I made sketches of many of the camps and of scenes in the vicinity. It is doubtful if this had ever been done before on an Indian campaign, and at that time I had no idea in the world that many years later I would be consulting this little book for data concerning our trip. On the first page I find entered, "Camp 1, on the Nutri. Sept. 22, 1885." And under this heading, in part, appears the following: "Left Wingate about 11 a.m., marched to the beautiful valley of the Nutri and went into camp at 5:30 p.m. Our camp is beautifully situated at the foot of a high, rocky bluff, and nearby is a running stream of clear, cold spring water. This is what is called Nutri River, but it is nothing more or less than a babbling, rippling brook. I am on guard tonight, and it is 1:40 a.m. I am writing this by the light of our campfire, assisted by a full, bright moon. The coyotes are giving a serenade while I write, and their distant howl and grating yelp lend a dreariness to the lonely hour."

Although I made no entry of some of the incidents of our first camp, I remember distinctly how the fellows yanked off their shoes, good old heavy regulation government brogans, and began doctoring blisters and sore spots, and that night how we gathered around the campfires, some laughing, some singing, and some, especially the recruits (we had a bunch of raw ones with us) casting furtive glances at the dark woods surrounding us and up at the towering bluff, as though expecting any moment to hear the crack of firearms and the war-whoop of hostile Indians. But most of us gave no thought to such things, and we grouped about the fires exposing ourselves as openly and brazenly as though there were no Indians within a thousand miles.

Once a "rookie" voiced aloud his thought. "I wonder if we will get to fight any Indians?" Sergeant Maguire, happening to overhear him, said, "Don't worry, me bucko, you'll get plenty of fighting before this thing is over; and if you'll take my advice, you'll write to your best girl and your mamma this very night, and tell them goodbye while you have a chance." Down in our hearts, we older soldiers wished only that he was right.

Everything in this world goes by contrast. Sometimes you conclude you are having it pretty hard unless you happen to think of a time when you had it much harder. Up in those mountains it gets exceedingly cold at night, even in midsummer, and while I was on guard I could hear the fellows turning and groaning as they tried to keep warm under a blanket or two and find a soft spot on which to rest their weary bones. But the rocks of New Mexico are not noted for being soft. I couldn't help but think, listening to the occasional growl of some poor rookie, about the time some nine months previously, in the dead of winter with snow and ice piled all around me, I had made camp with several other soldiers in that identical spot. We were then on an expedition from Fort Wingate to Fort Craig, New Mexico, and had followed the backbone of the Rockies through snow and ice all the way.

Finally, some of the rookies could stand it no longer, and out they piled and joined me at the campfire. One of them had a small photo at which he gazed intently, and by the firelight I caught a glimpse of a tear bedimming his

Private George Gould Whitaker successively served between 1882 and 1891 in the Twenty-first Infantry and First Infantry regiments. He was stationed in Arizona when he posed with his Springfield rifle. *Editor's collection*

eye. "Your sweetheart, Buddy?" says I. "Sweetheart, hell," says he. "That's my mother."

Although Geronimo was not a regular Apache chief, being more of a "medicine" man, he had a great influence over the members of his tribe—the

Chiricahua Apaches—and over a period of some ten or twelve years had frequently led bands of these Indians on raids through Arizona, New Mexico, and Old Mexico. One of his favorite tricks was to dash into Old Mexico, murder Mexicans right and left, stampede herds of their horses and other stock, and drive these up into Arizona. These exploits were both amusing and profitable to the Indians, but to those who were raided and who lived to tell the tale, they were anything but funny.

In May, 1885, having no doubt run out of supplies and feeling that it was about time to replenish the larder, Geronimo and several other so-called chiefs of the tribe organized another band of malcontents, several hundred in all, counting the squaws and papooses, and leaving the reservation behind again headed south toward the land of plenty. Thus began the historic Apache Campaign of 1885-1886, which was not brought to a close until September 4, 1886, when the hostiles surrendered to Brigadier General Nelson A. Miles at Skeleton Canon, not far from Fronteras, Old Mexico. Geronimo and all his followers were then placed on a train and taken to Florida.

During the period of the entire campaign, over two hundred citizens— ranchmen, miners, prospectors, women and children—were murdered in cold blood by these Indians. Very few soldiers were killed or even injured. Their engagements with the hostiles were few and far between and usually took place only when the Indians had everything in their favor or were forced to give combat. The truth of the matter is that the hostiles kept as far away from Uncle Sam's men as possible. They did not want to fight us—they knew better. So the campaign of 1885-1886 developed into a marching campaign, and I have no doubt that in this respect it was the greatest campaign of all time. General Miles had superseded Brigadier General George Crook in April, 1886, and he immediately started all available troops in hot pursuit of the hostiles, sometimes selecting for exceptionally long marches only such men as had been proved by experience to have the necessary stamina and courage to endure such an ordeal.

Here is what the general himself telegraphed the War Department September 6, 1886, concerning the troops and their marches: "Too much credit cannot be given to the troops for their courage, fortitude, and tireless endurance. Those gratifying results of the campaign, fraught with extreme hardships and difficulties, are due to their most laborious and dangerous service. The Indians have been pursued over two thousand miles in the heart of Arizona and Mexico, through the most rugged mountain regions. Captain Lawton's command alone has followed the hostiles over sixteen hundred miles, over mountains from 2,000 to 10,000 feet high, and through canons where every boulder was a fortress." Most vivid of all in my memory are those long grueling marches, often with no water, and sometimes with mighty little to eat—marches that exacted the last ounce of a man's strength, where literally a man had to do or die. For to be left behind on some of those vast stretches of burning sand would have meant certain death; a slow, lingering, horrible death, with the sun flaming above you like a ball of molten brass; and perhaps a few buzzards winging their indolent way across your field of vision, waiting, waiting, patiently waiting.

Taking into consideration the topography and extent of the territory covered, the extreme climatic conditions, the number of troops engaged, the length of actual service in the field and distances marched, the campaign of which I am writing should go down in history as one of the great epics of the ages. And I hope that my readers will not consider me egotistic if I suggest that it would be a most gracious and fitting gesture on the part of the government if it should bestow a distinguished service medal on each and every survivor of the campaign. For surely, no human beings ever rendered a greater service to humanity and civilization than the boys in blue who followed their leaders so faithfully through the trying years of 1885-1886 over the sun-baked plains and icy mountains of the Southwest. . . .

Immediately upon taking charge of the campaign, General Miles ordered out all available troops and dispersed them in such a way as to form a veritable ring of steel around the hostiles. The territory assigned to the companies of the Thirteenth Infantry was the northeast segment of this circle, the southwestern part of New Mexico Territory, the birthplace and former habitat of the notorious Geronimo. In guarding this section, our companies were shunted back and forth like the shuttle of a sewing machine. Upon consulting my diary, I find that we marched close to one thousand miles and made some fifty-six camps, sometimes camping at the same place five or six different times. Thus, we became pretty well-acquainted with the territory covered, and became quite expert in the matter of making and breaking camp.

When word would come that the hostiles were headed in our direction, detachments consisting of a non-com and five or six men would be sent out to protect the ranches in the vicinity. And there they would be welcomed with open arms and shown every courtesy. At most of these ranches the men would be given at least one meal a day, dinner usually, and surely the cooks must have enjoyed seeing them eat, for never were good meals more appreciated. Along in the spring of 1886, Geronimo headed for his old stamping ground, the Mogollon Mountains. . . . If Geronimo had concluded to go a little farther north instead of turning back to Old Mexico, the prophesy of Sergeant Maguire might have been fulfilled, and there would have been plenty of fighting for us. But I assure my readers that had he and his followers shown any signs of wanting to start something they would have met with a warm reception. For by this time we were thoroughly hardened soldiers, and almost every man was either a marksman or a sharpshooter. I am pretty sure that I myself was about the worst shot in the company, as I had never become even a marksman, but even at that I don't think Geronimo would have cared to have me draw a bead on him.

Besides shooting at targets, we had by this time had much experience in shooting at moving targets such as deer and antelope. And those old single-fire Springfield rifles, with their long bottle-necked [sic] .45 caliber cartridges could certainly send a ball a-whizzing. It was goodbye to anything it happened to hit. Each man carried a web belt of fifty of these death-dealers. And although we scarcely feared a night attack, we nevertheless, when in the immediate vicinity of the hostiles, slept with these belts encircling our waists and the good old trusty Long Tom snuggling beside us at the edge of our blankets.

When Geronimo and his followers surrendered at Skeleton Canyon in September, 1886, and allowed themselves to be bundled on a train and hustled out of the territory, the curtain fell on the most picturesque and stupendous drama that was ever enacted on the American continent. . . . On the 16th of September, 1886, we arrived, three companies of us, on the western slope of the Zuni Mountains overlooking Fort Wingate. About 150 of us in all, and the only way you could detect that we were Regular Army soldiers was by examining our arms and equipment. Aside from that, I must say that we looked more like tramps than soldiers. We went out dressed in blue flannel shirts and trousers, with the regulation campaign hats, boots, or shoes. We returned almost literally covered with buckskin, scarcely a patch of blue to be seen, and had on all sorts of hats, boots, or shoes, or what was left of them. Keeping ourselves well shod had been one of our greatest difficulties. One thing we had in plenty was whiskers, for it had been anything but easy to keep well shaved under such conditions. And sunburned?—don't mention it. We were as dark as Mexicans. As we sat there on the sun-backed mountainside, travel-weary and glum, looking down at the roofs of the fort, our features suddenly relaxed into a broad smile as we caught a glimpse of the glittering instruments of the band and knew that they were coming out to meet us. And this they did, marching toward us playing a welcoming air, and O how sweet that music sounded! For a long, drab year no such sounds had fallen upon our ears.

The command was given to fall in, and down the side of the mountain we went with a brisker and more cheerful step than for many a day. And as the band played, "Johnny Comes Marching Home," we swung along to the handkerchief waving and the cheering of the "stay-at-homes." Once again we were in front of the old familiar quarters, and [the] band had passed on. The command, "Break ranks, March," rang out, and the memorable Apache Campaign of 1885-1886 was at an end.

Service in Arizona, 1885 (By John P. Gardner, formerly of Companies E and K, Eighth U. S. Infantry. From *Winners of the West*, January 30, 1926)

Late in December, 1885, Company E, Eighth U. S. Infantry, was stationed at Fort Halleck, Nevada, and our captain, Egbert B. Savage, received orders to go to Arizona. In less than thirty minutes we were on our way to a railroad station some fifteen miles away. We were under light marching orders, and arrived at Bowie Station, Arizona, in the heart of the San Simon Desert, on New Year's Day, 1886. A few inches of snow covered the desert, the winds and sandstorms were fierce. We were allowed a tent to each two men and had to sleep on the ground. We remained here with other troops until April 7, and by that time twenty-seven of the thirty-two men of Company E were on sick report with lumbago, pleurisy, and rheumatism.

At this time they brought in a crowd of Indians to be transported to St. Augustine, Florida. The officers drew straws to see who the lucky company would be to escort the Indians, and our captain won, and the next day we set out for Florida with two coaches full of Indians, numbering in all seventy-six. It took us six days to make the trip, and the people at New Orleans went wild when we stopped there. We were a sight, with our dirty redwood jumpers and overalls and unshaven faces, but they had never seen an Indian before, and because of this they treated us royally and told us to stop over a day on our return trip. This we did and we had the time of our young lives, as the town was wide open to us and everything free.

We arrived back at Bowie on April 21st, having been just fourteen days in making the trip. The troops here had all left to head off Geronimo. Several companies, each of the Fourth and Sixth cavalry, several troops of colored cavalry, and Companies B, D, E, H, and K of the Eighth U. S. Infantry, were scattered out in all directions under General Nelson A. Miles. Renegades had tried to capture a supply train and in that fight Captain Crawford was killed [sic] and several men wounded. After taking the body to the station, we marched twenty-five miles away to guard a water hole in Apache Pass. The bacon that we got must have been left over from the Civil War, and the hardtack shot full of holes and bugs inside. The water we had to drink killed David Lahey of Company E. We were all hankering for fresh meat, so I started out one day to get a deer. I brought down a large buck, and while going through the thick brush to get him I saw four red devils going around a turn in the bottom of the ravine. I want to go on record as giving them the run of their lives. I showed them what a "Walk-a-Heap" could do when he got scared, and they were not even in the race. I was leading all the way to the camp. I surely lost my appetite for deer meat, and anyway I think he was too tough and so I left him for the redskins.

Rattlesnakes were thick and made life miserable, being almost as much dreaded as the Indians. We camped one night at an old abandoned blacksmith shop. The forge was all tumbled down; nothing was left of it but cinders and rocks, and as it made the ground higher, the boys laid their heads toward the forge. We were awakened during the night by groans, and lighting a stump of a candle we discovered one of the boys of Company B of the Eighth Infantry had been stung behind the right ear by a rattler. The rattler was under his coat, which he used for a pillow, and by turning in his sleep [he] must have pinched the rattler, which immediately stung him. He was at once taken to Fort Bowie, and lingered several months before passing away, and was then buried at the fort. We had lost our appetite for sleep that night and dug up the old forge and found five more rattlers, which we scalped pronto.

In October [September], Geronimo and his warriors were captured and also taken to St. Augustine, Florida, by Company K, Eighth U. S. Infantry. I will close with the war whoop poem of Company E, Eighth U. S. Infantry, of the wild and wooly West:

> Oh, we came to Arizona,
> To fight the Indians there;
> We thought we'd get baldheaded,
> But they didn't get our hair.
> As we lay among the briars,
> In the dirty yellow mud;
> We never saw an onion,
> A turnip or a spud.
> They brought in Chief Chiwawa [Chihuahua],
> Likewise old Chief Nan-Nai [Nana];

> We transported them to Florida,
>   Where they had no more to say.
> This was the year of '86, boys,
>   With Company E, the hungry Eighth;
> We came back to get Geronimo,
>   The dirty, pesky skate.
> We had bunions on our feet;
>   We had corns upon our toes;
> Lugging a gun in a red hot sun,
>   Put freckles on our nose. . . .

Trailing Geronimo by Heliograph, 1886 (By William W. Neifert, formerly a private in the U. S. Signal Corps. From *Winners of the West*, October 30, 1935)

Early in 1886 the Chiricahua Apaches had again broken loose to renew their old life of plundering, stealing, burning, and murdering. They were destroying ranches and torturing the inhabitants for sport, and finding shelter in their former mountain fastnesses. Of this tribe, Geronimo was the great war chief. His biographer says that his Indian name was Go-khla-Yeh, but the Mexicans at the battle of Kaskiyeh, Mexico, called him "Geronimo," a name that continued ever after, both among Indians and white men. He was born in No-do-yohn Canon, Arizona, in June, 1829, a son of Mangus Colorado, who was a villainous old genius for Indian warfare. Geronimo in the early raids of plunder was at first led by old Cochise, the hereditary chief of the tribe, and one of the most daring old renegades of the Southwest. He died in 1876, when his son, Naiche, became the head chief, and Geronimo finally succeeded him.

Early in April, Brigadier General Nelson A. Miles was ordered to Arizona, and with as little delay as possible proceeded to Fort Bowie, assuming command of the department on April 12, 1886. He had in previous Indian campaigns made efficient use of the heliograph, and soon after taking command of this section decided to make prominent use of the Signal Service. He so notified the chief signal officer, who promised to furnish twelve men with appliances for making such service useful and effective. Miles directed that signal detachments be placed upon the highest peaks and prominent lookouts to discover the movements of Indians, and to transmit messages between headquarters and the troops on the march or in camp. Six men were to be selected by competitive examination in the use of the

Signal Corps Private R. L. Sutton, in ca. 1885. The soldiers who operated heliographs during the Geronimo Campaign were attired similarly. *Editor's collection*

heliograph apparatus from the two classes of young men then undergoing the regular courses at the Signal Corps School of Instruction at Fort Myer, Virginia.

Notwithstanding the dangerous character of the prospective service, nearly every member at the school was anxious to be one of the squad soon to start for field service in Arizona. The result of the examination was eagerly watched, and the following winners were ordered to prepare for the journey: Charles C. Capwell, Henry Goucher, William W. Neifert (the writer), William A. Whitney, and James I. Wildmeyer, while Richard O'Dowd was subsequently selected and followed. In those days, privates did not ride in Pullman cars, and there was no "Y. M.[C. A.]" representative at the station to give us a supply of fresh fruit and chewing gum. The outstanding bright spot was a check signed by Wells Willard, Captain and C. S. [Commissary of Subsistence] in the amount of $9.00 for commutation of rations, six days, at $1.50 per day. We started from the old Baltimore & Ohio Washington depot on June 12 and six days railroad travel brought us to Bowie Station on the Southern Pacific [about fifteen miles north of Fort Bowie] during the forenoon of the 18th. On the surrounding prairie we found a lively scene with much noise and loud profanity from the troops, packers, mechanics, with their horses, mules, and all sorts of impediments, making up supply trains for the various military posts in the section. The stage agent got out a special coach to take our party to Fort Bowie, while the hazardous undertaking upon which we had embarked became more and more apparent, though we were "game" as we were in quest of laurels growing along Indian trails. The driver, of course, saw that we were "Tenderfeet, Oh! So Tender," and some of the bloodcurdling yarns that he related for our benefit added to our gloom. He particularly emphasized his remarks as we were passing the post cemetery that nestles on the mountainside in the canyon a short distance below the post, pointing out that at least half of the headstones gave a single line, "Unknown, killed by Apache Indians."

We reported at headquarters and were at once turned over to First Lieutenant Alfred M. Fuller, Second Cavalry, the signal officer for the Districts of Bowie and Huachuca, for general instructions and station assignments. We remained several days, when we separated for specially designated permanent stations in the line of communication that had just been established. In this arrangement, Fort Bowie was Station No. 1, and Bowie Peak (or sometimes called "Helen's Dome") was No. 2. The writer was ordered to station No. 8 on Mount Baldy, in the Santa Rita Mountains. This station was reputed to be one of the hardest of the system, not altogether because of the great amount of signaling, but because of its elevation above sea level (approximately 7000 feet) and the arduous climb several times each day from our camp in the canyon to the station on the peak. Six other Signal Corps men selected from western city weather stations were already in the field, though mostly in the New Mexico District, under First Lieutenant Edward E. Dravo, Sixth Cavalry.

My start for Mount Baldy was made without delay, going on the first lap of the journey to Fort Huachuca, where I was to pick up Private Landolen Bluste of Troop K, Fourth Cavalry, who had been detailed as an extra signalist. Here I was also to receive my "weapons of war," grub, and further details as to the duty on the mountain station. Lieutenant Fuller had been at the mountain during the previous week setting up the posts for the signaling apparatus, arranging camping details, etc. He was accompanied by Corporal Joseph Crowley of Troop K, Fourth Cavalry (who had been a telegrapher in his native Ireland prior to coming to America), and three men of the Eighth Infantry. In the chain, Fort Huachuca was No. 7, where Private Charles F. Von Hermann, Signal Corps, was already on duty. Anticipating my arrival, he was on hand to greet me when the mail stage rolled in from the railroad. He was an old frontiersman, so besides instructions in the work before us, he was in a position to assist me in other ways.

To reach Mount Baldy, we went by train to Crittenden, where a troop of the Tenth Cavalry was encamped. The commandant, Captain Alexander S. B. Keyes, had been instructed to furnish an escort, mounts, and pack train to take us to the station with our food, clothing, and camp equipment. In addition, he furnished three men from his force for our camp guard, cooks, etc. The detail was Corporal Edward Scott, Privates James H. Belden and Joseph Johnston. The guide to lead us was Mike Grace, an old timer reputed to be a member of the prominent New York family of the name. We started early the next morning on the twenty-mile trip—especially long to a tenderfoot unaccustomed to horseback riding. We went up and up over a trail that at many points was hard to follow, and as we ascended breathing became more difficult, requiring frequent stops for rest. We cleared the summit late in the afternoon and settled down to its occupation. After a meal, the escort and pack train started their return trip, taking with them the three infantrymen, who were to go to another state. We at once began our actual work, both on the station routine and [in] making the camp as comfortable as possible. We made "dugouts" between the rocks that furnished protection against attack and used Sibley tents for coverings—roofs so to speak. We were above the timber line, the crest being entirely of rocks, while at the camp there were a few straggling pine trees and some bunches of tough mountain grass. Otherwise, it was rock, and nothing but rocks, in which abounded chameleons, a few squirrels, some small birds, and short stuffy rattlesnakes. For our water we went to a spring a short distance from the camp down into Josephine Canyon. We used the mule ("Balaam" by name) with an aparejo for bringing it to camp over a circuitous trail of more than a mile. We also used the mule as transportation to make weekly trips to Crittenden for mail and such few supplies that we would bring in the saddlebags.

From the peak in that clear atmosphere we had an interesting view that covered many miles, even beyond the international border. Nogales, fifty miles away, was plainly visible, and away to the eastward one could see a surprisingly long distance. The heliograph, or "sun telegraph," as it was often spoken of on the frontier, is an instrument for signaling by sunlight reflected from a mirror. Metallic mirrors were originally used, but in service they were hard to keep bright and hard to replace if broken in the field. Consequently, glass mirrors were adopted and much successful work was accomplished by using this method of signaling in the armies of different nations, and at that time it was the most valuable instrument for field signaling. We used two 5-inch mirrors mounted on heavy wooden posts that were firmly set between the rocks. Vertical and horizontal tangent screws are attached to the mirrors by which they can be turned to face any desired direction and keep the mirrors in correct position with the sun's movement. As the flash increases about forty-five times to a mile, it could be read with the naked eye for at least fifty miles.

Equipped with a powerful telescope and field glasses, we made frequent observations of the surrounding country so that any moving body of troops or other men, as well as any unusual smoke or dust, might be detected and at once reported by flashing to headquarters. Troops in the field carried portable heliograph sets that were operated by specially trained and detailed soldiers, by this means communicating through the mountain stations with headquarters.

From our station we worked occasionally with Nogales, fifty miles [away,] and regularly with Fort Huachuca, thirty-seven miles distant. Then troops located at Calabassas and Tubac required some attention, and in addition, a station, No. 18, was later established at Crittenden with an infantryman named John V. Lovejoy in charge. We alternated in the weekly trips to Crittenden, going down usually on a Saturday and returning on Sunday. This gave each one an opportunity to procure several square meals at a dining room table. Furthermore, there was usually a Mexican baile [ball?] each Saturday evening. These were nice dances with plenty [of] refreshments, though the ladies did not smoke. Each man was required to "park his personal artillery" during the dancing. Considering the situation, we lived well. Joe Johnston was an excellent cook and furnished "well-balanced menus." We had a goodly supply of dried fruits and canned vegetables, besides the regular ration of flour, bacon, and other staples, all from the Huachuca commissary, and occasionally some game that our hunting parties brought in from the lower levels.

For the regular daily station work, but two men were required, so by this arrangement each operator could take advantage of every third day for rest or recreation. On such days, we usually made hunting trips in which I selected Scott for my associate. He joined the army shortly after the Civil War and he had the faculty of imparting the knowledge gained by his long service. He frequently related experiences of the early service in western Arkansas and eastern Indian Territory. We did not encounter any of the hostiles during the summer, though we had evidences that some parties crossed from one valley to the other over the hogback below our camp. We managed to keep well occupied—yet it was a long and tedious season—relieved by an occasional Crittenden journey or by scouting trips on the days that we were not on regular station duty.

The department commander carried on a vigorous campaign, and the troops gave the Indians no rest, pursuing them for nearly 2000 miles from New Mexico to Arizona, then to Old Mexico, and thence back into New Mexico again, over the most sterile districts of the Rocky and Sierra Madre mountains, beneath the burning heat of summer, until worn down and discouraged they found no peace in either country and were finally glad to lay down their arms and ask for mercy from the gallant officers and men who despite every hardship had achieved the success their endurance and fortitude so richly deserved.

[I learned that] when General Miles on the evening of September 3 met the troops with the renegades at the mouth of Skeleton Canyon—a fitting spot for the closing event of this extensive manhunt, Geronimo noticed the heliograph apparatus and, interested in the "sun telegraph," he asked the general to explain just how it worked. He was amazed when the operator on Bowie Peak threw a strong flash on the party while the surrender parley was in progress. He was astonished when told that each mountaintop was equipped with a similar instrument and the men were constantly on the lookout for him. On the evening of September 4th the Indians surrendered as agreed, and early the next morning the general started for Fort Bowie, taking with him Geronimo, Naiche, and four other Indians. The same day the troops started for the post with the main part of the Indians, and by making slow marches reached there several days later. The condition of their stock and their clothing showed that they had been relentlessly pursued, and the signal stations on the mountaintops played an important part at beating the Indian at his own game and in his own stronghold with everything in his own favor.

About the end of September we were ordered to close the station and report to Lieut. Colonel George A. Forsyth at Fort Huachuca. The order from district headquarters prescribing this movement was the first official intimation that we had received of the close of the campaign, although we were not unprepared for it, having heard of the occurrences at Skeleton Canyon. The guard was at once ordered in by Captain Keyes, though the three operators remained several days longer to salvage the property. Our rations were practically exhausted, though we had some flour and water was plentiful. We killed and ate some squirrels, and the small birds that we had fed all summer, until finally we waved "adios" to Mount Baldy and started on our last trek down the mountain and to civilization. Crowley and myself went by rail to Fort Huachuca, and Bluste rode "Balaam" back to the post.

At Station No. 8 we handled many hundreds of messages containing many thousands of words, and, in a final personal communication, Lieutenant Fuller wrote, "I was perfectly satisfied with your work, and considered that you had one of the hardest stations on the line on account of the cold weather (owing to its altitude) and the difficult ascent to the station from the camp each morning." In his report on the campaign, General Miles made the following reference to the system: "It was the most interesting and valuable heliograph system that has ever been established. These officers (Lts. Fuller and Dravo) and the intelligent men under them, have made good use of the modern scientific appliance, and are entitled to much credit for their important service." Awaiting assignments to permanent Signal Service stations, Von Herrmann, Whitney, and Neifert were at Fort Huachuca for several weeks enjoying a real rest after their arduous summer. On the day for final "goodbyes," Whitney started for Pensacola, Florida, Von Hermann for LaCrosse, Wisconsin, and Neifert for Fort Reno, Indian Territory.

What to do with Geronimo and his tribe was the last question. He pled to be left in the Arizona mountains, but General Miles said "no," knowing full well that they must be removed from those scenes which would at a time of anger rouse them to the warpath again. He urged that the children of suitable age be placed in the various industrial schools in order that the rising generation would not suffer from the acts of their fathers and that their present degraded condition might be materially improved. After an extended argument and discussion (mostly by wire) that seemed uncalled for, the renegades were placed in wagons and sent under heavy guard to Bowie Station, thence by rail to San Antonio, Texas, and soon thereafter to Old Fort Marion, Saint Augustine, Florida, thus ridding the territory of a foe that for three centuries had been a menace to prosperity. . . .

Remembrance of the Apache Campaign (By Samuel D. Gilpin, formerly of Company A, Thirteenth U. S. Infantry. From *Winners of the West*, October, 1938)

I want to make some observations as to the last Apache war, known otherwise as the Geronimo Indian War of 1885-86. . . . We were on our way [via train from David's Island, New York Harbor] to join our regiment, the Thirteenth Infantry, in New Mexico Territory, in September, 1885. In command was Lieutenant Moss [this officer remains unidentified], tall and gracious, and to him I reported every morning as he visited us from his parlor car on the trip of 2,500 miles to Fort Bayard. I recall more vividly the baked beans in cans than any other incident of that five-day trip. The recruits wanted second helpings so often! I fed them beans three times daily throughout the five days on the train. We had an old soldier with us, a friendly German, who emphasized the novelty of canned baked beans, saying he had eaten them before from a Dutch oven in the field. He was impressive also with stories of shooting buffalo from the porch at Fort Bayard in 1872. September 10, 1885, we recruits were lined up on the parade ground at Fort Bayard for inspection and then distributed to Company A or B, Thirteenth Infantry. And a month later a squad of us was sent to the field, fifteen miles from Fort Bayard, for thirty days with First Lieutenant George R. Cecil in command. To the recruit portion of our detachment, away from David's Island but a month, all was novelty. It was our first time in the field, and how novel it was to be cautioned to keep down the fire of heavy, hard mesquite at night! The loftiness of the mountains and the foe that might be lurking there filled the mind with awe. Between times it was novel to us recruits to dine on hardtack, bacon, beans, and a drink made by a decoction from Dutch-oven roasted coffee, pulverized with stones in a bag. Three times daily. A lonely old miner was a novelty with his self-imposed task of digging exactly $3 worth of gold from the side of the mountain fronting his shack before noon daily, together with his garden patch of tiny watermelons the size of a cannonball. It was a novelty also to sleep on the ground every night and to listen to Finnegan, my bunky, talk only in accordance with the strict rules of grammar. It was all sharply contrasted with our previous recruit life at David's Island.

The second field service was four months later, also fifteen miles from Fort Bayard. Here Patrick Sullivan, tall, bronzed, and with seven years' service, and I guarded the Southern Pacific Railroad station for thirty days, and I, for one, learned to cook, Sullivan knowing all about it. Biscuits I was taught to make by a Chinese cook at the laborers' boarding house at White Water. He mixed my first batch of flour with my yeast powder and cut the dough into biscuit form, and then he baked the panful in his kitchen oven . . . . From Mr. Farmer, the station agent, I next learned the American telegraph code, which incidentally did me some service a couple of months later. The result of all these episodes was that when my full Company A arrived at White Water in thirty days in pursuit of Geronimo, it found me a cook, a baker, and somewhat resembling a telegraph operator.

Next day, the march of my company was toward the Mexican line. Hachita and Almo Waco were our objective points. When we reached Separ in two days at fifteen miles per day, we had before us more than the usual fifteen-mile doughboy trek to Hachita. It was twenty-five miles from Separ to Hachita, and no water between. The twenty-five miles was made, however, in straggling formation in eight hours, but many of the boys turned up at Hachita plagued with soft corns. At daybreak the next morning, Captain John B. Guthrie selected a vanguard of twenty men, Second Lieutenant Charles S. Hall in command, to make camp at Almo Waco on the Mexican border. A ranch was there and our detachment from Company A relieved a troop of the Sixth Cavalry. . . . At Almo Waco we saw a white woman of refinement, a rare sight on this campaign, and we saw no other for six months. Among this lady's cowboys was Dr. Thad Updegraff, a young physician from Elmira, New York, out for a roughhewn life for a year to regain his health and on terms of fellowship and equality with Lieutenant Hall. There was nothing doing beyond watching at Almo Waco. Occasionally a squad of Mexican cavalry passed through the Almo Waco camp, making no inquiries, but seeking the common enemy and the latest burned ranch and terrorized ranchman.

In two months, my bunkie, Max Goldman . . . persuaded me, in view of the watching and uneventful life at Almo Waco so far, to transfer with him to Company A's headquarters at Hachita where the company was now mounted and had an auxiliary of mounted Indian scouts to guide it thru the mountain trails in an emergency. It was here at Hachita that Sergeant John Walton, a former medical student, and I were soon detailed as heliographers. Each morning thereafter we scaled the mountain to communicate with Fort Bayard, fifty miles distant, with Finnegan the grammarian at the Fort Bayard end. The first day on the mountain at Hachita, Finnegan heliographed an order to move a certain troop of the Sixth Cavalry out to a strategic point. I received this message. Sergeant Walton jotted down my reading on a pad. And soon the cavalry troop was off at a gallop. But alas! It was back in Hachita the next day saying the order must have been misinterpreted. Since I did the reading, it was up to me to don the dunce cap. But in addition, I lost all the prestige I had acquired from Mr. Farmer's telegraph key at White Water two months before. All that summer of 1886, Walton and I climbed to the mountaintop at 8 a.m. and returned at 3 p.m. to our orthodox hardtack, bacon, beans, and coffee.

By the way, since I am not disdaining episodes or names, let me say that our Company A, Thirteenth Infantry, was already identified as the outstanding company of the Thirteenth Infantry for drill and target practice results. Because it had four sharpshooters and a number of marksmen, Private Henry Frankenstein, our company tailor, naively thought Company A proficient enough in shooting Apaches to be ranked No. 1 when it got into action, and entitled to increased pay! Certainly, thirteen dollars a month was meager pay. And the daily ration was only ¾ lb. bacon, 1 ¼ lbs. flour, beans, yeast powder, and coffee. So far, in the summer of 1886, Company A and the troop of Indian scouts had galloped here and there on trips to investigate flying reports without any known authority for their truth, and the boys had found one Saturday afternoon a ranch burned, debris still smoking. On another occasion they discovered a ranchman who had fooled the Apaches that morning by crawling on his belly, he said, ten miles across a level prairie. But query: How did he escape the danger of their observation? On another of these winged expeditions we found a well and the old oaken bucket ruined and a dead cat lying nearby. The ranch was burned to the ground. Some gang of Apaches was traveling around the country exempt from punishment, and traveling within fifteen to twenty miles of our camp at Hachita. Geronimo was hardly with this gang, because Captain Henry W. Lawton and First Lieutenant John N. Glass were hot on his trail a little west.

There were intervening days when we played. Came July 4th and Company A met a cowboy baseball nine for two barrels of beer from Milwaukee. The cowboys' subsequent defeat was due, Captain Guthrie declared, to our excellent catcher, Private William H. Hyatt, who wore a regulation baseball mask. Where did Hyatt get the mask in that Godforsaken territory? Captain Guthrie umpired the game. On another occasion he ruled on the several horse races conducted by our Indian scouts—stoical, taciturn, and wary Indians. It was characteristic, be it known, for New Mexico to experience moonlight every night, or starlight. The frequent moonlight, the old boys of Company A will recall, . . . made Harry Green wonder if it were dangerous, and in what way. He had to sleep out in the moonlight a good deal. Would it impair his vision if he did not look at this satellite of the earth? As the months passed and those bi-monthly paydays went by without recognition from the paymaster, the boys reconciled themselves to the prospect of a long winter ahead lying on the ground with poncho and blanket for an improvised mattress and a greatcoat for a pillow. Payday would come only when and if that anti-social Geronimo bit the dust or was captured. On his account we had already missed three paydays, three $25.75's, but it constituted assets in Uncle Sam's hands that were good as gold. I had unfortunately, however, been seized with occasional vertigo and had my back sprained permanently from lifting bales of hay intended for our quartermaster mules and Indian scout horses. Ever since that summer, 1886, I have had both afflictions. "Go on the sick report," warned Sergeant Walton. But I declined. I was 20.

Finally, it was certain that New Mexico and Arizona people had Indian terrors while Geronimo was loose and a wholesome fear of all Apaches in their hearts. The entire population there lived in dread of Indian massacre. The Apaches had been out intermittently for fifty years. People today [1938] know nothing about it. Yet their fathers of those days of 1886 needed shelter from Indians almost as universally as shelter from weather in the Southwest. Geronimo's war whoops cost the War Department extraordinary expense and many soldiers' lives to protect the border settlements out there. But Company A, Thirteenth Infantry, notes with satisfaction that it was among "those present" when the Apaches were subdued forever in September, 1886. It put a quietus on our previous expectation of spending the winter in the field, though we former recruits deemed it fine and dandy to land at Fort Bayard from David's Island on September 10, 1885, and return to Fort Bayard from the field as Indian war veterans on September 10, 1886.

To and from Mexico, 1886 (By Albert Willis, formerly of Troop E, Fourth U. S. Cavalry. From *Winners of the West*, June, 1924)

On the 18th of August, 1886, the "general call" was suddenly sounded at old Fort Huachuca, Arizona Territory, and just a little after noon Troops D and E of the Fourth U. S. Cavalry received orders to saddle at once for field service and be ready at company front on the parade ground at 2 p.m. to leave for Old Mexico. They rode through the entire night, stopping only once to water their horses and fill their canteens. Up and down the mountain trails they went, sometimes leading their horses, then again riding rapidly to make time, as they were notified by Lieutenant Colonel George A. Forsyth ("Fighting Sandy") that their objective point was Fronteras, Mexico, which was just 101 miles from Huachuca. Morning came and we were still riding and we could see, over the old Mexican trails, through the valley, the town of Fronteras in the distance, which we reached at 4 p.m.

We halted at Cachula Ranch, five miles beyond, where we met First Lieutenant Charles B. Gatewood of the Sixth Cavalry, who had been the Indian agent in charge of the reservation from which the Indians we were trailing had escaped. From the information he gave us, and as soon as darkness had set in, we were ordered to form a skirmish line of five-yard intervals, keep a sharp lookout for Indians, and proceed slowly. At daybreak we learned that Captain Henry W. Lawton and his command of cavalry and infantry were just across a river from us, that a powwow had been held with the Indians and they had agreed to produce the head chief, Naiche, son of old Cochise, and also old Geronimo.

We then proceeded to Skeleton Canyon, where Brigadier General Nelson A. Miles joined us, and the surrender of the Indians was accomplished [on September 4, 1886]. We started next day for Bowie Station on the Southern Pacific Railroad and in three days the Indians were entrained and on the way to Fort Barrancas [sic—Fort Marion, Florida], Captain Lawton taking command of them. However, Lieutenant Charles B. Gatewood was the man who really got the Indians as he was the only officer they would talk to or surrender to. Captain Lawton got the credit, as "Fighting Sandy" Forsyth, the Beecher Island hero, also at Winchester with General Phil Sheridan, wanted no honors except to claim that his "boys" had made the longest ride in history on this occasion, 101 miles in 26 hours. After reaching their station in 1886, E Troop lost seventeen men who were discharged because they had broken down in health after that terrible ride . . . .

Present at the Surrender, 1886 (By Arnold Schoeni, formerly of Troop G, Fourth U. S. Cavalry. From *Winners of the West*, August 30, 1930)

After the surrender of Geronimo to Brigadier General George Crook in March, 1883, he got away again and the campaign for three years thereafter was more serious than ever. General Crook was relieved of the command on April 1, 1886, and was succeeded by General Nelson A. Miles. He selected Captain Henry W. Lawton, furnished him with the best riflemen and scouts, to follow the Apaches into Mexico as far as the Laqui River, some 200 miles from the border. In connection with Captain Crawford's Indian scouts, Captain Thomas C. Lebo's and First Lieutenant Charles B. Gatewood's help, they pressed the Indians to such an extent that Geronimo sent in word he would surrender to the chief.

General Miles, himself, arrived in Skeleton Canyon, and Chiefs Geronimo, Naiche, Chatto, and sub-chiefs were taken to Fort Bowie, Arizona Territory, in charge of General Miles, with a small detail, mostly selected from Troop G, Fourth U. S. Cavalry, of which detail I was a member. It is worth noting that General Miles, although he had an ambulance at his service, rode his horse the entire distance, some sixty-five miles, and on the route sat down with us to share a cup of coffee. The balance of the Indians arrived at Fort Bowie two days later. A great deal of this result was due to the heliograph service, which enabled the operators to flash news of the Indians' whereabouts to the nearest commands. I was in charge of the station at Steens Pass, New Mexico, previous to joining my troop in the field.

Will state that my captain, William A. Thompson of Troop G, Fourth U. S. Cavalry, was appointed acting adjutant general in the field, and First Lieutenant Wilbur E. Wilder commanded the troop. After the campaign came to an end, Captain Thompson commissioned me to make copies of all telegraphic and heliographic communications, to the end that a complete history could be assembled of the campaign while in charge of General Nelson A. Miles. . . .

Chasing the Apache Kid, 1892-1894 (By Richard F. Watson, formerly of Troop G, First U. S. Cavalry. From *Winners of the West*, July, 1939)

Of all the outlawed, renegade Indians that our government had to deal with, the Apache Kid was the worst by far. He was the most bloodthirsty, cruelest, most murderous outlaw in our history. He would kill the ranchers, steal their cattle and horses and, with his gang, make for the most isolated spots of the Table and Superstition mountains. From these hills, he would go on down into old Mexico, across the border, and there he would dispose of the cattle and horses.

On one of these trips over the high mountains and blistering desert, we trailed him to the Mexican border and, knowing he was over the line and in Mexico, we dropped the pursuit of him for a while. We were over our time and out of rations, so we returned to San Carlos. And a sight we were to behold—bewhiskered, dirty, tired, and hungry, our horses worn down to skin and bones, and our stomachs hollow.

In a few weeks we received word that the Apache Kid was back in Arizona and had made another big killing. We hit the trail again and kept after him. I am one of the few men who sighted him, twice through the field glasses of our commander, and that was away across a deep mountain gorge. He was on top of another range. In those terribly isolated mountains, the Kid always kept to the high trails, and it would often take a day's riding to get around to the point where he had been sighted. And so, with all the hardships and dangers that we experienced in trailing him, we never got him.

For years he continued on his bloodthirsty raids. The mention of his name in Arizona carried a shudder with it. He was the last and worst of that hostile band of Apaches. The partner of Wallapai Clark, an old government scout and miner, was killed and his horses stolen by the Kid. The Kid returned a year or so later, intending to make another raid on the cabin of Clark and he found Mr. Clark at home this time. Clark killed the Kid's squaw and wounded the Kid. It is believed that the Kid crawled into a cave somewhere in the mountains and died, as he was never heard of after that time.

Suggested Reading

For those readers interested in learning more about army life on the frontier, 1860s-1890s, and about the Indian campaigns treated in this book, or in seeking more context for the veterans' reminiscences presented herein, the following titles are among the best available.

Brimlow, George F. *The Bannock War of 1878.* Caldwell, Idaho: The Caxton Printers, Ltd., 1938.

Brown, Dee. *Fort Phil Kearny: An American Saga.* New York; G. P. Putnam's Sons, 1962.

Buecker, Thomas R. *Fort Robinson and the American West, 1874-1899.* Lincoln: Nebraska State Historical Society, 1999.

Coffman, Edward M. *The Old Army: A Portrait of the American Army in Peacetime, 1774-1998.* New York: Oxford University Press, 1986.

Cozzens, Peter (ed.) *Eyewitnesses to the Indian Wars, 1865-1890.* Vol. One, *The Struggle for Apacheria;* Vol. Two, *The Wars for the Pacific Northwest;* Vol. Three, *Conquering the Southern Plains;* Vol. Four, *The Northern Plains;* Vol. Five, *Army Life and Leaders.* Mechanicsburg, Penn.: The Stackpole Company, 2001-2004.

Faulk, Odie B. *The Geronimo Campaign.* New York: Oxford University Press, 1969.

Graham, William A. *The Custer Myth: A Sourcebook of Custeriana.* Harrisburg, Penn.: The Stackpole Company, 1953.

Gray, John S. *Centennial Campaign: The Sioux War of 1876.* Fort Collins, Colo.: Old Army Press, 1976.

Greene, Jerome A. *Morning Star Dawn: The Powder River Expedition and the Northern Cheyennes, 1876.* Norman: University of Oklahoma Press, 2003.

——. *Nez Perce Summer, 1877: The U.S. Army and the Nee-Me-Poo Crisis.* Helena: Montana Historical Society Press, 2000.

——. *Washita: The U.S. Army and the Southern Cheyennes, 1867-1869.* Norman: University of Oklahoma Press, 2004.

——. *Yellowstone Command: Colonel Nelson A. Miles and the Great Sioux War, 1876-1877.* Norman: University of Oklahoma Press, 2006.

Hedren, Paul L. *Traveler's Guide to the Great Sioux War: The Battlefields, Forts, and Related Sites of American's Greatest Indian War.* Helena: Montana Historical Society Press, 1996.

————. *We Trailed the Sioux: Enlisted Men Speak on Custer, Crook, and the Great Sioux War*. Mechanicsburg, Penn.: Stackpole Books, 2003.

Hoig, Stan. *Perilous Pursuit: The U.S. Cavalry and the Northern Cheyennes*. Niwot, Colo.: University Press of Colorado, 2002.

Hutton, Paul A. *Phil Sheridan and His Army*. Norman: University of Oklahoma Press, 1999.

Leckie, William H. *The Military Conquest of the Southern Plains*. Norman: University of Oklahoma Press, 1963.

Mangum, Neil C. *Battle of the Rosebud: Prelude to the Little Bighorn.* El Segundo, Calif.: Upton and Sons, 1987.

McDermott, John D. *Circle of Fire: The Indian War of 1865*. Mechanicsburg, Penn.: Stackpole Books, 2003.

Murray, Keith A. *The Modocs and Their War*. Norman: University of Oklahoma Press, 1959.

Rickey, Don, Jr. *Forty Miles a Day on Beans and Hay: The Enlisted Soldier Fighting the Indian Wars*. Norman: University of Oklahoma Press, 1963.

Robinson, Charles M., III. *A Good Year to Die: The Story of the Great Sioux War*. New York: Random House, Incorporated, 1995.

Sklenar, Larry. *To Hell with Honor: Custer and the Little Big Horn*. Norman: University of Oklahoma Press, 2000.

Stewart, Edgar I. *Custer's Luck*. Norman: University of Oklahoma Press, 1955.

Thompson, Erwin N. *Modoc War: Its Military History and Topography*. Sacramento, Calif.: Argus Books, 1971.

Thrapp, Dan L. *The Conquest of Apacheria*. Norman: University of Oklahoma Press, 1967.

Utley, Robert M. *Frontier Regulars: The United States Army and the Indian, 1866-1890*. New York: The Macmillan Company, 1973.

————. *Frontiersmen in Blue: The United States Army and the Indian, 1848-1866*. New York: The Macmillian Company, 1967.

————. *The Last Days of the Sioux Nation*. New Haven, Conn.: Yale University Press, 1963.

Vaughn, Jesse W. *The Reynolds Campaign on Powder River*. Norman: University of Oklahoma Press, 1961.

INDEX

About the Author:

Jerome A. Greene is a historian with the National Park Service. He is the author or editor of many books, including *Lakota and Cheyenne: Indian Views of the Great Sioux War, 1876-1877*, *Morning Star Dawn: The Powder River Expedition and the Northern Cheyennes, 1876*, *Washita: The U.S. Army and the Southern Cheyennes, 1867-1869*, and *The Guns of Independence: The Siege of Yorktown, 1781*. Mr. Greene resides in Colorado.